The Blacker the Ink

The Blacker the Ink

· ·

Constructions of Black Identity in Comics and Sequential Art

EDITED BY FRANCES GATEWARD AND JOHN JENNINGS

Rutgers University Press

New Brunswick, New Jersey, and London

Library of Congress Cataloging-in-Publication Data

The blacker the ink : constructions of black identity in comics and sequential art / edited by Frances Gateward and John Jennings.

pages cm

Includes bibliographical references and index.

ISBN 978-0-8135-7234-5 (hardcover : alk. paper)—ISBN 978-0-8135-7233-8 (pbk. : alk. paper)—ISBN 978-0-8135-7235-2 (epub)—ISBN (invalid) 978-0-8135-7236-9 (web pdf)

1. Comic books, strips, etc.—Social aspects—United States.   2. African Americans in literature.   3. African American cartoonists.   I. Gateward, Frances K., editor. II. Jennings, John, 1970- editor.

PN6725.B57 2015

741.5'973—dc23   2014035926

A British Cataloging-in-Publication record for this book is available from the British Library.

Visit our website: http://rutgerspress.rutgers.edu

Manufactured in the United States of America

This book is dedicated to the memory of Albert and Churie Thompson, Franklin Gateward, and Lee and Roz Desser.

Contents

Panel III: Black Tights

Panel IV: Graphic Blackness

Acknowledgments

An anthology is, by its very nature, a collaborative project. The editors would therefore first like to thank our contributors, whose patience matched their exemplary research. We feel very privileged to have had the opportunity to work with you.

A very special shout-out goes to Damian Duffy and David Desser, our supporters—not only with this project but for many over the years. Could not have done it without you!

Interestingly, we found from our many conversations with friends and colleagues that comic, comic book, and graphic novel readership is linked very closely to family. John would like to acknowledge his mother, Janie Lenoir, who purchased for John his first comics from the local stop-and-go. Little did either of them know that Thor and Spiderman comics would start a lifelong passion. Frances would like to thank her family—Dad, for taking her and her siblings to the Ft. Dix PX bookstore every Saturday for their weekly comic book fix; Mom, for never questioning or berating those reading choices; her sister, Cha, for introducing her to the medium through Richie Rich, Casper, and later Archie; her older brother Frank for expanding that interest to the world of caped crusaders; and Steven, for traveling to the cons and spending hours discussing issues of artists and story lines. Thanks to Sophie, a superhero in her own right, and David, for everything! We would also like to thank Leslie Mitchner at Rutgers, whose immediate enthusiasm was a big help in pushing this to its final stages, and Mekala Audain for her attention to detail and huge amount of assistance.

The Blacker the Ink

Introduction

• •

The Sweeter the Christmas

FRANCES GATEWARD

AND JOHN JENNINGS

> You have to have something to start with,
> and where you start has nothing to do
> with where you end up.
> —Bill Foster

If you are an avid reader of superhero comics, then you most likely smiled or chuckled at the reference in the title of this introduction to *Luke Cage, Power-man*'s signature "expletive" of shock used in the Marvel Comics character's early adventures. Luke Cage, like many other of his contemporaries, was an attempt to capitalize on the Blaxploitation film boom of the 1970s. He was the first African American superhero to be featured in his own monthly comic book. Cage's "Sweet Christmas!" catchphrase was his equivalent to Superman's "Great Scott!" or The Mighty Thor's "By Odin's beard!" or Robin's "Holy ——, Bat-man!" It was also an attempt of a white writer to create authentic street slang for a character that was born and raised in a space where he had most likely never visited. Even though the words were echoing from a pair of Black lips, a Black man's voice was not being heard. In reality, many of the Christmases the charac-ter would have experienced in the inner city would have been something far less "sweet" and far more foreboding. It was very difficult to negotiate the contrast between what was supposed to be an urban crime fighter and his costume of a steel tiara and steel wristbands with matching chain-link belt, accessorized with a bright yellow butterfly-collared shirt and boots. The shirt, by the way, was either always opened to expose his Black body or perpetually ripped to shreds each issue. Luke Cage is unremarkable insofar as many of the characters created in this era can be seen, in retrospect and most likely at the time, as being at the very least problematic. Jonathan Gayles's groundbreaking documentary from California Newsreel, *White Scripts and Black Supermen: Black Masculinities in Comic Books* (2012), deals with these issues head-on with interviews from Black male creators and scholars. Many of the men in the film openly express their love/hate relationship not only with Cage but also with The Black Panther, The Falcon, Black Lightning, and other Black male superheroes. So even though the catchphrase "Sweet Christmas" is now looked on as a well-intentioned faux pas, it and other racially centered missteps bring forth extremely interesting opportunities to explore the various modes and nuances of the representation of an underrepresented people via a historically misrepresented medium.

Comics traffic in stereotypes and fixity. It is one of the attributes at the heart of how the medium deals with representation. Comics abstract and simplify. Perhaps this adds to the negative connotation that comics have earned in our society. The use of pictures to tell stories is still seen as being juvenile even though we obviously live in a very image-driven and image-conscious world. The comics medium in its modern form has been defined as "juxtaposed pictorial and other images in deliberate sequence, intended to convey information and/ or to produce an aesthetic response in the viewer." This definition, posited by Scott McCloud in *Understanding Comics: The Invisible Art* (9), also lays out several questions as well. Whose images are being juxtaposed? What information is being conveyed? Which aesthetics are being valued? And as for McCloud's notion of "the invisible," what else *besides* comics can be thought of as invisible?

McCloud uses his very flexible definition of comics to include Trajan's Column, the Bayeux Tapestry, and even hieroglyphics into the canon of antecedents for the modern form of comics. If this is the case, then Black people have been making comics and seeing themselves as subjects for comics for thousands of years. It is not hard to see that Ghanaian Andinkra stamps, the geometric patterns of the Ndebele, and the Igbos' Nsibidi symbols also can be classified as a type of comic. Comics, in some sense already abstract, can also become *even more* abstract. One need only look at the amazing collection by Andrei Molotiu called *Abstract Comics* to see this. Abstract comics are sequential narratives that are actually nonobjective and utilize the conventions of comics, such as panels, words balloons, gutters, and the like. Using this example, African American quilts, for instance, can be seen as comics panels. So it would seem that, if viewed through an informed gaze, Blackness and comics have been intertwined for many, many years. Proclaiming something to be invisible is still a way of seeing.

When the collection of scholarly essays in your hands was entitled *The Blacker the Ink*, we were making an attempt to start constructing ideas around "Blackness" as a type of medium and how that medium has been used for various effects concerning peoples of African descent. The way that comics convey information is customarily by ink on paper. These days, the "ink" can also be digital, but the underlying idea is still there. The story comes first and then is translated into pencil drawings. The drawings are then made darker and enhanced by the inker. The inker uses her or his skills to bring out clarity and depth and to add form to the drawings. The colorist then gets the images and adds tone, atmosphere, and hue to the story. The final step is to add the dialogue, speech balloons, and captions. This job belongs to the letterer. The comics medium works very simply. It is a cognitive process: when you begin to perceive or order images in a sequence, your mind projects a story on them in order to make sense of the arrangement. This phenomenon is called *closure*. It seems ironic that this medium that functions by closure is actually one of the most ingenious and open forms of communication ever created. It is the openness and mutability of ink and how it mediates images that originally helped formulate the title and the conceptual framing of this collection.

The ink used in comics is not only physically and formally perceived to be the neutral of black; it also is the reification of "Blackness" in the modern sense. If you think of the ink container as the Black body, it completes this metaphor. The container is merely a vessel for the flexible, mutable, liminal nature of ink. It is no wonder that Rorschach tests are made with it. Ink holds vitality, potential, unpredictability, and the very nature of creation within its affordances, as does any medium for that matter. It resists being codified, tamed, or caged—Luke Cage notwithstanding. Ink is unruly and hard to deal with as a medium. You can ask any artist who has cursed at its pliable nature when attempting to learn the secrets of how to work with it. When a drop of ink hits a white piece of paper, something happens. Is the white paper now blemished by the aesthetically unpleasing dot, or is it made more interesting and nuanced? Is the spot truly a spot, or is it a hole into another space? Only when ink is applied and it dries does it become fixed. On the white Bristol board of the comics narrative, ink begins to take shape; as Gestalt theory's notion of "forms" has it, it begins to pull out potential stories. It defines the whiteness of the page, and in turn, the whiteness of the page begins to define it. Both become *fixed*, and in that fixity the art becomes valuable because it is now "camera ready" and perfect to be printed, mass-marketed, and consumed by millions of comics fans around the world. Capitalism hides process. It is the process of the creation and the various executions of these narratives with which this collection is concerned.

The Blacker the Ink was assembled to use closure in a different fashion than in McCloud's definition of the term. Whereas McCloud has a strictly textual definition of closure—the relationship between the reader and what is left out of the text (63)—we use the term somewhat differently. The book was conceived and executed to actually deal with a complex array of notions around Blackness, agency, and identity in the comics medium. Black people read comics, make comics, and are also the subject of comics. The subject of Blackness is as vast and deep as the images afforded by the aforementioned qualities of ink. Even as this publication is in the process of being edited, a plethora of insightful, diverse narratives about Black people have been produced or rereleased. The poetic and surreal *Pop Gun War* (2003) by Farel Dalrymple uses the metaphorical power of comics in his testimony to the painful task of being human. Ho Che Anderson utilizes a different graphic and color palette for each period in the life of civil rights leader Martin Luther King, Jr., in his magnificent *King: A Comics Biography of Martin Luther King, Jr.* (2005). James Sturm and Rich Tommaso provide a look at the extraordinary career of the baseball great Satchel Paige while situating his life within the terrible career of Jim Crow in *Satchel Paige: Striking Out Jim Crow* (2007). Craig Thompson's beautifully epic, yet problematic, historical romance narrative *Habibi* (2011) pushes the boundaries of the medium in both form and content. *Prince of Cats* (2012) by the illustrator and animator Ronald Wimberly recontextualizes the classic Shakespearean romance of *Romeo and Juliet*. And Max Brooks, along with the illustrator Caanan White, tells the exciting yet sad story of the 369th Infantry Regiment during the First World War—highly decorated for its battlefield heroics yet subject to intense discrimination back home—in *The Harlem Hellfighters* (2014). Blackness has a story, you see; and sometimes that story has one voice, and other times it has a collection of many voices. Comics can be made in solitude or created in intensively collaborative processes. It is this same idea that has created the notion of a "Black" identity. Blackness is a medium that Black people of the world have inherited and have added on to as the story has unfolded throughout history. The graphic, bold, instant gist of this story can be seen in the bright colors and unflinching line work of the modern comic. Comics, when created by a skillful and informed hand, can speak with the power of words and text combined. This power is many times more potent than either mediation can achieve on its own. In the United States, this power has been utilized mostly on the genre of the superhero. In fact, since the creation of the superhero in 1938, it has been a veritable index for the medium. This perception has played a great part in how comics have been severely limited in American popular culture. As a result, *The Blacker the Ink* seeks to broaden this perception of comics by having only a few chapters that deal with the genre of the superhero. It is not that the editors dislike superheroes. That could not be further from the truth. The intent is to illustrate that the Black experience in the comics medium is a diverse one and deserves as many approaches as possible to understand its complex and vital histories. The pieces centered on the superhero and modes of Black identity were chosen for how they deal with issues of performance around gender, race, and space in the comics medium. The genre of the superhero is very much a white-male-dominated power fantasy that is itself very much based in ideas around physical performance and power in relation to the negotiation of identity. Because the Black body has historically been linked to physicality and not intelligence, the depictions of Black superheroes already have inherent issues built into the very conventions of the genre. It is very hard for white men to see Black people as heroic outside the sports arena.

Take, for example, the fact that when in the fall of 2011 DC Comics decided to relaunch its entire line of monthly comics, it did so by ending over seventy years of continuity and beginning the entire roster of characters over with fifty-two new books under the general heading "The New 52." To put things into perspective, DC Comics is second only to Marvel as the largest publisher of comics in the United States. It is owned by Warner Bros., and its superheroes include some of the most recognizable in the industry. This list of characters includes Batman, Superman, Wonder Woman, Green Lantern, The Flash, and Aquaman. The relaunch was an attempt to secure the future of the publisher by supplying it with fresh readers. Much to the chagrin of comics retailers, "The New 52" planned to capture the interest of younger readers by simultaneously selling the online versions. Five of the fifty-two comics featured a Black character in the titular role: *Batwing*, *Static Shock*, *Mister Terrific*, *Voodoo*, and *The Fury of Firestorm: The Nuclear Men*. Three of these titles—*Fury of the Firestorm*, *Static Shock*, and *Mr. Terrific*—were canceled after just eight issues due to low sales. Some few months later, *Voodoo* followed suit. No "replacement" series featured a Black superhero. Only Batwing is still making his presence felt, with twenty-five issues as of this writing. However, *Batwing*, whose alter ego is a former child solider from the Democratic Republic of Congo, is basically "The Batman of Africa" and works under Batman's supervision. The other books in "The New 52" were in some ways more problematic. *Firestorm* is about two high-school teens, one Black and one white, who join together in one body. That body is racially coded as white. *Static Shock* was a remnant of Milestone Media, the first multicultural comics imprint featuring diverse characters. *Voodoo* is the story of an exotic dancer of mixed-race heritage who is also part alien and turns into a dragon-like monster. *Voodoo* was bought from Jim Lee, formerly of Image Comics and now publisher of DC Comics. *Mister Terrific* was the most progressive of these offerings, about an Olympics-level athlete whose primary superpower is his incredible intellect, which he showcases via his fourteen PhDs in various fields. However, despite the fact that only 10 percent of "The New 52" featured Black superheroes, it is fair to say that Black images in the comics have come a long way.

The first images of Black people in comics were loosely based on the stereotypes generated in blackface minstrelsy, stereotypes mired in the notion of fixity. These images dominated the mid-1930s until the mid-1940s. Characters such as Whitewash and Ebony White depicted Black Americans as dim-witted buffoons who needed the white male either to save them or to guide them in their lives. Whitewash appeared in the *Young Allies* comics from Marvel in the first half of the 1940s. He was a friend of Bucky Barnes, the spunky sidekick of Captain America. Whitewash's "superpower" seemed to be centered on speaking broken English and having the constant capacity for being captured and subsequently tied to various types of explosive devices. He was in constant need of recue. Ebony White, the sidekick to The Spirit, created by Will Eisner, was a collection of stereotypes reified in a sometimes childish and animalistic form.

Such depictions were challenged by alternative works. In 1947, Orrin C. Evans, a Black news reporter from Philadelphia, along with his brothers, created *All-Negro Comics*, the first comics anthology featuring Black characters. Even during this time, Black creators were playing around with the various modes of representation afforded via the comics medium. The collection featured action, romance, and comedy within its first issue. A subsequent issue was never to be. Once suppliers learned what Evans was doing, they refused to sell paper and ink to the newsman. Nevertheless, *All-Negro Comics* demonstrates what Black writers and artists can produce when allowed agency, access, and freedom of expression. Even within this first collection of comics, Black people were attempting not only to show the potential of comics but also to destabilize Blackness as an identity. So, to build on the Black-comics scholar Bill Foster's words of wisdom, this is where Black people started. Where have they ended up regarding comics?

In 1993, a Chicago-born surrealist artist and cartoonist named Turtel Onli posed a question relating to the "ages" of comics. The Golden Age of American comics runs from the 1930s into the late 1940s; the Silver Age goes from about 1956 to 1970; the Bronze Age of Comics is from 1970 to 1985; the Modern Age runs from 1985 to the present day. Onli's question was a simple one: "Where does the Black Age of Comics fall?" From that one query, an entire movement was spawned. Onli began to seek out comics created by Black people that featured Black characters. Once he found titles such as *Brotherman* (1990, from Black-owned Big City Comics out of Irving, Texas), *Heru, Son of Ausar* (published in 1993 by ANIA, a consortium of four small Black presses), and a handful of others, Onli began to distribute these books around the country from the trunk of his car, much as the independent filmmaker/novelist Oscar Micheaux did with his books and films decades before, during the period of the "race film." Onli used his position as an art teacher in Chicago's Kenwood Academy to launch the first Black Age of Comics Convention, turning the trunk of his car into a space of resistance. Now, on the eve of the twentieth anniversary of the Black Age of Comics, you can see the results of Orrin C. Evans's vision that started more than sixty years ago. Black images in comics now have an entire subculture and community connected to them. They have their own conventions, their own heroes and villains, their own superstar creators, their own awards ceremonies, and their own history. There are hundreds of Black creators of comics operating outside of the mainstream, making their own stories and their own futures with this amazing medium. However, even with all of this innovation and history, the notions of a Black superhero, a Black-comics publisher, and a Black-comics collector are still foreign concepts to many people.

The Blacker the Ink showcases scholarly work that examines these concepts with rigor, innovation, acumen, and reverence to the form of comics and sequential art. Our aim was to choose a wide breadth of topics that dealt with not only the formal aspects of comics but also the audience, execution, and content of various stories relating to or created by people of African descent. One thing is true when it comes to the politics around representation concerning Black people: no aspect of it can be taken for granted. There simply are not enough images of Black people in the mainstream not to be critical of the way they are constructed and portrayed. The Black image has had a very troubled history in the United States; so have comics, for that matter. In a sense, this collection seeks to investigate those histories and where those narratives overlap, create conflicts, and accent each other. The various explorations of Black identity in this volume are, again, an attempt to recontextualize the images connected to the Black body and its depictions in the comics medium while also offering alternative methodologies of dislodging Blackness as a monolithic identity.

The book is organized thematically, grouped under what we are calling "panels." We have four panels in tribute to the tradition of comics in the funny pages of newspapers, but we also wish to think outside the boxes, to expand not just the content and themes but the very form itself. It is also our intention both to intervene in existing scholarship on "Black comics"—comics and graphic novels made by Black artists and also comics that feature Black characters—and to expand the canon of what constitutes worthwhile objects of study within the broad area of Black comics. We make no claim to cover all artists or comics. We are ourselves aware of certain lacunae, but no one book can cover an entire field of study. Those who feel strongly that we have neglected a favorite book and/or missed the opportunity to discuss a significant artist are encouraged to get on board with us and produce the kind of scholarship that is worthy of your subject. And that is what we hope we have gathered together here.

We begin, then, with panel 1, "Black Is a Dangerous Color." Chapter 1, written by Daniel F. Yezbick, returns us to a time when Black indeed was looked on with suspicion and mistrust. For that matter, however, so were all comic books. In "'No Sweat!': EC Comics, Cold War Censorship, and the Troublesome Colors of 'Judgment Day!,'" the time is the 1950s during that period just after the so-called Golden Age of comics but before the Silver Age. It is the age when Fredric Wertham's zealously polemical anti-comic-book study *Seduction of the Innocent* appeared, the US Senate held hearings on comics' alleged impact on juvenile delinquency, and the resulting formation of the Comics Code Authority (CCA) put a damper on thematic explorations of various social issues as well as depictions of violence, sexuality, and depravity. Oddly, to our contemporary eyes, positive depictions of African Americans came under fire. They certainly did, as Yezbick ably rehearses, in the case of "Judgment Day!," coauthored by Al Feldstein and illustrated by Joe Orlando, which had originally appeared in the March–April 1953 issue of *Weird Fantasy* (#18). At the time of publication, the story received the kind of recognition rarely given to comics. But a year later, the Comics Code Authority was established, and an attempt to republish the story in 1955 met with resistance by CCA head Charles F. Murphy. The battle cry was sounded by EC publisher Bill Gaines, whose books had already come under close scrutiny. Gaines won the day, and "Judgment Day!" was reprinted without alterations in *Incredible Science Fiction* #33 in November 1955. Unfortunately, it was the last comic book that EC ever published. But the story does not end there. Yezbick goes on to perform a close reading of the text (something previous work on "Judgment Day!" does not do) in order to uncover what it was about this short work that provoked the CCA but that also makes it a rare and pioneering attempt to redress images of African Americans in comic books.

From African Americans, we turn to Africa itself. Perhaps less familiar to many readers of academic books on the subject of comics and to comics readers themselves are books created by Black African writers and artists. Sally McWilliams, the author of "Sex in Yop City: Ivorian Femininity and Masculinity in Abouet and Oubrerie's *Aya*," the subject of chapter 2, performs a great service to the field in introducing this work to so many of us. The writer Marguerite Abouet and the illustrator Clément Oubrerie have given us a graphic novel dealing with the bittersweet complexities of contemporary West Africa. *Aya* refuses the usual Western media's reductive iterations of an Africa always mired in diseases, disasters, and death. Instead, the graphic novel engages us with humorous depictions of gender constructions, sexual politics, and neocolonial class hierarchies in a progressive, urban West African locale. The series, originally published in France from 2005 to 2010 and recently translated into English, is set in the Côte d'Ivoire in the 1970s and focuses almost exclusively on middle-class characters.

In chapter 3, "A Postcolony in Pieces: Black Faces, White Masks, and Queer Potentials in *Unknown Soldier*," Patrick F. Walter takes us to contemporary Africa, to war-torn Uganda. *Unknown Soldier*, originally introduced by DC in 1966, is here reimagined by the writer Joshua Dysart (who is not African American) for a series that appeared in 2008. A frightening cover image—of a man with a completely bandaged face—stands in for the way both the main character and the country itself are torn apart and mended, stitched together but always in danger of collapsing into chaos and nothingness. The lead character, Dr. Moses Lwanga, is African by birth, African American by culture by dint of a long stay in the United States, and a returnee to his native land. The violence of the book is notable, and its themes are often difficult ones, such as the manipulation and degradation of the child soldiers of Joseph Kony and his Lord's Resistance Army. Thus, the comic book series was published by Vertigo, an imprint of DC that features more adult-minded and challenging books. No less challenging is Walter's intense analysis of the series, a deep and detailed reading of both the story and the art.

The second panel, "Black in Black and White and Color," takes us back in time to a period when there were no Black writers in the comic book world and Black characters, when present (and only rarely at that), were imaged in a typically racist manner. But we are gratefully reminded of a kind of Golden Age of Black authorship of comic strips, especially in the Black press of the 1930s–1950s. One essay discusses the work of a Black artist who was concerned with different aspects of Black life but always with an eye toward normalizing Blacks' desires, deeds, and comic devices. We are then introduced to a single-panel artist at work in a white-oriented magazine, followed by a discussion of what is certainly the most influential and controversial comic creation by a Black artist, *The Boondocks*.

A little background: The *Pittsburgh Courier* was the most influential and significant of the Black newspapers. By the late 1940s, the weekly publication could boast of having editions in fourteen major cities and a readership of over one million. It was modeled after mainstream newspapers, with its various sections of hard news, celebrity gossip, soft news, and the funny pages, where the comics lived. Of course, there were a couple of differences between the *Courier* and the vast majority of mainstream, which is to say white, publications. The *Courier* carried the stories of the United States' racial terror—of lynching, of Jim Crow laws, and of other indignities and outrages against Blacks. And on the funny pages, it carried the works of Black artists, including at least one notable woman. The *Courier* was host to a number of Black artists who had differing attitudes toward the racial components of their strips. William Holloway, the creator of *Sunnyboy* (sometimes called *Sunnyboy Sam*), and Bobby Thomas, the creator of *Bucky*, wrote gag comics, typically devoid of any particular racial component save that the characters were Black. *Society Sue*, by Samuel Milai, made race a more central concern, albeit in an atypical way in that the central focus is on a suddenly wealthy family. The comedy mostly concerns the working-class father's friction with the upwardly mobile Sue and her mother. Later in the series, a more nuanced image of Black culture appears as Sue's relationship with her boyfriend, Joe, gradually takes over. He introduces her to something more like Harlem street culture. We also get a glimpse of the prewar strip *Torchy Brown in "Dixie to Harlem,"* written by Zelda Jackson (Jackie) Ormes. But perhaps the most interesting of all the Black artists was Oliver Harrington. His *Dark Laughter* is the exception to the general tone of prewar *Courier* comics. *Dark Laughter* is a one-panel gag comic that Harrington continued to draw for most of the rest of his long career. Its main character, Bootsie, was born as Harrington's version of Harlem seen from below, or eye level, rather— life as lived by urban, working-class African Americans. This, of course, was a unique contribution to comics art, especially when we realize that Harrington has drawn an African American subculture. There are no white people at all in *Dark Laughter* until much, much later in its run, though there are sometimes references to them. Harrington shows a community of outsiders, who occupy a culturally distinct space. Things changed as World War II began, with the Black press under suspicion for possible sedition, and so became more overtly prowar. The funny pages of the *Courier* were no exception.

If *Dark Laughter* was an often caustic look at Black life, the work of Jackie Ormes was both a fantasy and a recognition of the aspirations held by many African Americans, especially women. Chapter 4, "Fashion in the Funny Papers: Cartoonist Jackie Ormes's American Look," by Nancy Goldstein (the acknowledged authority on Ormes), traces the life and career of the first African American woman newspaper cartoonist. She was a one-woman juggernaut of creativity: the author of four different strips throughout her career, two of which ran simultaneously in the *Courier*; a fashion designer; and overall a businesswoman of rare perspicacity. As Goldstein notes, at a time when images of African Americans in mainstream newspaper comics portrayed only derogatory stereotypes, Jackie Ormes defied the norm with her smart, beautiful women and children. It was gratifying for readers to turn to the pages of the Black press to see photographs and illustrations depicting attractive Black people, images not seen in the mainstream media. Ormes's characters, with their humorous but revealing names, such as Torchy, Candy, Ginger, and Patty-Jo, dressed in upscale attire as they commented on all manner of contemporary topics. Ormes gave to Black readers, especially women, a combination of down-home realism and a touch of fantasy.

And then there is *The Boondocks*. If figures such as Jackie Ormes require something like an archaeology of African American sequential or single-panel artists to assure their place in this evolving history, Aaron McGruder requires no such fieldwork—as the creator of the most controversial comic series ever by an African American artist (and probably any newspaper comic when you get right down to it). In chapter 5, Robin R. Means Coleman and William Lafi Youmans discuss the use of Black Nationalism in the discourse (and humor) for the character of Huey. Their essay, "Graphic Remix: The Lateral Appropriation of Black Nationalism in Aaron McGruder's *The Boondocks*," is an in-depth examination of how both the character and his creator appropriate Black Nationalism as a rhetoric and style. The concept of "lateral appropriation" is important here, the idea that one marginal group takes up the cultural or social capital of another marginal group. Huey spouts the slogans and ideals of Black Nationalism but at a time when it is a thing of the past, a nostalgic image for those who lived through it and a humorous (if still serious) one coming from the mouth of a ten-year-old boy.

There is little doubt that Huey would despise much of what passes for Black superheroes in mainstream comics. Yet the authors represented in panel 3, "Black Tights," boldly go where only an important few have gone before.

Building on the work of Jeffrey A. Brown, the author of *Black Superheroes, Milestone Comics, and Their Fans*, frequently cited in these essays, and Adilifu Nama's *Super Black: American Pop Culture and Black Superheroes*, contributors Conseula Francis, Andre Carrington, Reynaldo Anderson, and Blair Davis cast a critical eye on popular superheroes such as Captain America, Icon, and Luke Cage, among others. The authors in this section read closely and set their essays within richly drawn contexts.

First up in this section is Conseula Francis. Her essay, "American Truths: Blackness and the American Superhero," takes a perceptive look at the controversial miniseries *Truth: Red, White & Black*. This seven-issue series from 2003 reimagined the origin of the famed World War II fighting hero Captain America. *Truth* takes its controversial idea from the Tuskegee syphilis experiments, in which, over the course of forty years beginning in 1932, the US Public Health Service conducted an experiment on 399 Black men in the late stages of syphilis, without their knowledge, in an effort to study the effects of nontreatment. Written by the late Robert Morales with art by the influential Kyle Baker (the subject of chapter 12), *Truth* posits that the "Super Soldier" serum that eventually created Captain America was first experimented on unknowing Black soldiers. Francis also links these experiments to Nazi experiments on Jews in the concentration camps. This textual reading of the series reveals many insights into and issues in the American comic book, its fans, and its treatment of race.

With chapter 7, "Drawn into Dialogue: Comic Book Culture and the Scene of Controversy in Milestone Media's *Icon*," Andre Carrington examines the case of Milestone Media, a Black-owned company publishing comics about multiracial superheroes, carrying the well-known imprint of DC Comics. Carrington focuses most closely on the superhero Icon, who first appeared in 1993, the creation of the African American writer Dwayne McDuffie, one of the founders of Milestone, and the artist M. D. Bright. Carrington notes how the comic combined the figure of the superhero with the concerns of Black women, youth, and others living in urban America. In particular, he looks at the issue of teen pregnancy and abortion in a recurring story line in the comic that features a pregnant Rocket—Raquel Ervin, Icon's sidekick. The parallel stories of the alien superhero Icon and the very down-to-earth Rocket, whose superpowers come courtesy of a special belt, bring a new dimension, so to speak, to the superhero genre. Though the issue of teen pregnancy and abortion may have been unusual or controversial within the form, the comic's nomination for three Eisner Awards and its being honored three times with a Parents Choice Award testify to the skill, sensitivity, and artistry of the creators and the differing intentions of Milestone Media.

Chapter 8, "Critical Afrofuturism: A Case Study in Visual Rhetoric, Sequential Art, and Postapocalyptic Black Identity," takes us on an important tour of a number of theoretical issues within the fields of Pan-African and cultural studies and draws heavily on science fiction studies as well. Author Reynaldo Anderson positions his work on Afrofuturism against the Eurocentric tendencies of so many comic books, even progressive ones, and marshals his wide-ranging critical readings to explore the perhaps little-known comic *Ramzees* (1997), a publication of Ghettostone publications of Kansas City. *Ramzees* attempts to promote African cultural motifs in a postapocalyptic future United States. In this instance, it is the publisher, Michael R. Brown, who created an independent comic book imprint and with *Ramzees* secured national distribution. In this sense, *Ramzees* looks forward to the publication of graphic novels that bypass mainstream comic presses in favor of more freedom but sometimes less market penetration. According to Anderson, the appearance of *Ramzees* is emblematic of the political/cultural period of the mid-1990s in the United States, which experienced the emergence of the neosoul genre, globalization, and African-diasporic mobilization in the Million Man and Million Woman March.

A close reading of the visual motifs that characterize images in comic books forms the basis of chapter 9, "Bare Chests, Silver Tiaras, and Removable Afros: The Visual Design of Black Comic Book Superheroes," by Blair Davis. Davis's keen and sharp-eyed analysis of Black superheroes sets aside issues of characterization and narrative in favor of examining visual design, a somewhat neglected element of comics scholarship. Davis focuses on the visual elements that have proven common in the design of Black superheroes, how those particular elements function as signs that have larger symbolic meaning. Luke Cage, Black Lightning, Storm, Vixen, and Cyborg are the objects of his focus, with some particularly significant teasing out of underlying meanings in the way female characters are costumed.

Chapter 10, Kinohi Nishikawa's "*Daddy Cool*: Donald Goines's 'Visual Novel,'" inaugurates panel 4, "Graphic Blackness." In this section, the authors cover and perhaps uncover stories and art devoted to portrayals of African Americans in history and myth through the form of what has come to be known as the graphic novel. Appropriately, then, Nishikawa looks at the first graphic novel to have appeared under an African American author's name. *Daddy Cool* began life as a novel published by Donald Goines in 1974. Goines, a career criminal and drug addict who took up writing during one of his prison sentences, was shot to death in 1974. From 1969 through 1974, he published sixteen novels that today's publicity material acclaims as blood-soaked and almost unbearably authentic portraits of the roughest aspects of the Black experience. Yet as Nishikawa points out, *Daddy Cool* draws from the same arsenal of Blaxploitation stereotypes that are often linked to post-civil-rights superheroes' hypermasculinity and a penchant for violence. And the setting of stories amid urban crime scenarios appears to succumb to the kind of ideological particularity that has yoked visual stereotypes of race to notions of inner-city violence and criminality. As for the graphic novel, despite the attribution to Goines, *Daddy Cool* was written by Don Glut, a comics veteran and fringe Hollywood scriptwriter, and illustrated by Alfredo Alcala, a Filipino comics artist who specialized in spectacular images of masculine brawn and female eroticism. Neither man had known Goines, and each had only Goines's 1974 novel of the same name on which to base his adaptation. Yet for Nishikawa, it is worth examining the way in which the novel's adaptation into a graphic novel may allow it to lay claim to the uneasy title as the first Black graphic novel.

Chapter 11 takes as its subject a graphic novel devoted to a Black folk legend, though one would perhaps be hard-pressed to call him a hero exactly. *Stagger Lee* (2006), written by Derek McCulloch and illustrated by Shepherd Hendrix, is at its core a villain's story of origins, notes Qiana Whitted, in "The Blues Tragicomic: Constructing the Black Folk Subject in *Stagger Lee*." Using the notion of "blues comics," Whitted sees *Stagger Lee* integrating the formal and aesthetic structures of sequential art with the existential lament and intertextual dialogue of African American blues music. Though the subjects of blues comics may be accused of murder, Whitted argues that the authors are less interested in exonerating these men than they are in questioning notions of Black deviance and uncovering the racialized networks of power that contribute to their actions. As in the adaptation of Goines's *Daddy Cool*, *Stagger Lee* runs the risk of imaging the Black male as hyperviolent and brutal. But the dialogic and intertextual structure of the book problematizes simple readings of surface detail.

Another figure out of history—a history at once better known and more fraught with peril in the telling than that of Stagger Lee—forms the subject of chapter 12, "Provocation through Polyphony: Kyle Baker's *Nat Turner*," Craig Fischer's learned disquisition on one of the most extraordinary comic book series / graphic novels of the contemporary era. *Graphic novel* is truly the best term for the book, which is almost wholly wordless. Whether it was the subject matter—a historically accurate story of the famous leader of an 1831 slave rebellion—or the wordless nature of the panels, Baker decided not to approach Marvel or DC with his idea and published it himself under the imprint Kyle Baker Publishing. Strong reviews and word-of-mouth led to its being reprinted in graphic novel form by the famed art-book publisher Harry N. Abrams. Fischer examines the book from multiple viewpoints, but the bulk of the essay is devoted to an intense and intensive reading of the novel as a comic book per se—that is to say, a graphic novel with a focus on the graphics.

In chapter 13, we turn to another graphic novel of African American life, courtesy of Hershini Bhana Young and her essay, "Performance Geography: Making Space in Jeremy Love's *Bayou*, Volume 1." Young looks at this extraordinary graphic novel, a 2010 Eisner Award nominee for the Best Digital Comic, through a number of lenses, including the notion of "performative geography," slavery, and also the blues. Thus, *Bayou* bears resemblance to the stories told in *Nat Turner* and *Stagger Lee* and has something of their polyphonic nature as well. *Bayou* contains relatively little dialogue, concentrating for many panels on landscape—the swamp, the sky, and makeshift little towns. Perhaps some of its art and artistry may be owed to its origins as a webcomic, the most successful of

DC's zudacomics.com venture. If Kyle Baker was reluctant to take *Nat Turner* to DC, perhaps DC, in turn, was reluctant, at least initially, to issue *Bayou*, a story set in Mississippi in the 1930s and replete with all the horrors of lynching and Jim Crow nightmares, in print form. But it eventually did, and so what began as an experiment in new media entered the realm of the African American graphic novel—something of a new medium itself given its short history.

In chapter 14, "A Secret History of Miscegenation: *Jimmy Corrigan* and the Columbian Exposition of 1893," by James J. Ziegler, we are confronted by the case of a non–African American artist who has come to understand the centrality of race to the American experience in its erasure. Though it is often hard to describe or encapsulate the work of the artist Chris Ware, his *Jimmy Corrigan, the Smartest Kid on Earth* has a narrative and artistic drive that makes it one of the most lauded books in the comics medium, with awards ranging from a Harvey Award, an Eisner Award, and an American Book Award to recognition from *Time* magazine as one of the ten best graphic novels in the English language. What is at stake for our purposes here is the way in which *Jimmy Corrigan* critiques heroic public histories that narrate US national identity as if it were free from the vexations of race. In telling the story of Jimmy Corrigan—sadly, far from the smartest kid on Earth—Ware weaves a companion narrative, that of Jimmy's great-grandfather and the Columbian Exposition of 1893, which stands in the novel as a paradigmatic instance of how the disavowal of interracial identity has been a defining feature of US national culture. A story of miscegenation that took place during the Columbian Exposition (also called the Chicago World's Fair), *Jimmy Corrigan*, as Zeigler demonstrates, was controversial even at the time for completely ignoring the contributions to and even the very presence of African Americans in the American national character. The hidden secret of miscegenation at the heart of the novel is the way the Corrigans, like the United States itself, define their whiteness.

Chapter 15, "It's a Hero? Black Comics and Satirizing Subjection," by Rebecca Wanzo, closes our effort to survey the terrain of Black sequential art. She deals with two types of comics here, types we have previously looked at: comic strips and Black superheroes; and she focuses on texts we similarly have dealt with. Yet her perspective toward these texts is vastly different. She proposes the notion of a counterideal that arose in the 1990s at the time of the creation of these texts. Thus, she examines the characters of Raquel Ervin from *Icon* and of Huey Freeman from *The Boondocks* as launching satirical barbs: both satirize what it means that their bodies and speech cannot or should not be imagined in discourses of citizenship, that they should not exist in the genre they inhabit. Wanzo performs a sleight-of-hand on the concept of critical race theory and bends it to her use in what she calls "critical race humor," to demonstrate how the creators of both comics address the erasure of Black bodies in citizenship discourse.

So, what of *Luke Cage, Powerman* and his yuletide battle cry? Today, Cage enjoys a more modern-day vocabulary, mission, and appearance. He has become one of Marvel Comics' A-list characters and has even led an incarnation of *The Avengers*, Marvel's multimillion-dollar superhero team. In fact, Cage is now set to lead *The Mighty Avengers*. This is Marvel/Disney's new attempt to diversify its offerings by putting together an Avengers team that is composed almost solely of persons of color. The first Black superhero to have his own title has also been reimagined in other alternative titles such as *Earth X* and *Cage: Noir*, in which he becomes more like the legend of Stagger Lee. He has even survived a "thugged out" gangsta version of himself written by Brian Azarello and illustrated by the comics legend Richard Corben. The character was once *the* representative of the Black American in the superhero genre. He has now become something much more. Like Blackness, Luke Cage has seen fit to become flexible despite his superpowered, steel-hard skin. His exploits are now global, important, nuanced, relevant, and yes, sweet. This volume is a testimony to the amazing potential of the comics medium, its extremely fascinating histories while dealing with race, and its even more promising possible futures.

Works Cited

Brown, Jeffrey A. *Black Superheroes, Milestone Comics, and Their Fans.* Jackson: University Press of Mississippi, 2001.

McCloud, Scott. *Understanding Comics: The Invisible Art.* New York: HarperCollins, 1994.

Molotiu, Andre, ed. *Abstract Comics: The Anthology.* Seattle: Fantagraphics Books, 2009.

Nama, Adilifu. *Super Black: American Pop Culture and Black Superheroes.* Austin: University of Texas Press, 2011.

Wertham, Fredric. *Seduction of the Innocent: The Influence of Comic Books on Today's Youth.* New York: Rinehart, 1954.

Panel I

Black Is a
Dangerous Color

• •

Chapter 1

"No Sweat!"

· ·

EC Comics, Cold War Censorship, and the Troublesome Colors of "Judgment Day!"

DANIEL F. YEZBICK

> The construction of Black identity and stories about Black people is at once a negotiation, a vocation, and a creative enterprise.
> —Stanford W. Carpenter

> The Black body also functions as a political referent with broader social discourses projected across it.
> —Adilifu Nama

The Battle of the Space "Negro": EC Comics' Racial Delinquency

As comics studies—both historical and aesthetic—has developed vociferously in recent years, Fredric Wertham's zealous anti-comic-book campaign and polemic study *Seduction of the Innocent*, the Senate hearings on comics' alleged impact on juvenile delinquency, and the resulting formation of the Comics Code Authority (CCA) have garnered a great deal of renewed critical interest, much of it wisely crafted and extremely incisive.[1] Yet the racial dimensions and ethnic implications of the movement to "clean up" the comics have never been adequately discussed, especially with regard to the racial elements of a few key pre-Code tales.

One such story, "Judgment Day!," turns on the revelation of the protagonist's racial identity. In the story, William Gaines and his collaborators at EC Comics concoct a fantasy shocker rooted in the reader's ethical alignment with a responsible, handsome, and somewhat tragic African American role model who is neither stereotyped nor caricatured according to traditional codes of cartooning and comics art. In fact, Tarlton, the black "Earthman," in "Judgment Day!" is greeted with cheers as the near-savior of Cybrinia. He is welcomed as a respected authority figure—an inspector, teacher, and judge who serves an almost heraldic role in this cybernetic world as the "representative of our creators." As Tarlton's robot guide announces, "If you find that we are ready, all of the wonders and greatness of Earth will be ours." As it turned out for "Judgment Day!," neither Cybrinia nor the United States could make the cut.

It all began more or less like this. When Bill Gaines first published "Judgment Day!," coauthored by Al Feldstein and illustrated by Joe Orlando, in the March–April 1953 issue of *Weird Fantasy* (#18), the story received a kind of recognition quite rare for science fiction comic book yarns. "Judgment Day!" is "an obvious commentary on the practice of racial segregation," and its narrative exemplifies "just the type of 'twist' ending that Gaines liked" (Nyberg, "No Harm" 43). In it, "an astronaut visits a planet of orange and blue robots; he witnesses the robots' mutual prejudice and concludes that the planet is not ready for admission into the Galactic [Republic]. Returning home, the astronaut takes off his helmet to reveal himself as a Black man" (Strömberg 111). EC's intensely devoted readers, among the first to establish loyalty clubs around a comic book publisher and its signature themes, wrote enthusiastically to comment on what remained its "strongest statement about racial intolerance" (Benson 43). The *Chicago Defender* commended EC's attack on institutionalized bigotry (Hajdu 322). Even Ray Bradbury, on whose socially conscious science fiction "Judgment Day!" may have been loosely based, declared that the story "should be required reading for every man, woman, and child in the United States." He told Gaines, "You've done a splendid thing here, and deserve the highest commendation" (qtd. in Geissman 142).

Then, in winter 1954, Fredric Wertham, a Bavarian-born psychiatrist and "liberal progressive concerned about the poor and disadvantaged," published *Seduction of the Innocent*, a four-hundred-page screed on the social evils and psychological dangers involved in reading comic books (Wright 93). Wertham's text was "pompous, polemical, and sensational" and "aimed to impress a popular audience with professional expertise and moral outrage" (Wright 157–158). Despite some protest from the comic book industry and a few concerned supporters, "Wertham affirmed parents' worst fears: that comics were rotting our brains and turning kids into potential degenerates" (Rhoades 58). In "the considerable Cold War hysteria at the time," the resulting public outcry led, in the spring and summer of 1954, to a witch hunt surrounding Senator Estes Kefauver's Subcommittee to Investigate Juvenile Delinquency (Lopes 37). In April and June, the committee conducted "hearings on the comic book industry" in New York that "called twenty-two witnesses and accepted thirty-three exhibits as evidence" (Nyberg, "No Harm" 28). Among them were both Wertham and Bill Gaines, whose line of EC Comics came under particularly harsh scrutiny. By August, a number of concerned publishers had formed the Comics Magazine Association of America (CMAA), which decided to adopt a strict code of self-regulation, the Comics Code Authority, patterned somewhat after the Hollywood studios' Hays Office of the 1930s. EC originally refused to join the CMAA or subscribe to its censor's code, but it relented when "distributors . . . aware of Gaines' notoriety, refused to handle the EC line without the 'Seal of Approval' on the cover" (Nyberg, "William Gaines" 13). Thus, the political fallout from Wertham's "smoothly written, alarmist, often smarmy book" led to a new phase of self-censorship in the American comic book industry (Jones 270).

Unfortunately, the CMAA and its Comics Code gravely disappointed both Wertham and Gaines. Wertham, an associate of Theodor Adorno and a subscriber to his theories on the implicit dangers of popular media to the masses, who were supposedly "far more susceptible to such mechanical deception than the educated classes," had lobbied mostly for age-based restrictions (Jones 273). During the Kefauver hearings, Wertham suggested "that the sale and display of crime comic books to children under 15 be forbidden" (qtd. in Sabin 158). As one critic has phrased it, "*Seduction* may have been his *Mein Kampf*, but his 'final solution' for comics was definitely not blanket censorship" (Sabin 158). As a "left-wing Jew whose politics and social views" were largely in tandem with "intellectuals who had fled the Nazis," Wertham was all too familiar with the dubious role censorship could play in "modern brutishness" (Jones 272). As it turned out, his fears about the CMAA were well founded, and the resulting Comics Code of 1954 became "a rigorously conservative political manifesto" that "made no concessions whatsoever to the age of comics readers" (Sabin 161). It seemed, in fact, specially crafted to crush the EC line of comic books and their "forthright political themes," which were flagrantly "anti-McCarthyite" and largely devoted to "social commentary" that "laid waste to family values" (Sabin 159–160). Gaines and Wertham both complained vociferously in the popular and trade press; but as Roger Sabin observes, "by then, nobody was listening," and the Comics Code Authority began to repress any "potentially subversive conduit for anti-establishment ideas" in mainstream comic books under the guise of eliminating adult or inappropriate content "for the good of the children" (Sabin 159).

By 1955, EC was facing serious troubles with both CMAA censorship and poor sales. That summer, EC editor Al Feldstein had a story for *Incredible Science Fiction* rejected by the head of the CMAA, Charles F. Murphy.[2] Though the specific details of that story or how it violated the CMAA code remain uncertain, Feldstein and Gaines decided to "pull out an old one." Feldstein chose "Judgment Day!," long one of his favorites and among what Feldstein called EC's most successful "preachies." Two years after its celebrated publication in *Weird Fantasy*, post-Wertham, post–Senate hearing, and post-CMAA, the story was rejected on grounds that it violated "the code's prohibition against ridicule or attack on any racial group" (Nyberg, "William Gaines" 13). Murphy's personal objection is said to have been, "You can't have a Negro" in the story (Hajdu 322). The 1954 Comics Code simply declares that "ridicule or attack on any religious or racial group is never permissible," but Murphy may have been invoking the Code's much more general potentially sinister catch-all tenet that "all elements or techniques not specifically mentioned therein, but which are contrary to the spirit and intent of the Code, and are considered violations of good taste or decency shall be prohibited" (Nyberg, *Seal* 167). Such generality with regard to both "good taste" and "decency" involving "the spirit of the code" certainly empowered the censors with enough leeway to pursue their own ideological agendas in the suppression of questionable content.

According to David Hajdu's *The Ten-Cent Plague*, the most detailed treatment of the affair, Gaines called Charles Murphy directly and threatened to "have a press conference . . . to tell the public that the comic-book industry is a racist authority that will not permit black people to have equal depiction" in their medium (322). The CMAA chief relented "on the condition that the beads of perspiration on the black astronaut's face be removed" from the last panel's surprise finale. Gaines reportedly said, "'Fuck you,' hung up on Murphy, and published the story intact" (Hajdu 323). "Judgment Day!" was reprinted without alterations in *Incredible Science Fiction* #33 in November 1955. The book carried the CCA seal of approval, though it was never officially sanctioned by the agency itself. It represented "the last comic book EC would ever publish" (Hajdu 321). EC's official resignation from the CMAA was accepted in October 1955, and "Judgment Day!," a gripping and innovative sci-fi parable that dared to focus on a dignified Black man in a responsible position of authority, came to signify the final skirmish in "the battle over EC Comics" and its caustic critiques of American mores (Nyberg, "William Gaines" 14).

That is roughly how it went for EC and "Judgment Day!" according to more or less every major history of American comic books (Nyberg, *Seal* 123). Yet, as Amy Kiste Nyberg has repeatedly stated, the specifics concerning the rejection of the story that EC first submitted to Murphy and the CMAA remain vague, and "there are differing accounts as to why he ruled against 'Judgment Day!'" (Nyberg, "No Harm" 43).[3] In any event, what anecdotes and scraps do exist provide a fascinating perspective on the racially motivated censorship of popular entertainment in the middle 1950s, when "the heightened state of Cold War anxiety now raised the pitch of the debate over youth culture to such a hysterical extent that" comic books were easily positioned as "a threat to the nation's social fabric" (Wright 87).

We might ponder the extent to which Murphy and the CMAA used the Comics Code not only to sanitize the tainted medium and save the comic book industry but also to assist in "an agenda of cultural containment" that would promote and reify strictly conservative norms while suppressing a "menacing youth culture that violated and mocked traditional values" (Wright 88). If Feldstein's account of the angry exchanges between Gaines and Murphy surrounding the rejection of "Judgment Day!" is indeed accurate, they inspire a number of useful queries about race, freedom of speech, and the implicit prejudices of institutional surveillance of the media.

First, Feldstein recalls that Murphy insisted on reading EC's submissions personally: "I'd go in there with the pages, and all the little old ladies were reading everything else, and I'd have to wait until Murphy personally read our pages" (qtd. in Hajdu 321). Feldstein's reminiscence also suggests that Murphy himself first refused to approve Tarlton, the protagonist of "Judgment Day!," on purely racial grounds: "I say you can't have a Negro" (qtd. in Hajdu 322). We should consider Murphy's many possible motivations. Was he actually concerned with the offensive representation of a "sweaty" African American male? Was he personally offended by the suggestion of a professional "Negro" astronaut? Did he ask for the change in order to uphold CMAA guidelines meant to squelch controversy by weakening the signifying power of comic books, thereby "forcing the comic book creators into such a narrow range of possibilities" to ensure "the industry would publish only banal and formulaic" and therefore safe and conventional work (Nyberg, "No Harm" 45)? In doing so, would Murphy have been consciously promoting the general reaction of "sources of traditional values" against the role comic books played in the "commercialization of [adolescent] peer culture" (Wright 87)? Was he simply committed to giving Feldstein and his publisher an especially hard time as payback for their public attacks "on the association, despite having an agreement with the CMAA not to do so" (Nyberg, "William Gaines" 13)? Or was Murphy, as tends to be the case with most censors regardless of era or medium, simply committed to busting the chops of any mavericks, wiseacres, or iconoclasts who generally refused to conform to prevailing views and dictums?

To remain fair, we might also consider whether EC strategically chose "Judgment Day!"—a race-based tale—to test the limits of the CMAA's seemingly "autocratic, self-appointed" manipulation of its editorial freedoms and commercial interests. All of these speculations hinge on the use of a "science fiction allegory about race," segregation, and equal rights at a time when such concerns were still fairly discomforting in mainstream American discourse (Hajdu 320). So the complete story, as full of holes and assumptions, protest and provocation, reprimand and repression as it is, prompts us to explore just what it is in the narrative development of "Judgment Day!" that could produce these severe responses in an era when comic books, nationalism, and racial equality were all about to erupt into very turbulent times. As Paul Lopes observes, "the specific crusade against comic books, therefore, is linked to a Cold War hysteria that generated fears of a morally, socially, and politically vulnerable America threatened by oppositional voices and deviant culture" (37).

Mining this "backlash in civil society," Gaines produced comic books that aligned themselves with kids and teenagers against oppressive authorities, good manners, wholesome attitudes, and false ideals (Lopes 37). Developing suspense-based, socially conscious narratives for the 1950s that were in line with Arch Oboler's radio thrillers and propaganda plays from an earlier decade and were prescient of Rod Serling's *Twilight Zone* TV broadcasts, which began less than four years after EC shut down all titles save *Mad* magazine, EC's iconoclastic comic book auteurs remediated the stock figures of horror, action, adventure, mystery, war, and perhaps most importantly, science fiction, with an interest in absolutely riveting and, therefore, potentially *swaying* entertainment. At the same time, EC's trademark stories "imitated the radio suspense shows [EC's staff] liked," but their comics enjoyed "the freedom to expose the nastiness of modern life that radio didn't allow, and they devoted themselves with wicked chuckles to turning American sentimentality inside out" (Jones 256):

> Drawing on the popular culture of their time and place—motion pictures, radio, pulp fiction, detective novels, and science fiction—and giving the artists unprecedented freedom in their work with more editorial encouragement than control, the talented staff proceeded to carry the comic book into new frontiers of artistic accomplishment. Among innovations the EC staff brought into comic book art were the use of highly literate and stylistically effective narrative captions, realistic dialogue which permitted characters to use blasphemy (though without obscenity or cursing), an engaging plot line which always concluded with an ironic twist or a surprise ending, and some of the most distinctive visual effects ever produced for the pages of comic books. Here was creativity of the first order, an inspired blending of the visual and literary media. (Inge 117)

Unlike most postwar publishers, EC also "dared to get political" with "stories about lynch mobs, racists, and small-town cops who frame innocents"

(Jones 257). One editor, Harvey Kurtzman, the founder of both of EC's war titles and eventually *Mad* magazine, also caught the wrath of the US Army and the FBI for his bitter, unglorified portrayals of modern warfare (Jones 257). As M. Thomas Inge observes, "Specific experiences in reading these stories contributed to the readers' education and provided philosophical epiphanies of a sort, after which they probably never thought the same about a particular subject again" (Inge 129). As Robert Warshow argued in his 1954 essay for *Commentary*, EC's uniquely irreverent perspective on hypocrisy, vice, and folly fostered a peculiar "sense of identification with this publishing company and its staff" among self-professed "EC Fan-Addicts," but its material was not to most readers' taste (67). EC's market share was predominantly male, adolescent autodidacts, "young men who saw through their trash but still loved it, who were inventing something unimaginable and profoundly unacceptable to their parents' generation" (Jones 275). They thoroughly enjoyed how EC's comics pursued "bad taste" as an "especially effective and satisfying route to notoriety" during "a time when public conformity and forced decorousness are given great meaning" (Jones 257). As Warshow described his own eleven-year-old son's allegiance to EC, "the comic books are not a 'universe' to him, but simply objects produced for his entertainment" (70). Still, "in a society as repressed as 1950s America," not all comic book readers were entertained by EC's parade of zombies, vampires, aliens, addicts, and psychotics (Sabin 158).

EC comics were among the most evocative of their era, but they never enjoyed the enormous popularity of such mainstream publishers as George Delacourte's Dell Comics, which retained licensing rights to "Disney, Lantz, MGM, and Warner characters" (Gabilliet 32). "EC titles themselves never overwhelmed newsstands" with the multimillion-copy circulation of Dell's *Walt Disney's Comics and Stories*, but "histories of American comic books have traditionally presented 1950–1954 as the age of EC. Never has a niche publisher been so closely associated with a period (with the exception of Marvel and the renaissance of superheroes at the start of the 1960s)" (Gabilliet 40). In fact, for many critics, EC Comics developed "in a five year period" material "that many consider the supreme works of the Golden Age of comic books" (Inge 117). Though its titles also trafficked in largely repetitive, openly grotesque, and often sexist power fantasies, EC became one of the few voices in any medium with the chutzpah to present openly subversive morality plays that regularly questioned concepts of liberty, equality, faith, and justice despite frequently pandering "to male adolescent fantasies and daydreams" with "stories about future sex, alien sex, and weird sex," especially in the science fiction and horror series (Benson 39).[4]

Under Gaines's guidance, EC had developed a rather outrageous set of house themes that ranged from the "wild hilarity" of *Mad* magazine and *Panic!* to the perverse gross-outs of *Tales from the Crypt* and *The Haunt of Fear* (Warshow

68). Flying in the face of propriety and pretension, EC was devoted "to a wild, undisciplined machine-gun attack on American popular culture," and race-based controversies were often deployed in its assault (Warshow 68). EC may have developed hundreds of science fiction stories "carefully plotted to deliver a surprise-twist ending with a heavy helping of irony and cynicism," but the narrative impact of "Judgment Day!" remains the most multivalent in its representation of race (Benson 38).

"Judgment Day!" is hardly unique among EC comics in its use of race for provocation. Other EC genre tales such as "The Whipping" from *Shock SuspenStories* #13 toyed with themes of interracial romance involving middle-class Anglos and "dirty Mexicans" or "spics." Another *Shock SuspenStories* tale, "In Gratitude," "pointed to the hypocrisy of a nation that purported to champion freedom and equality in the Cold War while denying the same to its own citizens" when a black soldier, killed in action, is refused a plot in a segregated cemetery (Wright 137). Two of EC's undisputed masterpieces, Bernie Krigstein's "Master Race" and Harvey Kurtzman's "Corpse on the Imjin," also employed war-based scenarios to introduce themes of Nazi genocide and interethnic conflict. Each story focuses on how political and racial "others" are needlessly abused and murdered out of sociopolitical allegiance to a supposedly higher cause.

Race is also a recurrent theme in EC's domestic tales, and the publisher seems to have taken special pleasure in continual references to small-town ignorance, clandestine KKK-esque societies, and lynchings of both Caucasians and Blacks. Its horror, suspense, and crime titles continually featured cover designs emphasizing public executions such as decapitations and hangings, mob violence, and secretive assemblies of armed, angry villagers. Such "enthusiastic and irreverent" treatment of particularly touchy or taboo subjects surely packed, as Bradford Wright has phrased it, "a devastating cultural punch" to the "prevailing mores and conventions of mainstream America" (137). EC's science fiction titles, however, were particularly "willing to make moral statements about bigotry, prejudice, and racial inequality" (Benson 43). Examples subsequent to "Judgment Day!" include the satire "The Teacher from Mars," wherein "Earth boys hate their Martian teacher out of blind prejudice"; "The Mutants," depicting "rigorous and unreasonable segregation"; and "Close Shave," a "daringly sympathetic" cautionary tale concerning interracial human-alien marriage (Benson 42). In each case, comic book narrative becomes a method of "unmitigated political and social commentary" in which shock, revulsion, ridicule, and irony work at confronting "harsh realities and contentious issues, such as racism, violence, war, drudgery, and poverty, elevating them to a plane where they can be understood, dissected, disarmed, and rethought through laughter, enjoyment, pleasure, and honest dialogue" (Regalado 98). EC's science fiction series "dared," especially, "to make . . . readers think and question some of their basic beliefs by showing the 'other' side of the issue" (Benson 45). Still, whether that "other" was Black, Asian, Martian, or robot, "Judgment Day!" represents EC's most effective installment in an assortment of recalcitrant condemnations of humanity's and, more particularly, the United States' failings.

In EC's heyday, then, its comics—outrageous and overwrought though they were—performed, as Aldo Regalado observes in "Modernity, Race, and the American Superhero," the most laudable service any comics can, which is to "playfully challenge the world to be different, without necessarily seeking to subvert established social realities through politics. Instead, they present new ideas for consideration, but they do so in an often-contradictory fashion" (98). Though such stories clearly contribute to this tradition of dissenting discourse, "Judgment Day!" is also unique in its construction of allegorical signs involving race, segregation, and democracy.

Considering how thoroughly EC developed and disseminated its angry little fables across various genres and markets and how vociferously multiple elements of the political spectrum responded to the antisegregation themes of "Judgment Day!," it might be time to look a bit more closely at just how scrupulously the story itself mediates its pithy contradictions.

Strange "Suit": The Arthrological Agendas of Race in "Judgment Day!"

"Judgment Day!" holds a pivotal position in the development of the American comic book industry. It has been frequently cited, quoted, and summarized, but no study has accurately parsed the actual mediating strategies that animate its multivalent address. As comics studies continues to gain legitimacy and precision in the post-McCloud era of criticism, theoretical advances in the poetics of the medium have provoked new insights into just how all those "juxtaposed pictorial images in deliberate sequence" work as communicative texts (Rhoades 2).

In English-language comics scholarship, current theoretical investigations into the mediating power of comics frameworks include Neil Cohn's 2014 *The Visual Language of Comics*, Barbara Postema's 2013 *Narrative Structure in Comics: Making Sense of Fragments*, Hannah Miodrag's 2013 *Comics and Language*, and Jared Gardner's 2012 *Projections: Comics and the History of Twenty-First Century Storytelling*. Earlier valuable studies include Charles Hatfield's pioneering 2005 *Alternative Comics: An Emerging Literature*, Douglas Wolk's 2007 *Reading Comics*, and the continuing works of Roger Sabin and Paul Gravett in the United Kingdom. More recent translations of French semiotic theories of comics-based systems of articulation by Benoit Peeters and Thierry Groensteen, especially Groensteen's 2013 *Comics and Narration* and Jean-Paul Gabilliet's 2010 *Of Comics and Men: A Cultural History of American Comic Books*, have also added immense conceptual weight and aesthetic accuracy to the theorizing of comics as an art form and an industrial mass medium, an endeavor that more or less began with Gilbert Sedes's 1924 *Seven Lively Arts* in the United

States and with Reinhold Reitberger and Wolfgang Fuchs's McLuhan-driven
1970 *Comics: Anatomy of a Mass Medium,* and Pierre Couperie and Maurice
C. Horn's 1968 *The History of the Comic Strip* in Europe. Though none of these
works deals extensively with the articulation of race vis-à-vis comics mediation,
they all do acknowledge that the medium's uniquely sequential visual representation preserves or proliferates a number of ethnicity- and identity-based issues
and problems. Taking a few figurative "biopsies" from the organic mise-en-page
of Joe Orlando's "Judgment Day!" will help to clarify just how intrinsically comics in general and this story in particular can initiate readerly comprehensions or
suppositions in their "figurative narrations" of race (Peeters).

First, the basics: "Judgment Day!" is a seven-page story, composed of predominantly normative paneling, captions, and lettering for its era. There are
few, if any, illustrative or, as Benoit Peeters might call them, "tabular" flourishes
of drawing or design that overthrow the linear narrative's rhetorical supremacy.
In fact, its forty-five total frames are arranged into fairly conventional two-
and three-strip tiers per page, which facilitate comprehension of the extremely
heavy dialogue and descriptive text that largely defined EC's "densely plotted,
overnarrated, luridly descriptive" techniques (Jones 256). There are no silent
panels, contradictory word-image pairings, or unanticipated leaps in continuity between individual panel gutters or specific sequences—nor are there any
signs of an interest in realigning a reader's interstitial orientation to particular images or cues for surprising interruptions of the effusive and periodically
redundant prose narrative. With the exception of the opening "splash panel"
depicting Tarlton's arrival in "Cybrinia, the planet of Mechanical Life," each
frame of "Judgment Day!" is utterly orderly in its size and shape, though there is
frequent and fluid variation in nearly every two- or three-panel progression to
develop visual diversity. The basic mediating multiframe of the layout presents
a methodical and accessible but purposely lively and diversified mise-en-page
that consciously eschews the harsh regulation and arbitrary conformity of the
world it depicts. Peeters classifies such design as "typically rhetorical," meaning that the "dimensions of the panels," while somewhat regular and obvious,
still "conform to the action being described" so that "the whole page layout is
placed at the service of a pre-existing narrative for which it serves to accentuate
the effects." In simplest terms, the very structure of the story seems to side with
Tarlton's view that, while advanced and sincere, Cybrinia has somehow missed a
basic step in its development as a free and fair society.

Orlando's page designs were often prized for their vigorous detail, especially
with regard to outlandishly intricate backgrounds and vivid shading (Geissman 141). With a heavy "reliance on caricature and exaggeration," his figures
are generally lanky with distinctly expressive gestures and evocative poses—no
small feat considering the tight compositions required by EC's overloaded
text boxes and dialogue balloons (Inge 119). In fact, for "Judgment Day!" to
remain effective, Orlando has an extra challenge. He needs to keep readers

not only interested but ethically aligned with Tarlton as he surveys Cybrinia with his facial features completely obscured by his helmet. Thus, the character's physical stance across panel-to-panel transitions and in-panel posture become especially meaningful. Orlando's subtle positioning of Tarlton's body evinces the character's influence, as well as his amiability and patience. He is rarely depicted in passive poses, and his ironically white-gloved hands continually move to acknowledge, direct, or instruct his companions. At one point, he runs his hands approvingly over a "twentieth century level mobile-car" developed by the cyborg "N-R-E Phord." In another frame, his arched shoulder evinces surprise when he learns of the color-based segregation on Cybrinia's public bus system.

Of all Tarlton's gestures, the only repetition involves his inclination to stand proudly with his hands at his hips while the Cybrinians introduce him to the achievements that define their world. Tarlton stands silent, hands again at his waist and elbows out, six times out of twenty-nine discernable partial body poses. In every case, either he is concerned about the cultural repercussions of a particular Cybrinian "advance" or he lectures his hosts on the limitations of their bigoted perspective, which "differentiates between blue robots and orange robots" in an elaborate condemnation of the "separate but equal" fallacy. During his tour of Cybrinia, he encounters segregated orange and blue bus stops, "Blue Only" signs on the backs of buses, a "Blue Town" ghetto in "the seedy section of the city" where "the buildings no longer shined" and the "streets were crowded," and a dingy blue "Construction Line and Assembly Plant," which lacks the funds and upgrades of the orange robot generator. Yet, as Tarlton points out with one hand at his hip and another hoisted toward the production line, the blue "internal units" display the "same designs" with "no improvements" or structural "difference" from their privileged orange counterparts. Tarlton's pose seems especially stiff when he encounters the "educator" machines that charge robotic minds with "all knowledge available to society" before new units are rolled out and made "free to follow his choice of endeavor." Educators, he learns, are the "parents, relatives, and the environment and the school all rolled into one." He soon discovers that the "Blue Educator" lacks "the advantages of the Orange" models, and once again, one hand at his hip, he points to his guide and explains that Cybrinia's "free enterprise society" is fundamentally flawed because the "differences between you and the blue robots are taught in your educator," and therefore blue Cybrinians' "choice of endeavors" are "limited."

Tarlton's final hip-resting stance occurs as he prepares to leave, after rejecting Cybrinia's bid to join the great galactic republic. Stopping "below his gleaming rocket," he explains with one hand raised in professorial mode, "For a while, on Earth, it looked like there was no hope! But when mankind on Earth learned to live together, real progress first began. The universe was suddenly ours." Three panels later, Tarlton's rocket blasts "into the endless cosmic vacuum," and as he removes his helmet between frames, "the instrument lights made the beads of perspiration on his dark skin twinkle like distant stars"; and the beginning of the end of EC's dissident science fiction comics is assured.

Orlando's composition of the final panel, which caused so much debate with the CMAA in 1955, is a simple low-angle head shot. The hotly contested perspiration comprises little more than a dozen tiny beads matched with four or five reflecting sparkles that dignify the rich, dark texture of Tarlton's high cheek bones, pensive eyes, and close-cropped hair. His facial features are quite handsome and, thankfully, hardly a cartoon caricature of established African American icons. He is neither Joe Lewis nor Jackie Robinson, not Paul Robeson or Sidney Poitier, not Harry Belafonte, Chuck Berry, or Nat King Cole. He is, rather, an utterly innocuous Black man of the future, for whom the usual daily struggle of prejudice and preconceptions has been somewhat reversed. Rather than learning to negotiate the twentieth-century injustices and inequalities of widespread racism and organized segregation, Tarlton, whose Earth has been ethically and scientifically galvanized by the extinction of such prejudice, must wrestle with the dubious privilege of monitoring a developing civilization's persistent urge to generate damaging hierarchies of power and culture rooted in physical or ethnic differences as artificial and random as the color of their robotic shells.

Throughout "Judgment Day!," Orlando's use of color and blocking also enhance the eventual shock of the story's superbly timed climactic panel. Using repeating visual relations and rhythms across panels, strips, and pages, Orlando develops an intensely suggestive graphic or "iconic solidarity" employing an illustrative framework that Groensteen has recently dubbed "braiding" (*System* 19). He conceives of the comics page as a reverberating plastic "spatio-topical" system that operates arthrologically, or through units of interactive, visually timed articulation, with essential "active collaboration provided by the reader" (21). Groensteen's ideas offer a great deal to the study of "Judgment Day!" (10).

1.1 The oddly hotly contested perspiration in the final panel of "Judgment Day!"

Braiding, for example, generally refers to how isolated points or details of the mise-en-page "can be linked in series (continuous or discontinuous) through non-narrative correspondences" (Beaty and Nguyen ix). Braided, otherwise minor points or details may create facile, accessible signposts suggesting linear continuity across time, space, or action, but they can also operate above or beyond the narrative matrices of the story itself, creating a fresh and, in the case of "Judgment Day!," intimately inclusive metastatement about the entire comics experience or systemic "multiframe" (Groensteen, *System* 22). Most obviously in Orlando's layouts, Tarlton is immediately braided to the orange Cybrinian ambassador who guides him through the robot population. From the initial image of Tarlton exiting his rocket ship, forty-one of the story's forty-five panels include insistent visual pairings wherein the two characters physically mirror each other in the compositions. Sometimes these are standard medium two-shots or balanced medium long shots with each one balancing out the other on opposite sides of the frame. In other examples, they appear from extreme distances, silhouetted against futuristic cityscapes, in cars, or through bus windows—but always together in equal proportion. From extreme high and low angles, Orlando presents this persistently braided, systemic suggestion that these two figures are almost too insistently equal in spatial and narrative value. Once Tarlton enters the blue assembly plant, a third blue Cybrinian guide is introduced, and for six consecutive panels, until the astronaut openly censures the oblivious orange representative for his bigotry, the three characters are practically glued together in space. The exact composition and distance of Orlando's three-shots may differ extensively, but it is impossible not to notice how blue, orange, and human seem crunched together in an extended braid of metaphoric sameness, unity, and equality.

Aside from the recurring motifs of orange and blue, the colors of Orlando's backgrounds are also arthrologically significant. The story's dominant color scheme involves blue, yellow, black, and some orange, with Tarlton's reddish spacesuit, and eventually his brown skin, popping out against this palette. In the very first panel, Orlando employs alternating blue and yellow spaces to develop depth and perspective. In the extreme foreground, the interior of Tarlton's ship is blue, followed midframe by the general congregation of orange Cybrinians assembled to welcome him in an enormous yellow antechamber. Behind them sits a distant blue wall, which gives way to another huge, yellow observation deck cut off from the open air. In it sit the throngs of equally excited blue Cybrinians, who doubtless know that Tarlton's arrival can only assist their struggle against the ignorance disseminated through the orange educators. Similar rhythms of alternately blue-yellow, yellow-black, and orange-blue are used throughout "Judgment Day!" within panels and across whole page layouts to braid in clues about the obsessive separation of different colors, the boundaries involved, and the agents responsible for them.

1.2 The two robots and Tarlton are practically glued together in space as Tarlton points out the bigotry of the orange robot.

Finally, Tarlton's spacesuit initiates one of the story's most nuanced arthrological games. The first panel that depicts Tarlton's arrival includes, in the extreme right foreground, an enormous spherical piece of futuristic navigational equipment. EC artists always delighted in "filling in the holes with funny machinery and buildings and landscapes and things" to increase the visual weight and wonder of their compositions (Benson 49). In this case, the weird machine resembles some type of pneumatic astrolabe, with gears, hoses, and circuits connecting it to the rest of Tarlton's complicated rocket. Following the gizmo's erect arm up into the rest of the frame, we are drawn immediately to Tarlton's head as he exits his ship. Orlando includes another braided visual comparison, in which the huge machine and its attendant hoses clearly comment on the design of Tarlton's face-obscuring helmet and its air intake. The link is unmistakable, suggesting, from the very beginning of the story—amid shouts of "Welcome! Welcome Earthman, to Cybrinia! To the planet of Mechanical Life!"—that, at first glance, the visitor appears almost as artificial as the resident robots. The irony sets up the final panel's payoff, when we encounter the first truly human face in the entire spatiotopical experience and, regardless of his race or appearance, cannot help but identify with his noble, pensive, resolutely unrobotic features. The thoughtfully prepared twist represents a remarkable alternative to the long, painful tradition of racist stereotypes in American science fiction, which as Adilifu Nama argues, is rooted largely in "crude construction of the

1.3 Background design and mechanical gear link Tarlton to the robots, though later he will be differentiated by his humanity.

black male body as a phallic threat," an expendable, exoticized companion, or a gruesome alien other (81).

Nama's 2008 study *Black Space: Imagining Race in Science Fiction Film* also offers one final key to the persuasive potency of "Judgment Day!" In most cases, he argues, the spacesuit, "one of the most iconic symbols of SF cinema," has been employed as a tool of "racial stigmatization." As a "second skin" that allows the wearer to survive in the vacuous cosmos, it also functions as a traditionally white "symbol/signifier" that conjures themes of "antiseptic, hyperrational, and chaste morality" rooted in the Caucasian dominance of space exploration (Nama 85). In such cases, the spacesuit "underscores the transcendent aura of the astronaut" as an advanced, noble—and at times imperialist—pioneer (Nama 85). It can also perpetuate the questionable racial and colonial themes of "juvenile" pulpy "cowboys-and-Indians-in-spaceships science fiction like Buck Rogers" (Benson 37). With the emphasis on a fire-engine-red spacesuit, "Judgment Day!" once again goes against the grain, using Tarlton's second skin to mask social codes and individual assumptions associated with his actual organic epidermis until the story's end. Instead of a technological fetish or totem employed to perpetuate the traditionally "standard absence and token presence" of nonwhite protagonists in science fiction, Tarlton's bright red suit keeps clashing with the rest of Orlando's color scheme (Nama 10). It hints, again and again, from panel to panel, that something about this astronaut and his skin will mark a profound and disturbing change not only in the annals of imperfect Cybrinia but also in the conventions of science fiction and, unfortunately for William Gaines and his startlingly belligerent publications, the future of the US comics industry.

To further comprehend how singular the revelation of Tarlton's race might have seemed to a comics-reading public, we should step outside the contexts of the Senate and the CMAA, civil rights and science fiction, and look briefly at how few heroic African American comic book characters actually existed before all the trouble over "Judgment Day!" The numbers, as we might expect, are surprisingly few, but Tarlton's scarce ancestors are especially revealing.

Race Comics B.E.T.: Before EC's Tarlton

The ironic finish of "Judgment Day!" trades on the unexpected shock of revealing that Tarlton is, in fact, a righteous and responsible Black man. This celebration of a heroic Black protagonist's intelligence, responsibility, and tutelage is not only surprising for its time; it is nearly unique in comics—and exceedingly scarce in media history—before 1960. In terms of 1950s science fiction, the story is unprecedented in its use of race as a criticism of democratic progress. In radio, TV, or cinema up to 1955, few fantasies were as specifically accusatory concerning segregation. Nama's *Black Space* salutes later works such as *The Outer Limits*, *Star Trek*, and *Space: 1999*, but there is little reference to positive race-based allegories before the early 1960s. Except for a rare metaphor for the "erosion of white imperialistic hegemony" in *When Worlds Collide* (1951), the science fiction of the time was largely rooted in the "political gamesman-ship" of Red Scare allegories such as *The Day the Earth Stood Still* (1951), *The War of the Worlds* (1953), and *Invasion of the Body Snatchers* (1956) or nuclear panic films such as *Them!* (1954) and its host of radioactive, colossal, shrink-ing, overwrought, underplotted brethren (Nama 14)[5]. Even *Sight and Sound*'s more comprehensive time line of international science fiction media from 1895 to 1996 suggests little room in the genre of *Gojira* (1954) and *The Giant Claw* (1957) for statements on prejudice or segregation beyond the tangential cautionary messages of Don Siegel's *Body Snatchers* and Fred Wilcox's *Forbid-den Planet* (1956) (Allan et al.). In comic books, one generally finds the same recurrence of slight but highly compromised caution, cruelty, and control with regard to representations of race.

As Christian Davenport points out in his "examination of ethnic stereo-types" in comic books, "Black Is the Color of My Comic Book Character," comics-based depictions of "Blacks (whether they appeared on a street corner or on Mars) would be represented by characteristics that were/are usually asso-ciated with African Americans, such as a threatening demeanor, high levels of athletic prowess, low intellectual capabilities, exotic and mysterious backgrounds, residence within an inner city, and menial employment or unemployment" (22). Charles Hardy and Gail Stern's *Ethnic Images in the Comics* also confirms that Tarlton's heroic features and thoughtful demeanor are well ahead of his time. From 1900 to 1960, African American characters were decidedly stereo-typed as ignorant, savage, servile, or grotesque—a representative lineage clearly tied to established blackface minstrel traditions (Hardy and Stern 13). Of the nearly two hundred images surveyed in Fredrik Strömberg's *Black Images in the Comics*, only four of the forty-one prior to 1960 depict consciously positive representations of African Americans, and only one—a brief untitled backup story about a Black war hero in *World's Finest* #17 from 1945—appears in comic book form before EC's "Judgment Day!" (97).[6] Nearly everything else, not surprisingly, conforms to Charles Johnson's observation that Ameri-can comics' "cornucopia of culturally sedimented images" shows that most of their creators "knew nothing—absolutely nothing—about their black sub-jects" (6, 11). Aldo Regalado's inquiry into racism in superhero comics expands on Johnson's comment, noting that "writers, artists, industry executives, and audiences have historically, although often unconsciously, employed an often divisive, exclusionary, and oppressive vocabulary of themes and images in the creation of characters, landscapes, and narratives that sell the dream, but not the reality, of individual liberation and social transgression. Of these discourses, none is more insidiously prevalent than that of race, as is evidenced by the over-whelming majority of white, muscled, male heroes that populate the genre, as well as by the negative stereotypes of Asians, Native Americans, African

Americans, and other ethnic groups that often manifest in the face of comic book villainy" (86).

Even beyond the superhero genre, "comic book creators and audiences engaged the language and imagery of race, either consciously or unconsciously, because it existed (and continues to exist) as part of their lived experience. Appropriating this racial language, comic book creators manipulated its contours, and employed it in giving voice to their own desires, fantasies, and longings. . . . This process of individual or group affirmation has often entailed an objectification or vilification of ethnically or racially defined others" (Regalado 86). The rampant desecration of African American identities, especially their bodies and faces, in American comics before 1960 was, in fact, one of the first offenses that Fredric Wertham cited in his influential crusade against the comics. Concerned, at first, with the "ideological content" of comic books, Wertham "especially despised the racist, imperialistic, and pornographic images littered throughout the jungle comics" and their space-opera derivatives (Wright 94). Wertham himself hardly fits the image of a typical censor or crusader (Beaty 135). He was, by all accounts, a "liberal progressive concerned about the poor and disadvantaged," with a particularly commendable record with regard to race: "He was . . . among the few psychiatrists at the time who would see black patients. . . . [He] personally opened the LaFargue Clinic in the basement of Harlem's St. Philip's Episcopal Church, where he and his staff offered psychiatric service to poor clients, most of whom were African Americans, at a cost of twenty-five cents per visit," and he was eventually responsible for "a set of arguments later used in the Supreme Court's landmark *Brown vs. Board of Education* desegregation ruling" (Wright 93). How ironic, then, that Wertham's efforts to purge the comics of politically dangerous and ethnically offensive material would ultimately lead to the squelching of the publisher whose output included the forward-thinking "Judgment Day!," among other tales of tolerance and protest.

As far as current scholarship can fathom, Tarlton in "Judgment Day!" has an extremely small ancestry of nonbigoted Black comics characters. Jackie Robinson had become the subject of several inspirational one-shot comics, and the achievements of a few other African American athletes and celebrities had been documented in the pages of some lesser-known news-based "True Facts" titles. For the most part, supposedly nonthreatening Black servants or mascots, sweet Topsys, and grinning "pickaninnies" were present in every form of American comics, from World War II propaganda to cross-marketed Hollywood novelties: "*The Young Allies* had Whitewash, Will Eisner's popular *The Spirit* had as his side-kick Ebony, *Classics Illustrated* had published 'Uncle Tom's Cabin' (No. 15, November 1943); Walt Kelly had inked covers for *Our Gang Comics* showcasing black children, and African Americans had appeared throughout the newspaper strip reprint titles and in other comics as background characters. But you had to stretch to find them. Moreover, there was not a single lead character, certainly not a lead or secondary superhero to be found!" (Weist 106).

Limiting the search to Black comic book characters involved in any form of racial awareness or social activism makes Tarlton's legacy even more astonishing. Here, the dignified Black astronaut stands or "sweats" alongside only a few known antecedents. Among them are Roy Ald and Alvin Hollingsworth's short-lived, three-issue experiment in *Negro Romance* from Fawcett and the anonymous propaganda piece at the back of *World's Finest* #17, detailing the exploits of Sgt. Ralph Jackson, who led "a battalion of Black American soldiers against the Nazis," and concluding with "living examples" such as "Joe Lewis, Paul Robeson," and Marian Anderson, who proclaim, "thousands of negroes of every profession have shown the world that your race can do anything any other can" (Strömberg 97). Though inspiring for such innovative efforts, these abortive series and brief "feel good" tales, relegated to the backs of superhero comic books, apparently caught little fire with the public ("Race"). The stylish and frequently politicized works of Jackie Ormes, E. Simms Campbell, Morrie Turner, and Ollie Harrington, distributed through either African American newspapers or periodicals such as *Esquire* and *Ebony*, provided a more consistent but still marginalized and largely underappreciated set of voices and talents.

Next, there were the witty personalities who inhabited the Philadelphia-area Black journalist, activist, and entrepreneur Orrin C. Evans's *All-Negro Comics* of June 1947. They included the lead hero, Ace Harlem, a hard-boiled proto–Easy Rawlins, conceived to "point up the outstanding contributions of thousands of fearless, intelligent Negro police officers." Then came the jungle feature "Lion Man and Bubba," which "hoped to give American Negroes a reflection of their natural spirit of adventure and a finer appreciation of their African heritage" (Evans, qtd. in Weist 106). *All-Negro Comics* "might have achieved great goals," and "thousands of African Americans across the country would have rejoiced"; but like "Judgment Day!," the material was suppressed, and "external forces made the first issue a one-shot" (Weist 106). The series was refused newsprint and "stonewalled by suppliers in the Philadelphia area," and it remains uncertain whether Evans's groundbreaking use of positive Black characters ever "received wide distribution" (Weist 106). Less than a decade later, when an established white publisher faced similar resistance to a story that had previously won it kudos from both Black and white readers, it, too, eventually gave up the ghost. We must also mention the groundbreaking 1957 one-shot *Martin Luther King and the Montgomery Story*, which was published by the Fellowship of the Reconciliation and became an important tactical document in the promotion and proliferation of the civil rights movement as well as a seminal moment in the history of African American comic art.

Yet one other substantive and largely underrecognized example of American comics' "positive" use of racial conflict and political awareness before 1960 exists. In this case, the book circulated with considerable impact without any blowback from censors, but its origins are somewhat surprising. Ironically, it arose as a conservative, faith-based tool for alerting America's Cold War youth to threats of Communist terrorism and subterfuge. It was the product of the same "small Catholic publisher" that produced the Christian-themed *Topix* and *Treasure Chest* comic book lines.⁷ *Is This Tomorrow? America under Communism* appeared in 1948 with a hellish, apocalyptic cover design that must have hit the majority of Americans as if Satan himself had hurled an atomic bomb at the United States. At any rate, this and other "anticommunist propaganda pamphlets" circulated freely at home and abroad (Gabilliet 36). Distributed through the American Catholic Church, ten- and fifteen-cent copies were delivered to "parishes, youth clubs, boy scouts, and other groups" nationwide (Gabilliet 36). *Is This Tomorrow?* boasts one of the era's most serious portrayals of African Americans on a high-circulation comic book cover. As the Stars and Stripes are consumed in a holocaust of fire and violence, an elderly white man viciously punches an African American soldier or vet, while another soldier in Communist uniform overpowers a priest with a "half-nelson." Center cover, a lascivious, grinning assailant strangles a well-dressed woman in one of the strongest coded metaphors for bigotry, sacrilege, and rape ever assigned to popular comics in the United States.

The nightmares within *Is This Tomorrow?* are equally appalling. The dystopian epic reveals an intricate "Commie plot" to undermine American capitalist democracy in total and ends with the shooting of the president himself. Early in the conspiracy, Communist agents incite dissension and disorder by antagonizing the racial and spiritual fault lines of the American populace. In one harrowing phase of the takeover, immediately after a fuming mob has ruthlessly pulled a bespectacled intellectual from his home and lynched him, the "red plan" employs "a flood of intolerant pamphlets" to turn Catholics and Jews against each other, but the coup de grace comes when their attention turns to African Americans.

To initiate a race riot that leaves the majority of an unnamed American city ablaze and leads to an industry-crippling general strike, a beautiful, white Red agent is ordered to "start something with those two negroes" at an amusement park. In a frightening parallel to the Emmett Till lynching, the woman turns toward two well-dressed Black men who are quietly engaged in a carnival game and shouts, "That man insulted me!" The next panel shows her physically wrestling with one of the thoroughly confused African Americans while a mob of outraged white men, laced with clandestine Communist agents, falls upon them both. Two panels later, the city has burned for four days, and the riot has spread across the country. The book's general depiction of African Americans is somewhat sympathetic. Though they are positioned as hapless, innocent victims of Communist conspiracy and rampant racial hatred, the story also emphasizes that their worst enemies are the Anglos who are so easily misguided and cajoled into acts of racist violence. On the cover and throughout the text, no Black character ever rises up or resists the onslaught of the mindless white oppressors—though plenty of African Americans are depicted as victims, prostrate or recoiling from

1.4 The apocalyptic cover design of *Is This Tomorrow?*, an anti-Communist pamphlet.

the blows of easily manipulated white hordes. Wertham and his constituents worried over the suggestive powers of comic book imagery with regard to delinquency and fascist ideology, but *Is This Tomorrow?* suggests that such concerns could also work to encourage the opposite result, that of gross reactionary intolerance through sequential suggestions of Communist-induced interracial rape, lynching, and rioting.

The final irony might be that *Is This Tomorrow?* likely reached more young Americans than any other pro- or quasi-pro-Black comic book. As an organ of the Roman Catholic Church, its distribution system worked outside established commercial networks and beyond the purview of most censors. Compared to either *All-Negro Comics*, the Martin Luther King, Jr., one-shot, or the two EC editions that contained "Judgment Day!," *Is This Tomorrow?* may have scared more kids straight into epiphanies about race and class than most comics and their makers ever would have conceived or attempted. To exploit such an opportunity, the book's back cover boasts a handy checklist that advises readers on how to "fight Communism with the Ten Commandments of Citizenship." Its succinct creed includes statutes such as "Be tolerant of other races, religions, and nationalities" (number 4), alongside tenets of critical awareness such as "Know your government" (number 1), "Practice your own religion" (number 5), "Read newspapers and magazines critically" (number 6), and "Be American first" (number 10).

The book's sixth commandment is especially amusing considering the storm of controversy and derision that comics were to encounter in years to come. Still, *Is This Tomorrow?* is not so different from "Judgment Day!" as we might wish. Both were designed as racial polemics by and primarily for a white readership. Both stories depict exaggerated future worlds where racial prejudice and widespread segregation retard the progress of democracy while assisting and sustaining its industrial and imperialist systems of control and exploitation. Both also offer sympathetic and respectable portrayals of non-Anglo protagonists, both Black and blue. In terms of narrative, each story also reveals a shocking potential truth as its finishing punch. In one scenario, humans have overcome their racial biases and men such as Tarlton have arisen to take their rightful place in "the great Galactic Republic." The other warns that tolerance is not enough, as the enemies of freedom and democracy will gladly exploit existing faults and prejudices to destroy the freedoms of the future. One wonders if *Is This Tomorrow?* would have garnered approval from Murphy and the CMAA despite its many violations of CCA guidelines pertaining to violence and criminal activity (Nyberg, *Seal* 166).

"Judgment Day!," with its stunning finish and its affable Black protagonist, ultimately signifies a watershed moment in three distinct contexts. First, it offers a surprisingly positive reversal of the standard racial dynamics of American science fiction, in which a solitary enlightened Black man stands alone against a blatantly prejudiced, ignorant society. At the same time, Feldstein and Orlando's clever mise-en-page engenders what Groensteen would describe as a uniquely compelling comics *multiframe*, in which readers are carefully encouraged to identify with the perspectives and goals of African American equality without pandering to established cartoon stereotypes. Lastly, the fracas between EC and the CMAA over the censorship of "Judgment Day!" provides us with a fascinating example of how easily supposedly protective forms of regulation and censorship may be appropriated and deployed to limit or stifle potent social protest or political dissent. In fact, from our twenty-first-century post-Obama perspective, it is quite fitting that Orlando's "Judgment Day!" has grown in stature and import with other EC shockers such as Bernie Krigstein's "Master Race" and Harvey Kurtzman's "Corpse on the Imjin" to become one of the most respected and influential tales of tolerance in American comic books.

Notes

1   Recent examples include Jean-Paul Gabilliet, *Of Comics and Men* (2010); Paul Lopes, *Demanding Respect* (2009); Randy Duncan and Matthew J. Smith, *The Power of Comics: History, Form, and Culture* (2009); David Hajdu, *The Ten-Cent Plague* (2008); Shirrel Rhoades, *A Complete History of American Comic Books* (2008); and Bart Beaty, *Fredric Wertham and the Critique of Mass Culture* (2005). Excellent earlier histories include Amy Kiste Nyberg's *Seal of Approval* (1998) and James Gilbert's *A Cycle of Outrage* (1986). Carol L Tilley's 2014 article "Seducing the Innocent: Fredric Wertham and the Falsifications That Helped Condemn Comics" is an even more focused and recent reassessment of Wertham's influence.

2   *Incredible Science Fiction* was the retitled version of *Weird Science-Fantasy*, a change necessitated by the Comics Code's infamous decision to forbid such key words as *weird* and *horror* while severely restricting the use of the word *crime*—all key components in the titles of EC's pre-Code "New Trend" comic book series (Nyberg, *Seal* 166–167).

3   Nyberg's scrupulously researched publications all provide excellent summaries of the many variations of what may have happened between the CMAA and EC with regard to "Judgment Day!" Bart Beaty also comments on the "historical amnesia" involved in how "EC publisher Bill Gaines has recast the history of the Comics Code as an attempt to drive his 'subversive' company out of business" and observes that "a large number of commentators have come to accept as truth this myth, which gained force in early EC comics fan circles and subsequently spread" (203–204). For example, David Hajdu privileges Al Feldstein's account of events surrounding the post-Code reprinting of "Judgment Day!," and Ron Mann's 1989 documentary *Comic Book Confidential* includes Bill Gaines's own summary of the affair, in which he calls "Judgment Day!" the "finest story we ever wrote."

4   Even "Judgment Day!" is guilty of overemphasized patriarchy since it posits the utterly masculine homosocial world of Cybrinia, where mothers, wives, sisters, and lovers are replaced by the assembly line and the Educators. To ensure some "responsibility toward propagation," each newborn Cybrinian must "work for a time on the assembly line." This is one of the few aspects of Cybrinian culture of which Tarlton clearly approves, signaling in part that he too is somehow implicated in the future's erasure of femininity. If the makers of "Judgment Day!" had been truly committed to testing the full revolutionary power of their art, they might have revealed Tarlton as an African American woman astronaut.

5   A rare and obscure but fascinating exception to the generally race-oblivious nature of 1950s American science fiction cinema is the still underappreciated Arch Oboler chamber drama *Five*, focusing on the world's last handful of postnuclear survivors, one of whom is African American while yet another is a neo-Nazi. With much of the same candor as Oboler's equally progressive "Strange Morning" propaganda play for the World War II radio series *Plays for Americans*, *Five* digs deeply into the

racial politics of atomic apocalypse where more conventional, mainstream narratives ignored or marginalized issues relating to civil rights, interracial understanding, and African American pride.

6 The last two examples are both somewhat-little-known works by African Americans. One is Jackie Ormes's *Torchy Brown* newspaper strip, which began before "Judgment Day!" in 1937 and was distributed by Afro-American Continental Features Syndicate to "Black-owned syndicates and papers" (Stromberg 109; see also Nancy Goldstein's chapter 4 in this volume). The last is "another comic printed in the Black press" around 1959, Tom Feelings's strip for the *New York Age*, *Tommy Traveller in the World of Negro History* (Stromberg 115).

7 *Treasure Chest Comics*, a sort of Catholic blending of *Boys Life*, *Classics Illustrated*, and Dell's humor books, also periodically featured positive portrayals and even cover designs based on the newsworthy achievements of African Americans.

Works Cited

Allan, Vicky, Ben Bachley, Leslie Felperin, and Nick James, with Philip Strick, eds. "Cloning the Future: Science Fiction Film 1895–1996." Special supplement of *Sight and Sound*, November 1996.

Beaty, Bart. *Fredric Wertham and the Critique of Mass Culture*. Jackson: University Press of Mississippi, 2005.

Beaty, Bart, and Nick Nguyen. Foreword. *The System of Comics*. By Thierry Groensteen. Jackson: University Press of Mississippi, 2007. vii–x.

Benson, Mike. *The Illustrated History of Science Fiction Comics*. Dallas: Taylor, 1992.

Carpenter, Stanford W. "Authorship and the Creation of the Black Captain America." *Comics as Philosophy*. Ed. Jeff McLaughlin. Jackson: University Press of Mississippi, 2005. 46–62.

Cohn, Neil. *The Visual Language of Comics: An Introduction to the Structure and Cognition of Sequential Images*. New York: Bloomsbury Academic, 2014.

Comic Book Confidential. Dir. Ron Mann. Strand Releasing, 1988. DVD.

"Comics Magazine Association of America Comics Code: 1954." *Seal of Approval: The History of the Comics Code*. By Amy Kiste Nyberg. Jackson: University Press of Mississippi, 1998. 166–169.

Couperie, Pierre, and Maurice C. Horn. *A History of the Comic Strip*. Trans. Eileen B. Hennessy. New York: Crown, 1968.

Davenport, Christian. "Black Is the Color of My Comic Book Character: An Examination of Ethnic Stereotypes." *Inks: Cartoon and Comic Art Studies* 4.1 (February 1997): 20–28.

The Day the Earth Stood Still. Dir. Robert Wise. Perf. Michael Rennie, Patricia Neal. 20th Century Fox, 1951. Film.

Duncan, Randy, and Matthew J. Smith. *The Power of Comics: History, Form, and Culture*. New York: Continuum, 2009.

Feldstein, Al, and Joe Orlando. "Judgment Day!" *Weird Fantasy* #18 (March–April 1953). EC Comics.

———. "Judgment Day!" *Incredible Science Fiction* #33 (January–February 1956). EC Comics.

Five. Dir. Arch Oboler. Perf. William Fipps, Susan Douglas Rubbes. Arch Oboler Productions, 1951. Film.

Forbidden Planet. Dir. Fred M. Wilcox. Perf. Walter Pidgeon, Anne Francis, Leslie Nielsen. MGM, 1956. Film.

Gabilliet, Jean-Paul. *Of Comics and Men: A Cultural History of American Comic Books*. Trans. Bart Beaty and Nick Nguyen. Jackson: University Press of Mississippi, 2010.

Gardner, Jared. *Projections: Comics and the History of Twenty-First Century Storytelling*. Stanford, CA: Stanford University Press, 2012.

Geissman, Grant. *Foul Play! The Art and Artists of the Notorious 1950s EC Comics!* New York: HarperDesign, 2005.

The Giant Claw. Dir. Fred F. Fears. Perf. Jeff Morrow, Mara Corday. Clover Pictures, 1957. Film.

Gilbert, James. *A Cycle of Outrage: America's Reaction to the Juvenile Delinquent in the 1950s*. New York: Oxford University Press, 1986.

Gojira. Dir. Ishiro Honda. Perf. Akira Takarada, Momoko Kochi. Toho Film, 1954. Film.

Gravett, Paul. *Comics Art*. New Haven, CT: Yale University Press, 2014.

———. *Graphic Novels: Everything You Need to Know*. New York: Harper Design, 2005.

Groensteen, Thierry. *Comics and Narration*. Trans. Ann Miller. Jackson: University Press of Mississippi Press, 2013.

———. *The System of Comics*. Trans. Bart Beaty and Nick Nguyen. Jackson: University Press of Mississippi, 2007.

Hajdu, David. *The Ten-Cent Plague: The Great Comic Book Scare and How It Changed America*. New York: Farrar, Straus, and Giroux, 2008.

Hardy, Charles, and Gail Stern. *Ethnic Images in the Comics*. Philadelphia: Balch Institute for Ethnic Studies, 1986.

Hatfield, Charles. *Alternative Comics: An Emerging Literature*. Jackson: University Press of Mississippi, 2005.

Inge, M. Thomas. *Comics as Culture*. Jackson: University Press of Mississippi, 1990.

Invasion of the Body Snatchers. Dir. Don Seigel. Perf. Kevin McCarthy, Dana Wynter. Walter Wanger, 1956. Film.

Johnson, Charles. Foreword. *Black Images in the Comics*. Ed. Fredrick Stromberg. Seattle: Fantagraphics, 2003. 6–19.

Jones, Gerard. *Men of Tomorrow: Geeks, Gangsters, and the Birth of the Comic Book*. New York: Basic Books, 2004.

Lopes, Paul. *Demanding Respect: The Evolution of the American Comic Book*. Philadelphia: Temple University Press, 2009.

Martin Luther King and the Montgomery Story. Fellowship of the Reconciliation, 1957. Available at *Martin Luther King, Jr. and the Global Freedom Struggle*, The Martin Luther King, Jr., Research and Education Institute, Stanford University. Web. http://mlk-kpp01.stanford.edu/primarydocuments/Comic%20Book%201957.pdf. Accessed 20 December 2013.

Miodrag, Hannah. *Comics and Language: Reimagining Critical Discourse on the Form*. Jackson: University Press of Mississippi, 2013.

Nama, Adilifu. *Black Space: Imagining Race in Science Fiction Film*. Austin: University of Texas Press, 2008.

Nyberg, Amy Kiste. "'No Harm in Horror': Ethical Dimensions of the Postwar Comic Book Controversy." *Comics as Philosophy*. Ed. Jeff McLaughlin. Jackson: University Press of Mississippi, 2007. 27–45.

———. *Seal of Approval: The History of the Comics Code*. Jackson: University Press of Mississippi, 1998.

———. "William Gaines and the Battle over EC Comics." *Inks: Cartoon and Comic Art Studies* 3.1 (February 1996): 2–15.

Peeters, Benoit. "'Four Conceptions of the Page' from 'Case, planche, récit: lire la bande dessinée.'" Trans. Jesse Cohn. *ImageTexT: Interdisciplinary Comics Studies* 3.3 (2007). Web. http://www.english.ufl.edu/imagetext/archives/v3_3/peeters. Accessed 27 August 2012.

Postema, Barbara. *Narrative Structure in Comics: Making Sense of Fragments*. Rochester, NY: RIT Press, 2013.

"Race, Romance, and the Comic Book." *History Detectives*. Episode 56. PBS.org. 12 July 2011. Web. Accessed 10 April 2013.

Regalado, Aldo. "Modernity, Race, and the American Superhero." *Comics as Philosophy*. Ed. Jeff McLaughlin. Jackson: University Press of Mississippi, 2007. 84–99.

Reitberger, Reinhold, and Wolfgang Fuchs. *Comics: Anatomy of a Mass Medium*. New York: Little, Brown, 1971.

Rhoades, Shirrel. *A Complete History of American Comic Books*. New York: Peter Lang, 2008.

Sabin, Roger. *Adult Comics: An Introduction*. New York: Routledge, 1993.

Sedes, Gilbert. *Seven Lively Arts*. 1924. Mineola, NY: Dover, 2001.

Strömberg, Fredrik. *Black Images in the Comics: A Visual History*. Seattle: Fantagraphics, 2003.

Them! Dir. Gordon Douglas. Perf. James Whitmore, Edmund Gwenn. Warner Brothers, 1954. Film.

Tilley, Carol L. "Seducing the Innocent: Fredric Wertham and the Falsifications That Helped Condemn Comics." *Information & Culture* 47.4 (2012): 383–413.

The War of the Worlds. Dir. Byron Haskin. Perf. Gene Barry, Ann Robinson. Paramount, 1953. Film.

Warshow, Robert. "Paul, the Horror Comics, and Dr. Wertham." 1954. *Arguing Comics: Literary Masters on a Popular Medium*. Ed. Jeet Heer and Kent Worcester. Jackson: University Press of Mississippi, 2004. 67–80.

Weist, Jerry. 100 *Greatest Comic Books*. Atlanta: Whitman, 2004.

When Worlds Collide. Dir. Rudolph Mate. Perf. Richard Derr, Barbara Rush. Paramount, 1951. Film.

Wolk, Douglas. *Reading Comics: How Graphic Novels Work and What They Mean*. Cambridge, MA: Da Capo, 2007.

Wright, Bradford. *Comic Book Nation: The Transformation of Youth Culture in America*. Baltimore: Johns Hopkins University Press, 2001.

Chapter 2

Sex in Yop City

• •

Ivorian Femininity and Masculinity in Abouet and Oubrerie's *Aya*

SALLY McWILLIAMS

> She was back in Africa. And that felt like
> fresh honey on the tongue: a mixture of
> complete sweetness and smoky roughage.
> — Ama Ata Aidoo

> Graphic narratives, on the whole, have the
> potential to be powerful precisely because
> they intervene against a culture of invis-
> ibility by taking the risk of representation.
> —Hillary Chute and Marianne DeKoven

In Ama Ata Aidoo's 1977 tour de force, *Our Sister Killjoy*, a young West African woman returns to Africa after experiencing the racial prejudices and poverty
of Germany and England; the novel's protagonist, Sissie, acknowledges the
problems confronting her postcolonial homeland and her commitment to the
possibilities it has to offer. This combination of sweetness and harshness speaks

to the multifaceted feelings that many African women writers draw on in their literary representations of Africa and its peoples, societies, politics, and histories. The first in the series of graphic novels written by Marguerite Abouet and illustrated by Clement Oubrerie, *Aya* centers on the bittersweet complexities of West Africa.[1] The graphic novel's form and content intervene in what Hillary Chute and Marianne DeKoven in this chapter's epigraph call "the culture of invisibility"—an invisibility understood to mean a lack of representations showing Africa and Africans to be more than victims of colonialism, tribally motivated aggressors against one another, or the displaced black-skinned pawns in global conflicts over natural resources, land, and power. With evocative, colorful images by Oubrerie and engaging characterizations by Abouet, *Aya* redirects our attention away from the Western media's reductive iterations of an Africa always (and seemingly forever) mired in diseases, disasters, and death.[2] Employing the register of the everyday and social comedy, *Aya* refuses the invisible "single story" of Africa[3] and instead opens the way for critical engagement with humorous depictions of gender constructions, sexual politics, and neocolonial class hierarchies in a progressive urban West African locale, in what Guy Lancaster terms "an era of cultural transformation" (944). The text uses stock characters, illustrative colors, exaggerated proportions, multiple points of view, and braiding of panel sequences to construct a feminist narrative that resists any moribund interpretation of Yop City's gender and sexual politics.[4] *Aya* represents what Abouet claims to be the reality of Africa: for as she says, Africa endures despite everything "because, as we say back home, life goes on" (qtd. in Reid).

Abouet and Oubrerie's collaboration to produce a graphic novel about West Africa is a risky literary venture. Not only do graphic novels continue to have a troubled relationship to the literary, but the difficulties in representing Africans in this medium are particularly treacherous because of the problematic relationship between African peoples and the way cartooning has historically depicted them.[5] Abouet and Oubrerie are undaunted, however; they boldly use visual and narrative strategies based on hybridity, contrasts, and contingency to position *Aya* within the global arena of contemporary comics. Ivorian locales, French-inspired fashions, neocolonial architecture, and linguistic play all bespeak *Aya*'s participation in "the global flux of ideas and images in a world undergoing rapid changes" (Repetti 18). The book's reputation as an award winner reveals how graphic novels about Africa are beginning to claim their rightful place within this burgeoning field of literary production.[6]

Aya establishes its own credentials as a postcolonial feminist space of interrogation through its deployment of social comedy. In the introduction to the collection titled *Cheeky Fictions*, Susanne Reichl and Mark Stein argue that the pairing of the postcolonial with humor has been seen as not only oxymoronic but also disrespectful of the serious nature of the postcolonial project to question the ideological discourses and actions of (neo)colonialism (2). They theorize that "while the complex postcolonial relationships between centre and margin (or centres and margins) are far from humorous, the specific settings, however diverse, regularly include conditions in which laughter and humour can release some of the tension and relieve some of the potential aggression" (9). In the case of *Aya*, the interrogative power of humor goes even further as its feminist impulses function to destabilize not only prescribed categories of gender and patriarchal ideology but the postcolonial social order itself.

Feminist humor is multifaceted, resistant, and piquant. Wendy Siuyi Wong and Lisa M. Cuklanz assert that the use of humor by women "is in itself a politically charged act" (71). They explain that "feminist humor in general has been characterized as having four defining elements: directly attacking or critiquing gender roles, exposing the realities of gender inequality and discrimination under patriarchal ideology, expressing elements of experience that are shared by women generally, and expressing hope toward a vision of change" (72). Feminist humor also helps to overcome the kinds of images that characterize Africa in Western media as well as helps to dissipate some of the egotism and misogyny of male humor. Jaye Montresor writes, "Because humor that relies on the arrogant perception of traditional male humor to get laughs reinforces the fear, anger, and hatred that are at the root of so many of our social problems, sharing a laugh that promotes awareness and identification rather than arrogance and estrangement is one way we can overcome . . . negative perceptions" (338).

Black feminist humor goes further than simply interrogating gender politics; it takes on neocolonialism, racialism, Western feminism, and Black patriarchal modes of power. Calling attention to the ideological shortcomings and quagmires created by hegemonic discourses and actions, it disallows a monolithic rendering of nationalism at the expense of gender awareness and refuses to privilege Black masculinity at the expense of Black women's agency. It challenges the presumed and presumptuous arrogance of neocolonialism. It shuns the monofocal aspects of Western feminism when its practitioners are immobilized by their well-meaning, albeit stereotypical, views of the "poor" African woman in need of rescue. Black feminist humor shows the serious side of laughter as being a survival strategy, a mode of reaching out for and creating happiness. Speaking about African American women, Daryl Cumber Dance writes, "Humor . . . has rather been a means of surviving as we struggled. We haven't been laughing so much because things tickle us. . . . We laugh to keep from dying" (xxi–xxii). African women, like their U.S. counterparts, deploy humor "to speak the unspeakable, to mask the attack, to get a tricky subject on the table, to warn of lines not to be crossed, . . . to speculate, to gossip, to educate, to correct the lies people tell on us, to bring about change" (Dance xxii). Such humor riffs on African women's sexuality, their bodies, their ways of walking and talking, and the actions of their male counterparts. African women's humor shows us society through the African woman's dark-eyed "squint"—a critical perspective that sees more than most when it comes to the personal and public power relations between men and women, among nations, and across cultures.[7]

Circulating Stories of Modernity

Abouet and Oubrerie's novel begins with the eponymous nineteen-year-old female narrator contextualizing the image of her country, the "Ivory Coast, my beautiful country," circa 1978.[8] Instead of telling us about her fellow citizens or the country's achievements, Aya describes what we see on the TV screen, namely, the first TV ad campaign for the country's most popular beer, Solibra, represented by a popular male comedian's physical prowess. Aya's simple yet heartfelt honorific—"my beautiful country"—humorously challenges the image of the beer-fueled male bicyclist outpacing public transportation. Her understated sarcasm refuses to fall prey to sentimental patriotism or unqualified adoration of Ivorian masculinity; yet her tone is not disrespectful of her nation or its male citizenry. She respects Ivorian modernity enough to be able to laugh at and along with her countrymen; and yet, rather than being fueled by Solibra, Aya's commentary is fueled by keen feminist insights about gender, power, and national identity.

But more than double-edged sarcasm is at work in this opening panel. Abouet and Oubrerie script the Ivory Coast's entrance into the global age of media production and consumption while at the same time ironically equating empowered Ivorian masculinity with a comedian who drinks the local brew.[9] The captioned introductory page cleverly provides intertwined references and images of Black masculinity, heterosexuality, lineage, consumerism, and globalization within a West African context. The TV, the paradigmatic marker of global consumerism, is itself situated between two other types of pictures: in the upper left-hand corner is a family portrait (with the father's face obscured by the caption); the second, located below the TV, is a framed photograph of a well-dressed Ivorian man and woman in a dancers' embrace. Reproductions of familial longevity (the family portrait), nationalized Black masculinity as comedic (the TV ad), and committed heterosexual relationships (the framed photograph) suggest that the Ivory Coast of 1978 is already deeply implicated in the production, circulation, and consumption of images and discourses of African modernity.[10]

Indicatively, this foregrounding of image making (TV ads and framed photographs as two examples) is a metatextual moment, for not only are the images in the panel working to frame our understanding of Aya's country, but the caption and the white space around the full-page panel also suggest a self-reflexive stance toward the representations of society and culture. Aya as narrator heightens our awareness that the images, stories, and discourses that circulate about

1978 was the year that Ivory Coast, my beautiful country, got to see its first television ad campaign. It was for Solibra, a local beer popular in all of West Africa. Dago, a comedian who was big at the time, took a swig, and suddenly he had the power to blow by buses on his bicycle.

2.1 A TV screen shows the first ad campaign for a popular beer in *Aya*.

Africa are rarely those created and voiced by young West African women. As *Aya* assumes the role of storyteller, then, her insights guide us in our interpretation of her "beautiful" country: we must read both inside and between panels to negotiate the complexities and even the contradictions in the existing and imagined relations of gender, bodies, politics, and spaces. *Aya* deftly foregrounds its own textuality, not to discount that construction but rather to emphasize that the only way one can know a culture and society is to interpret the images and stories that move from storyteller to listener, reader to reader, place to place.

Unsettling Stock Characters: Good(-Time) Girls Unite

Abouet's narrative unfolds within the prevailing, everyday ideologies that circumscribe gender and sexuality in West Africa. This is done by invoking and then complicating two stock female characters: the good-time girl and the good girl. Stephanie Newell explains that African women writers who produce popular fictions disrupt gendered discourses by writing against the grain: "Rather than overthrowing existing gender ideologies, these writers work *within* them and rewrite the most rigid beliefs about the moral qualities that make women into good wives, spiritual mentors or good-time girls. Positioned thus, they might problematise the figures of the ideal wife, the rural mother or the good-time girl, but they do not necessarily reject these popular constructions of femininity" (8; emphasis in original). And yet by working within established gender parameters, these women writers refuse to accept any naturalization of these constructions. The use of stock characters, or recurring stereotypical characters, is a common practice not only in African popular fiction but also in cartooning. Charles Hatfield reminds us that "stereotypes are the raw material of cartooning, hence of comics," hastening to add, in a paraphrase of the master graphic novelist Art Spiegelman, "[the] sustained comics narrative has the power to individualize the stereotype, dismantling it in whole or in part" (115).[11]

If at the start of *Aya* Ivorian masculinity is sarcastically equated with beer drinking and comedic superhuman feats of power (similar to how U. S. commercials combine sports with alternately comic and masterful depictions of men to create positive associations with the brands being marketed), femininity is superficially aligned with the spectacle of women's bodies and their circulation in the games of sexual politics. Abouet invokes the stereotypical "good-time girl" in her depictions of Bintou and Adjoua, two of Aya's closest friends. And yet in these characterizations Abouet reveals the struggles in young women's lives and concomitantly their joie de vivre even as they confront sexism, neocolonial class privilege, and masculinized nationalism. Through her female characterizations, Abouet invokes and at the same time problematizes the impulse to categorize and judge women because of their sexual and class politics.

The equation of women's power with their sex appeal is underscored in several scenes that include dancing at a local open-air restaurant, or *maquis*. For example, early in the novel Adjoua and Bintou hit the dance floor after Bintou has deflected her new boyfriend's jealousy toward a young man she claims to be her "cousin." The two women enthusiastically "roll their tassabas" to the lively sounds of a song whose lyrics declare, "I sailed off by day under a burning sun, leaving my father and country" (Abouet and Oubrerie, *Aya* 11). The suggestion of breaking away from the patriarchal and by extension the nation is emphasized by the young women's gyrations; they are happily unconcerned at this moment with the male spectators who are busy eyeing all their moves. This sequence of panels highlights for us how these young women refuse to be positioned as merely passive objects or simple, rapacious competitors in the national discourse of sexual politics.[12]

Conscientious, responsible, analytical, and forward thinking as well as pretty, Aya seems to stand in contrast to her "good-time girl" counterparts. But instead of pigeonholing her as the morally upright and uptight African woman, the novel creates humorous connections among this "good girl" and her "good-time" girlfriends. While her friends dance away from a patriarchal world, Aya has the strength of character to slough off the sexist views of her father, who would keep her from becoming a doctor (22). In the tradition of stock characters that embody "goodness," Aya is the voice of reason among her female and male friends. And yet her reason is the springboard into different forms of logic. For example, the day after Bintou and Adjoua's night at the maquis, Aya comes over to Bintou's compound to have one of their "endless discussions" (16). When Bintou teases Aya, saying she acts like she is going to university, Aya responds, "I am! I don't want to wind up in the 'C' series" (18). Bintou and Adjoua are amused when Aya reveals that the "C" series she is referring to is "combs, clothing, and chasing men" rather than the science series that "C" typically refers to in Ivorian high schools.

Aya's refusal of the "C" series is supposed to be a putdown of her friends' lack of ambition. But Abouet is not satisfied with a playful rewriting of reason that only leaves a class hierarchy of values in place; instead, after Aya airs her witty logic, her girlfriends twist her vision back on itself to empower their working-class aspirations for female autonomy. Contrary to Aya's expectation, her two friends disagree with her, claiming that they want her version of the "C" series: "That's a good one, Aya," chuckles Adjoua. "But I'd take the 'C' series. I can see myself owning a fancy hair salon, paid for by my man" (18). And the same is true of Bintou, who declares, "And how about my dressmaker's shop, with all the rich ladies in Abidjan coming to have dresses made" (18). Adjoua's and Bintou's visions of their futures, albeit "paid for" by men, include businesses that the women can own and run successfully. Here what might be seen as the "good-time girl's" hedonism is translated into a business plan for her future well-being as a mature Ivorian woman. Aya's refusal of the "C" series is juxtaposed with her working-class friends' views of life after high school, deflecting the humor of her joke into a space to imagine a productive way of life for young, working-class women.

While Adjoua's and Bintou's dreams may seem highly problematic because of the means they want to use to reach them, the text neither silences nor condemns them. In fact, it is Aya's attempt to cross class lines that is summarily challenged throughout the novel. At one point, Adjoua castigates Aya for thinking she is the only "brain" who can use big words in Yop City (49). At another juncture, Hervé, Bintou's cousin, says of Aya, "Boy, you can really talk white, huh" (44), invoking class through race. Ultimately, both stock representations of African young women—whether "good-time girls" or "good girls"—are dislodged and rewritten as the text unveils the class and gender discourses at work.

The moral politics underpinning the suggested dichotomy between "good-time" and "good" girls also comes in for closer scrutiny as a rivalry emerges between Bintou and Adjoua for one man's affections. The code of civility by which a "good girl" should live is lampooned when Aya attempts to stop Bintou, who, in a jealous rage, picks a fight with Adjoua. The sequence of panels shows Aya literally tackling Bintou around the legs. The panels are energized with drawings of Bintou's screaming face and the physical confrontation of the two women, with stars, shoes, and braids flinging across the panel; all the while, Aya hangs on to Bintou's legs for dear life (85). And although Bintou cannot break the tackle, it does not stop her: she merely drags Aya with her. Comically, even while Aya exerts all her strength to drag Bintou away so that she will not hit Adjoua, she respectfully makes excuses to Adjoua's mother about the interruption and intrusion. Aya's attempt to restrain her friend, as powerful as it tries to be, is meaningless. Bintou's superhuman power, fueled by sexual jealousy, echoes the novel's beer-fueled depiction of the Ivorian popular comedian on his bike that opened the novel. The "good" girl cannot stop the "good-time" girl, but neither will she abandon her. Aya's middle-class aspirations are not outside the physical circle of her working-class female peers, but they do not dominate either. It is only the mature African woman, Adjoua's mother, who can get Bintou under control, by wresting her away from Aya. This depiction proves to be a humorous tribute to the power of the adult African woman, thereby trumping either version of "girl"-hood.

African womanhood in its mature glory stands in contradistinction to the superhuman iconography of other popular graphic novel heroes, humorously named the "spandex wall" by the critic Douglas Wolk.[13] In Abouet's world of the graphic novel, the everyday accomplishments of women, at whatever age, become beacons of impressive inspiration. In the novel's presentation of working-class women's bodies as pleasure seeking and self-confident, *Aya* also represents women's bodies as laboring bodies. Even the "good-time girls" Adjoua and Bintou are shown doing the household chores. Throughout the text, we encounter women—working and middle class, young and old—doing lots of physical labor and emotional counseling, while the young men are depicted as lounging around the streets, kiosks, discos, and family compounds. And it is not only young men who are shown as slothful; many of the middle-aged Ivorian men also come in for critique. They are represented as seducing the daughters of

2.2 Only the mature African woman can get a furious friend under control in *Aya*.

their friends, as in the scene where Hyacinthe, Adjoua's father, is shown dancing with Bintou while Bintou's father, Kofi, is dancing with another woman, who is his daughter's age. Even Ignace, Aya's father, is shown as playing a sexually suggestive bartering game with a young girl selling plantains along the road when he is traveling on business in his new position as national sales representative for Solibra Beer. The women, on the other hand, work in the marketplace, hold managerial positions in corporations, tend to the material and emotional needs of their extended families, and do the physical labor associated with domestic work. While masculinity may be fueled by Solibra (and the capitalism associated with the beer industry, as in the case of Mr. Sissoko, Ignace's boss), its representations underscore masculinity's ineffectiveness in contributing much more than sexual innuendo, sex, or capitalistic greed in the course of everyday life. It is the labors of women's bodies that keep Yop City going and growing. If the equivalency between sex appeal and femininity were the predominant quality in the characterization of these young Ivorian women, then *Aya* would only participate in the weary stereotype of the hypersexualized Black woman as the "good-time girl" who ultimately is punished for her freewheeling lifestyle. But with the inclusion of the daily reality of women's work lives, such a stereotype is problematized and displaced.

The Color and Proportions of the Postcolonial

Social comedies derive much of their humor from taking seemingly mundane details or actions and highlighting them so that they reveal the absurdities, ironies, and possibilities that constitute the everyday. In graphic novels, such humorous twists occur not only through the sequencing of panels and the resignification of stock characters but also through the visual play of color and proportions. In *Aya*, these aspects of the visual register complicate and intervene in this soap operatic tale of sexually active youth. While *Aya* in one sense is written against Eurocentric discourses that marginalize Africa from the space and time of modernity (underscoring the cult of invisibility mentioned in the opening of this chapter), in another sense the text relies on a visualization of the invisible—in this case, of darkness—to reveal a space unrestricted by capitalism and traditions of reason.

The novel uses a "splash" panel with a dark-blue wash to produce a space of intimacy.[14] Oubrerie's blue wash intensifies the starry night sky while it cloaks the identities of the young men and women waiting for their respective dates or already in the embrace of their lovers. Within a Eurocentric grammar of progress, a space with no electricity or bricks-and-mortar hotels might symbolize lack, whereas for the Yop City youth, the unlit space of the open-air marketplace becomes their terrain for nocturnal trysts. This space of daytime activity even gets renamed, discursively transforming it from vacant lot to libidinous site of nightly encounters: our narrator tells us, "Evenings, young people in Yopougon used to meet in secret at the market square, also called the 'Thousand Star Hotel'" (28). In contrast to the bright yellows and ochres used in daytime scenes, Oubrerie's color choice acts as both a material marker of time and a metonymic marker of youthful, heterosexual desire. The colors of the Thousand Star Hotel scenes function as a comic foil to the scenes of parental reason and capitalism. The views of human figures from behind, the careful use of shadow to obscure faces and physiques, and the playful encounters of mistaken identity intentionally disrupt the logic of progress and development that the older generation of Ivorians desire to see embodied and enacted by their children. In other words, the darkness that allows for and sustains the encounters at the Thousand Star Hotel ironically reveals the generational differences and sexual politics at the heart of postcolonial Abidjan.

Class privilege, like sexual politics, comes in for critique, this time through the play of proportions. Instead of using color as the tool of destabilization, exaggeration of proportions satirizes the neocolonial aspects of the new African middle class. Mr. Sissoko (Moussa's father and Ignace's boss) and the Sissoko family compound are depicted as larger-than-life figures and spaces. Having seen the single-story, modest homes that line the narrow streets of Yop City, readers are startled by the full-page panel of the Sissokos' pink, multistoried house qua mansion (30). An unattributed speech balloon, emerging from the house, functions like a sign on the side of the house telling all visitors that this supersized structure—this marker of capitalist wealth—"This is beautiful" (30). The owner, like his house, is also represented as an imposing figure, one out of proportion in comparison to the other characters. Mr. Sissoko's girth is emphasized by the *boubou* he wears, a style of clothing that marks him as traditional and yet, because of the cloth and cut, equally of the newly monied middle class of Ivorians (in contrast to Ignace, Aya's father, whose ill-fitting Western suit emphasizes his own uneasiness with being in a room full of the newest Parisian furniture).

Mr. Sissoko's status as owner of Solibra Beer is indicated by the consumerist trappings of the home's in-ground pool, interior furnishings, his wife's wardrobe, and high-end car—all of which construct an oppressive space for his previously carefree son, Moussa. In one panel, the pink mansion nearly swallows Moussa as he slouches home after finding out that he is the father of Adjoua's baby (68). What is unmasked through the exaggerated proportions of Mr. Sissoko and his home is the ambivalence at the core of the new African middle class. No longer subjects of colonial rule, these new Africans attempt to inhabit and wear both the trappings of the colonizers—only bigger and better—and the cloth of Afrocentric sensibility while failing to bring them together in acceptable proportions. The satirical size of Sissoko's home and self reveal the ambivalent authority that class elitism attempts to assert for itself in modern West African society.

Typically in a social comedy, the confusion of mistaken identities and cross-class alliances are put to right by a class-appropriate heterosexual marriage. However, the trajectory of this novel refuses to impose a happy ending that would reaffirm the differences between classes and quell the sexual playfulness of the youth. The wedding between Adjoua, from working-class Yop City, and Moussa, from the heights of Solibra industrial fame, becomes the site to satirize new money and old morals. For example, the novel turns a humorous eye on the neocolonial-inflected class elitism exhibited by the older Sissokos, who take great pains not to spend much money on the forthcoming wedding. Differentiating themselves from their working-class soon-to-be in-laws, Mrs. Sissoko tells the caterer, "no cutlery, they'll use their hands," while Mr. Sissoko demands that his lackey "dig up a few liters of that gutrot Koutoukou. Peasants love that stuff" (86). But the joke is on the Sissokos because the Yop City community turns the grudging spirit of the wedding into another great local party. The neocolonial privilege embodied by Mr. Sissoko is deflated by the assemblage of working-class Yop City residents who converge as our narrator, Aya, recounts that "on Saturday, the 22nd, despite everything, Yopougon got to see its biggest wedding ever, thanks to all the surprise guests who came" (89).

And while the wedding has temporarily stanched any scandal that might have stained Mr. Sissoko's socioeconomic status had the sexual exploits of his son with a girl from Yop City became front-page news in the aptly named newspaper, *The Calamity Morning News* (where Adjoua's father, Hyacinthe, is a reporter), the birth of Moussa and Adjoua's child does not seal the happy ending expected of most social comedies. In sharp contrast to the didacticism of certain African popular fiction, which points to the correct pathways to gain moral knowledge about being a "good girl" (Newell 9), we have only Adjoua's claim about the father's identity since as readers we never literally see them together at the Thousand Star Hotel. And the text does not privilege her words. Adjoua's declaration about Moussa's paternity is undercut by the quizzical facial looks of and comments by Bintou and Aya once they see the new baby, wondering aloud whom he looks like. The question of paternity is left open: a tactic to indicate the forthcoming sequel but also an indicator of how *Aya* invokes the contemporary attributes of playfulness, contingency, and open-endedness.[15] Thus, the wedding and the child's birth take on a lighthearted resonance that inspires good-natured laughter at the neocolonial reasonings and class dynamics at the heart of African modernity.

Taking Another Look at Uncontested Male Privilege

Lest these scenes from *Aya* seem overly judgmental in satirizing gender, sexual, and class relations in the Ivory Coast, Abouet and Oubrerie insist on intertwining laughter with critique. The surprises in the text propel readers to reflect on earlier scenes and panels to make sense of the unexpected disruptions to the narrative of postcolonial modernity. Sequential narratives such as comics and graphic novels rely on their readers to interweave images from multiple panels or sequences of panels to produce meaning. Thierry Groensteen explains, "An image is interpretable in the sense that . . . it is always close to other images, situated before and after in the course of the story. . . . Comics should be apprehended as a networked mode that allows each panel to hold privileged relations with any others and at any distance" (126). In a later chapter, he writes that braiding creates the discursive whole among panels, whether adjacent or distant: "Braiding deploys itself simultaneously in two dimensions, requiring them to collaborate with each other: synchronically, that of the co-presence of panels on the surface of the same page; and diachronically, that of the reading, which recognizes in each new term of a series a recollection or an echo of an anterior term. A tension can be established between these two logics, but far from ending in conflict, it resolves itself here in a semantic enrichment and densification of the 'text' of the comic" (147). A particularly exemplary braiding sequence surfaces in the subplot of the "unannounced male visitor," that is, the unexpected appearances of the character Mamadou throughout the story.

Through the braided repetition of Mamadou's unannounced appearances into spaces populated by women, the novel creates a moment of resistance to the cavalier presumption of postcolonial, masculinized privilege and power in Ivorian society.[16] During the first episode at the *maquis*, a tall, Afro-coiffed man appears from out of the crowd, is passed off as Bintou's cousin, and just as quickly leaves, but not without having fired up Moussa's jealousy. The next day, Aya drops by to chat with Bintou and Adjoua. The splash panel that introduces this sequence positions readers at the same level as Aya, seated on a low stool with her eyes focused on her friends Adjoua and Bintou (16). As they wrap up their discussion of the "C" series and the role men play in their future plans, an unannounced male visitor enters through an open door into the compound (18). Mamadou fills the doorway and creates the uncanny impression that he has been listening to the women's conversations all along. In a third series of panels, the same formula is used: Aya has stopped by to visit an ailing Adjoua. The first panel in this sequence has an open door to the left of the sofa on which Aya is comforting her sick friend. Adjoua reveals that she knows all about Aya's date with Hervé, to which Aya responds, "News sure travels fast around here" (48). Two panels later, Mamadou enters through the open door. His entrance is unsettling to the women-only dynamic.

The fourth instance disrupts this pattern as readers are aligned directly with Mamadou. We look over his shoulder as he eyes Aya's backside from the doorway into Bintou's compound (63). For the first time, readers are explicitly positioned to look at women's bodies through the voyeuristic gaze of a particular male spectator. While this positioning in itself is not violent, it does implicate us in the consumption of women's bodies from a heterosexual position of male desire. We become aware once again of the text's reflexivity and in this instance how readers become interpellated into being consumers of women's bodies. Matthew Jones writes, "Reflexivity is not something that is located in the text itself; rather it is something that the author engages in while creating and the audience engages in while consuming" (270). And reflexivity can occur by making the spectator (reader) aware of his or her status as spectator (reader): "the reader of the comic becomes conscious of him/herself . . . through an awareness of the gaze" (Jones 279). In this moment of self-awareness, readers are not only complicit in ogling Aya's "tabassa"—her sexualized body—but also in the itinerant masculinity that Mamadou represents.

This textual reflexivity relies on our remembering the previous entrances by Mamadou; this echoing of previous instances of his presence—the braiding of anterior scenes with the present as we read both synchronically and diachronically—is both humorous and problematic. Mamadou is presented as a harmless young man who just happens to show up when the young women are sharing time together. And yet the repetition of his uninvited arrivals disrupts the women-only spaces in such a manner that Aya becomes suspicious of his actions: "Just passing by, I bet," she remarks cynically with her arms crossed against her chest. "Yup, just passing by," replies Mamadou (63).

Our awareness of how the novel has striated humor and surprise with suspicion regarding male privilege makes one final turn as the novel closes with a quick shift in point of view. Being literally drawn into and self-reflective about

Mamadou's scopophilia, readers are caught off guard when the final scene reverses the gaze. This quick volte-face challenges gender inequalities and male control, a move that capitalizes on the novel's humorous feminist critiques of Ivorian male privilege and status. In the penultimate panel, five women—Bintou, Aya, Adjoua's mother, Adjoua, and Adjoua's mother-in-law, Mrs. Sissoko—are gathered at Adjoua's bedside to see her newborn baby. In the panels immediately preceding this one, their conversation has turned to insinuations that the baby might not be Moussa Sissoko's after all. The penultimate panel shows us the five women staring wide-eyed at someone outside the frame; a speech balloon linked to the as-yet-unseen speaker startles the women with the words "Hello there, Girls!" (96). The next, and final, panel shows Mamadou in the hospital room's doorway seemingly flustered with all these women's incredulous eyes on him. After echoing a by-now-much-used line—he "was just passing by"—his self-confident tone turns to a queasy interrogative: "Why's everybody looking at me?" (96). The power of the gaze is reversed in this panel, for he is positioned as the women see him: a possible disruption in the presumed parental relationship between Adjoua and Moussa and an interloper into the female community. This deliberate shift in perspective dissipates Mamadou's previous control of the space that the women's bodies inhabited.

Abouet's story line braids a recursive sequencing of panels that involve Mamadou, networking all into a significant subplot (or "densification" of the text, to return to Groensteen's language). This subplot intensifies the challenge to gender relations that the novel puts forward. The recurrence of Mamadou is at first humorous, but the repetition creates a disequilibrium. This instability reveals the possibility that young Ivorian women are always under surveillance by their male counterparts. No longer simply the "unannounced male visitor," Mamadou becomes a "marked" man in terms of both the questions about paternity and the control of the gaze. The isolated young Ivorian man now stands in the bright light of critical analysis emanating from the Ivorian women's shared space of communal viewing. This framing of Mamadou acts as a contrast to the novel's opening panel: Ivorian masculinity is no longer isolated by the disinterested gaze of the TV screen and fueled by Solibra; instead, Mamadou stands in the liminal space of the doorway, neither setting the pace of Ivorian development nor representing the uncontested power of masculinity associated with the space of the nation. It is the women's gaze that sets the scene for the next iteration of life in Yop City.

Ivorian Bonus: Feminist Humor Alive and Laughing

Speaking to an audience at the 2007 PEN World Voices Festival in New York City, Marguerite Abouet emphasized that the media shows how Africans die but not how they live ("Conversation"). Her graphic novel reverses that discursive and representational tendency by providing readers with the richly comical and serious nature of the everyday lives of men and women living in West Africa. The setting conveys the dynamism of the Ivory Coast after the departure of the French colonizers. In creating an African urban space free from the threat of HIV/AIDS, civil strife, and multinational corporate greed, Abouet has opened up her project to criticism that she is depicting an idealistic and idyllic version of the Ivory Coast, or a "nostalgic anomaly," as one critic begrudgingly said of the text.[17] And yet what this historical setting calls forth is closer attention to the continuity and contradictions of daily African life within modernity. In choosing to focus on the gender and sexual politics in the working-class suburb of the "Paris of West Africa," as Abidjan has been called, Abouet rewrites the discourse of postcolonial nation building. Resisting an impulse to Africanize her subject matter with the sheen of nationalistic liberation, Abouet provides the space for a feminist analysis through which readers can interpret how the complexities of Ivorian relations constitute the postcolonial rather than being erased by Western media-dictated versions of Africa.

Whether we are reading across panels to understand the dynamics of gendered relations and sexuality, the class constructs in a postcolonial Ivory Coast, or the modern configurations of African communities in an age of burgeoning consumerism, we as readers are actively engaged in the production of meaning in *Aya*. Susanne Reichl and Mark Stein theorize that while laughter is subjective, it is also informed by the company we keep, the interpretive community we are part of, the "communities of laughter" to which we belong: "Laughter, too, presumes shared worlds, shared codes, and shared values. . . . Postcolonial literatures . . . speak not only to local but also to international readerships, which often find cues in the texts that enable access to their comic potential. Laughter and humuor are therefore 'test cases' not for cultural belonging, but for transcultural competence" (13). The prescriptive images of Africa as "Other" with which many readers might approach the text soon fade away as the novel's transcultural humor of social comedy reverberates. Engaging in this complex set of affairs, the non-African U.S. reader must step up to confront the challenge of developing new ways of seeing and reading the cultural and gender politics of Africa via the hybridic form of the graphic novel or be left behind in the tracks of an exhausted "us" versus "them" binary and two-dimensional point of view. But the text also reminds us that our "shared codes" will fall short, as the novel provides new representations that disrupt old neocolonial taxonomies.[18] Readers have to think carefully and cautiously about how race, class, gender, sexuality, and cultural context are at work in the frames and in the larger ways we frame the reading experience of the African graphic novel itself. *Aya* is not an escapist comic but rather a deftly entertaining interrogation of modern Ivorian sexual and gender politics. Instead of the gutters between panels being the space for a neocolonial culture of invisibility to maintain its power to defame and distort representations of Africa, the interstitial spaces call forth interpretations of images, ideas, and insights about the vivacity of postcolonial West African nations. If we are to trust Scott McCloud's statement that "in an incomplete world, we must depend on closure for our very survival" (63), then this closure must surely involve the feminist-inspired laughter that *Aya* calls forth.

Notes

1 The series, which began with *Aya* (2007), includes four other titles, all published by Drawn and Quarterly.

2 In the opening chapter in *Cartooning in Africa*, John A. Lent points to the general "ignorance of African culture and society" found in "Western media's (including the comics') stereotyping of the continent as dark and uncivilized" (1).

3 I invoke Chimamanda Ngozi Adichie's insightful reference to the single story that we impose on African representations ("Danger of a Single Story"). For an analysis of how social comedy is infused with popular media across the four volumes of *Aya*, see Harris.

4 The graphic novel is often categorized as young adult fiction. Instead of situating *Aya* as an educative tool for young readers (see Anderson or Jorgensen and Lechan for such readings), my analysis positions the text as a feminist intervention into the multidimensionality of Ivorian gender and sexual politics in the 1970s.

5 Rebecca Wanzo points to the challenge of depicting Black characters since the creators of such characters "recognize that blacks are always already stereotyped when their bodies are represented" (97). Qiana Whitted provides a close readings of this problem and the way *Aya* and certain U.S. comics "restore the agency of a Black speaking, seeing subject" (2), capturing the "multi-dimensional black experience" (14).

6 Repetti explains how a "rising generation of African comic-book artists is gaining a growing fan base. . . . Their comics have also started to win prizes at prestigious international festivals" (28). *Aya*, for instance, was awarded the Best First Album at the preeminent Festival International de la Bande Dessinée d'Angoulême in 2006.

7 The subtitle of Ama Ata Aidoo's *Our Sister Killjoy*—"Reflections from a Black-Eyed Squint"—underlines how Sissie's encounters with racism, sexism, and xenophobia have expanded her vision and understanding of gender, race, class, and neocolonial and neoliberal relations in Europe and Africa.

8 Lancaster reminds us in his review that the story is set during the thirty-year period of unprecedented economic growth of the independent Ivorian nation (942).

9 For an analysis of the metonymic use of "strong men" ads, see Whitted.

10 Whitted sees the juxtaposition of the TV and the two photos as "evidence of material success, middle-class respectability, and domestic life" (15).

11 Elana Anderson makes a similar argument when she writes that the graphic narrative, while invoking stereotypes, also slips beyond them, representing "new and visually stimulating forms through the use of color and technique," thanks to Oubrerie's artistry and collaboration with Abouet (7). See Gardner (142) on how Asian American graphic narratives can destabilize racism while deploying racial stereotypes.

12 See Anderson for a different interpretation of this scene and of Aya's level-headedness.

13 In a discussion of the gendered aspects of the comics industry, Wolk comments on the conflation of superheroes and the comics medium (89).

14 Will Eisner defines the term "splash" as referring to the qualities of the first page of a graphic novel: "Properly employed it seizes the reader's attention and prepares his [*sic*] attitude for the events to follow. It sets a 'climate.' It becomes a 'splash' page

proper rather than a simple 'first page' when the artist designs it as a decorative unit" (62). These qualities equally describe how Abouet and Oubrerie open each new section of *Aya* with its own "splash" page.

15 The sequel, *Aya in Yop City*, picks up the question of paternity and humorously continues to explore the gender and sexual politics of African postcolonialism.

16 See Jordanna Maltron's analysis of marginalized Abidjanais masculinity in relation to barbershop signage and the co-optation of masculinized success in the African diaspora.

17 Refer to Alisia Grace Chase's preface to the graphic novel for this critique.

18 Focusing on the metarhetorical work that the *pagnes* accomplish in the novel, Whitted reminds non-African readers that we may lack the "specialized knowledge to decode" certain textual messages, and the glossary at the end of the novel functions to complicate, rather than explain, such embodied signifiers (18).

Works Cited

Abouet, Marguerite, and Clément Oubrerie. *Aya*. Trans. Helge Dascher. Montreal: Drawn and Quarterly, 2007.

————. *Aya of Yop City*. Trans. Dag Dascher. Montreal: Drawn and Quarterly, 2008.

Adichie, Chimamanda Ngozi. "The Danger of a Single Story." TED Global. October 2009. Web. http://www.ted.com/talks/chimamanda_adichie_the_danger_of_a_single_story. Accessed 27 February 2014.

Aidoo, Ama Ata. *Our Sister Killjoy, or Reflections from a Black-Eyed Squint*. New York: Longwood, 1977.

Anderson, Elana. "The Graphic Novel: Re-imag(in)ing Africa." *Sankofa: A Journal of African Children's and Young Adult Literature* 9 (2010): 6–17.

Chase, Alisia Grace. Preface. *Aya*. By Marguerite Abouet and Clément Oubrerie. Montreal: Drawn and Quarterly, 2007.

Chute, Hillary, and Marianne Dekoven. "Introduction: Graphic Narrative." *Modern Fiction Studies* 52.4 (2006): 767–775.

"Conversation with Neil Gaiman and Marguerite Abouet." PEN 2007 World Voices Festival. Sean Wilsey, moderator. 26 April 2007. Web. http://www.pen.org/book/conversation -neil-gaiman-marguerite-abouet-with-sean-wilsey. Accessed 1 September 2008.

Dance, Daryl Cumber. "Introduction." *Honey, Hush! An Anthology of African American Women's Humor*. New York: Norton, 1998. xxi–xxxv.

Eisner, Will. *Comics and Sequential Art*. Tamarac, FL: Poorhouse, 1985.

Gardner, Jared. "Same Difference: Graphic Alterity in the Work of Gene Luen Yang, Adrian Tomine, and Derek Kirk Kim." *Multicultural Comics: From Zap to Blue Beetle*. Ed. Frederick Luis Aldama. Austin: University of Texas Press, 2010. 132–147.

Groensteen, Thierry. *The System of Comics*. Trans. Bart Beaty and Nick Nguyen. Jackson: University Press of Mississippi, 2007.

Harris, Marla. "'Sex and the City': The Graphic Novel Series *Aya* as West African Comedy of Manners." *International Journal of Comic Art* 11.2 (2009): 119–135.

Hatfield, Charles. *Alternative Comics: An Emerging Literature*. Jackson: University Press of Mississippi, 2005.

Jones, Matthew T. "Reflexivity in Comic Art." *International Journal of Comic Art* 7.1 (2005): 270–286.

Jorgensen, Anna, and Arianna Lechan. "Not Your Mom's Graphic Novels: Giving Girls a Choice beyond Wonder Woman." *Technical Services Quarterly* 30.3 (2013): 266–284.

Lancaster, Guy. "*Aya* (review)." *Callaloo* 31.3 (2008): 941–944.

Lent, John A. "African Cartooning: An Overview of Historical and Contemporary Issues." *Cartooning in Africa*. Ed. John A. Lent. Cresskill, NJ: Hampton, 2009. 1–38.

Maltron, Jordanna. *"Il est Garçon*: Marginal Abidjanais Masculinity and the Politics of Representation." *Poetics* 39 (2011): 380–406.

McCloud, Scott. *Understanding Comics*. Northampton, MA: Kitchen Sink, 1993.

Montresor, Jaye Berman. "Comic Strip-Tease: A Revealing Look at Women Cartoon Artists." *Look Who's Laughing: Gender and Comedy*. Ed. Gail Finney. Amsterdam: Gordon and Breach, 1994. 335–347.

Newell, Stephanie. Introduction. *Readings in African Popular Fiction*. Ed. Newell. Bloomington: Indiana University Press, 2002. 1–10.

Reichl, Susanne, and Mark Stein. Introduction. *Cheeky Fictions: Laughter and the Postcolonial*. Ed. Reichl and Stein. Amsterdam: Rodopi, 2005. 1–23.

Reid, Calvin. "*D&Q* to Publish *Aya*, Angoulême Prize-Winner." *Drawn & Quarterly* 1 May 2006. Web. http://www.drawnandquarterly.com/newsList.php?item. Accessed 5 May 2008.

Repetti, Massimo. "African Wave: Specificity and Cosmopolitanism in African Comics." *African Arts* 40.2 (2007): 16–35. Web. http://www.mitpressjournals.org. Accessed 7 January 2008.

Wanzo, Rebecca. "Black Nationalism, Bunraku, and Beyond: Articulating Black Heroism through Cultural Fusion and Comics." *Multicultural Comics: From Zap to Blue Beetle*. Ed. Frederick Luis Aldama. Austin: University of Texas Press, 2010. 93–104.

Whitted, Qiana. "'And the Negro Thinks in Hieroglyphics': Comics, Visual Metonymy, and the Spectacle of Blackness." *Journal of Graphic Novels and Comics* 17 December 2013: 1–22.

Wolk, Douglas. *Reading Comics: How Graphic Novels Work and What They Mean*. Cambridge, MA: Da Capo, 2007.

Wong, Wendy Siuyi, and Lisa M. Cuklanz. "Humor and Gender Politics: A Textual Analysis of the First Feminist Comic in Hong Kong." *Comics and Ideology*. Ed. Matthew P. McAllister, Edwards H. Sewell, Jr., and Ian Gordon. New York: Peter Lang, 2001. 69–97.

Chapter 3

A Postcolony in Pieces

• •

Black Faces, White Masks,
and Queer Potentials
in *Unknown Soldier*

PATRICK F. WALTER

> Fi all them fucking people whose only
> concern in life is to mine our permanent
> state of hesitancy.
> —Spaceape

> We might reach this result: man-
> kind retaining this fire through
> self-combustion. Mankind set free,
> and digging into its own flesh to find a
> meaning.
> —Franz Fanon

Franz Fanon famously likens being colonized to being ripped apart and stitched back together. On one hand, for both the individual and the collective body, colonization is mutilation. "What else could it be for me," Fanon asks, "but an amputation, an excision, a hemorrhage that spattered my whole body with black blood" (112). On the other hand, it is also a process suturing bodies into a sort of patchwork of racist stereotypes. "The white man," Fanon says, "had woven me out of a thousand details, anecdotes, stories" (111). As recounted by Fanon, this process of dismemberment and suturing, then, is as much about physical bodies as it is about texts; the colonized body is torn apart by *but also composed of* racist discourses that are themselves textual scraps.

I begin with these famous passages from Fanon's *Black Skin, White Masks* because it is precisely this bodily and discursive dismemberment that is at work in Joshua Dysart's *Unknown Soldier*, a comic book about the political situation in postcolonial Uganda. This study focuses on two intertwined sorts of fragmentation depicted in the first two volumes of *Unknown Soldier*: the mutilation of bodies and the ripping apart of media discourses. Like Fanon's colonized body, the discursive and material bodies of *Unknown Soldier* seem to be composed by the spectacle of their own dismemberment. The postcolonial world depicted in the comic is, to use the titular hero's imagery, "a grinding machine, fueled by corruption, greed, fanaticism, stoked by the world at large, by our so called leaders by ourselves, and we are all meat in its gears" (Dysart, *Unknown Soldier, Vol.* 1 [*US1*] 143). The panels of artists Alberto Ponticelli and Pat Masioni show us bodies and texts being torn to pulp and mended by each other, and in fact, our titular hero's "white mask" of bandages barely holds his gnarled face together. Together, these fragmented bodies and texts articulate an *absence* central to colonial conceptualizations of the black subject and Africa more generally. Fanon formulates this absence of the colonized, maintaining that "not only must the black man be black; he must be black in relation to the white man" and thus "has no ontological resistance in the eyes of the white man" (110). That is to say, the black subject is entirely subordinated to the material and discursive domination of the colonizing white perspective whereby his black body is repeatedly "burst apart" and "woven together." Beyond this colonial regime, the black subject amounts to a gap, an open question, a void.

Achille Mbembe makes a similar point regarding the negativity of the concept "Africa." "More than any other region," Mbembe tells us, "Africa thus stands out as a supreme receptacle of the West's obsession with, and circular discourse about, the facts of 'absence,' 'lack,' and 'non-being,' of identity and difference, of negativeness—in short, of nothingness" (4). By making "Africa" signify all that differs from the West, colonial discourse has ultimately posited the continent as a sort of "absent object," a stand-in for nothingness as such (241).[1] As with Fanon's notion of a black body woven entirely from racist caricatures, the African "postcolony," in Mbembe's theory, amounts to an assemblage of "detail, anecdotes, stories" in which "one takes anecdotes, fragments of the real world, scattered and disconnected things" and thereby "makes furtive sketches, scenes rearranged as one likes, pictures full of movement—in short, a dramatic story in which words and images, in the final analysis, amount to very little" (177). These colonial collages produce the overarching impression of Africa as a half-sketched, fractured, irrational, and unfathomable chaos of textual bits and image shards. Like the black body, then, the African postcolony is composed of these discursive scraps, beyond which it is, again, an absence, an open question, a void.

Texts such as *Unknown Soldier*, which attempt to make sense of contemporary African postcolonies, must always contend with this discourse through which the colonized subject and Africa have been equated with abjection, chaos, and ultimately absence. Thus, while *Unknown Soldier* often makes critical gestures toward this colonial discourse and, more specifically, the geopolitical relationship between the Ugandan government, global capitalism, and the violence inflicted on the Acholi people of the country's northern region, these critical gestures are just as often undermined by spectacles of mutilated bodies, religious fanaticism, and chaotic political turmoil—spectacles that reify colonial discourse. The cover of the first volume exemplifies these conflicting *critical* and *reifying* impulses at work throughout the comic (see fig. 3.1). Like Fanon's colonized body, the unknown soldier's face here is literally "woven" out of "details, anecdotes, stories" from a newspaper, his bandages seeming to merge with scraps on which we can make out a map of Africa, youthful soldiers, and a prostrated corpse situated alongside the word "war." Fragmented glimpses of a continent torn away from the rest of a world map, child soldiers, dead black bodies, and allusions to military conflict: this assemblage of textual bits reflects, with striking conciseness, our current neocolonial media discourse that has cast Africa, and specifically contemporary northern Uganda, as a "dark and chaotic" void.

Throughout the 1990s and the first decade of the twentieth century, the Western media often deployed just such fragmented and sensationalized images to depict the conflict between the Ugandan military and the rebel group the Lord's Resistance Army (LRA). This theater of "terrorism" concocted by the mainstream media cast the LRA leader, Joseph Kony, as a monstrous religious zealot who, for no apparent political reason, was kidnapping Acholi children of northern Uganda and forcing them to become soldiers and concubines. Thus, Acholi children were, in turn, placed in the roles of psychologically and physically maimed victims, with the typical story providing ample photographs and litanies of their mutilated and otherwise victimized bodies.[2] From the briefings in the *Economist*, Kony emerges as a "witchdoctor-turned-warlord," "shrouded in an aura of fear and mysticism," who "intends to turn Uganda into a theocratic state governed by the Ten Commandments." We hear that his army is forcing children "to club, stamp and bite to death friends and relatives, sometimes even their own parents, then lick their brains, drink their blood and even eat their flesh." At the same time, we are presented with descriptions of children who "had lips, noses, breasts and limbs hacked off."[3] *Maclean's* offers us a similarly spectacular depiction of what it deems "one of the most brutal and senseless emergences to hit this corner of Africa in recent years," characterizing Kony as a "former faith healer" "who at times dresses in women's clothing and claims that

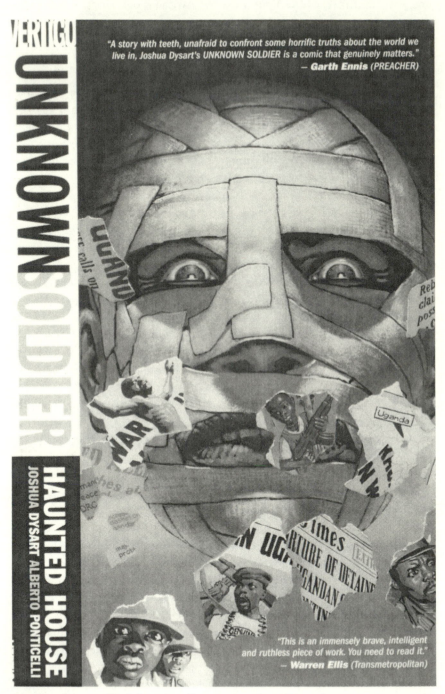

3.1 The unknown soldier's face is literally woven out of anecdotes and stories, newspaper strips that also merge with a map of Africa.

he speaks directly with God" and who forces Acholi girls to become sex slaves and Acholi boys to become ruthless killers. We learn of a boy who attempted to escape and whose "mouth was padlocked shut, with the lock's metal hood driven through his upper and lower lips." These highly detailed anecdotes are accompanied by the typical array of photographs displaying maimed black bodies.[4] Likewise, Elizabeth Rubin's more extended and "literary" piece in the *New Yorker* suggests that Kony "slunk into hiding" and "flipped through his Bible until he alighted upon the punishments he was looking for in Mark 9." Kony's perverse interpretation of scripture, then, apparently leads to his terroristic killing. "Jesus's metaphors," according to Rubin, "provided Kony with a useful instruction manual. He unleashed his few hundred remaining followers, and they set about cutting off lips, ears, legs, hands, breasts, and genitals of suspected government informants" (60). These presentations of Kony as a troll-like religious quack, the LRA as a band of duped butchers, and the colonized as a series of raped, mutilated, and murdered body parts do more to reiterate classic colonial discourses of "Africa" than to make sense of the politico-economic situation of northern Uganda. Repeating certain racial and sexual stereotypes ad nauseam, this coverage presents the LRA and its leader, Joseph Kony, as a demonic threat to Western institutions, which are in turned aligned with the heterosexual family and other heteronormative social formations. While, indeed, the LRA and the Ugandan military appear to have perpetrated such atrocities against the Acholi, largely missing from these catalogues of brutality in the Western media are any clear articulations of the way the Ugandan government, the governments of other nations, and multinational investors have contributed to the violence of northern Uganda, a topic discussed in more depth later.

Instead, this mainstream coverage produces something akin to the tattered newspaper clippings of dead black bodies, child soldiers, and fragmented text depicted on the cover of *Unknown Soldier*. More specifically, these images of the LRA as violent "sexual deviants" who threaten the heteronormative institution of the family and other "normal" social formations reappear throughout *Unknown Soldier*. Unlike this media coverage, however, the political status of this cover image on the first volume, and of *Unknown Soldier* more generally, is ambiguous. By presenting us with newspaper images of Uganda, this cover art seems to frame and thus critique the mainstream media's discourse on northern Uganda. At the same time, however, this cover image reproduces this same discourse, albeit within a frame. That is to say, this cover is at once both a fragmented depiction of Uganda and also a critique of these fragmented depictions as they are produced by the Western media. Indicative of the aesthetic at work throughout the comic, then, this cover both reiterates popular stereotypical notions of Africa and at the same time foregrounds the way the media propagates these stereotypes.

Of course, these conflicting impulses reflect the comic's position as both *critical of* and also *a part of* the mainstream media, *Unknown Soldier* being a popular release from the DC Vertigo imprint. At a more fundamental level, however, these cross-purposes are a product of the colonial discourse with which the comic must always contend. As Mbembe points out, insofar as Africa "exists only as an absent object," all discourses about the postcolony necessarily involve the repeated fabrication of this object—the repeated making present of this absence. According to Mbembe, these discourses "are deployed only by replacing this object, creating it, erasing it, decomposing and multiplying it. Thus, there is no description of Africa that does not involve destructive and mendacious functions" (241–242). Since Africa and the colonized body have been constructed precisely as either complete voids or monsters of colonial fantasy, any attempt to articulate the African postcolony and the black subject must necessarily reiterate, however critically, these same images of colonial discourse. Thus, while much of my reading of *Unknown Soldier* looks at how the comic reiterates these colonial stereotypes, this analysis is not intended as a simplistic and dismissive indictment of this comic. Indeed, within mainstream comics, *Unknown Soldier* is singular in its serious attempt to engage with these discursive complexities of the postcolony.

These conflicting critical and reifying impulses of *Unknown Soldier* are staged most vividly by one of the primary plotlines of the comic book, the attempted assassination of the celebrity humanitarian Margaret Wells. The character of Margaret Wells references any number of current celebrity humanitarians in the Western media, such as Madonna, Angelina Jolie, and Bono, who indeed provide publicity for dire situations in sub-Saharan Africa but, in doing so, frame these situations within colonialist terms in which African children supposedly need to be rescued from apolitical states of "African chaos" by heroic Western subjects. Speaking at a charity benefit for northern Uganda, Margaret claims, "The Lord's Resistance Army has been kidnapping and forcing children into soldiering for over fifteen years. What are the figures? 15,000 kids? 20,000? Every night tens of thousands of children walk up to six miles to find a safe place to sleep . . . and why are the world's cameras not trained on this terror?" (*US*1 2–3). Casting the postcolony as a miasma of religious fanaticism and victimized children, Margaret reiterates the view of northern Uganda constructed in the mainstream media and thereby "trains the worlds cameras" on Uganda but only by presenting the postcolony precisely as a site of monstrous "terror." To this extent, her character provides a figure through which the comic can critique Western media coverage of Africa. But her status as the "damsel in distress" of the narrative tends to reify the very stereotypical images the comic is attempting to critique. The attempted assassination of Margaret, wherein she is cast as the heroine in peril, epitomizes a "blackface/whiteface duality," which Angela Grzyb identifies in media coverage of Darfur and Sudan. This duality reduces the African subject to a blackface image of terror, famine, genocide, and madness and thereby subordinates this black subject to a white subject that is supposedly threatened by this "African abjection." As Grzyb puts it, African bodies are thus "transformed into a murky but monolithic blackface that is thrust into the back-ground and replaced by a whiteface narrative that is preoccupied with the safety of Westerners" (76). In popular representations of Uganda, including those of *Unknown Soldier*, this "murky but monolithic blackface" consists of mangled corpses, religious fanaticism, and victimized children.

Conversely, the privileged whiteface is composed of a singular life that is in peril, on the brink of being extinguished and thus in need of protection. Nowhere is this racial duality made more apparent than in the African eco-nomic liberation movement's plan to kill Margaret. "Will you continue to kill countless children or take out a single celebrity?" a member of the movement asks. "One bullet can move a mountain. It is only a question of where that bullet is aimed" (Dysart, *Unknown Soldier, Vol.* 2 [*US*2] 65–66). The implication here is that, because the slaughter of "countless black children" carries no symbolic weight, such massacres cannot ultimately change international politics; these black bodies do not count. The symbolically charged assassination of Margaret would perhaps have the capacity to change international policy; her white body *would* count. In a political maneuver discussed in more depth later, the Afri-can economic liberation movement, then, appropriates the same racial duality that Margaret herself employs during her speech. For the movement, as much as for Margaret herself, the political situation of Uganda remains stuck in a black-face/whiteface opposition in which Africans remain a nameless and faceless mass and Westerners remain the privileged subject. A page-sized illustration depicts this duality perfectly (see fig. 3.2). A blunt articulation of the color line, one side of the page depicts "countless" massacred black bodies; the other, one white body. The miniature scale of the black bodies here literally disfigures them, presenting them more as deindividualized corpses than as human figures, whereas the detailed rendering of Margaret lends her a subjective individual-ity. In this representational logic, blackness amounts to a faceless mass while whiteness achieves individual identity and selfhood. The metaphysical status of these bodies underscores their racialized difference. While black bodies here are presented as a tangle of objectified corpses that are *already* dead, Margaret is captured at the melodramatic moment of death, her body reeling backward from the gunshot, lending her figure a subjective dynamism that is lacking in the mass of corpses with which she is juxtaposed. In this way, blackness serves as the background of death for the dramatic depiction of a single endangered white life.

In this respect, *Unknown Soldier* itself shares in, even as it critiques, this racial duality. Throughout the comic, similar images of wounded and/or amassed black bodies, particularly those of children, provide an objectified backdrop for the action. In the first volume (*Haunted House*), one of the first images of rural Acholiland, a panorama of an internally displaced person (IDP) camp, again presents blackness simultaneously as both a faceless statistical mass and a dismembered body. Taken together, the miniature scale to which these people

3.2 Countless massacred black bodies juxtaposed with one white body in *Unknown Soldier*. For quality reasons, this image has been revised slightly.

and huts are drawn along with the caption giving us population statistics and panels depicting a young amputee reiterate an all-too-familiar constellation of facelessness and dismemberment at work in the popular image of the postcolony. While the intent of such images might be to provide readers with a notion of the catastrophic scale of the situation in northern Uganda, the effect is still a generalized and thus depoliticized sense of suffering and bodily mutilation that

recalls Western stereotypes of the postcolony. Indeed, the narrative is punctu-
ated by such images of black bodies going to pieces.

In both of these images, black bodies are already in fragmentary pieces and
ultimately dissolve into the orange flare of bomb blasts, losing any individual
consistency. The black body is thereby depicted precisely as objectified meat, as
a representational figure that is disintegrating into a smear of ink. These eviscerated bodies then provide the negative background for a bodily integrity
that is always tacitly aligned with whiteness and the West. In fact, the eviscerated corpses depicted in the second panel literally take the place of Margaret's
body, their truck having accidentally hit a roadside bomb intended for her car.
At the level of image, then, even *Unknown Soldier* itself cannot break with the
blackface/whiteface duality in which Africans are already dead, *disfigured*, corporeal objects while Westerners are living, legible figures of identification. And
at the level of narrative as well, the comic tends to transfer our sympathies from
these colonized subject to white, Western subjects. The Margaret Wells plot-
line, for example, resolves by directing our sympathies toward her character,
who laments, "If I start to believe that the efforts I make here are valueless or
wasteful . . . I don't know what I'll do. I can't . . . I can't believe that. It'll kill me"
(*US2* 144). Thus, Margaret's anxieties about her ineffectual and/or interloping
position efface the oppression of the colonized, who in turn become a negative
backdrop for this Western subject.

Aside from privileging the white subject, however, these images of mutilated black bodies frame the socioeconomic and political inequalities faced by
northern Ugandans as essentialized differences of race and desire. As with many
mainstream representations of the conflict in northern Uganda, the two main
central figures in *Unknown Soldier*—the unknown soldier and child soldiers—
align mutilated blackness with notions of "deviant" sexual desire and thereby
associate "normal" sexuality with whiteness and the West. Casting the colonized
as violent sexual deviants and the West as an ideal of "normal" desires, the sexual
aspect of this racial duality then functions as an alibi for conflict in northern
Uganda and thus overshadows the geopolitical complexities of the region. The
unknown soldier's visage is perhaps the overarching visual metaphor for the
racial and sexual dynamics at work in these spectacles of gore (see fig. 3.3). Here,
the unknown soldier seems to be maddeningly ripping open himself and escaping from himself, but inside himself is another surface. The confluence of surface
and depth in this splash page—which is also quite literally a confluence of black
skin and white masks, of blackface and whiteface—articulates the *absence* central to dominant notions of the postcolony and the colonized body. Beneath the
bandages, it would seem, is not some authentic being but instead yet another
layer of constructedness. Beneath his racialized, corporeal surface is not some
authentic psyche but instead another surface. In fact, the unknown soldier's
psyche, which, on one hand, appears to have been programmed by Western

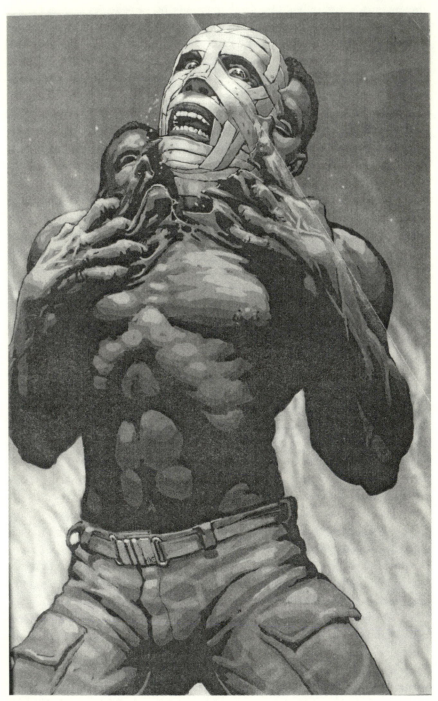

3.3 The unknown soldier tries to rip himself open, but inside is another surface.

imperial powers in some secret lab, also, on the other hand, appears to have been already shaped by postcolonial violence from within the womb (see fig. 3.4). Here, a bluish-green aura of emaciated infants, children with weapons, and screaming soldiers surrounds the brownish-orange fetus and thus locates the supposedly distinct, external world of political violence within the biological site of the womb. Locating this postcolonial violence within the womb presents

3.4 Postcolonial violence shapes the unknown soldier even in the womb.

a paradox: it depoliticizes and thereby essentializes a violence that is, at the same time, completely political. That is to say, the *political* violence represented by the bluish-green images become internalized, pathologized, and thus naturalized; external and internal forces become indistinguishable. It would thus appear that the body of the colonized is doomed to be fractured by and thus perpetuate this bluish-green miasma of "terror" because according to the logic of these images, this colonized body is, *from before birth*, mired in this "terror." In this way, the comic depicts the violence of the postcolony as *both* a political phenomenon *and also* an "insane" force of the colonized subject that exceeds political roles. The unknown soldier occupies multiple and often conflicting geopolitical positions precisely because this "violent impulse" that possesses his character is political but also lacks an ultimate political consistency. He is his "actual," diasporic self, Lwanga Moses, who is already both a native Ugandan and a pacifist Western doctor, but he is also a faceless soldier embroiled in a global conspiracy who is driven by his violent pathology.

This politically fragmentary "impulse" inhabiting the unknown soldier takes the visible shape of his own self-mutilation, and moreover, scenes of mutilated black bodies provide visual metaphors for this "deviant," politically schizophrenic, drive that seems to inhabit not only the unknown soldier but northern Uganda more generally. During the pivotal scene of transformation, Moses, guided by his preprogrammed alter ego, kills an LRA soldier and then slashes his own face with a stone. This self-defacement culminates with a splash panel of Moses's disfigured body flanked by the body of a Ugandan military officer and an LRA child soldier. The victim of his own "insane," self-inflicted violence who is positioned between a symbol of the postcolonial state and a symbol of terrorism, the unknown soldier's mangled face here stands in the precise space of the colonized subject, namely, the much-stigmatized Acholi of the northern region, whose wounded bodies are indeed often caught between the state and so-called terrorist and who, much like the unknown soldier, tend to be aligned with notions of pathological and self-destructive violence. As Sverker Finnström points out (61), the Acholi have been stereotyped as a backward and essentially violent ethnicity, and the historical racialization of the Acholi follows a pattern not unlike that of the pathologization of the unknown soldier. In the same way that the comic presents the unknown soldier's violent alter ego both as a preprogrammed construct of the colonization and as a natural biological attribute, popular opinion and ethnographic scholarship has figured the violence that has plagued Acholi society as both the result of British colonization and also an essential characteristic of Acholi ethnicity. Based on the fact that British colonizers recruited and trained the Acholi as a military force, these popular and scholarly discourses conclude that the Acholi are essentially a militaristic ethnicity.[5] This stereotypical notion of the Acholi, which also contributes to the popular monstrous characterization of the LRA, places the political conflict of northern Uganda in a Manichean framework in which the self-destructive evil of terrorists imperils the unquestioned goodness of the Ugandan state.[6] The political violence of the LRA has thus been attributed to the senseless, apolitical, and self-destructive "nature" of the Acholi themselves.

In *Unknown Solider*, this pathologically self-destructive violence that is so often attributed to Acholi and to Africa more generally takes the specific shape of nonheteronormative desire. As figures for this queer desire, the unknown soldier and the child soldier (see later in this chapter) straddle the racial duality. On one hand, these are blackface monsters with "deviant" impulses who are bent on senselessly mutilating themselves. On the other hand, however, they are whiteface victims of this self-destructive impulse who are on their way to being "healed," which, in the narrative logic of the comic, means taking on Western, heteronormative social formations and being reintroduced into a capitalist order of things. This racial and sexual ideology at work in *Unknown Soldier*, then, is intimately bound to the political hegemony of global capitalism. As the dominant narrative device through which the political situation of northern Uganda has been interpreted, this blackface/whiteface duality, which is also a sexual duality, ultimately legitimates neoliberal African states such as Uganda and, moreover, restates the opposition between "market free democracy" and "fundamentalist-terrorist-totalitarianism," an opposition that, as Slavoj Žižek has suggested, everywhere provides ideological support for global capitalism. That is to say, neoliberal "democracies" such as the Ugandan government and "fanatical terrorists" such as the LRA do not represent political alternatives but instead represent a false contradiction that is manufactured and imposed on us by the dominant political order. These racialized spectacles of religious fanaticism, deviant desires, and brutalized children demand that we position ourselves in alliance with the state and against this blackface stereotype of "terrorism." As Žižek puts it, "one of the basic operations of hegemonic ideology is to *enforce a false point*, to impose on us a false choice" (384–385). And as figures who stand at this false point between "terrorism" and the state, between blackface and whiteface, between queerness and heteronormativity, the unknown soldier and the child soldier constantly offer up this false choice.

Even as *Unknown Soldier* tends to reiterate these dualities, however, it also hints at a more complex geopolitical situation. Before further analyzing the racial and sexual dynamics of the unknown soldier and the "child soldier," then, I will briefly summarize the geopolitical situation of northern Uganda, which so often gets reduced to these simplistic dualities. Early in the comic, the cynical secret agent Jack Lee Howl soliloquizes, "It's the easiest thing in the world for a European to get the permits and licenses to do business in Africa, but for an African to import to Europe or Asia or the States? Shit, the paperwork is staggering, virtually impossible. This is one of the most resource-diverse places there is, and the whole world just picks the living meat right off its bones" (*US*1 137). Likewise, while raging against the exploitative "humanitarianism" of Margaret and her press entourage, the unknown soldier exclaims, "Investment in our markets, honest trade with the outside world, micro-loan agencies, stable banks, leaders who give a fuck, that's what we need. We need the world to stop stealing from us with one hand and giving back crumbs with the other" (*US2* 95). Rare moments such as these, when characters remark in passing on trade imbalances, unstable financial institutions, and corrupt government leadership, allude to what David Harvey terms "accumulation by dispossession" (145), a global system of economic exploitation to which northern Ugandan and many other African postcolonies have indeed been subjected.[7] This violent process of seizing lands and displacing local populations, usually administered by the military and police apparatuses of the state, produces new property and labor pools for capitalist investment. As Harvey explains, this is a process whereby the state engages in "taking land, say, enclosing it, and expelling a resident population to create a landless proletariat, and then releasing the land into the privatized mainstream of capital accumulation" (149). Especially in regions with vulnerable peasant populations, such as northern Uganda, capitalism then produces and thrives on these forced displacements.

Rather than a simple Manichean opposition between terrorists and the state, then, the war in northern Uganda might be more accurately understood as just such a process of accumulation by dispossession, whereby the Acholi have been deprived of their land and turned into a displaced industrial labor force. A case study in neoliberal reforms such as these, the Ugandan government—the National Resistance Movement (NRM) headed by Yoweri Museveni—has been a major participant in structural adjustment programs prescribed by the World Bank and the International Monetary Fund. These reforms have done little to curb extreme conditions of poverty, particularly in the rural areas of the north.[8] What is more, these structural adjustments have been abetted by the authoritarianism of Museveni's "no party" regime, which has received a good deal of criticism for both its militaristic approach to dealing with the LRA and its general oppressiveness with respect to political opposition.[9] Opposite Museveni's neoliberal regime, the LRA has played the role of the "fundamentalist terrorist." Although the LRA has inflicted numerous acts of violence on the Acholi population and has been identified as war criminals by the U.S. government and the International Criminal Court, the extent to which we can read the conflict between the LRA and the Ugandan government as a clear-cut opposition between the "bad" terrorists and the "good" state is questionable. Employing Carol Nordstrom's concept, Finnström instead characterizes the conflict as a "dirty war" in which *both* rebel forces and the state wage a perpetual campaign of terror against civilian populations (13). Similarly, critics such as Peter Eichstaedt and Mahmood Mamdani have argued that, instead of attempting to eliminate the LRA, Museveni's government has intentionally perpetuated a low-level war against the rebel group in part as a way to justify the internment of over 90 percent of the Acholi population, roughly 1.5 million people, in IDP camps. Mamdani gives a vivid picture of this internment program:

It took a government-directed campaign of murder, intimidation, bombing, and burning of whole villages to drive the rural population into IDP (internally displaced persons) camps, complete with enclosures guarded by soldiers. The government called the camps "protected villages"; the opposition called them "concentration camps." The camp population grew from a few hundred thousand by the end of 1996 to almost a million in 2002. By then nearly the entire rural population of the three districts of Acholiland had been interned in official camps. According to the government's own Ministry of Health, the excess mortality rate in these camps was approximately one thousand persons a week. (280)

Conditions in these camps have garnered suspicion that this forced internment amounts to, at best, systematic economic disempowerment and, at worst, an intentional ethnic cleansing of the Acholi, perpetrated by the Ugandan government. In essence, Acholi who were not confined to camps were considered members of the LRA and thus targets of the U.S.-backed Ugandan military aggression. Caught between the LRA (whose tactics include kidnapping, mutilation, and mass murder) and the Ugandan military (whose tactics include similar acts of violence along with forced internment), the Acholi population became a sort of bare life.[10] That is to say, deprived of any rights as citizens, the Acholi were only recognized as either civilians or terrorists insofar as they were either incarcerated or killed. The demonic portrayal of the LRA then provided Museveni with an alibi for this internment and subjugation of the Acholi. As Eichstaedt concludes, "The continued existence of the LRA was a useful evil. It gave Museveni the excuse he needed to exert near-total control over the Acholi and Langi" (137–138).

Whether or not this internment and perpetual war has been an intentional attempt at ethnic cleansing, it appears to have only further economically disenfranchised the Acholi. While the full socioeconomic impact of this mass internment has yet to be properly assessed, the few studies and reports that are emerging suggest something akin to accumulation by dispossession, one of the main forms of which is the privatization of land once held communally by the Acholi. Indeed, the popular "theory" among the Acholi is that the mass internments were carried out for the express purpose of "opening" the land of the northern region to private international investment.[11] The reputation of the Ugandan military along with a number of current government policies and land deals do little to abate such suspicions.[12] With interned Acholi only recently beginning to return to their land, and the conflict having wreaked havoc on their system of communal ownership, northern Uganda has certainly been left "open" for capitalist accumulation. For the past few years, the *Daily Monitor* has reported on attempts by the government to hand over large portions of northern land to corporate interests, a major one being the Madhvani corporation, with the implication that displaced Acholi would serve as the surplus labor for this privatized program of agricultural industrialization.[13] Ronald R. Atkinson's

research also chronicles a number of attempts at privatization and industrialization of this land by the Ugandan government.[14] Moreover, as thousands of
Acholi peasants are being evicted from their land and as many have yet to return
from IDP camps, the government's 2007 Land Amendment Bill and Egypt's
announcement that it will be leasing substantial portions of land in the north
for large-scale wheat production have all met with a great deal of skepticism
from Acholi people, political groups, and activists.[15] In short, although it may
be a bit hasty to term the fallout from the twenty-three-year-old war a "land
grab," what is clear is that the massive internment of the Acholi has traumati-
cally transformed their communal system of ownership into a system based on
privatization, industrial production, and international investment.[16] And while
the "conspiratorial" notion that the Ugandan government *intended* this dispossession is debatable, the massive displacement certainly did not help the Acholi
to defend themselves against predatory economic interests.

Like much of the Western media, however, *Unknown Soldier* often reduces this
complex geopolitical relationship to the blackface/whiteface duality of terrorism
versus the state. Not merely reductive, however, this racialized discourse of "deviant" terrorists at war with the "normal" state actually inverts the power dynamics
that have shaped the political struggle in the region. That is to say, the dominant
narrative through which this struggle has been interpreted, the tale of monstrous
Acholi rebels attacking their own families and children, recasts the neoliberal state
as a whiteface victim of the fanatical, blackface terrorism. Although *Unknown
Solider* makes vague allusions to the complex geopolitical situation just summarized, the comic often deploys this reductive specter of a horrific, terrorist desire.

As this monstrous drive is embodied by the unknown solder, it is defined by
its very difference from, and hostility toward, heterosexual relationships, particularly his relationships with his African wife, Sera, and his American ex-wife,
Rachel Callos. Again, these depictions of the monstrous drive do not so much
deny the geopolitical situation of the region as they do essentialize this political
strife. Political violence is presented as "deviant" sexual pathology. Embroiled
in a firefight between the Ugandan government and the LRA, the unknown
soldier hears the strains of Carl Weber's "Ozean, du Ungeheuer" playing in his
head. This aria, which supposedly reoccurs "every time the carnage starts," effectively attributes this *political* violence to a natural and monstrous force internal
to the unknown solider. While the unknown soldier does refer to the aria as a
"white man's music" and thus alludes to a history of colonization, the title of the
aria, which translates as "Ocean, thou Mighty Monster," lends a quality of naturalness and inevitability to the conflict between the Ugandan government and
the LRA (*US2* 33–34, 44, 80). With this aria as background music, political
violence takes on the aspect of an ineluctable, oceanic, and musical force. Lacking coherent explanation, it would seem that this force ripping the colonized
body apart is precisely an essential aspect of this same body, in a cyclical logic
that, of course, recalls the unknown soldier's own *self*-disfiguration.

If the blackface dimension of the unknown soldier amounts to these spectacles of "monstrous" drive, then the whiteface aspect of his character consists of a "normal" desire that is always, supposedly, threatened by this force. The closer the unknown soldier gets to this violent aria of postcolony, the further he gets from *both* whiteness *and* heterosexual formations. His initial choice to do humanitarian work in Uganda severs his engagement with his Western fiancée, Rachel Callos, whose separation from "Africa" is underscored by the very first image we get of her. Framing Rachel within the flashback setting of the Western supermarket, the panel removes her character spatially and temporally from the Ugandan setting, but she is also *racially* removed "far from the wilderness" that is constitutive of the unknown soldier. This "wilderness," another term for the monstrous force possessing the unknown soldier, takes its shape from its apparent hostility to these heterosexual formations. The voice of the unknown soldier's sinister alter ego emerges during a dream in which he murders his Ugandan wife, Sera, and moreover, the mass of dead bodies and violent "madness" that constitute the unknown soldier's world provide a threatening backdrop not only to whiteness but to heterosexual ideals as well (see fig. 3.5). Here, the mass of dead black bodies quite literally serves as a background for an image of heterosexual love; fighting contrasts with fucking. The erotically charged "hunger" and "aliveness" of the unknown soldier functions as a dual opposite to an idyllic image of heterosexuality.

If these figures of nonheteronormative "hunger" and "aliveness" simultaneously function as stereotypes of blackness, they also bind heteronormativity to whiteness. That is to say, the color line that these figures of monstrous desire establish sets up a racialized order of sexuality in which whiteness appears as a white *straightness* that is always being terrorized by a *queer* blackness. While the unknown soldier's violent alter ego appears to endanger his relationships with both white and black women, the comic tends to equate threatened heterosexuality specifically with threatened whiteness. Indeed, the narrative trajectory of Sera bears out this logic. Although the African liberation movement's plot to kill Margaret imperils the three women in the unknown soldier's life—Sera, Rachel, and Margaret—Sera's character is subordinated to the drama surrounding Rachel and Margaret. Leading up to the attack, we see numerous panels in which Sera is consoling Rachel and Margaret, and when the action commences, the central concern of the narrative becomes Rachel, who appears to be fatally wounded. As with the depiction of Margaret's assassination, the melodramatic images of Rachel being shot capture her *on the verge* of death and are juxtaposed with images of a shattered, already-dead black body of a rebel.

In comparison to Rachel's wounded body, whose face is given a startled expression, the wounded black body is shattered, its face literally disintegrating into red smears of blood. Blackness is again aligned with the bodily fragmentation of a corpse, a "piece of shit" that is *already dead*, whereas whiteness is equated with a life in peril. And Sera, for her part, is placed in a subservient

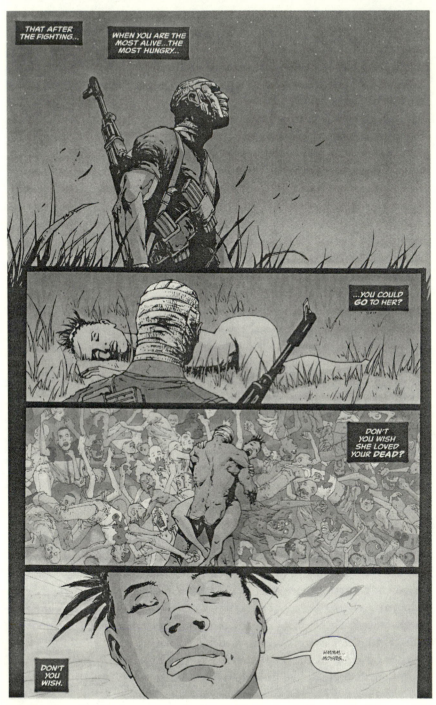

3.5 The mass of dead bodies serves as a background for an image of heterosexual love in *Unknown Soldier*.

position with respect to this latter threatened white subject. Although we see Sera whisper, "Don't you walk out on me again," as she spies the unknown soldier escaping the banquet hall, she is for the most part depicted providing medical attention to Rachel and consoling the traumatized and guilt-ridden Margaret, in a rehearsal of the "black people helping white people" stereotype (*US2* 142–144). In this way, the "terrorist" violence, of which the unknown soldier is a part and which threatens to destroy his heterosexual relationship with Sera, is framed as the endangerment specifically to white, Western subjects.

The unknown soldier, then, embodies both terms of the racial duality at work in colonialist discourse. He is, as Sera puts it, "two very different things at the same time," an eviscerated black body and a wounded white visage, a monstrously violent desire and a pacifist, heteronormative Western subject who has lost his way (*US2* 112). In occupying these two positions, the unknown soldier reifies the two options—a queer black terrorism and a heteronormative white liberalism—that constitute the dominant political hegemony of globalization. Indeed, his blackface and whiteface aspects illustrate how heteronormative ideology functions with respect to this racial ideology underlying global capitalism. The same can be said for the other embodiment of this duality offered in the comic: the child soldier. Like the unknown soldier, the child soldiers depicted in the comic—not to mention in the Western media more generally, where these figures have become the catchall symbol of military conflict in Africa— are dismembered bodies and "deviant" sexualities as well as threatened or wounded "innocents" that are on their way to being protected, healed, and thus transformed into heteronormative Western subjects. Nowhere is the blackface dimension of child soldiers more apparent than in the many spectacles of their obliterated bodies cited earlier. These depictions of the child soldier conjure bodily and representational disfigurement, masses of corpses, psychic fragmentation, and ultimately deindividualization—that is, all those modes of abjection at work in colonialist notions of blackness. If the wounded yet animated and whole bodies of Margaret and Rachel always stand at the melodramatic precipice of death, these obliterated corpses of child soldiers are already dead. Much like zombies, they are both physically mutilated and psychologically automatized, and in fact, they often appear to the unknown soldier as zombie ghosts of his past victims. When not *in fact* corpses or zombies, these child soldiers are often depicted as killing machines on par with the psychologically programmed unknown soldier himself.

At the same time, however, the very notion of *childhood* at work in the image of the child soldier points toward an idyllic heteronormativity and subjective wholeness that the comic aligns with Western institutions and whiteness. By standing for the blackface threat of the LRA's "senseless" terrorism, the child solider also amounts to a subject who needs *to be saved*, and in many ways, "salvation," as its presented in this comic, amounts to a white mask. The figure of the child soldier, then, implies a narrative arc whereby a "lost" subject moves from being victimized by the monstrous drive associated with blackness to being saved by and thus taking on institutional, economic, and sexual formations associated with whiteness. The first child soldier depicted in the comic exemplifies the racial and sexual dynamics of this "redemption" narrative. In a condensed rehearsal of this arc, we first encounter him just after he has raped a young girl and only see him again in a makeshift IDP hospital as he is about to be handed over to the International Red Cross, which will in turn place him in an Acholi foster family (*US1* 20–76). Exemplary of the "child soldier" narrative trajectory, this character transforms swiftly from a "deviant" sexual threat into a victim in need of psychological healing and family guidance administered by Western institutions. The two lone-wolf and cub subplots of the comic, in which the unknown soldier shepherds a girl, Anyayo, and a former child soldier, Paul, through the northern region, repeat this same normalizing arc. In Anyayo's story, "home" is a colonial Catholic school filled with Christian iconography, while for Paul, "home" is a series of IDP camps; in fact, both of these Western institutions, the church and the camp, include a white mother figure. The head of the Catholic school, a nun who heroically pursues the LRA through the bush in order to rescue her kidnapped pupils, references an actual nun, Rachele Fassera, who gained international press coverage when she performed a similar feat during the highly publicized Aboke abductions. Receiving extensive coverage in the *New York Times Magazine* and the topic of two documentary films and one documentary novel, *Aboke Girls* (1995), which is reported to be subject of a forthcoming film starring Uma Thurman, the Aboke incident did much to make the situation of northern Uganda visible to Western audiences but visible again within the familiar narrative framework of victimized African children, demonized African "rebels," and white, Western heroism.[17] Thus, the threat to Anyayo's childhood innocence is cast as a threat to this white, Western institution, and in turn, this institution is made to symbolize the "salvation" and the "normalcy" to which Anyayo supposedly belongs. The presence of Margaret Wells within the IDP camps lends a similar air of white maternalism to these neoliberal formations. A number of panels depict Margaret in these camps watching children play and carrying infants (see fig. 3.6). This Madonna with Child iconography ascribes a symbolic matrix of whiteness and heteronormativity to the setting of the IDP camp, to which Paul returns and where he is supposedly "healed." Aside from this iconography, however, as discussed earlier, the IDP camps are themselves an oppressive social formation administered by state forces and global "humanitarian" organizations, where thousands of Acholi have been interned and many have died. To say the least, these are problematic sites for the comic book to call "home." As Paul himself suggests, these camps are, in a sense, a "government trap," and "it is no different inside the fence than outside" (*US2* 36, 155). When Paul returns to his extended family, who have been living in a camp, he might very well take part in what appears to be traditional Acholi "cleansing" rituals and thus reenter a properly "African"

3.6 The maternal embrace of Western benevolence in *Unknown Soldier*.

community, but he does so within the confines of these global institutions and thus under the auspices of the neoliberal project of accumulation by dispossession to which the Acholi have been subjected. For these child soldiers, then, returning home, where they are physically and psychologically "redeemed," means returning to a maternal embrace of Western benevolence, an embrace that, at least in a politico-economic sense, has attempted to crush the Acholi.

Like the unknown soldier, then, the child soldier's position at the divide between blackface and whiteface also marks an opposition between "bad" and "good" sexual formations, between "deviant" impulses and "normal" psychic desires. Generally speaking, this dualistic image of the child soldier at work in *Unknown Soldier* concurs with the dominant humanitarian narrative of children in combat. As David Rosen observes, "In humanitarian accounts, child soldiers are either victims or demons, or, better yet, they are demons because they are victims. Neither demons nor victims are rational actors" (134). As both demon and victim, the "child soldier" then requires the tutelage of a Western caregiver and thereby promotes the authority of Western "rationality" and, in turn, the subordination of non-Western "irrationality." This is not to deny the reality of young Ugandans being raped and forced into soldiering, but how these children have been represented in popular media has more to do with the dominant ideology concerning the postcolony than with the actual plight of displaced people such as the Acholi. In this respect, it is telling that, as Finnström notes, both the LRA and the Ugandan government have employed child soldiers and otherwise brutalized the young Acholi population, yet the image of the child soldier that is constructed time and again by the mainstream media points specifically to those postcolonial political groups that oppose emerging neoliberal states (91). As Rosen concludes, this figure of the "child soldier" arises at a particular moment of postcolonial politico-economic reform when "the international community of humanitarian and human rights groups and of governments, once avid supporters of the armies of national liberation, have now redefined all rebels and their leaders as apolitical criminals and child abusers" (14). This image of the "child soldier," then, not only legitimizes neoliberal states such as Uganda but binds this neoliberal system to a racialized image of sexual normativity. If the rebels are always "child abusers," then the state becomes the locus of "normal" child rearing, heterosexual reproduction, and familial bonds.

In this respect, the image of the child soldier functions much like the image of the child more generally. As Lee Edelman argues, insofar as the popular image of endangered childhood stands for a social order that needs to be preserved, this image necessarily equates this valued social order with heteronormativity. That is to say, the unquestioned mandate to "protect the Child" in contemporary political narratives such as *Unknown Soldier* directs all politics toward a "reproductive futurism" that necessarily privileges heterosexual social formations. As Edelman puts it, any politics "remains, at its core, conservative insofar as it works to *affirm* a structure, to *authenticate* social order, which it then intends to transmit to the future in the form of its inner Child. That Child remains the perpetual horizon of every acknowledged politics, the fantasmatic beneficiary of every political intervention" (3). The image of the child, then, is synonymous with conservative politics, and what this politics of the child seeks to conserve is always a heteronormative notion of an "authentic social order." If the image of the child places heterosexuality at the center of this "authentic social order," the *racialized* version of this image—the child solider—links this privileged heterosexuality to a fantasy of neoliberal whiteness. In a symbolic order governed by the "child soldier," the social formations that supposedly need to be preserved are implicitly white, Western, and heteronormative.

The unknown soldier and the child soldier, then, both embody the two political options that limit the political sphere: on one hand, a blackface image of terroristic desire in which bodies and psyches are blown to pieces and, on the other hand, the whiteface image of Western and heteronormative "home" in which bodies are stitched together often through appeals to essentialist racial stereotypes, neoliberal institutions, and ideals of whiteness. Thus, there is a false choice: either we submit to the terrorist violence supposedly perpetrated by the colonized on themselves or take refuge in Western camps and Western fantasies of the neocolonizers; either we are mired in a queer black mass of dismembered corpses or "saved" by a heteronormative white subject and thus restored to bodily integrity. Indeed, breaking with this ideological double bind seems an arduous task both to enact and to theorize. Žižek has suggested that, faced with such false choices, a properly emancipatory politics must begin by identifying and affirming a "third element" that has been subtracted from this hegemonic duality of *either* terrorism *or* global capitalism (386). And from the perspective of queer theory, Edelman argues for a similar affirmation of the missing element. According to Edelman, in order to break with the order of "reproductive futurism," in order to develop a politics that is not subordinated to the heteronormative image of the child (or the child soldier, as the case may be), it is necessary to embody the "gap" within, and constitutive of, this heteronormative order. For Edelman, affirming this queer element would amount to "a movement beyond the pleasure principle, beyond the distinctions of pleasure and pain, a violent passage beyond the bounds of identity, meaning, and law" (25). In other words, affirming this queerness that is always subtracted from the heteronormative symbolic order would mean exceeding the sensory, identitarian, linguistic, and legal categories that structure the social sphere, and I would add that such a radical affirmation would necessarily mean exceeding the racial dualities of colonial discourse as well since these racial dualities are themselves bound to normative sexual ideology. This affirmation, however, would not simply leave these sexual and racial orders behind. Instead, this embodiment of the absent element would found a politics around the perpetual inability of these sexual and racial orders to fully encapsulate the dynamic relationship between the social, the sexual, and the political.

It is precisely this affirmation of a subtracted term that *Unknown Soldier*—both the comic and the character—struggle with, and I will conclude this study by looking at one instance when the comic both articulates and forecloses on this emancipatory potential: the character of T'Anay, the leader of the African economic liberation movement. Though entirely subsumed in the racial and sexual dualities constitutive of the postcolony, T'Anay, much like the unknown soldier, embodies this subtracted element. While the comic ultimately attempts to close this gap and reinsert these characters into the dominant political narrative, the *very serial form of comic books as such* helps to undermine this narrative and political closure. Although T'Anay is a marginal character, she shares with the unknown soldier a lack of fidelity to any of the political positions offered by the hegemony of the postcolony. Consisting of "political refugees from all over D.R.C., C.A.R., Chad, Rwanda, the children of the Afar people of Ethiopia," her movement traverses national boundaries and appears to have ties to various, contradictory, political organizations (*US2* 40). Also like the unknown soldier, T'Anay and her movement operate within the terms of the dominant racial and sexual order. As discussed earlier, their plan to assassinate Margaret

Wells appropriates and, to a certain extent, supports the racial dualities of the postcolony.

In fact, the movement's engagement with these racial politics might very well be seen as a self-defeating strategy that resembles the unknown soldier's own self-mutilation. Recalling this self-mutilation, the scarification on T'Anay's face underscores these similarities between the two characters' contradictory political positions. The difference between these scarred faces, however, illustrates a key distinction between their characters. Unlike the unknown soldier's mass of slashes, which never stops underscoring his frenzied self-destructive impulses, T'Anay's scars mark a calculated aesthetics of body modification. Whereas the unknown soldier's mangled face presents an eviscerated blackness barely held together by a white mask of bandages, T'Anay's scarification presents something far more unsettling to the dominant order of racial and sexual dualities—a "wounded" blackness that has been intentionally affirmed, aestheticized, and politicized. It is this point of *affirmation* where the narrative paths of the unknown soldier and T'Anay diverge significantly, the former tending toward a blackface/whiteface narrative of loss and redemption, the latter offering a radical potential that the comic both demonizes and leaves largely unexplored. During a violent confrontation with the unknown soldier, T'Anay exclaims, "You think it is easy hiding my compassion!? Acting like something I am not so I can change this mavi world!? You think I am a monster!? I am just more courageous than you" (*US2* 136). As T'Anay suggests, her difference from the unknown soldier is both very slight and also quite profound. Although both characters occupy a liminal subject position, the unknown soldier longs for *who he was*, while T'Anay struggles to continue being *something she is not*. The question for the unknown soldier is whether he can be "healed," whether he will stay in the IDP camps and assist the Acholi, whether he will return to his old world or survive within the world of the postcolony *as it is*. Conversely, the question for T'Anay is *changing this mavi world*. T'Anay's plan, then, refuses the standard redemption narrative whereby the colonized subject is "healed" or rather transformed from a demonic blackface stereotype into an angelic whiteface stereotype.

T'Anay also complicates the heteronormative opposition between violent drive and heterosexual ideals at work within this racial duality. When the unknown soldier pins her down atop a dead body, T'Anay responds by saying, "You want to fuck me now? Fuck me on this man you killed? I understand. I understand you." She then touches the unknown soldier's cock and continues, "Yes, see, there it is. Your body knows. Go on. Do it" (*US2* 134). T'Anay's ploy recalls the unknown soldier's fantasy of fucking Sera atop a mass of corpses, but whereas the unknown soldier's anxiety-laden fantasy framed these violent impulses as a potentially catastrophic threat to the heteronormative social order, T'Anay's calculated play affirms this anxiety-laden threat as a political weapon. Her "cock teasing" locates this violent threat to heteronormativity *within* heterosexual desire as such and furthermore suggests that this self-overturning, nonnormative potential of heterosexual formations, or at least normative anxiety about this potential, can be appropriated for her larger political project. In touching the unknown soldier's cock, she gestures toward a bodily affect that exceeds and indeed fragments the boundaries of unitary selfhood, sexual norms, and political intentionality, but she does so precisely in order to *play with* the fantastical connotations of this affect and play them against other characters. Thus, in keeping with this tactical sexuality, we see T'Anay sleeping with Jack Lee Howl, presumably in order to draw him into her plan, and attempting a similar liaison with the unknown soldier as well. In this way, T'Anay refuses the supposedly clear opposition between violent drives and heteronormative sexual formations. The sexuality affirmed by her character is political precisely because it operates within but exceeds the dualities of the dominant political and sexual order. Like T'Anay herself, this sexuality indeed always acts like something it is not.

My suggestion here that T'Anay and her movement might represent a radical, emancipatory politics is of course precarious. After all, from a certain vantage, their planned assassination of Margaret only reiterates the dominant racial duality in which tragically victimized whiteness takes precedent over countless dead black bodies. Likewise, T'Anay's sexual machinations might be seen as merely a reification of the fetishistic association of the colonized body with violent, nonnormative sexual deviance. Given this precariousness, T'Anay's assertion that she is "more courageous" than the unknown soldier could not be more accurate because there is no assurance that her movement will have its intended effect and not the diametric opposite. Rather than a calculated future, the movement's agenda is based on the present refusal of the political positions offered by the racial and sexual hegemony of the postcolony. To put the matter differently, the movement rejects both the blackface visage associated with the LRA and the whiteface visage of the neoliberal state. What is more, the movement refuses the narrative trajectory of "healing" exemplified by the unknown solider and child soldiers, for whom this middle ground is simply an anxious transition from a nightmare of the violent impulses to a resolution of heteronormativity. The movement thus denies every signifier of selfhood and identity offered by the dominant symbolic order and thereby exemplifies *courage*, which, as Alain Badiou puts it, "amounts to the force to traverse anxiety since this means nothing else but the capacity to consider oneself null" (315). By affirming a subtracted void within the dominant order, by "acting like something she is not," T'Anay wagers that actualizing the imaginary danger to whiteness and heteronormativity that is always attributed to the colonized, enacting the violence for which the colonized is always condemned *before the act*, might actually transform the world.

On the basis of neither a dramatic longing to be redeemed nor the stable positions within the dominant symbolic order of racial identities and sexual orientations, T'Anay presents a significant challenge to narrative closure, political or otherwise, which the comic book attempts to contain by ascribing homophobic beliefs to her and, finally, literally removing her from the narrative altogether. During her confrontation with the unknown soldier, she shouts, "Msenge wewe! Goat fucking homosexual!" an accusation that displaces the comic's own heteronormative ideology onto T'Anay (*US2* 136). Attributing these epithets to T'Anay offers us, as readers, another false point and a false choice between the overt homophobia of her character and the implicit homophobia of the comic itself. More simply, though, this characterization of T'Anay as homophobic demonizes her revolutionary politics, casting it as the "bad intolerant other," the mirror opposite of a supposedly tolerant Western democracy. Indeed, the deployment of the Swahili "Msenge wewe" emphasizes the association of this overt homophobia with non-Western, "African" culture.

There is a glaring irony to T'Anay's homophobia here, given that recently the most visible example of homophobia with respect to Uganda has come *not* from any rebel group but instead from the Ugandan government itself. In 2009, as a way of "strengthening the nation's capacity to deal with emerging internal and external threats to the traditional heterosexual family," and in conjunction with representatives from the Western Evangelical movement, Museveni's regime proposed an antihomosexuality bill that attempted to further criminalize "homosexuality," further systematize the incarceration of "homosexuals," and make "aggravated homosexual acts" punishable by death.[18] Given this context, to make the head of an international revolutionary group the mouthpiece for homophobic intolerance seems, at best, misleading and, at worst, an attempt to stigmatize antistate forces of "terrorism" while at the same time eliding the homophobic terror perpetrated by the state itself. Thusly stigmatized as homophobic fanatics, T'Anay and her movement literally disappear from the narrative, which reverts to concerns about protecting the white femininity of Margaret and Rachel, "healing" of the unknown soldier's "wounded" masculinity, and returning the child solider to his "home" in an IDP camp.

Yet the political potential embodied both by T'Anay and, to a certain extent, by the unknown soldier himself haunt these all-too-tidy conclusions. By literally writing T'Anay and her movement out of the narrative, the comic leaves open the possibility that she and her movement might return in future issues to further trouble the political and narrative order. Indeed, the most recent installments of the comic, which find the unknown soldier still living in an IDP camp, undermine the reconciliatory note that concludes the first two volumes. In this way, the seriality of the comic book, that is to say, the open-endedness of the comic book format as such, has been conducive to characters such as T'Anay and the unknown soldier, who always are "something they are not." In fact, the most valuable contribution of the *Unknown Soldier* is to present the political situation of Uganda within this serial structure because in doing so the comic book can provide us with wounded bodies that never quite heal and a political play that is never finally harnessed by the terms of any racial or sexual duality. Characters such as T'Anay and the unknown soldier are most powerful, however, *not* because they survive these wounds but because they ask whether their mangled bodies might be the sites of a revolutionary politics.

Notes

1 As Mbembe further explains, these colonialist "systems of reading the world" have secured authority by "assigning Africa to a special unreality such that the continent becomes the very figure of what is null, abolished, and, in its essence, in opposition to what is" (4).

2 For an example of the typical photographic treatment of Acholi children in the mainstream press, see especially Stevens.

3 For this terminology used in the *Economist*, see especially this series of briefings: "Thou Shalt Not Kill," "Africa's Most Wanted," "Catching a Ugandan Monster," "Hunting Uganda's Child-Killers."

4 For this terminology and photographic imagery see Lovgren; Nutt and Hoskins.

5 For a history of colonial, popular, and ethnographic perceptions of the Acholi, see Finnström 55–61, 78–81.

6 This racist framework ignores the Ugandan government's politico-economic exploitation of the Acholi and also misrepresents the political motives of both the Acholi in general and the LRA specifically. Finnström's ethnographic work suggests that many Acholi express a great deal of frustration with the Ugandan government's neoliberal economic programs. Furthermore, Finnström claims that there are a number of manifestos produced by the LRA that reiterate the Acholi's political dissent and present the rebel group less as religious fanatics and more as a politicized resistance movement. For a rare in-depth account of the political situation of northern Uganda and the LRA specifically, including a brief study of LRA political manifestos, see Finnström 99–126.

7 For an extensive account of how this neoliberal policy of accumulation by dispossession has effected Africa as a whole, see Bond.

8 Surveying a 1997 study by the World Bank, Susan Dicklitch notes that, although Uganda boasted one of the fastest growing economies in the world, the population nonetheless experienced an increase in economic inequality, higher death and infant mortality rates, and lower per capita incomes and life expectancies than did many low-income countries (63, 69). As in many developing countries, neoliberal reform in Uganda has resulted in massive layoffs in the civil sector and drastic cuts in social services, education, and health care—policies that certainly do not foster improved living conditions for the working poor. As Geoffrey B. Tukahebwa argues, neoliberal structural adjustment and the trend toward privatization have actually exacerbated unemployment and have done nothing to address social inequality and poverty. Michael Twaddle and Holger Bernt Hansen concur that the neoliberal agenda of Museveni's government, while resulting in overall economic growth, "has not increased employment opportunities at all significantly. Nor has it enlarged the number of Ugandan entrepreneurs. Poverty too, has not been reduced so far by privatization" (14). For these examinations of Uganda's neoliberal policies, see Dicklitch 63–72; Tukahebwa 59–72; Twaddle and Hansen 10–17.

9 Citing both indirect and direct election misconduct, human rights violations, and the violent suppression of political party activities, strikes, and student demonstrations,

Dicklitch concludes, "the NRM regime is promoting economic liberalization to the exclusion of political liberalization and democratization" (121). Finnström also provides a useful corrective to the dominant characterization of the LRA as the sole perpetrators of "terrorism" in the war by documenting the mass internments and property dispossessions committed against Acholi peasants by the Ugandan military. See Dicklitch 96–122; Finnström 71–74, 84–91.

10   As one Al Jazeera documentary on the war puts it, "In the official parlance of this war, the dead are always described as rebels. Those taken alive are described as rescued abductees." For more detailed accounts of how the Acholi are violently appropriated by the conflict, see Al Jazeera English; Finnström 88–91.

11   For recent ethnographic studies of Acholi perspectives on their own politico-economic situation, see Rugadya ii–vi.

12   The Ugandan military has a documented history of stealing property from Acholi farmers, particularly cattle, and, what is more, UN investigations have linked top-ranking military officials to massive lootings of natural resources in the Congo. See Finnström 71–74, 176–177.

13   For reports from the *Daily Monitor* on the Madhvani land deals, see Egadu, "Investors" and "Museveni"; Mugerwa; Nalugo; Lawino.

14   Along with the Madhvani case, Atkinson documents a 2008 land deal between the Ugandan government and the Amuru District Community Farmers Association, in which control of once-communal land would be placed in the hands of a small group of investors, with the Acholi population being thus repositioned as tenant farmers. He also cites plans developed by the military in the late 1990s for the privatization of northern Ugandan farm land and, perhaps most significantly, a plan developed by the company Divinity Union Ltd. (headed by Museveni's brother) to convert large amounts of this land to industrial-scale grain farming. See Atkinson 7–9, 17–19.

15   More recently, the *Daily Monitor* reported that the Madhvani group has attempted to evict twenty thousand people from the eastern Jinja region in order to further expand land holdings, and Egypt's land leases have been suspected of furthering a trend toward accumulation by dispossession. See Wanyera and Muyita.

16   Aside from agriculture, oil is another major northern Ugandan commodity that is being tapped by international interests, with Heritage Oil announcing in 2009 the discovery of Uganda's largest oil field in Amuru. In recent years, government dealings with Heritage Oil have been a point of political contention. See Biryabarema; Ssenkabirwa and Mugerwa.

17   See Thernstrom; Finnström 109–111; BBC News.

18   For a copy of this bill, see Gettleman.

Works Cited

"Africa's Most Wanted." *Economist* 3 June 2006: 44.

Al Jazeera English. *America's New Frontline: Diplomats or Warriors.* Sept. 2009. Web. http://english.aljazeera.net/programmes/witness/2009/09/2009910121135544650.html. Accessed 25 June 2010.

Atkinson, Roland R. "Land Issues in Acholi in the Transition from War to Peace." *Examiner: Quarterly Publication of Human Rights Focus* 4 (2008): 3–9, 17–25.

Badiou, Alain. *Theory of the Subject.* Trans. Bruno Bosteels. New York: Continuum, 2009.

BBC News. "Hollywood to Tackle Uganda Rebels." 28 Aug. 2009. Web. http://news.bbc.co.uk/2/hi/8226675.stm. Accessed 25 June 2010.

Biryabarema, Elias. "Biggest Oil Well Found in Amuru." *Daily Monitor* 14 Jan. 2009. Web. http://www.monitor.co.ug/News/Education/-/688336/693726/-/yy12x9/-/index.html. Accessed 25 June 2010.

Bond, Patrick. *Looting Africa*. New York: Zed Books, 2006.

"Catching a Ugandan Monster." *Economist* 22 Oct. 2005: 48–50.

Dicklitch, Susan. *The Elusive Promise of NGOs in Africa: Lessons from Uganda*. New York: St. Martin's, 1998.

Dysart, Joshua. *Unknown Soldier, Vol.* 1: *Haunted House*. Illustrations by Alberto Ponticelli and Pat Masioni. Cover art by Igor Kordey and Dave Johnson. New York: Vertigo, 2008.

———. *Unknown Soldier, Vol.* 2: *Easy Kill*. Illustrations by Alberto Ponticelli and Pat Masioni. Cover art by Igor Kordey and Dave Johnson. New York: Vertigo, 2010.

Edelman, Lee. *No Future: Queer Theory and the Death Drive*. Durham, NC: Duke University Press, 2004.

Egadu, Samuel G. "Investors Are Turning to Northern Uganda to Take Full Advantage." *Daily Monitor* 23 Sept. 2007. Web. http://www.monitor.co.ug/Business/Business%20Power/-/688616/782102/-/kkfba1/-/index.html. Accessed 25 June 2010.

———. "Museveni to Meet Acholi Leaders Again." *Daily Monitor* 14 Dec. 2007. Web. http://www.monitor.co.ug/News/Education/-/688336/799724/-/10iryky/-/index.html. Accessed 25 June 2010.

Eichstaedt, Peter. *First Kill Your Family: Child Soldiers and the Lord's Resistance Army*. Chicago: Lawrence Hill Books, 2009.

Fanon, Franz. *Black Skin, White Masks*. Trans. Charles Lam Markmann. New York: Grove, 1967.

Finnström, Sverker. *Living with Bad Surroundings: War History and Everyday Moments in Northern Uganda*. Durham, NC: Duke University Press, 2008.

Gettleman, Jeffrey. "America's Role Seen in Uganda Anti-Gay Push." *New York Times* 3 Jan. 2010. Web. http://www.nytimes.com/2010/01/04/world/africa/04uganda.html. Accessed 25 June 2010.

Grzyb, Amanda F. "Media Coverage, Activism, and Creating Public Will for Intervention in Rwanda and Darfur." *The World and Darfur: International Response to Crimes against Humanity in Western Sudan*. Ed. Amanda F. Grzyb. Montreal: McGill-Queen's University Press, 2009. 61–91.

Harvey, David. *The New Imperialism*. New York: Oxford University Press, 2003.

"Hunting Uganda's Child-Killers." *Economist* 7 May 2005: 41–42.

Lawino, Sam. "Acholi Agree to Give Land to Madhvani." *Daily Monitor* 24 Feb. 2009. Web. http://www.monitor.co.ug/News/National/-/688334/698118/-/vhc2sh/-/index.html. Accessed 25 June 2010.

Lovgren, Stefan. "Childhood Lost." *Maclean's* 14 Dec. 1998: 38–39.

Mamdani, Mahmood. *Saviors and Survivors: Darfur, Politics, and the War on Terror*. New York: Pantheon Books, 2009.

Mbembe, Achille. *On the Postcolony*. Berkeley: University of California Press, 2001.

Mugerwa, Yaslin. "Museveni to Meet Acholi Leaders over Amuru Land." *Daily Monitor* 9 July 2008. Web. http://www.monitor.co.ug/News/Education/-/688336/743390/-/10f118m/-/index.html. Accessed 25 June 2010.

Nalugo, Mercy. "Elders Petition Museveni over Amuru Land Takeover." *Daily Monitor* 9 Sept. 2008. Web. http://www.monitor.co.ug/News/Education/-/688336/749946/-/10fpbq5/-/index.html. Accessed 25 June 2010.

Nordstrom, Carolyn. "The Backyard Front." *The Paths to Domination, Resistance and Terror*. Ed. Carolyn Nordstrom and JoAnn Martin. Berkeley: University of California Press, 1992. 260–274.

Nutt, Samantha, and Eric Hoskins. "The Unknown War." *Maclean's* 12 Jan. 2004: 16–18.

Rosen, David. *Armies of the Young: Child Soldiers in War and Terrorism*. New Brunswick, NJ: Rutgers University Press, 2005.

Rubin, Elizabeth. "Letter from Uganda: Our Children Are Killing Us." *New Yorker* 23 Mar. 1998: 56–64.

Rugadya, Margaret A. *Northern Uganda Land Study: Analysis of Post Conflict Land Policy and Land Administration: A Survey of IDP Return and Resettlement Issues and Lesson: Acholi and Lango Regions*. Washington, DC: World Bank, 2008.

Ssenkabirwa, Al-Mahdi, and Francis Mugerwa. "Banyoro: We Want Our Land, Jobs Back." *Daily Monitor* 14 Aug. 2009. Web. http://www.monitor.co.ug/News/Education//688336/715664/-/10drugu/-/index.html. Accessed 25 June 2010.

Stevens, Bruno. "Night Flight." *Foreign Policy* Mar.–Apr. 2006: 74–77.

Thernstrom, Melanie. "Charlotte, Grace, Janet and Caroline Come Home." *New York Times Magazine* 8 May 2005. Web. http://www.nytimes.com/2005/05/08/magazine/08UGANDA.html?pagewanted=all&_r=0. Accessed 25 June 2010.

"Thou Shalt Not Kill." *Economist* 6 Sept. 2003: 43.

Tukahebwa, Geoffrey B. "Privatization as a Developmental Policy." *Developing Uganda*. Ed. Holger Bernt Hansen and Michael Twaddle. Athens: Ohio University Press, 1998. 59–72.

Twaddle, Michael, and Holger Bernt Hansen. "The Changing State of Uganda." *Developing Uganda*. Ed. Holger Bernt Hansen and Michael Twaddle. Athens: Ohio University Press, 1998. 1–18.

Wanyera, Dalton, and Solomon Muyita. "Madhvani to Evict 20,000 from Jinja." *Daily Monitor* 30 Mar. 2010. Web. http://www.monitor.co.ug/News/National/-/688334/889212/-/wjvph4/-/index.html. Accessed 25 June 2010.

Žižek, Slavoj. *In Defense of Lost Causes*. New York: Verso, 2008.

Panel II

Black in Black-and-White
and Color

Chapter 4

Fashion in the Funny Papers

●●●●●●●●●●●●●●●●●●●●●●

Cartoonist Jackie Ormes's American Look

NANCY GOLDSTEIN

> Didja ever see a dream running? Well we did—It's Torchy crossing 7th Avenue thru an imaginary traffic rush; she dreams up a lovely dress shop and dashes over to get herself some New York finery.
> —Jackie Ormes, *Torchy Brown in "Dixie to Harlem"*

At a time when images of African Americans in mainstream newspaper comics portrayed only derogatory stereotypes, cartoonist Jackie Ormes (1911–1985) defied the norm with her smart, beautiful women and children. It was gratifying for readers to turn to the pages of the black press to see photographs and illustrations depicting attractive black people, images that would not be seen in the majority media. Characters such as Torchy, Candy, Ginger, and pint-size Patty-Jo dressed in upscale attire as they commented on all manner of contemporary topics, from U.S. nuclear armament in the Cold War to the vagaries of Christian Dior's hemlines. Indeed the built-in obsolescence of designers' seasonal mandates and consumer appetites for ever-new trends provided a constant source of humor for Ormes. But just as important, the visual representation of chic clothing and modish interiors in the funny papers gave her the opportunity to report on modern lifestyles to a large African American readership and to advocate inclusion in a more prosperous America. At the same time, Ormes's interpretations of Paris couture, American sportswear, and Hollywood glamour came together to create what could be called a unique American look, at once elegant, active, and hip. Along with visual presentations, her characters often verbally described clothing, hats, gloves, and shoes, sometimes in exacting detail. Colorful Torchy's Togs, a half-page panel of paper-doll cutouts, further expanded Ormes's fashion reportage. Dressed in the latest fashions and ensconced in upscale lifestyles, Torchy, Ginger, and Patty-Jo were models of the middle-class American dream that served to promote racial advancement.

Cartoon historians consider Jackie Ormes to be the first African American woman newspaper cartoonist. With coast-to-coast distribution and artistic production that was completely her own, she is certainly the first who compares to contemporaneous syndicated cartoonists. Ormes entered the national scene with a comic strip that ran from 1937 to 1938. She took an unexplained break for seven years, resuming to draw from 1945 to 1956. Ormes's four cartoons and comic strips were *Torchy Brown in "Dixie to Harlem," Candy, Patty-Jo 'n' Ginger*, and *Torchy in Heartbeats*, with the latter two running simultaneously for some years. Most of Jackie Ormes's work appeared in the *Pittsburgh Courier*, one of the largest black weekly newspapers. In the late 1940s, the *Courier* claimed a readership of over a million and had fourteen big city editions, allowing Ormes to display her sense of humor as well as her fashion sense to a national audience. Ormes lived in Chicago during most of her adult life, and some attractions she depicted in her cartoons, such as the Chicago Park District and International Style buildings, would have been familiar to readers of the *Courier*'s Chicago edition. One imagines that savvy Chicago readers may also have caught her visual references to fashions seen on the streets of Chicago or in the fashion shows that Ormes produced for groups such as the Urbanaides, a chapter of the Urban League, and the Chicago Negro Chamber of Commerce.

In this chapter, I discuss only newspaper comics and cartoons since this is where Jackie Ormes's work appeared; she was not known to have produced art for comic books or magazine or book illustrations. This chapter also puts by the story of her political life, already described in my 2008 biography of her (Goldstein). But I would be remiss not to mention Ormes's political activism and her FBI file of nearly three hundred pages that the Justice Department compiled during twelve years of the communist-hunting days of the 1940s and 1950s. Although she was certainly not a communist, her left-leaning activities and some of her associations nevertheless made her a target for investigation. Despite what must have been a worrisome situation, her cartoons continued to criticize such powerful entities as segregated school systems and the U.S.

military machine, defying some of the most entrenched American institutions. Ormes was also probably the first cartoonist anywhere to take on the subjects of industrial pollution and environmental justice, as she did in 1954, the last year of *Torchy in Heartbeats*. Finally, although hair and makeup are essential elements of a fashionable look—elements Ormes never neglected in her real life or in her cartoons—their practice in African American grooming and commercial entities has been written about extensively elsewhere and is only briefly touched on in this chapter.

The Fashionista Cartoonist Emerges

Jackie Ormes grew up in a middle-class home and mixed-race neighborhood in the small city of Monongahela, Pennsylvania, about twenty-five miles south of Pittsburgh, where she was born. She and her husband, Earl, later lived in Pittsburgh before relocating in Salem, Ohio, to ride out the Depression with his family. In 1942, they moved to Chicago, where she lived for the rest of her life. From here, she mailed her work to Pittsburgh to be made up into newsprint that would reach all corners of the country.

Her first published cartoon was a full page of caricatures for the Monongahela High School yearbook of 1930, the year she graduated. The artist signed her work Zelda Mavin Jackson, her given and maiden name; "Jackie," the name most people called her, was short for Jackson. High school provided an ample supply of personalities for her to satirize on the yearbook page, and Jackie included herself in this rogues gallery. There is a drawing of a disreputable little car titled "Exclusive photo of Ed Ewing's flivver" and another of a leggy young woman giving herself a dope-slap, aghast at the run in her nylon stocking ("ping!"), "Ila Ward's hose misbehavin'—'Another runner!'" Along with jokes about her classmates, this teenager was beginning to observe and parody people and events in the larger world. Referring to the stock-market crash of 1929, she included on the page a sketch of a fat little man holding a ticker tape, falling back on his heels in dismay: "And the stocks descended and men yelled, and so did Mr. Haskins!" Off to one side of the page, however, was a self- portrait. Here we see a young woman dashing to beat the tardy bell: "Last minute champ of 207—Z. Jackson!" Dust clouds puff up around her feet as she trips along in heels (in high school, mind you); little sweat bullets spring from her brow, along with sound effects, "puff-puff-puff," but every hair on her head is miraculously in place; and in her haste, her coat flaps open, allowing us to admire the coat's smart print lining—no matter that the real-life attire for this teenager was more likely a simple blouse, trim skirt, and saddle oxfords. She was never one to let reality get in the way of creating a more glamorous identity for herself or for her characters on the page.

While in high school, Jackie had done some stringer reporting for the *Courier*, and after graduation she moved to Pittsburgh and became a proofreader and sometime feature writer for the newspaper. Here she met and married Earl Ormes, and in a year their daughter, Jacqueline, was born. But tragedy struck when the little girl developed a brain tumor and died at age three and a half. They were to have no more children, but they did have a happy forty-five-year marriage. Perhaps as a way to help assuage her grief, she returned to the drawing table in 1937, with a one-year contract to produce a comic strip for the *Courier*.

From the start, people noticed that Jackie Ormes looked a lot like her attractive female cartoon characters. She was not known to have live models and probably used a mirror to capture pose, movement, and expression. In interviews some time after Jackie Ormes's death, her sister, Delores Towles, was asked how the cartoon characters' long-legged, statuesque physiques compared to the real-life cartoonist. Smiling, Delores replied that her sister drew the imaginary women as "her perfect self" (personal interview, 2003) —no wonder her women looked like her, and why not? She was shapely and pretty, though at five foot one inch too short to do the runway modeling that Delores once said she probably would have loved. To complete the fantasy, every week Jackie clothed idealized cartoon bodies in something new, different, and interesting. The fashion historian Valerie Steele quotes the linguist and literary critic Philip Thody that "clothes express our freely elected vision of ourselves," adding her own caveat: "But, above all, clothing and adornment are significant because of their connection with the self. Clothing expresses a particular image of the physical body, the individual's self-awareness, and his or her social being" (45–46, quoting Thody 1199). With Ormes as her own model and with an imaginative vision of her body and wardrobe, it is not surprising that she represented her own physical likeness in her cartoons. Other women cartoonists of the time did the same. Gladys Parker, best known for nearly three decades of *Mopsy* (1939–1965), depicted herself in her earlier *Flapper Fanny* in the late 1920s, prompting "herstorian" Trina Robbins to note how the character "grew to closely resemble her delineator, one of several cases where a woman drew herself as the heroine of her own strip" (33). Robbins includes in this convention Dale Messick, whose *Brenda Starr* started in 1940 and who "had identified with her creation to the point of dyeing her own hair red and naming her daughter Starr" (68). In effect, what Jackie Ormes could not achieve in real life—several inches in height and carte blanche at the House of Dior—she could accomplish on the page with cartoon stand-ins. Interestingly, she reinvented a few aspects of her actual self as well, claiming to be years younger than she was and attempting to wear smaller shoe sizes, the latter turning out to be a bonanza for her sister-in-law, who really could wear the petite footwear after Ormes cast them off.

Ormes once told an interviewer that she had no formal art training but rather taught herself to draw by copying comics out of the newspaper. It appears that both Parker's and Messick's work influenced Ormes. When asked in a 1947 interview if it was unusual for females to make it in what was considered a man's profession, she commented, "Women cartoonists are not as rare as you think," no doubt referring to Parker, Messick, and a small host of other women cartoonist predecessors (Thompson 116). Ormes's signature drawing style of crisp black lines seemingly carved into ample white space bears a remarkable likeness to Parker's drawings, and the 1950s independent, adventurous Torchy character strides onto the page with a take-charge attitude like Messick's Brenda. One of *Brenda Starr*'s most popular elements was the accompanying paper-doll cutouts with sumptuous wardrobes, a selling feature that was not lost on Ormes when she added a similar panel, *Torchy's Togs*, to her 1950s *Torchy in Heartbeats*. Of course Ormes would have read the work of male cartoonists such as Edgar Martin's *Boots and Her Buddies* (1924–1969) and Russ Westover's *Tillie the Toiler* (1929–1951), both notable for their fashionable characters and paper-doll cutouts, as well as Paul Robinson's *Etta Kett* (1925–1974), a strip whose title was a play on words for its etiquette tips and one that may have inspired Ormes to offer rules of dress and decorum in the 1950s *Torchy's Togs*. And George McManus's highly successful *Bringing Up Father*, which ran from 1913 to 2000, apparently caught Ormes's eye. Both *Bringing Up Father* and Ormes's 1937 *Torchy* told a rags-to-riches story, and both strips' drawing styles were remarkably similar, with delicate black outlines of characters dressed in high style. In one *Bringing Up Father* series, Jiggs and Maggie travel to Europe on a Grand Tour that of course includes shopping and fittings at fancy Paris design houses, in scenes that bear similarities to some of Ormes's work. Just as fine-art artists borrow from their predecessors and peers, Ormes obviously sampled others' styles and stories, learned from them, and created a vision all her own.

No doubt *Courier* editors were convinced that Ormes's emphasis on upscale fashion and lifestyle would be good for circulation and for business. Dressed head to toe in detailed attire, her beautiful black women offered fashion news for female readers and provided eye candy for men, two compelling reasons to buy a paper. Stylish characters such as Torchy, Ginger, and even Patty-Jo fit in nicely with the *Courier*'s society page, which was filled with photographs and stories describing attractive females dressed for travel, luncheons, and evening fêtes. Such attention to social life and glamorous entertainments not only provided evidence of racial progress but also enticed advertisers to buy space. In fact, the stories and layouts on the social page were often situated next to ads for beauty products and classifieds for mail-order jewelry and hair products, advertising that helped keep the paper afloat. (Longed-for display advertising from the likes of Marshall Field's or General Electric rarely made it to black-press newspapers at this time [Walker].)[1] Aside from the entertainment value in Ormes's funnies, her curvaceous, sexually charged female images could be said to extend what Kim T. Gallon describes as the black press's role to provide "a space and a way for 'ordinary' African Americans to view and publicly discuss sexual representations and ideas" (1). Whether dressed or undressed, appearing in modest attire or edgy underwear and poses, Ormes's females verify Gallon's thesis that "editors believed that sensationalism played a vital role in their ability to sell newspapers to a mass black readership" (3).

In addition, Ormes's elegant interiors and clothing would have been appreciated for their aesthetic value, providing variety on the funnies page, where the other—all-male—cartoonists more typically simply drew people in plainer clothes, often in lower social-economic settings. At the peak of the *Courier's* circulation, in the late 1940s, its black-and-white funnies made up most of the page on which they appeared, with two single panels on the left side (Oliver Harrington and Jackie Ormes) and five or six cartoonists' strips on the right (Harrington, Wilbert Holloway, Samuel Milai, Clovis Parker, Jerry Stewart). The single panels are first to command the reader's attention. Harrington, who has been called the Michelangelo of black-press cartoonists, filled his *Dark Laughter* panel in a painterly style reminiscent of the lush chiaroscuro of Italian Renaissance art. His much-loved character, Bootsie, was a good-natured lower-class everyman usually seen in a barroom or his tenement neighborhood and more often than not the butt of the joke. Ormes's *Patty-Jo 'n' Ginger*, usually placed just below, made a striking contrast. Her characters emerge in fine black outlines with curves, edges, and angles that stretch across the ample white space of the panel, delineating people in such settings as well-appointed interiors, art museums, theaters, or fancy department stores. With dramatically different style and content, and along with the talented strip cartoonists, Harrington and Ormes created a page as handsome and appealing as any on the newsstand. At the same time, Ormes connected her own image to characters in ways that helped build her public persona as a businesswoman. The real-life Jackie Ormes eventually channeled her fashion aspirations into producing fashion shows, running her own business training fashion models, and modeling shoes for photographic newspaper ads.

Some *Courier* editorials and editorial cartoons advised readers on deportment and correct dress that they considered elements of racial advancement, a primary mission of the black press. Ormes extended that mission by promoting what Susannah Walker calls "consumer citizenship," a term that defines full participation in the marketplace and signifies entry into the American middle class. While fashion and beauty products were heavily advertised to women of all races in America, for African American women the shopping experience was different—and less. Racist attitudes dictated that there would be no blacks in major manufacturers' beauty, clothing, or homemaker ads, nor could a black woman always expect respectful service in a store or restaurant, even in many northern big cities (Walker 11–28). The publisher John H. Johnson gave full voice to consumer freedom in the pages of *Ebony*, the Chicago-based magazine that Ormes certainly would have read. His famous 1949 editorial "Why Negroes Buy Cadillacs" could be read as a corollary to Ormes's encouragement of fine fashion and high style. The cultural historian Jason Chambers analyses Johnson's editorial: "Americans judged one another based on their clothes, choice of liquor, and the cars they drove. Therefore, an African American that drove a Cadillac gave an immediate impression of lofty status. Further because blacks were judged as a group rather than individuals, the success of one translated in some small way to improving perceptions of the group" (65).

Exuding confidence and economic power, Jackie Ormes's black characters cast off the limitations of the marketplace, breezily traversing contested sites such as hotels and eateries while claiming equal ownership of lifestyle and taste that signifies membership in the middle and upper-middle class. She pictured college graduations, travel on airplanes, shopping in air-conditioned stores, and children's nurseries chock-full of toys, providing a kind of freedom for her readers: the all-American freedom to want more.

Torchy Brown in "Dixie to Harlem," 1937–1938

In the late 1930s, Jackie and Earl were still recovering from the death of their daughter. *Torchy Brown in "Dixie to Harlem"* helped provide much-needed psychological and emotional release, according to a sister-in-law who also lived with them in the family home in Salem, Ohio. Jackie, drawing at her table, sometimes late into the night, escaped her lingering sorrow, if only for a few hours. *Torchy Brown in "Dixie to Harlem,"* her first nationally published comic strip, appeared in the *Pittsburgh Courier* from May 1, 1937, to April 30, 1938. It could be argued that Jackie Ormes was at her most inventive, humorous, and delightful in *"Dixie to Harlem,"* a lighthearted black-and-white strip about a Mississippi farm girl who grew up to find fame and fortune as an entertainer at New York's Cotton Club. Star power obviously impressed Ormes, and this strip among all her others bears the most influence of Hollywood, theater, and popular musical performance with its several visual and verbal references to recognizable entertainers. Paradoxically, at this time Ormes herself was a young wife and homemaker living in her in-laws' modest house, dressing economically and working part-time on cartooning. Without the ways or means to realize her dreams, she let her cartoon characters do the talking, traveling, dressing up, and strutting. As her doppelganger Torchy said in 1937, "I've got to get away from here. I belong in big places!"

The series opens with the two adorable teens, Torchy and her friend Bones, exclaiming over the news that Bones's cousin, glamorous New Yorker Dinah Dazzle, is coming for a visit. "So this is Dixie!" beautiful Dinah says as the amazed girls watch her unpack hatboxes, trunks, and suitcases in the farmhouse guestroom. When Aunt Clemmie calls everyone to the table—"Th' biscuits is on the table chillen . . . git down heah!"—Torchy and Bones are left alone with the finery, and they proceed to try on dresses from Dinah's trunk. "Oh! Jus' look at me. . . . Y-E-E-E-S-M!" exclaims Torchy in a slinky, ruffled white gown. Many readers would recognize this as the Letty Lynton dress, possibly the most famous single design of the decade and one that the fashion scholar Christopher Breward calls "almost an icon of its age" (137). A frothy, white, many-layered organza confection designed by Adrian for Joan Crawford in the 1932 film *Letty Lynton*, the dress had sensational wide, flounced sleeves that retailers soon transplanted onto various designs that became hot on the market (see fig. 4.1). "Even as the movie appeared, the dress was on the street," Patricia Campbell Warner observes in her discussion of retailers' deals with the studios. "Macy's claimed to have sold 50,000 copies of the dress the year the movie came out" (85). Today we take for granted that movies and movie stars affect consumer choices, but seventy years ago the case still had to be made. These were the have-not days of the Great Depression, and movies importantly delivered much-needed escape for audiences that could vicariously savor a richer life. Designer-label wardrobes were beyond average women's reach, but those who could sew would be able to craft a star-power garment with "Hollywood Patterns" that cost fifteen cents and were put out by the publisher Condé Nast from 1932, complete with a photo of a popular movie star on the package.[2] "Everybody in the trade scoffed

4.1 Most readers would recognize the version of the Letty Lynton dress that Torchy wears in the *Torchy Brown in "Dixie to Harlem"* comic strip. *Pittsburgh Courier*, 15 May 1937.

at the idea at first. They said movies had no influence on fashion," the film critic Margaret Thorp is quoted as saying about the film industry in the late 1920s. By 1939, Thorp amended her comment, writing about films in *America at the Movies*, "The American public today is convinced that they have an influence on practically everything" (Thorp 110, qtd. in Warner 85). It is possible that the silver screen made an especially indelible impression on Ormes from a young age since her father had owned an open-air movie theater in Pittsburgh. Delores, who passed away in 2011 at the age of 101, remembered how in warm weather she and Jackie as children would join the crowd sitting on benches to watch silent films. Jackie, in her adult life, whether or not she saw *Letty Lynton*, surely would have recognized the name of Adrian and would have seen the dress in *Photoplay* or other movie magazines that had circulated since the early days of silent films. Other mainstream journals, such as *Life* magazine, were beginning to run fashion photography, sometimes featuring stars such as Crawford, Hedy Lamarr, or Katharine Hepburn posing languorously in gorgeous gowns and backlit in unforgettable luminosity.

Alluring black actresses would not have appeared in mainstream magazines in the late 1930s, nor were there many parts for them in Hollywood. Those roles that did emerge were usually stereotypes, such as domestics, or what the film historian Charlene Regester calls "shadow or Other" roles that provided counterparts for white actresses (2).[3] No doubt Ormes would have seen the few Hollywood movies with major black roles, such as *The Emperor Jones*, a 1933 Warner Bros. film starring Paul Robeson and the actress Fredi Washington, who in one scene wears a voluminous ruffled-sleeve dress similar to the Letty Lynton dress. The African American filmmaker Oscar Micheaux presented heroic and attractive black characters, along with less laudable persons, in musical, romantic, dramatic, and comic parts. He sometimes dressed his actresses in glamorous gowns, as in *Underworld* (1936), or had them sing and dance in smart outfits, as in *Swing* (1938). Ormes may not have seen a Micheaux movie at this time since the closest big city to Salem was Pittsburgh, which apparently did not have a "race film" theater. But she would have seen photos and read about Micheaux's actors in the *Pittsburgh Courier*. One can also imagine Earl and Jackie occasionally driving to nearby Youngstown, Ohio, to take in the big bands and their glamorous singers who appeared there. And she may have seen black musical theater that traveled throughout the country bringing some of the vibrant Harlem creative community to smaller cities. *Dixie to Broadway*, starring Florence Mills, was one such traveling show, and Ormes obviously referenced its title, story line, and female lead in *"Dixie to Harlem."*

Ormes selected widely from Hollywood trends, though she never actually named a designer or female star whom she may have been following. One *"Dixie to Harlem"* episode especially evokes the dream factory that was Hollywood. Torchy is asleep, dreaming that she has landed on Seventh Avenue, New York's garment district, where women walking on the street are turned out from top to toe. She eyes a lady in a wide-brim picture hat in the style of those made fashionable by Greta Garbo in several films, and she sees another woman in a conical little number reminiscent of the geometric designs of Elsa Schiaparelli, a top designer for films whose clients included Mae West and other stars. "Golly gee—I guess all New Yawk gals are pretty nifty . . . I'm gonna get me a hat like that." Soon she finds herself inside a stylish boutique trying on dresses and gowns. "Clothes do make the woman," the shop girl tells Torchy, who, more than a little out of her element, replies, "Sho' nuff?" Ormes punches up the humor with a satirical comment on fashion extremes with Torchy looking at herself in a mirror, wide-eyed and nearly knock-kneed in a silly, overdone dress and cape that swallows the wearer. In another panel, Ormes clearly covets fashion's inherent glamour, posing Torchy looking like Jean Harlow in a shimmering body glove of a gown.

Once awake, the dream inspires Torchy to go to Harlem, and she begs Dinah Dazzle to take her along. In language that defines Dinah's sophistication and distinguishes her from her southern kin, she protests, "Of course Torchy Darling—but don't you see I can't take you as long as Aunt Clemmie objects! It's madness—why—it—it's preposterous, no less!"[4] But Torchy runs away from home and heads north, making for week after week of funny and sometimes poignant encounters as she conquers the city to become a headline entertainer at the Cotton Club.

Earlier, as a young woman living in Pittsburgh in the early 1930s, Jackie and her sister, Delores, had been acquainted with Lena Horne, the African American singer and actress who sometimes lived with her family there. Delores once described how the three young women would give each other tips on hairstyles and sometimes for fun would cut each other's hair. (personal interview, 2003) Horne's route to stardom via a stint at the Cotton Club must have impressed Ormes, who modeled Torchy's progress much along the same lines. About the time of "Dixie to Harlem," Horne was traveling with Noble Sissle's Orchestra, gaining fame for her torch songs and her elegance. No doubt Ormes admired the beautiful evening gowns that Horne wore on stage and her now professionally coiffed, sometimes upswept hair fastened with a glittery flower. Once Torchy becomes a singer and dancer in the Cotton Club, her clothes and hair often resemble Horne's or, occasionally, the singer Billie Holiday's. One series shows young gentlemen in white tie and tails escorting Torchy and her friends out nightclubbing. A handsome man leads her onto the floor: "Torchy Brown, eh? . . . Shall we dance?" And she spins across the floor, in a backless dress, wide hem swirling, reminiscent of Katherine Dunham, at the time a well-known African American stage dancer and choreographer whose career Ormes would certainly have followed.[5]

Ormes prepared readers for the extraordinary fashion show to come by establishing Torchy's well-formed body. Lissome and athletic, she bends, crouches, kneels, and dances with actions and movements that set the narrative in motion. But sometimes Ormes presented the body for its own appeal. Throughout her career, she would often draw women half dressed in poses that draw attention to their shapely torsos and long legs. One *"Dixie to Harlem"* panel that probably would have been censored out of the mainstream press shows a nearly nude Torchy emerging from her bath with a view of her breast and hip. Scenes in the nightclub dressing room afford more opportunities to see and enjoy Ormes's nearly nude females as they primp and banter about their clothes and boyfriends. Torchy sometimes wears scanty, feather-festooned getups in her Cotton Club routines like those worn by Josephine Baker, another dancer who wore edgy costumes, or very little. When asked about Ormes's aesthetic choices, her friend and cartooning colleague Chester Commodore said, "Jackie knew where her bread was buttered," suggesting that her eye-catching motifs were good for business (Goldstein 60). But the body images and fashions of *"Dixie to Harlem"* were not strictly confined to trim figures. Torchy shares a Harlem apartment with Dinah and another friend, Bumps, a character whose rounded body contrasts with her svelte roommates'. Other cartoonists usually exaggerated full-bodied persons and dressed them for laughs in dowdy clothes, but Ormes draws Bumps's body with restraint, clothing her in similarly imaginative and detailed dresses and gowns.

Cameo appearances of real stars add color to the story, and their signature costumes provide humorous visual recognition. Torchy finagles an audition with Leonard Reed, in real life a dancer and longtime emcee at Harlem's Apollo Theater. Wearing his rehearsal getup of short-sleeve shirt and loose-fitting pants and suspenders, Reed first discourages Torchy but ends up hiring her, humorously scratching his head in wonder at the ability—and gusto—of the young woman from Dixie. The bandleader Cab Calloway introduces Torchy's solo debut dressed in his trademark white suit and tails. Another panel names and shows the entertainment columnist Billy Rowe, in a business suit of course, smiling and enjoying the show. A delightful sequence of panels has Torchy and Bill "Bojangles" Robinson tap-dancing together as Torchy begs, "Hey Bill—take me to Hollywood nex' time you go, will ya, huh?" Drawn in a surreal, dream-like style, their darkly inked bodies and clothing, profiled against a white background, with the two dancers' legs and arms in unison, seem to float in space. Later, wearing street-appropriate clothes, Torchy pushes her way into an RKO Pictures casting call with Mr. Blank—a real person in RKO's production team—Franklin, and Blank. "Can you give me an audition an' screen test an' put me in the MOVIES?" she wheedles. The year-long *"Dixie to Harlem"* strip ends with a bang when the mystery woman who is Torchy's mother appears in the unmistakable profile of Josephine Baker, her hair topped with a gaggle of exotic flowers, and cries out, "My Baby!"

Candy, 1945

Now living in Chicago, Ormes plunged into the social and cultural life of the city and the South Side where she and Earl resided. She took a several years' break from cartooning while doing a little stringer reporting and writing a social column for the *Chicago Defender*. Eventually she said, "Well that's fun, but I want to draw!" and presented her idea to the editors (Goldstein 32). It was wartime, and the *Defender*'s editorials encouraged readers to capitalize on labor shortages by pressing for better working conditions and wages for household domestics. An eye-catching cartoon of a shapely, smart, and sassy housemaid would fit perfectly with the *Defender*'s current topic, Ormes argued, and the paper gave her a try, placing *Candy* on the editorial page alongside columns by such notable writers as Walter White, S. I. Hayakawa, W.E.B. Du Bois, and Langston Hughes. For reasons that were never explained, *Candy* lasted only four months. But the short run gave Ormes a chance to develop the beautiful, long-legged, and buxom female figure that was to become her mainstay for future cartoons and comics. E. Simms Campbell, a black artist, illustrator, and cartoonist, had paved the way with cartoons of sexy females in the *Courier* with his 1930s single-panel *Harlem Sketches*. Other black-press cartoonists, such as Wilbert Holloway and Jay Jackson, followed with the kind of pinup images that had become ubiquitous on posters, calendars, and matchbooks and were directed at soldiers as wartime "morale boosters." With a curvaceous body often dressed in scanty attire and a direct, insouciant gaze, Candy follows in the lineage of the great pinup art of the era (Goldstein 82–84).

Candy also prompted Ormes to teach herself the art of the single-panel cartoon. Her previous published work, *"Dixie to Harlem,"* was a comic strip that in its most basic definition is a storytelling sequence of panels, read from left to right and usually ending with a suspenseful cliff-hanger or a humorous remark. A single panel works differently. The cartoonist must engage and hold the reader's attention in one space, directing the eye around the panel's interesting details, finally leading the reader to the bottom and to the caption that reveals a gag or bit of insight (see Eisner; McCloud). Ormes first captures our interest with Candy's curvaceous physique and her playful, wide-eyed expression that accentuates the verbal zinger at the bottom of the panel. Most of Candy's comments poke fun at her detested mistress while she filches clothes from the woman's closet: "Gee, I hope Mrs. Goldrocks doesn't gain any more weight, I can't possibly wear a size larger," she says as she pulls out sweaters, furs, shoes, and black-market nylon stockings.

The government's War Production Board (WPB) had essentially frozen the dress silhouette in 1942 by prohibiting nonessential production. In better days, garment factories were able to make the time-consuming adjustments to their machinery required for new fashions, and their suppliers provided ample amounts of woolens, cottons, silks, and elastics to construct the latest styles. But now manufacturing machinery and resources were fully committed to producing the materiel of war, such as uniforms and combat boots. To conserve wool for winter uniforms, for example, fashionable skirts were held at a seventy-two-inch circumference at the bottom, with a maximum two-inch hem; jackets could be only a certain length and limited to one patch pocket; and coats were made without a back pleat and sometimes no collar or front overlap (Milbank 138). But Mrs. Goldrocks found ways to get around the WPB rules. As an antidote to Mrs. Goldrocks's extravagant wardrobe, Candy's clothing captures the essence of wartime rationing in the few simple dresses she wears. Her knee-length skirts flow straight down to narrow hems, as dictated by the fabric restrictions of the WPB, and her practical underwear is missing much of the fancy trim we had seen in *"Dixie to Harlem."* It must have been difficult for Ormes to limit her characters to such sparse clothing; and even when the war was over, shortly into the *Candy* series, she probably was dissatisfied with the sartorial options afforded by a housemaid character, often confined to a black dress and white apron. That was soon to change. *Candy* ended in late July, and by September 1, the fashion mannequin Ginger, a Candy look-alike, arrived in the *Pittsburgh Courier*'s single-panel *Patty-Jo 'n' Ginger*, Ormes's longest-running cartoon.

Patty-Jo 'n' Ginger, 1945–1956

Well before the turn of the twentieth century, Paris was setting fashion rules that were followed by upper levels of American society, eventually trickling down to nearly every woman. Haute couture dictated, for instance, how nineteenth-century crinolines would replace petticoats, then how bustles replaced crinolines, until the early 1900s, when design required that women put small pads in the rear to balance the S-shaped corsets that gave them fashionable curves. One exception to Paris's domination was the popular Gibson Girl silhouette, inspired by the turn-of-the-century drawings of the American illustrator Charles Dana Gibson. With a large bust and hips and a tiny waist, the Gibson Girl exemplified a certain type of woman who was at once modern and feminine, independent and sexually alluring. Her flared skirt and practical shirt-blouse were tailored for clerical work in a business office but could also move freely when she played lawn tennis or cycled. The healthy athletic lifestyle implied in the Gibson Girl look planted a foothold on the public imagination for what came to be called sportswear, an American fashion breakthrough. But ironically it was the hard times of the Great Depression and World War II that eventually freed American clothing designers and manufacturers from the domination of Paris couture. High-society women who could no longer travel to Europe turned to American designers such as Claire McCardell and Mainbocher, and middle-class women followed these and other homegrown designers' "American look" of moderately priced, mix-and-match, go-anywhere blouses, sweaters, and skirts, as well as dresses. "The rise of American fashion—and New

York as a fashion center—had more behind it than a few years of independence from Paris," Caroline Rennolds Milbank explains. "What rendered New York so important was demonstrated competence, skill, and ingenuity; the clothes it produced were stylish, appropriate for Americans, and well made even in the thousands. . . . Ready-to-wear was no longer considered a necessary evil; it was modern, it was democratic, and New York had proved that it was stylish" (143). California designers added outdoorsy, athletic elements to the American look with such clothing as swimwear, golf togs, and frocks for patio dining.

Jackie Ormes returned to the *Courier* with fashions that reflected fresh American styles from both coasts and included her own selections from everyday Chicago street wear. The war had ended, and American manufacturing was gearing up to satisfy the country's long-suppressed appetite for the better things in life, including a plentiful supply of attractive clothing. For Ormes's cartoon characters, the war's end meant going about town turned out in the latest suits, hats, gloves, stockings, and shoes or lounging decoratively in a well-appointed home. The little-sister-big-sister duo in *Patty-Jo 'n' Ginger* not only provided a template for humor and satire but also gave Ormes opportunities to draw clothing for a beautiful woman as well as for a little girl. A mainstay among her cartoon themes was Patty-Jo teasing her big sister about her clothing, her figure, or her boyfriends, a gag theme that draws attention to fashion of the day and to a curvaceous body. In the first *Patty-Jo 'n' Ginger*, Ormes establishes a humorous dynamic between the cute, outspoken Patty-Jo—the only one who talks in the cartoon—and her big sister, whose role is to look beautiful—and astonished—at Patty-Jo's words. Hoping to cadge a few coins from Ginger's boyfriends, Patty-Jo explores the armistice's pecuniary potential: "Now that the war's over I guess I'll see what the man shortage had to do with that no-nickel Jody we been puttin' up with!" Ginger registers wide-eyed surprise at her sister's remark as we view her from the back in an simple, wartime A-line dress with gathered, slightly padded shoulders and a small, defined waistband, and, of course, nylon stockings identifiable in the cartoon by their perfectly straight seams that run up the backs of her long legs.

About this time, Jackie Ormes took some life-drawing classes at the School of the Art Institute of Chicago, and she satirizes the experience in an original cartoon that was found in her papers but never published. "Oh sure, Mr. La Gatta—my folks say I'm positively a 'natural.' Where's my easel?" the fresh-faced young woman says in what is obviously a self-parody (Goldstein 24). Here Ormes references John La Gatta, an illustrator known for his well-dressed, sensuous women on the covers of prominent magazines such as *Fortune* and the *Saturday Evening Post*. La Gatta taught drawing in his later life, but it is not known if Ormes was ever in his class since transcript records cannot be found at the Art Institute. But apparently she was impressed with La Gatta's mastery of the female form since he was on her mind as she began to flesh out Ginger in her new cartoon.

Ormes's fashion instincts were not limited to adult women, however. Patty-Jo showed up each week in different dresses, hats, pinafores, pajamas, robes, and skating and cowgirl costumes, as well as all manner of sunsuits and winter and spring coat sets, no doubt making her the best-dressed child in all of cartoon history. Now in the economic boom of postwar America, parents were showering their children with the richness of new inventions, and girls wanted the new hard, plastic dolls that came with huge wardrobes. But when African American mothers and fathers went shopping for toys for their children, they found stereotypical and poorly made Topsy- or mammy-type dolls and rarely could locate a realistic black doll of quality. By 1946, readers were asking Ormes to produce a Patty-Jo doll based on her adorable little cartoon character. The next year, she signed a contract to design a doll for the Terri Lee Company of Lincoln, Nebraska, and the Patty-Jo doll was on store shelves in time for Christmas (see fig. 4.2). Terri Lee was a new company whose forte was a large wardrobe of doll clothing made from the best fabrics and trims and carefully crafted to hold up in children's vigorous play. It seemed like a match made in heaven: for Ormes, her little girl character would become a well-made doll with a large, quality wardrobe; for Terri Lee, a new market of African American consumers opened up. The company began to place ads in the *Courier* and in *Ebony*

4.2 Jackie Ormes and the Patty-Jo doll in a 1953 film documenting prominent African American women. At this point in the movie, the narrator says, "Her Patty-Jo doll is the achievement Jackie Ormes is proudest of. Happiness is her trademark!"

magazine. Patty-Jo dolls started to pop up in the newspaper cartoon, often carried by the little-girl Patty-Jo character dressed in Terri Lee clothing; in one panel, she has in her hand an order coupon with Jackie Ormes's home address. But apparently the doll did not sell well, and in late 1949 Ormes's contract was not renewed. It is interesting to note that Ormes was ahead of her time in recognizing that dolls can have a profound significance as self-identity for a child. A few years later, the "doll test" was instrumental in the arguments in *Brown v. Board of Education*, which overturned segregation in public schools. In the test, psychologists offered African American children white or black dolls, and when the children said they preferred white ones, calling them "nicer" and "prettier," it was interpreted to indicate an epidemic of low self-esteem among black children (Goldstein 159–161). The efficacy of the test was questioned at the time and has since been repeated by psychologists, with varied results. But clearly the time for change had come, and the doll test seemed as good a reason as any to desegregate America's schools.

In the five-hundred-some *Patty-Jo 'n' Ginger* cartoons Jackie Ormes produced over eleven years, Christian Dior particularly fascinated her and was the only designer she mentioned by name. The Frenchman's 1947 "New Look," with its hourglass silhouette of prominent bust line, small waist, and bouffant skirt, restored to Ormes's characters the feminine beauty that had been missing in her austere wartime drawings (see fig. 4.3). "To the wartime generation, the New Look was the rediscovery of happiness," Marie-France Pochna declares, and indeed among Dior's first postwar creations was a dress the designer called "Happiness" (153). Americans who had loved the curvaceous yet practical Gibson Girl look earlier in the century fell immediately for a like-minded New Look. The novelist Colette wrote, "It took one swish of the hips and America was won," and when Christian Dior toured the United States at the invitation of Dallas's Neiman-Marcus store, one of his most important stops was at Marshall Field's in Chicago, where Jackie Ormes lived (qtd. in Pochna 154). According to Jackie's sister, Delores, Marshall Field's was prominent in Jackie's life. She sometimes modeled for the company's shoe advertising, followed its ads in the *Chicago Tribune*, shopped there, and eventually had an arrangement with its furniture department to help find antiques and artwork. Clearly it was Marshall Field's that Ormes had in mind when Patty-Jo in a summertime cartoon advised her little friends to visit a store for its air-conditioning and when Ginger tried on especially luxurious garments in a well-appointed fitting room. Field's was the most stylish place to shop in the Midwest and "bought more couture than any other retailer back then," Teri Agins reports (175).

Field's landmark limestone and granite building with a glittering Tiffany-glass vaulted ceiling at this time featured eleven restaurants, a dry cleaner, and a charm school along with merchandise of apparel, furniture, and housewares. Inside Field's entrance at 28 East Washington Street, wealthy women boarded a private elevator that whisked them to the sixth floor's "28 Shop," an exclusive

COPYRIGHTED 1948 JACKIE ORMES FEATURES

"Guess what, Sis. Miss Loyalouse says our school is 'WAY behind the times . . . Mostly on account of we're still using OLD picture lessons showin' ALL races are EQUAL!"

4.3 Ginger's Dior-inspired outfit features her coat with a prominent bust line and cinched waist above a flared hem, all over a hobble skirt. On her feet are boot heels, and her hat, purse, and belt sport a chic animal-print design. Patty-Jo emerges from the schoolhouse also dressed to the nines. Jackie Ormes, *Patty-Jo 'n' Ginger, Pittsburgh Courier*, October 23, 1948.

boutique carrying designer originals including Christian Dior. "Knockoffs came out of the 28 Shop and trickled all the way down to the budget floor," Agins explains, making the New Look available to middle- and working-class women as well as to rich socialites (175). Through Ormes's cartoons in the *Courier*, Paris designs traversed all classes of African American readers and helped promote her espousal of "consumer citizenship," discussed earlier. Sexual desirability was the essence of Dior design, and his attention to a woman's curves must have appealed to Ormes as an element that would certainly catch the reader's eye. Ever the humorist, she appropriated the human comedy inherent in controversies that surrounded Christian Dior. Each season he reinvented the New Look, causing women to run to their seamstresses for adjustments or to shop for something new. As Patty-Jo quips when she sees Ginger holding a newspaper with an ad for Dior's latest style, "Gee . . . it must be awful to have that Dior fella switch rules on you in the middle of the game!"

In the early 1950s, Ormes began producing fashion shows for the Urbanaides, a volunteer group of career women who raised money for the Urban League of Chicago's programs to end race discrimination. No doubt the shows provided a fresh supply of ideas for dressing cartoon Ginger. As Ormes chose fashions and negotiated between stores, catalogue dealers, models, photographers, and fashionable patrons, she would have instinctively absorbed the latest in fashion, but she was also taking in Chicago street wear, which she translated to everyday attire in *Patty-Jo 'n' Ginger*. Some of the most delightful cartoons have Ginger in outfits straight from the street, like one of a rainy day when Ginger wears a practical clear, plastic raincoat and see-through plastic galoshes, a fad at the time but never considered fashionable, or a cartoon with Ginger in simple shorts and peasant blouse, her hair in a casual updo. Ginger's shoes always add a little frisson, with everything from platform heels to lace-up string sandals. A few times she surprises us by stepping out of the frame and into the white space below or, as readers may experience it, nearly into our laps. The cartoonist and comics scholar Scott McCloud has defined this empty gutter space as "closure," a narrative tool to transition from one idea to another (60–94). When Ginger's well-shod foot slips over the edge of the frame and into the gutter, Ormes achieves closure with a dynamic transition from the visual image to the caption below.

Torchy in Heartbeats, 1950–1954

Splashed in full color across the page, *Torchy in Heartbeats* was one of eight comics in a tabloid-size insert designed to lure readers to buy the *Courier*. Women's interests were now a larger part of 1950s newspaper economics, and clearly the *Torchy* strip was intended to exploit a growing market of women consumers. In the 180-some extant *Torchy in Heartbeats* comics, Torchy pursues adventure and romance and occasionally strikes pinup poses that capture attention. Of course, Torchy is well dressed, but sometimes the story line limits her wardrobe, as in the series in which she works in a clinic and is confined to a nurse's white uniform. A separate "topper" panel with *Torchy's Togs* paper doll and clothing cutouts solves any sartorial conflict and becomes a stage on which to present a beautiful black woman's body and to adorn her with smart, imaginative designs.

4.4 Torchy invites female readers to play with fashion by dressing this paper-doll cutout: "Follow my lines girls, with a carefully wielded scissors, and I'll show you how fine a girl can look in a 'paper' wardrobe!" *Torchy's Togs* "topper" panels often accompanied the *Torchy in Heartbeats* comic strip in a full-color, tabloid-sized comics insert. Jackie Ormes, *Torchy's Togs*, *Pittsburgh Courier*, February 3, 1951.

Torchy in *Torchy's Togs* wears a variety of smart American sportswear, Paris-style evening dress, and occasionally ordinary clothing, sometimes athletic, easy, and comfortable and other times elegant, feminine, and ladylike. In what is undoubtedly a unique narrative device for paper-doll cutouts, Torchy speaks directly to readers, telling them how and when to wear their clothes. In one *Torchy's Togs* panel, for instance, she is in a bra, girdle, and nylons and says, "These undergarments are a must for proper grooming." Fashions are attuned to the seasons, and Torchy provides apt descriptions such as, "Want to whirl in his arms as gay as an autumn leaf? Then try this date dress with the large leaf pattern," and "Here are four neat little numbers for my summer weekend trip." In 1951, at the height of the Korean War, Torchy shows "a romantic quartet of fashion hints just for those days when your fighting man comes home on leave." Indeed the paper-doll clothing is a panoply of early 1950s fashion, with such styles as full or pleated skirts, toreador pants, cocktail dresses, and one-piece bathing suits with matching cover-ups. Ormes describes materials and cut in detail, verbally reveling in the sumptuousness of luxury fabrics, as in these side commentaries: "White sharkskin suit with bold black touches at collar, buttons and pocket, smart as a new penny" and "A silk shantung hostess gown—royal blue with gold pleated chiffon draped diagonally." Sometimes Torchy invites readers to send in their own drawings, crediting them by name and city, a convention made popular in *Katy Keene* comic books and in other cutout top-pers. On one occasion, Torchy informs readers that they can order the clothing from a Florida catalogue address, with a coupon included in the *Torchy's Togs* panel; presumably, Ormes had some business connection with the catalogue company and used its designs to create her drawings. Other times, Torchy likens the cuts of necklines, sleeves, and hemlines to "the latest styles," and a few times, she compares her clothing to couture designs by Christian Dior or "a famous designer" or drops the name of Artie Wiggins, a well-known African American hat designer in Chicago, or refers to such trends as an "important French silhouette in the 1953 forecast—mink-flared chiffon over velvet!" Indeed, the popularity of paper dolls has waned since the days of the Great Depression and World War II, when cutouts were a favorite and inexpensive amusement. Though they had a relatively short lifetime and abrupt end, Jackie Ormes's paper dolls reflected fashion news in an imaginative way, entertained with charming banter, and demonstrated a proud vision of black female beauty.

A sensual female form and suggestive commentary was acceptable in black newspapers and even celebrated—as well as criticized—as Gallon has demon-strated. Occasionally Jay Jackson's work, which appeared in both the *Defender* and the *Courier*, had examples of risqué cartoons that probably would never have made it into many mainstream papers. One 1943 Jackson cartoon in the *Defender*, for instance, shows a shapely woman sitting in a deep chair with only her legs and arms showing: "What have I got on tonight? Not a thing, not a thing!" And the next year, Jackson offered a display ad: "Pin Up Girl—She's here, she's fine . . . so fall in line and knock yourself to this gorgeous babe! Drawn by that 'send-sational' glorifier of sepia sweeties!—From Jay Jackson's Sketch Pad." In contrast, Jackie Ormes's partly clothed paper dolls remained within the boundary of good taste and acceptability. As with counterpart newspaper paper dolls such as Brenda Starr, Mopsy, Boots, Tillie, and Jane Arden, Torchy appears in bathing suits or underwear, ready for dressing. But occasionally Torchy wears lingerie or swim attire that were edgy for their time, such as strapless and back-less bra tops and bikini-cut briefs. Combined with her friendly chatter and the virtuous characterization in the comic strip, however, the portrayal is one of wholesome sexuality. Torchy is the girl next door who might tease just a little but is never naughty. Although the social-realism story lines in the comic strip and the sophisticated fashions and commentary in the paper-doll panel appear to be directed at an adult readership, nevertheless Torchy conformed to standards of modesty as befit Ormes's idea of a family newspaper. But Ormes's enjoyment at showing off Torchy's beautiful body and her clothes is unmistakable. Striking a pose that recalls the heyday of wartime pinups, paper-doll Torchy at one time invites people to admire her body, saying, "get out your scissors, gals, but for a guy, a pin is all you need!"

According to a magazine article published a year and a half after the comic strip's first appearance, the *Courier* "found in a recent survey that *Patty-Jo 'n'*

Ginger tops all its other features in reader popularity" (Thompson 118). But looking at the cartoon now, one must ask, what made *Patty-Jo 'n' Ginger* so popular, and what accounts for its eleven-year run? Naturally people enjoyed the little girl's antics and her outspoken criticism of government or politics and her humorous riffs on social mores. As Langston Hughes wrote in the *Defender*, "If I were marooned on a desert island, . . . I would miss . . . Jackie Ormes's cute drawings" (14). But today we cannot help but notice Ormes's sometime repetition of setting and jokes and the last few years' decline in technique as she increasingly became afflicted with rheumatoid arthritis in her hands. Furthermore, what was the appeal that kept a very feminized *Torchy in Heartbeats* and *Torchy's Togs* running for four years alongside the testosterone-spiked cowboy, detective, fighter-pilot, and foreign-intrigue strips? And two decades before, what attracted editors to hire this untried young woman cartoonist to draw *Torchy Brown in "Dixie to Harlem"*? Surely at least some of the answers lie in the powerful visual impact of Ormes's attractive, smart African American women and their fashionable, painstakingly drawn attire. Cartoons, combining as they usually do both text and art, depend on a visual vocabulary to say what words fail to convey. Ormes's upscale settings and fashions visually delineated lifestyle in ways far more nuanced and complex than most other black-press comics did, implying material consumption as a marker of economic prosperity and entry into the middle class. The first step, her settings and characters implied, was a shopping trip to the finest store; it was understood that the next step would be employment at the store, a role in management, and, maybe one day, even ownership.

Notes

1   Susannah Walker explains, "With rare exceptions, companies underestimated the African American market and showed little interest in targeting it directly," despite the best efforts of black businesspersons such as the publisher Claude Barnett, who targeted market research exposing how, in his words, white advertisers had "built up a defense mechanism against using Negro newspapers which is marvelous and indicates concerted thinking and agreement" (16).

2   Vintage Hollywood Patterns can be found on eBay. A mid-1930s dress pattern with a photo of Claudette Colbert on the front sold in October 2010 for $28.55. Another sale was for the "SUMMER 1938 issue of the HOLLYWOOD PATTERN BOOK, a magazine-format catalog containing 50 pages. This issue contains illustrations of fashions available as patterns from the Hollywood Pattern Company and articles on films and film stars of the time. Feature articles on various stars and full page photos of Bette Davis in Warner's 'Jezebel' and of Ginger Rogers on location for the film 'Having Wonderful Time' are in this issue."

3   "As I use the term and concept in this study, a shadow self is a reflection of another subject, darker and less distinct in form and substance than the subject the shadow reflects. In its basic definition, Otherness refers to difference and usually carries an

array of negative connotations. . . . The black actress was the 'dark' self and usually a reflection of the white female" (Regester 2).

4 Edward Brunner illuminates Ormes's use of language in *"Dixie to Harlem."*

5 Dunham went on to appear in *Stormy Weather*, a 1943 film with a nearly all-black cast. The film included a breakthrough role for Lena Horne as a jazz singer.

Works Cited

Agins, Teri. *The End of Fashion*. New York: William Morrow, 1999.

Breward, Christopher. *Fashion*. New York: Oxford University Press, 2003.

Brunner, Edward. "'Shuh! Ain't Nothin' to It!': The Dynamics of Success in Jackie Ormes's *Torchy Brown*," *MELUS* 32.3 (2007): 23–49.

Chambers, Jason. "Presenting the Black Middle Class: John H. Johnson and *Ebony* Magazine, 1945–1974." *Historicizing Lifestyle: Mediating Taste, Consumption and Identity from the 1900s to 1970*. Ed. David Bell and Joanne Hollows. Burlington, VT: Ashgate, 2006. 54–69.

Eisner, Will. *Comics and Sequential Art*. Tamarac, FL: Poorhouse, 1985.

Gallon, Kim T. "Between Respectability and Modernity: Black Newspapers and Sexuality, 1925–1940." Ph.D. dissertation, University of Pennsylvania, 2009.

Goldstein, Nancy. *Jackie Ormes: The First African American Woman Cartoonist*. Ann Arbor: University of Michigan Press, 2008.

Hughes, Langston. "Colored and Colorful." *Chicago Defender* 26 June 1948: 14.

Johnson, John H. "Why Negroes Buy Cadillacs." *Ebony* September 1949: 34.

McCloud, Scott. *Understanding Comics*. Northampton, MA: Kitchen Sink, 1993.

Milbank, Caroline Rennolds. *New York Fashion: The Evolution of American Style*. New York: Harry N. Abrams, 1989.

Pochna, Marie-France. *Christian Dior: The Biography*. New York: Overlook, 2008.

Regester, Charlene. *African American Actresses: The Struggle for Visibility, 1900–1960*. Bloomington: Indiana University Press, 2010.

Robbins, Trina. *A Century of Women Cartoonists*. Northampton, MA: Kitchen Sink, 1993.

Steele, Valerie. *Fashion and Eroticism*. New York: Oxford University Press, 1985.

Thody, Philip. "The Semiotician in the Wardrobe." *TLS* 16 October 1981: 1199.

Thompson, Maxine. "Woman Cartoonist Turns to Doll Designing." *Toys and Novelties* November 1947: 116–118.

Thorp, Margaret Ferrand. *America at the Movies*. 1939. New York: Arno, 1970.

Walker, Susannah. *Style and Status: Selling Beauty to African American Women, 1920–1975*. Lexington: University Press of Kentucky, 2007.

Warner, Patricia Campbell. "The Americanization of Fashion: Sportswear, the Movies and the 1930s." *Twentieth-Century American Fashion*. Ed. Linda Welters and Patricia A. Cunningham. New York: Berg, 2005. 79–98.

Chapter 5

Graphic Remix

• •

The Lateral Appropriation of Black Nationalism in Aaron McGruder's *The Boondocks*

ROBIN R. MEANS COLEMAN AND

WILLIAM LAFI YOUMANS

In April 1999, then-twenty-five-year-old Aaron McGruder, creator of the comic strip *The Boondocks*, signed a national, daily syndication contract with Universal Press Syndicate, the world's largest independent, international newspaper syndicate. The publishing deal put the comic strip in over 160 newspapers, with 40 more by the year's end, resulting in one of the biggest launches of a strip in the history of comics (McGrath). The syndication of *The Boondocks* introduced American newspaper readers to McGruder's cutting, satirical take on contemporary politics, pressing social issues, and popular events, all from one African American male's perspective. *The Boondocks* strip entered (seemingly permanent) hiatus in 2006 to make way for McGruder's animated series of the same name on the Cartoon Network.[1]

One of *The Boondocks'* most intriguing features is the way it worked as an assemblage of Black American sociopolitical currents, as they were personified in the characters. The strip's central figure, Huey, represents an earlier school of thought, 1970s Black nationalism, to which McGruder has been publicly sympathetic. However, McGruder's own connection to that movement was not through direct involvement but was mediated through hip-hop music. Huey, then, came about through an intragroup appropriation, as a creation of strategic nostalgia, adapted to a very different setting. Thus, this chapter contends that cultural appropriation can be seen as crossing boundaries of time and space, not just social markers of difference. Hip-hop relates in two ways. First, hip-hop was one of the first channels by which McGruder became familiar with Black nationalism's symbols. Second, the appropriations in his strip can be analogized to the work of a hip-hop DJ, who samples and remixes past styles to create new music. Instead of music as the medium, for McGruder, it was the nexus of images, themes, and ideologies of Black sociopolitical life since the 1960s.

In attending to McGruder's use of a media-informed Black Power–era nationalism in *The Boondocks*, this chapter considers what Whitney Anspach et al. have theorized as "lateral appropriation." Lateral appropriation describes taking up the capital of one marginalized group by *another* marginalized group. Lateral appropriation works to reveal that cultural appropriations are not, as Bruce Ziff and Pratime Rao define, singularly "the taking—from a culture that is not one's own—of intellectual property, cultural expressions or artifacts, history and ways of knowledge" (1) without considerations of positionality and power. Through McGruder, lateral appropriation serves to advance a Black cultural assertion; that is, it functions to press for the protection of Blackness from a postindustrial and seemingly postracial society. It is a theory that reveals that appropriation conversations need to consider that "sometimes the in-ness or out-ness of a particular individual" (Ziff and Rao 3) makes the ethnoracial groups and the lines between them variable, elusive, and amorphous. The process of appropriation, then, can be seen within differently positioned members or generations of one group.

For McGruder, the nostalgia of the Black Power era is indirect, only experienced in mediated forms, and then further mediated through the strip. Nostalgia, writes Tina Steiner, "functions strategically," providing characters with "an imaginary, often idealised memory of the past, which becomes the basis of their critique of the present" (9).[2] Hip-hop was an initial channel for McGruder's nostalgic appropriation. The role of hip-hop in his political socialization makes appropriate an analogy: McGruder as a DJ who sampled the past and repurposed its iconography, slogans, and frameworks to speak against other sociopolitical trends in Black America. *The Boondocks* in general, and Huey specifically, was a remix with a cause.

The Strip, the Author, the Message

The Boondocks features the ten-year-old radical, Black-nationalism-inspired Huey Freeman and the eight-year-old gangsta wannabe Riley "Escobar" Freeman, siblings originally from the South Side of Chicago. Central to the strip's overarching story line is that the boys have found themselves abruptly relocated by their "Granddad," the integrationist Robert Jebediah Freeman, a retiree, to the predominantly White, "upscale" suburb of Woodcrest (hence, the "boon-docks"), with the "stink" of clean air (McGruder, *Right* 13). The move represents a dream fulfilled for Granddad—who has "survived nearly seventy years on this earth as a Black man"—by trading in "the problems of the city" for "really big oak trees in the yard and lakes nearby to go fishing" (13). Another character is the racially conflicted Jazmine DuBois, a biracial girl, and her guilty-liberal lawyer parents, Sarah, who is White, and Tom, who is Black. In addition, Huey's best friend, Caesar, a Black Woodcrest transplant from Brooklyn, is ideologi-cally aligned with Huey but far less fatalistic. Cindy, a cheery yet naïve White girl, comes to understand Blackness entirely through media. There is also an array of other characters that come and go in the strip—teachers, neighbors, politicians, and even a *Star Wars* fanatic.

Among this cast of innovative characters, Huey stands out as the strip's star and antihero. The well-informed, militant-minded Huey often utters the most scathing critiques of party politics, race relations, and current affairs. For exam-ple, when Tom DuBois kidnaps the 2004 presidential candidate Ralph Nader because Tom does not want "Bush to destroy the world," Huey displays his engagement in current affairs by countering that "Al Gore didn't lose because of Nader. Al Gore lost because Katherine Harris hired Choicepoint/DBT to illegally block 58,000 people from voter rolls, claiming they were convicted fel-ons. Turns out 95% of them never committed a felony" (McGruder, *Right* 143). In other strips, Huey takes on misogynist rap videos on Black Entertainment Television (BET), Ronald Regan's funding of terrorists in Afghanistan, and Condoleezza Rice's private life.

Born in Chicago, Illinois, in 1974, McGruder spent the earliest of his years living on the city's South Side. Just before he entered elementary school, the McGruder family moved to the predominantly White Baltimore, Mary-land, suburb of Columbia.[3] A *New Yorker* columnist described Columbia as "a planned community—envisioned as a sort of integrationist, post-civil-rights

5.1 The difference between the inner city and the suburbs is humorously illustrated in this caustic exchange. *Boondocks*, © Aaron McGruder.

utopia—developed by the Rouse Company in the mid-nineteen-sixties, and featuring an official town 'Tree of Life,' and streets and neighborhoods with names like Hobbit's Glen, Morning Walk and Elfstone Way. (Huey and Riley live on Timid Deer Lane, one block over from Bashful Beaver.)" (McGrath). Negotiating Chicago's and Columbia's evolving interracial race relations and stutter-step integration efforts seemingly worked to have a profound impact on the way McGruder interrogated his world. His worldview was further honed as he earned a degree in African American studies from the University of Maryland. In short, the strip worked to confront the realities represented by both Chicago and Columbia for McGruder. On interrogating the complexities of race relations, he explained, *The Boondocks* examined "the racial diversity and complexity of our world" through "the terrain where dashikis and Brand Nubian CDs meet The Gap and Hanson" (*Boondocks* website). McGruder was described by the *Washington Post* as the "Garry Trudeau of the hip hop generation" (Sessions Stepp). He cited hip-hop music as being most influential to his thinking and, subsequently, to the strip. In a 2004 interview, McGruder was quoted as saying, "I look at everything from a hip-hop perspective. My point of view on that is very obvious: get off my dick. Leave my shit alone" (McGrath).

McGruder's affinity for hip-hop was not singularly focused on the art form's entertainment and aesthetics. Rather, McGruder identified hip-hop as providing him an early, if flawed, introduction to Black nationalism: "When I was in high school, we went through a short nationalistic phase in hip-hop. It was the right time to be 15 or 16, because it felt like there was a movement going on. There wasn't. We didn't realize that it was just a soundtrack and not a movement. We realized that these guys were not politicians, they were just rappers" (Datcher). Yet hip-hop proved to be a spark in McGruder's interests.

Through Huey, named for the Black Panther Party cofounder Huey P. Newton, McGruder did more than explore intersectionalities between place, class, and race relations. Huey reflected the kind of nationalism attractive to hip-hop-inspired youth, as well as revealed that the ideological outlook of the hip-hop generation was informed by 1970s Black Power movement rhetorics. Simply, Huey represented McGruder's nostalgic fondness for the moment in his youth when hip-hop expressed the symbols and sentiments of the pro-Black, anti-integrationist period. Huey served to communicate that such a political orientation should be understood as relevant today, particularly urgent in this purported post-civil-rights society. Howard Winant characterizes the post-civil-rights era as amounting to a "substantial modification of the previously far more rigid lines of exclusion and segregation, permitting real mobility for more favored sectors (that is, certain class-based segments) of racially-defined minority groups" (43). This description fits perfectly with McGruder/Huey's experiences of upward class mobility to the suburbs. In the strip, Granddad embodies the aspirations of integration and mobility, as symbolized by the civil rights movement, and mainstream Black institutions and leadership. Huey's brother, Riley, signifies more recent mainstream rap culture and its values, which are mocked and critiqued by Huey. McGruder as an author used Huey to bring back a past social movement and its philosophy to challenge the world that McGruder was writing and drawing in, one marked by shifting discourses of race and racism moving through, and even past, rhetorics of multiculturalism toward postracialisms. In short, McGruder's continuation of debates about the ideologies of the civil rights movement, the Black nationalist movement, and hip-hop's brand of Black nationalism is not him coming late to the discussion. Instead of a lag, the strip is a reflection of McGruder's persistent struggle to keep at the fore Black culture and politics even as, according to Decker, notions of "pluralism and the ethnic melting pot in the U.S. threaten the Black community with the loss of a collective identity" (55). For McGruder, the threat is reality.

Appropriating Black Power: The Remix

In the strip, McGruder does not present a wholesale rejection of all past generations' efforts at Black comeuppance. Rather, his concern is over what he perceives as the failures of accommodationist strategies. As the historian Derrick Alridge explains, there is continuity from the rhetoric, beliefs, and even behaviors of the Black Power era to those of the hip-hop generation. For Alridge, the conduits were the young adults of the 1980s, reared during the 1970s, who brought the political anthem of the Black Power era to their hip-hop music—Public Enemy, Brand Nubian, Afrika Bambaataa, KRS-One, to name a few—with "black nationalist and other groups, inspired by the Nation of Islam, the Five Percent Nation of Islam and the resurgence in the popularity of Black nationalist icons such as Malcolm X, . . . weighing in on the Black condition and espousing a philosophy of self-determination" (235). Likewise, for McGruder, Black nationalism was, quite literally, music to his ears:

> My political perspectives as a young adult were shaped by hip-hop's political era. . . . We had Public Enemy, KRS-One, X-Clan, Brand Nubian and all those very overtly political groups. . . . It was actually Black nationalism; it was racial socialism. There was no Black leadership supplying these political ideals to the next generation, and what few people there were, a lot of us—particularly those of us who grew up in the suburbs—discovered that through hip-hop. We discovered who Louis Farrakhan was through hip-hop. When the trends changed, most people changed with it, and a handful of us were put on this path to become politically oriented, because of hip hop. (*All the Rage* 171)

And yet McGruder was not an adult in the 1980s. Rather, as he reveals, he was a teen when he began to hear and make sense of Black Power–infused hip-hop offered up by those (men) born at least ten years before him. In short, McGruder borrowed from the borrowers. This lateral appropriation, through the medium of hip-hop, sheds light on the at times purposeful sociopolitical hyperbole in *The Boondocks*. Huey can be understood as an artistic, embellished construction of a strategic nostalgia, not a reflection of actual lived experience. The construction of Huey is not without risk, in that he may function to reduce the politics of Black Power to a punch line. Angela Davis effectively elaborates on what is lost politically when sociohistorical context is misplaced in a shift of temporality:

> Most young African Americans who are familiar with my name and twenty-five-year-old image have encountered photographs and film/video clips largely in music videos and in Black history montages in popular books and magazines. Within the interpretive context in which they learn to situate these photographs, the most salient element of the image is the hairstyle ["the Afro"], understood less as a political statement than a fashion. The unprecedented contemporary circulation of photographic and filmic images of African Americans has multiple and contradictory implications. On the one hand, it holds the promise of visual memory of older and departed generations, of both well-known figures and people who may not have achieved public prominence. However, there is also the danger that this historical memory may become ahistorical and apolitical. (38)

Can McGruder's borrowing and adaptation be understood in terms of appropriation? Appropriation is defined, in its simplest form, as "any instance in which means commonly associated with and/or perceived as belonging to another are used to further one's ends" (Shugart 210–211). However, Eric Lott challenges us to consider the important distinction in acts of appropriation, whether they are "love" or "theft." Both are consumptions and re-presentations of that which belongs to another, while raising questions around the nature of the encounter—either the fetishistic (theft) or the celebratory (love). In considering this dichotomy, McGruder's appropriation of Black Power rhetoric calls for a consideration of the different ways in which cultural forms and identity practices are adopted and toward what ends and with what results.

This form of appropriation, it should be noted, has an analogue in hip-hop music, in which sampling—the borrowing and reusing of others' music—has been a central and controversial (with regard to intellectual property) element. Sampling has been used for overt commercial purposes and as a form of homage to past masters, roughly mirroring Lott's distinction between theft and love. In music, a remix is simply a "re-interpretation of a pre-existing song" (Navas 159). Given the centrality of hip-hop in McGruder's identity and political development, this is an especially appropriate analogy. Sampling as a creative act of borrowing and reusing is inherent to art formation, in general, even outside the digital era. Henry Jenkins notes that the "story of American arts in the 19th century might be told in terms of the mixing, matching, and merging of folk traditions taken from various indigenous and immigrant populations" (135).

Appropriations by external groups have been problematized by many scholars. Sean Tierney reveals an appropriation along the lines of Edward Said's critique of Western imperialism and the cultural representations it spawned in *Orientalism* (1978). Western imperial powers appropriated and represented the colonized "Other" in processes of knowledge production. This served and emanated from the logics of racial superiority. This stringent assignment of superior-inferior roles, according to Tierney, can best be seen in films such as Quentin Tarantino's *Kill Bill* (2003–2004). The White heroine not only appropriates Asian culture (in this instance, represented stereotypically as samurai sword fighting) but also does so with superiority over Asians and, importantly, in their own countries. As such, appropriation is not just happenstance; rather, it is first largely considered in cultural studies as a practice of power (Ashley and Plesch 3). Appropriation's directionality is not singular, however, even when power is seen as the fulcrum on which it swings. Research on appropriation has also looked at cases of weaker groups taking on elements of dominant culture (Anspach, Coe, and Thurlow). What marks McGruder's appropriation as different from that defined and described by Lott, Tierney, Helene Shugart, and others is, perhaps, his sincere identification—the mixing, matching, and merging—with the Black Power movement as a past framework to be applied to contemporary times, a transference over space, urban to suburban, and time, the 1960s to the turn of the millennium.

Anspach et al. introduce a new, more nuanced understanding of appropriation through their theorization of "lateral appropriation." Lateral appropriation is defined by the authors as the "usurping of one marginalized group's capital by another marginalized group" (100). An example they provide is the use of the terminology "come out of the closet," typically associated with the queer movement but taken up by the atheist movement. That is, just as it is politically and socially safer for people of minority sexual orientations to hide their identities, so too is it less risky to "closet" one's minority religious identity (or even perhaps a dual gay-atheist identity). McGruder, it may be argued, engaged in a sort of *intra*racial lateral appropriation by taking the cultural capital of one marginalized group (Black nationalists of the 1970s) as a member of another marginalized group—Blacks of the late-twentieth-century/hip-hop generation. McGruder easily portrayed this borrowing, as he appeared unencumbered by and immune to asymmetrical power hierarchies that are more apparent in, say, Blacks appropriating Asian popular culture (e.g., the Wu-Tang Clan) versus Asians appropriating Black popular culture (e.g., "blackfacers" adopting Black style).[4] One cannot lose sight of the fact that McGruder, just as the rap artists who inspired him as a youth, offered a largely symbolized form of nationalism that was not necessarily in *direct* contrast to the philosophies of the civil rights movement, even if the source, the Black Power movement, was. New, conscientious hip-hop groups responded to a bland, commercialized hip-hop/pop-music industry that bore little relation to an increasingly impoverished, neglected, and crime-ridden urban America during the Reagan presidency. They were not doctrinaire artists, not to the extent of Huey, for example. Rather, they confronted the failures of the mass media arts to reflect real life. This gap between image and reality was not just happening in music. Television presented so-called White savior themes in *Diff'rent Strokes* (1978–1986) and *Webster* (1983–1989), while movies resurrected integration themes through the police buddy film, as seen in 48 *Hrs.* (1982), *Running Scared* (1986), and *Lethal Weapon* (1987).

New movements in film mirrored the rise of conscientious hip-hop in the late 1980s. McGruder would not have been able to ignore one of (Black) popular culture's most influential creative talents—Spike Lee. Lee spoke the language of Black nationalism: "I've never believed in that melting pot shit. You have to be White for that" (Nicodemus). By the time McGruder was eighteen, he was among a generation of moviegoers inspired to see the biography of one of America's most famous Black nationalists while proclaiming, "I am Malcolm X," at Lee's insistence.[5] More specifically, in a 2004 interview, McGruder expressed his fondness for the rap artist Chuck D of Public Enemy and his song "Fight the Power," which was the anthem for Spike Lee's 1989 film *Do the Right Thing* (McGruder, *All the Rage* 187). Lee's mainstream success, then, opened the mainstream door for McGruder's similarly profitable brand of racial discourse.

The Civil Rights Movement: Silent, Absent, Obsolete

Lateral appropriation in *The Boondocks* meant the importation of a key debate from the 1960s–1970s political era into the Freemans' home. Through the strip, McGruder implicitly tackles the civil rights movement, which was premised on the notion that social change and empowerment for Blacks could come through integration. The civil rights ethos is manifested through the representation of Granddad, who possesses a largely single-minded interest in peace and quiet, an orientation toward the world that often clashes with Huey's. Huey's politics can be described as a form of Black nationalism that is anti-integrationist and invested in self-empowerment as it was manifested in movements such as the Black Panther Party. McGruder thus draws on the tensions between the two formative movements, civil rights and Black Power. However, what is key here is *how* McGruder presents these tensions aesthetically—pitting Black Power's iconography against civil rights' but also adding to the mix an opposition to gangsta rap's gangsterism, with its focus on self-aggrandizement and consumption.

McGruder casts Granddad's act of integration as, at best, pragmatic work on behalf of improving the boys'—and thereby the Black—condition. From the most critical standpoint, Huey's, Granddad's efforts to transplant the family betray Black communalism and cause psychological damage and harms to the cultural identity of the children. Ignoring Huey's plea to be homeschooled, Granddad enrolls the boys into Woodcrest's J. Edgar Hoover Elementary— named for the longtime director of the Federal Bureau of Investigation (FBI) whose antipathy for both the civil rights and Black Power movements is well-known (Kiel; Cunningham; Nash). Whereas Granddad sees working within the system as viable, Huey lectures the school's administration that "public educational facilities such as this are the cornerstone of the institutionalized racism that continues to oppress Black people" (McGruder, *Right* 27). McGruder is also drawing on a Black nationalist axiom that, according to Noliwe Rooks, stated that White education systems "intentionally instilled a sense of racial inferiority in Black students. In order to shed that sense of inferiority and find a healthy identity, such students needed special courses on the 'Black experience' taught by Black professors" (64). In the face of such sociopolitical assertions, either Granddad is left out by McGruder, therefore having no credible response to Huey's brand of Black empowerment, or when Granddad does appear, he is cast as an apolitical traditionalist—inattentive to and unquestioning of political affairs. In this sense, the civil rights movement is represented as complicit in institutional exclusions.

Granddad represents the purported irrelevancy or even conservatism of the civil rights movement's vestiges. In a 2003 interview, McGruder made obvious his belief in the presence of a generational political friction when he said, "Marches are not gonna do it anymore. . . . We need guys who will change the world and no one will know their names. *We need gangsters.* We need people who have figured out what to do when you walk into the room of power and the only person in the room is the devil—because that's where we're at today" (Datcher; emphasis added). In the strip, McGruder continues to highlight the divisions. When Granddad learns that the Iraq War is costing the United States $143 million per day, McGruder portrays him as being outraged. But far from someone who knew what to do about the condition of (Black) America, Granddad protests that he could buy "143 million lottery tickets" with all of that money (McGruder, *All the Rage* 31). Simply, McGruder uses his wit to expose that Granddad, or those who share his politics, is not the "gangster" who is going to bring change to the Black world.

Against the image of Huey as a wise (cracking) neorevolutionary, Granddad is cast as plain-speaking, simple, kindly, and well-meaning but ultimately flawed. Granddad, cast as a symbol of an obsolete civil-rights-era generation, is often shown to be hypocritical. For example, when Granddad tries to ban the use of the "n-word" in his home, he is exposed as ideologically flawed when he scolds a confused Huey by yelling, "n****, you know which 'n-word' I'm talking about!" (McGruder, *All the Rage* 35). Granddad also sides with fellow integrationist Bill Cosby, first giving him a pass for what is called throughout the strip his "drug and rub" scandal and then later agreeing with Cosby's speeches in which the

5.2 Bill Cosby's controversial statements about African Americans' responsibility for their own social problems is sarcastically highlighted in a typical manner for the equally controversial McGruder. *Boondocks*, © Aaron McGruder.

comedian/actor indicts the Black underclass for being deficient: "By the time you are 12, you can have sex with your grandmother. You keep those numbers coming. I'm just predicting" (an actual quote from Cosby printed in the strip). To which Granddad responds supportively, "Really disgusting, Cos, but I'm still with you!" (McGruder, *Public* 148).

The strip was not so unsophisticated as to paint Huey as good and the others as bad. McGruder presented Granddad at his political best when he is serving as foil to Huey's and Riley's attempts at imitative, empty performative and aesthetic alignments with their derivative understanding of Black nationalism and/or hip-hop culture. He demands that they pull their sagging pants up, he forbids Riley to have his hair cornrowed (braided), and he derisively rejects "Black English Month" when it is explained to him by Huey that it is "when we take time out to celebrate the richness and creativity of African American speech" (McGruder, *Public* 45). As such, Granddad evidences an ideological foothold within Blackness that is markedly different from both Huey's and Riley's; he represents those who see the toughest of race relations battles finally behind them and relishes in the victories over an era fraught with lynchings, bombings, black codes, and Jim Crow.

On the Margin of the Margins: Huey and the Challenge of McGruder's Appropriation

Through gangsta-rap-loving Riley, Huey's younger brother, it is apparent that Huey's political program faces an uphill battle. Huey's ideological obstacle is not just Granddad's uncritical traditionalism and its embedded integrationist attitude but also the even more youthful direction of hip-hop since Black Power's reincarnation and demise. Gangsta rap, which gave shape to mainstream rap, grew dominant by glorifying sex and violence, the pursuit of personal (not collective) power and money, and having a flair for gross self-aggrandizement and machismo. This version of hop-hop is as constitutive of Riley as the Black Power movement is of his brother, Huey.

Riley's self-assigned moniker is indicative of his values. He adopts the name Riley "Escobar," thereby expressing his fealty to the Medellín cocaine-cartel leader Pablo Emilio Escobar Gaviria, "who insisted on living the hedonistic life of a rock star—while making millions from one of the most ruthlessly violent drug gangs in history" (Riegel). In the strip, Riley proclaims, "Chief Mafioso thug kingpin 'Riley Esco' is now in charge! I'm packin' heat, I hate cops, I don't fear jail! WHAT!!!! Hold on to your jewels 'cause Riley is takin' your loot— BELIEVE DAT!!" (McGruder, *Boondocks* 20). In response, Huey rejects Riley's celebration of gangsta-rap artists, lyrics, and seemingly empty rhetoric by dismissing Riley's heroes: "I'm allergic to studio gangsters" (20). For Huey, these artists were frauds who glorified the wrong types of gangsters. While McGruder once intimated that "we need gangsters" to serve as new Black power brokers through earned respect and backroom dealings with big shots, these politically minded gangsters are not the kind that Riley emulates. Riley personifies a component of the hip-hop generation that stands in contradistinction to McGruder's generation, so Huey is the voice of McGruder's criticism.

Thus was the challenge that McGruder faced: how could he effectively appropriate a past political discourse that many twenty-first-century youth have no connection with? The disconnect that McGruder faced with the generation after his could have to do with the evolution of racism in the United States. John Jackson in his book *Racial Paranoia* summarizes the ideological dilemma that people such as McGruder face: "In some ways, race was easier to understand and discuss when it was that obvious impetus for public water hosings and police dog attacks, when it was emblematized by socially meaningful lines separating the fronts from the back of buses. Fortunately, that version of racial reality is dead. . . . [However,] the farther we advance from overt racist doctrines and laws, the more material traces those past sins leave behind, which means all the more surfaces to which contemporary racially charged paranoia might stick" (10, 95). Jackson analyzes contemporary responses to racism by considering those who simply use their "racism detector" to note perceived prejudices (95). Hidden-beneath-the-surface racisms are not easily evidenced in this age of covert, enlightened racism. Jackson explains, "so, Mos Def raps about how a racist cop will never explicitly say that he stopped a young Black man because of race, but they'll both still 'know' the unsaid truth" (159). The taken-for-granted nature of racism is symbolized by the strip's settings, which typify the post-civil-rights era's false sense of a postrace America. Huey's discomfort in the suburbs, themselves often the result of urban "White flight," has to do with his attention to the structural, increasingly depersonalized nature of racism. Riley's rap gangsterism offers no response to this other than noting the taint that a suburban address leaves on one's claim to street credibility; for Granddad, such an address is aspirational. Huey is therefore out of place.

For the rank materialists, such as Riley, and the integrationist Granddad, Huey is seen as paranoid. Calling out structural racism demands what can be called instinctual responses, which is inherently difficult to show to others even if, for example, Mos Def's description of actor cognizance is true. Reporting hidden and highly nuanced racism is difficult for those who are untrained in critical studies or not highly attentive to current affairs. McGruder seems to engage this lacuna playfully at times even as he seeks to overcome the perceptual gap. In one strip, Huey is comical when he reviews conspiracy theories such as the World Trade Center being blown up from within but turns serious when he reminds readers that the government was capable of blowing up of the levees in New Orleans to flood the poor Black parts during Hurricane Katrina because "they did it in 1927" (McGruder, *All the Rage* 95).[6] Yet McGruder himself relies on racial intuition, sans facts, to reveal how some Black Americans work to make sense of their lives and the myriad obscured "forces potentially allied against them" (Jackson 7). For example, McGruder's intuition was on display when, at an awards ceremony, he called Secretary of State Condoleezza Rice a murderer. On hearing McGruder brag about his real-life confrontation with Rice, the syndicated columnist Armstrong Williams protested, to which McGruder responded, "she's a murderer because *I believe* she's a murderer" (McGruder, *All the Rage* 184; emphasis added). Huey also speaks often from this instinctual consciousness, one that has proven not to transfer to Granddad or Riley.

In considering McGruder's appropriation of his understanding of 1960–1970s Black Power, it is imperative to probe its fit in the post-civil-rights era. Clearly, McGruder does not find much hope in Black institutions and leaders. In taking on leaders of the civil rights (and Granddad's) era, McGruder describes traditional civil rights organizations as "outdated" (Datcher). McGruder derides Jesse Jackson ("he's old" and "he doesn't speak for me") as well as Al Sharpton ("you'll never be taken seriously with a perm" [McGruder, *All the Rage* 158]). As for protest rallies, McGruder has rejected them in the tenor of a Malcolm X: "Marching isn't doing it." He argues that they failed because the powers that be have no "fear" of Blacks. He contends, "If the best you can do is march on the Capitol 20-deep, they know you've got nothin' up your sleeve." His model for success is, oddly, the "Right Wing," which "lies, cheats, steals, and kills." Lessons can be learned from them, he says: "If you want to win, that's what you have to do. Do whatever it takes to win. They have no rules; you shouldn't" (McGruder, *All the Rage* 158). This ethos is a rejection of Granddad's quietism. However, the question remains whether Huey's worldview offers a compelling alternative.

It is not clear that McGruder was fully vested in Huey as a response, though he *mostly* was. As a satirical figure, Huey presents a caricature of are-you-Black-enough Black nationalists, while simultaneously circulating their concerns all the same. Moreover, added to these sociopolitical concerns is a contemporary anxiety over the depoliticization of hip-hop. For McGruder, and by extension Huey, the music genre faced diffusion and mainstream popularity, threats to its authenticity. The multicultural threat to the sanctity of hip-hop is presented in *The Boondocks* as a similar problem for all of Blackness. The young White girl Cindy embodies McGruder's obvious concerns about hip-hop going mainstream and quite literally the selling out of hip-hop on networks such as MTV and VH1. To illustrate, Cindy encourages Huey to say "hooo hooo . . . like the song" when she chants "holla back" to him. When he silently refuses to participate, Cindy wonders, "you don't know a lot about Black people do you, Huey" (McGruder, *Right* 214).

However, the treatment of the biracial Jazmine harkens another concern for McGruder that is not singularly about racial/cultural dilution. Until Huey's arrival in Woodcrest, Jazmine lived comfortably postracial, not being moved to claim any particular group identity. She happily existed in a moment that, for her, transcended race. It is Huey who demands that Jazmine consider where, socially, her authentic racial identity lies and that she in fact must choose. In the strip, Jazmine eventually concedes that she has some racial identity quandaries, only to have Huey coldly dismiss her concerns, assigning her an essential identity: "You're BLACK. Get over it" (McGruder, *Boondocks* 27). Huey applies his own one-drop rule by placing Jazmine on the side of Black. For those who are invested in discourses such as multiculturalism, this type of essentialism is an alien, if not a wrongheaded, notion. The politics of the activist Huey place him well into the margins of a marginalized group, something McGruder forwards effectively as a device in the strip's narrative.

Like so many earlier comic creators (e.g., Charles Schulz's *Peanuts*, Bill Watterson's *Calvin and Hobbes*, Ray Billingley's *Curtis*), McGruder delivers his provocative social commentary through the mouths of babes, which works to heighten the comedic factor while moderating the analytical blow—most likely an ingredient in the strip's commercial success. What sets McGruder, and therefore his strip, apart is that Huey often defines solutions reflecting panhumanist harmony as culturally dangerous for Black identity—a notion contra the logic of the civil rights movement, which suggested that Black identity would be safe. Therefore, one can see just how subversive is Huey's implicit view that the embrace of postrace ideologies, multiculturalism, integration, or hybridity and syncretism is a foolhardy move toward sacrificing Blackness—while Whiteness maintains its identity whole and full. Huey reminds those whose ideologies are different from his that they are first and foremost, that is essentially, Black—the categorical imposition of essential identity that Huey imposes on the biracial Jazmine.

The Boondocks was a graphic assemblage of hip-hop culture, Black American political history, and the lessons of African American studies scholarship. Each helped McGruder make retrospective sense of his own city-to-the-boondocks racialized experiences within the longer story of the struggle for equality in America. While McGruder was certainly not the first to appropriate Black nationalism to form a sort of "hip hop nationalism" (Decker 54), his brand of appropriation resonated with many readers. He strategically placed into the strip's characters different currents of thought and lifestyle in Black sociopolitical history, one of which, Huey, reflects a strategic nostalgia. The strip was furthered by the intentional tension between the characters and their associated ways of being. Huey's leftist Black nationalism was deployed as a framework of commentary on contemporary times as well as a counterpoint to the outcome of the civil rights movement—yet it was nostalgic to the point of caricature, a way of essentialist thinking that was incongruent with the mainstream of Black America, its organizations and figureheads. McGruder's borrowing intraracially and across generations of political thought, then, effectively further complicates understandings of cultural appropriation—getting beyond initial binaries of idolization or theft. His borrowing sheds light on how same-group borrowing can differ from extragroup borrowing and on how making social context central functions to redress what might be lost ideologically in this temporal shift. Specifically, in his appropriation, McGruder's strategic nostalgia-turned-remixing reveals how such borrowing can simultaneously drop off, in this case the complex politics of liberation, in favor of an aesthetic (style and humor), while also giving formation to powerful, historically embedded critiques of Black culture, organizations, celebrities, and other agents of representation.

Hip-hop played a central role in *The Boondocks*. It was fundamental as an analogy for the strip's creative production: McGruder fashioned the strip through sampling and remixing the imagery, slogans, and figures of the Black Power, civil rights, and post-civil-rights eras, thereby acting in part as a DJ, albeit a visual one. It was musical hip-hop that first introduced him to these histories. On a more direct level, McGruder used the strip, especially the juxtaposition between Huey's and Riley's tastes, to critique the music as it existed in the strip's time. Huey's view about hip-hop was that without its Black Power influences and consciousness-raising aspirations, it ran the risk of simply being about all that Riley's heroes represented—hypermaterialism and violent bravado. Todd Boyd suggests that hip-hop's tradition of presenting Blackness in ways that reflect nobly and positively on Black people was replaced by a hyperindividualistic "niggaz for life" art form that celebrated non-collectively-enriching values. The hip-hop generation did not invest in uplifting rhetoric, role-model behaviors, or (political) actions that cast them as anything but possessing "cool detachment and defiance" (Boyd 19). Importantly, Boyd goes on to assert that gangsta rap does, indeed, have its political dimensions, while Black-nationalist-inspired rap has not been immune to braggadocio and commercialism. For McGruder, the fluidity of hip-hop's politicization poses a dilemma and demands a careful balancing act. Mark Anthony Neal credits McGruder and his use of hip-hop for challenging "general perceptions among older generations of Blacks that a 'mythical' vibrant and engaged Black intellectual and moral life—which ironically was intimately connected to Black youth culture during the civil rights movement—is consistently eroded by the post-soul and hip-hop generations" (169). However, in Huey's world, the rhetorical strategy of relying on binaries of the engaged versus the obtuse, that is, the pitting of one movement against the other, is deemed persuasively necessary—even if it is a falsehood. For Huey, nuance in understanding most starkly emerges when he tells readers that today's youth are not cognizant of either the civil rights or Black Power movements. Huey argues that youth who have little coming their way substantively and politically cannot carry the blame for their obsessions with self and material consumption. For McGruder, the only solution was to reach back in time and appropriate what he believed were the last, best forces of Black liberation—even if they put him on the margins of a community he thought needed shaking up.

As expected, the strip was received quite differently by Black and white readers (Rockler). As a controversial strip, *The Boondocks* was removed from newspapers across the nation numerous times. One newspaper, the *Durham [NC] Herald-Sun*, canceled the strip entirely for its provocative content. The official *Boondocks* website featured messages from readers accusing McGruder of race-baiting, a lack of patriotism, and promoting Black stereotypes; some posted their own messages of vitriolic hate against the strip.[7] However, *The Boondocks* gained wide acclaim—especially from Blacks. Tavis Smiley, the former host of *BET Tonight*, praised McGruder as a "true credit to his race" (McGruder, *Boondocks*, back cover). In 2002, McGruder won the NAACP Chairman's Award for his work on the strip. The *USA Today* columnist DeWayne Wickham praised it: "I think his comic strip . . . is brilliantly funny and purposefully shocking. McGruder doesn't just want to make his readers laugh; he works mightily to make them think." By the end of the strip's seven-year run in 2006, its distribution rose to over 350 newspapers, making it one of the most syndicated strips in the country at the time. That is significant, especially for a strip tackling the weighty issues of identity, power, and culture in Black America. McGruder's strategic appropriation of past Black experiences in different times and places, and the expressions of critique it produced, gave the strip its power. Though the appropriations in *The Boondocks* were driven by a very particular authorial background, McGruder's own experiences and political education, they were connected to larger cultural movements and spoke within a time in which race was widely represented as moot after the civil rights movement. That the strip resonated with so many people suggests that *The Boondocks* was a unique pop-cultural footnote on mediated proclamations of a post-civil-rights America.

Notes

1   In February 2006, it was reported that McGruder was taking a six-month hiatus. By September 2006, Universal threw in the towel on McGruder and *The Boondocks* by issuing this statement through its president, Lee Salem: "Although Aaron McGruder has made no statement about retiring or resuming *The Boondocks* for print newspapers . . . newspapers should not count on it coming back in the foreseeable future. . . . Numerous attempts . . . to pin McGruder down on a date that the strip would be coming back were unsuccessful" (Sessions Stepp).

2 Steiner's analysis of strategic nostalgia comes from an analysis of the Egyptian-Sudanese writer Leila Aboulela. The term has also been used by Myria Georgiou in her study of Arab television viewers in Europe.

3 In addition to Aaron, the immediate McGruder family includes his mother, Elaine; father, Bill; and political-cartoonist brother, Dedric. According to McGruder, the family lived in Champaign, Illinois, and Louisville, Kentucky, for a couple of years, but he grew up in Columbia, Maryland (*All the Rage* 170).

4 On Japanese youths' complex appropriation and performance of Black fashion, hairstyles, vernacular, music, and even skin color, see Wood.

5 In a 2002 *USA Weekend* interview conducted with McGruder and the filmmaker Reginald Hudlin (Hudlin and McGruder cowrote the screenplay and subsequent 2004 comic novel *Birth of a Nation*), McGruder recalls consuming Lee's films but says directly to Hudlin, "Spike Lee's films were very heavily racialized and politicized but they didn't resonate with me as much as yours did." Here, McGruder describes Hudlin's "very realistic portrayal of what young black kids are actually like as opposed to the Hollywood ghetto-ized version" (Anderson). Hudlin is, perhaps, best known for directing the 1990 comedy film *House Party*, starring the rap duo Christopher "Kid" Reid and Christopher "Play" Martin.

6 Since Hurricane Katrina struck the Gulf Coast, there has been renewed interest in a similar flood in 1927. A levee protecting St. Bernard Parish (a poor community) was exploded with dynamite in an attempt to protect the city of New Orleans (a wealthier one).

7 For an analysis of *The Boondocks'* reception by readers, see Cornwell and Orbe.

Works Cited

Alridge, Derrick P. "From Civil Rights to Hip Hop: Toward a Nexus of Ideas." *Journal of African American History* 90 (Summer 2005): 226–252.

Anderson, Sara. "Pop Culture: Reginald Hudlin and Aaron McGruder." *USA Weekend* 17 February 2002. Web. http://159.54.226.237/02_issues/020217/020217bhm_pop.html. Accessed 8 June 2011.

Anspach, Whitney, Kevin Coe, and Crispin Thurlow. "The Other Closet? Atheists, Homosexuals and the Lateral Appropriation of Discursive Capital." *Critical Discourse Studies* 4 (March 2007): 95–119.

Ashley, Kathleen M., and Veronique Plesch. "The Cultural Process of 'Appropriation.'" *Journal of Medieval and Early Modern Studies* 32.1 (2002): 1–15.

The Boondocks website. Home page. http://www.gocomics.com/boondocks. Accessed 8 June 2011.

Boyd, Todd. *Am I Black Enough for You? Popular Culture from the 'Hood and Beyond*. Bloomington: Indiana University Press, 1997.

Coleman, R. Means, ed. *Say It Loud! African-American Audiences, Media, and Identity*. New York: Routledge, 2002.

Cornwell, Nancy C., and Mark P. Orbe. "'Keepin' It Real and/or Sellin' Out to the Man': African-American Responses to Aaron McGruder's *The Boondocks*." *Say It Loud! African-American Audiences, Media, and Identity*. Ed. R. Means Coleman. New York: Routledge, 2002. 27–43.

Cunningham, Kevin. *J. Edgar Hoover: Controversial FBI Director*. Minneapolis, MN: Compass Point Books, 2006.

Datcher, Michael. "Free Huey: Aaron McGruder's Outer Child Is Taking on America." *Crisis* September–October 2003. Web. http://findarticles.com/p/articles/mi_qa4081/is_200309/ai_n9297778/pg_1?tag=artBody;col1. Accessed 8 June 2011.

Davis, Angela Y. "Afro Images: Politics, Fashion, and Nostalgia." *Critical Inquiry* 21 (1994): 37–39, 41–43, 45.

Decker, Jeffrey Louis. "The State of Rap: Time and Place in Hip Hop Nationalism." *Social Text* 34 (1993): 53–84.

Georgiou, Myria. "Between Strategic Nostalgia and Banal Nomadism: Explorations of Transnational Subjectivity among Arab Audiences." *International Journal of Cultural Studies* 16 (January 2013): 23–39.

Jackson, John L., Jr. *Racial Paranoia: The Unintended Consequences of Political Correctness*. New York: Basic Civitas Books, 2008.

Jenkins, Henry. *Convergence Culture: Where Old and New Media Collide*. New York: NYU Press, 2006.

Kiel, R. Andrew. *J. Edgar Hoover, the Father of the Cold War: How His Obsession with Communism Led to the Warren Commission Coverup and Escalation of the Vietnam War*. Lanham, MD: University Press of America, 2000.

Lott, Eric. *Love and Theft: Blackface Minstrelsy and the American Working Class*. New York: Oxford University Press, 1993.

McGrath, Ben. "The Radical: Why Do Editors Keep Throwing 'The Boondocks' Off the Funnies Page?" *New Yorker* April 2004: 3. Web. http://www.newyorker.com/archive/2004/04/19/040419fa_fact2. Accessed 8 June 2011.

McGruder, Aaron. *All the Rage: The Boondocks Past and Present*. New York: Three Rivers, 2007.

———. *The Boondocks: Because I Know You Don't Read the Newspaper*. Kansas City, MO: Andrew McNeel, 2000.

———. *Public Enemy #2: An All-New Boondocks Collection*. New York: Three Rivers, 2005.

———. *A Right to Be Hostile: The Boondocks Treasury*. New York: Three Rivers, 2003.

Nash, Jay Robert. *Citizen Hoover: A Critical Study of the Life and Times of J. Edgar Hoover*. Chicago: Nelson-Hall, 1972.

Navas, Eduardo. "Regressive and Reflexive Mashups in Sampling Culture." In *Mashup Cultures*. Ed. Stefan Sonvilla-Weiss. New York: Springer-Verlag, 2010. 157–177.

Neal, Mark Anthony. *Soul Babies: Black Culture and the Post-Soul Aesthetic*. New York: Routledge, 2002.

Nicodemus, Katja. "Sit, Wagner!" *Sign and Sight* 23 March 2006. Web. http://www.signandsight.com/features/673.html. Accessed 8 June 2011.

Riegel, Ralph. "Medellin Inspired Chainsaw Killing Scene in 'Scarface.'" *Independent* (Dublin) 24 July 2008. Web. http://www.independent.ie/national-news/medellin-inspired-chainsaw-killing-scene-in-scarface-1439085.html. Accessed 8 June 2011.

Rockler, Naomi. "Race, Whiteness, 'Lightness,' and Relevance: African American and European American Interpretations of *Jump Start* and *The Boondocks*." *Critical Studies in Mass Communication* 19.4 (2002): 398–418.

Rooks, Noliwe M. *White Money / Black Power: The Surprising History of African American Studies and the Crisis of Race in Higher Education*. Boston: Beacon, 2006.

Said, Edward. *Orientalism*. New York: Pantheon Books, 1978.

Sessions Stepp, Laura. "Syndicate Says 'Boondocks' Won't Return." *Washington Post* 26 September 2006. Web. http://www.washingtonpost.com/wp-dyn/content/article/2006/09/25/AR2006092501391.html. Accessed 8 June 2011.

Shugart, Helene A. "Counterhegemonic Acts: Appropriation as a Feminist Rhetorical Strategy." *Quarterly Journal of Speech* 83 (1997): 210–229.

Steiner, Tina. "Strategic Nostalgia, Islam and Cultural Translation in Leila Aboulela's 'The Translator' and 'Coloured Lights.'" *Current Writing: Text and Reception in Southern Africa* 20.2 (2008): 7–26.

Tierney, Sean M. "Themes of Whiteness in *Bulletproof Monk*, *Kill Bill*, and *The Last Samurai*." *Journal of Communication* 56 (2006): 607–624.

Wickham, DeWayne. "'Boondocks' Comic Echoes African-American Thoughts." *USA Today* 21 October 2002. Web. http://www.usatoday.com/news/opinion/columnist/wickham/2002-10-21-oped-wickham_x.htm. Accessed 8 June 2011.

Winant, Howard. *The New Politics of Race: Globalism, Difference, Justice*. Minneapolis: University of Minnesota Press, 2004.

Wood, Joe. "The Yellow Negro." *Transition* 73 (1997): 40–66.

Ziff, Bruce, and Pratime V. Rao. "Introduction to Cultural Appropriation: A Framework for Analysis." *Borrowed Power: Essays on Cultural Appropriation*. Ed. Ziff and Rao. New Brunswick, NJ: Rutgers University Press, 1997. 1–27.

Panel III

Black Tights

•••••••••••••••••••••

Chapter 6

American Truths

• •

Blackness and the American Superhero

CONSEULA FRANCIS

In 2002 Marvel Comics announced a seven-issue limited series that would shed new light on the origins of one of its most popular and long-standing heroes, Captain America. The series, titled *Truth: Red, White & Black*, would expose the racist origins of the Super Soldier program that created Captain America and reveal that Steve Rogers was not the only man to wear the Captain America uniform during World War II. The premise of this prequel is that before Dr. Reinstein deemed the top-secret formula safe enough to test on all-Americans such as Rogers, he first worked out the formula's kinks on a group of black soldiers. *Truth* is based largely on the Tuskegee syphilis experiments, in which, over the course of forty years, the U.S. Public Health Service conducted an experiment on 399 black men in the late stages of syphilis, without their knowledge, in an effort to study the effects of nontreatment. Similarly, subjects of the Super Soldier program in *Truth* are being used to gather data. After being injected with the serum, these black soldiers will be sent out into the field both to conduct the business of war and to allow Reinstein and others to observe the effects of the formula. *Truth* tells the story of this group of black soldiers, draws parallels between the U.S. government's treatment of black men and the Nazis' treatment of Jews, and deconstructs the American superhero.

This kind of retconning (the deliberate revision of established facts in works of serial fiction) is common in superhero comics. Marvel's *Captain America*, in fact, is a slight retcon of Timely Comics' original version of the character. And Marvel, as I am writing this, is in the midst of a retcon of the entire Super Soldier / Weapon X program. So, again, while the retooling of Captain America's backstory is simply business as usual in the world of comic books, the fan reaction to this particular retool is quite interesting. Alex Alonso, the editor of *Truth*, told *Entertainment Weekly* that criticism of the story fell into three camps: "the fanboy purists who don't like Marvel messing with sacred cows; those who worry the series will somehow besmirch Steve Rogers' legacy; and 'outright racists who just don't like the idea of a black man in the Cap uniform'" (Sinclair). Many of these reactions appeared on message boards and websites and did indeed fall into the three camps, though those in the third camp seemed especially numerous and vociferous. Even more interesting were the reactions from those outside the fanboy community, such as the *New York Times* editorial writer Brent Staples, who, after reading the first issue, praised the series for shedding new light on the untold stories of black World War II veterans, or Michael Medved, who, writing in the *National Review Online*, criticized Marvel for publishing Captain America stories that challenged American international and domestic policy. (Remember that *Truth* was published in 2002. In the wake of the September 11 attacks, many Americans had little patience for anything they deemed unpatriotic.) For Medved, *Truth* was the final straw in a deliberate campaign to attack the country through its greatest comic icon. He writes, "We expect such blame-America logic from Hollywood activists, academic apologists, or the angry protesters who regularly fill the streets of European capitals (and many major American cities). When such sentiments turn up, however, hidden within star-spangled, nostalgic packaging of comic books aimed at kids, we need to confront the deep cultural malaise afflicting the nation on the eve of war." Medved here echoes readers' assertions, which I discuss later in this chapter, that comics are "light" entertainment that should not be sullied with politics, particularly the politics of race. His comments also highlight, though, the ideological work done by comic books, particularly ones such as *Captain America*, which make use of actual American history and events. If questioning American foreign policy or racial history in a comic book provides a challenge to the status quo, as Medved implies, then certainly the status quo is upheld by that same comic when no challenge is present.

Reactions such as Medved's make *Truth* a perfect case study for examining the role that race plays in American superhero comic books. It is entirely possible that a successful black American superhero is impossible because it seeks to combine two ideals that are antithetical to each other: superheroes and American racial thinking.[1] We project onto superheroes our basic ideas about humanity (no matter what distant imploded planet those heroes hail from), and they, in turn, reflect back the kind of heroism we would like to imagine we are capable of. Captain America, whose origin story is tweaked (though, importantly, not altered) in the *Truth* series, is particularly resonant in this regard. Steve Rogers, through the miracle of the Super Soldier serum, becomes a walking, talking, (near) indestructible symbol of American courage, strength, and virtue.[2] To place a black man in this uniform calls into question those virtues and makes many things we would rather not see, such as the whiteness of American heroism, visible.

Truth, I argue, tells a superhero story from a black point of view, and that point of view provides an opportunity to look at the role that race plays in readers' interpretations of superhero comics and the role that race plays in this particular story. In this chapter I am interested in answering three questions: Why is a black point of view so disruptive to a superhero narrative? What is revealed when we tell a superhero story from a black point of view? And, finally, what happens when this black point of view becomes canonized?

Comics Are Supposed to Be Fun

Readers bring very specific formal and generic expectations to a superhero comic book. Readers expect comic books to be "light" entertainment. Small-group participants in Naomi R. Rockler's study of black and white readers' interpretation of comic strips confirmed this expectation. Said one participant, "Comics are supposed to be fun" (Rockler 412). In particular these readers, who were looking at two strips, *Jump Start* and *Boondocks*, both drawn by black men and featuring blacks as main characters, rejected the possibility that a comic strip was the appropriate venue for any discussion of race. Interestingly, particularly when thinking about superhero comics, the white readers felt that race was too politically charged an issue to inflict on the comics form. Their "concerns reflected a desire that comic strips be escapist and deflect attention from uncomfortable topics such as racism" (Rockler 412). Black readers, on the other hand, felt the form was too insignificant to do the subject of race justice.

Readers' expectations of the form are important to take into consideration because of the way the form works. In the seminal *Understanding Comics* (1993), Scott McCloud attempts to provide a theory of comics, an explanation of the formal characteristics that distinguish comics from other written and visual forms. Perhaps the most useful term/concept he offers is "closure," the thing that happens in the "gutter," that is, the space between comics panels. For McCloud closure is crucial because only a fraction of the action in any given comic occurs on the page. The rest happens in the gutter. The reader, according to McCloud, has to supply the missing action. For instance, if one panel shows a close-up of a gun being fired and the next panel shows an image of a woman screaming in horror, the reader must fill in the violent act. If one panel shows the sun low on the horizon and the next shows a starry night, the reader fills in the actual sunset. While closure in electronic media is "continuous, largely involuntary, and virtually imperceptible," closure in comics is "far from continuous and anything but involuntary" (68). McCloud goes on, "Closure in comics fosters an intimacy surpassed by the written word, a silent, secret contract between creator and audience. How the creator honors that contract is a matter of both art and craft" (69). This idea of a "contract" is crucial to beginning to understand how race can be so disruptive to the superhero narrative. If readers have expectations of the comics form, then they certainly also have expectations of the superhero genre. These expectations are driven, at least in part, by this "contract" between creator(s) and readers.

Jeffrey Brown's book-length study *Black Superheroes, Milestone Comics, and Their Fans* (2001) considers this contract important in theorizing the reading practices of superhero-comic readers. Rather than trying to determine whether these readers interpret with or against the hegemonic grain, Brown instead posits that for the "devoted comic book fan interpretation is a complex process shaped by inter- and intratextual information shared with, and about, other fans and the creators themselves" (2). Because information about individual characters and titles, about the history of particular universes, about creators and behind-the-scenes business practices is shared between fans, creators, and publishers, a kind of contract develops. Each party has expectations of what the others bring to the genre, and fulfillment of these expectations plays into readers' interpretation of any given superhero story: "Through contact at conventions and comic book specialty stores and with fanzines, electronic bulletin boards and, monthly letters-to-the-editor columns, readers can feel like active participators in the medium's construction. For comic book fans, interpretation of meaning does not necessitate a counter-hegemonic stance against monolithic ideologies but often a form of negotiated understanding" (Brown 92). While Brown's theory of readers' interpretive strategies rightly pushes us out of the complicit/resistant binary, his conceptualization of the "negotiated understanding" that happens when the expectations of readers, creators, and publishers are met and his insistence that comics culture's "social infrastructure" (92) plays the most significant role in readers' interpretation of texts raises some questions. Namely, what happens to the readers who are marginalized by dominant "monolithic ideologies" or whose experiences do not necessarily make up the "social infrastructure" of comics fandom? What expectations do these readers bring to the superhero comic? For, while fandom can certainly be a welcoming and nurturing space for all those, regardless of race, gender, sexual orientation, and so on, with fannish interest in any given media product, it is nevertheless still a culture in which people of color, women, gays, and so on long for stories and characters that reflect their experiences. Before tackling this issue, however, let me say a little more about expectations in the superhero genre.

It goes without saying that the stories in comics are fantasies. But they are a very particular kind of fantasy, one that posits the ability of an ordinary citizen to become an extraordinary hero, all in a world that looks remarkably like our own. Superman may be a superpowered alien from a distant planet, but his superhuman feats happen on the streets, and in the skies, of Metropolis, USA. Daredevil may have superhuman reflexes and the ability to battle crime bosses despite his blindness, but he does so in Hell's Kitchen. Superhero comics are full of men (and the occasional woman) who represent the "ultimate power fantasy" invariably wrapped up in an "idealized image of heroism that [is] explicitly honest, law abiding, chaste, excessively masculine, and above all, white" (Brown 3). So when a reader comes to a superhero comic, he typically does not want a Batman who has teamed up with the Joker or a Peter Parker who is sleeping his way through the female population of Empire University or a Green Lantern who is afraid of a fight. Nor, it seems, does he want a character who is black. In the case of *Truth*, it seems it is the racial aspect of the story rather than the retconning of Captain America's origin that constitutes the more grievous breach of contract. As the white readers in Rockler's study and many of the readers in Brown's book state, the issue of race does not belong in comic books. The fans in Brown's book were particularly wary of "black" comic books because of their knowledge of past attempts at black superheroes. Perceiving these attempts as poorly done and/or overly politicized, fans were skeptical that the new black superheroes from Milestone would live up to their expectations, that is, that they would fulfill the terms of the contract. Beyond this, though, is readers' assumption that black equals political and that political equals bad or, at least, unentertaining, art. As Brown writes, "If mass-produced texts appear to be too politically informed they are often ignored as merely ideological preaching, complaining, or propaganda" (55).

And yet black readers long for black superheroes (as female readers long for female heroes and gay readers long for gay heroes, and so on), despite their knowledge of and participation in the "social infrastructure" of comics fandom. What accounts for this? I argue that black fans, and other fans marginalized by the "negotiated understanding" created from the shared "intra- and intertextual information" of comics fandom, bring other interpretive frames to superhero comics. In the case of black fans, and pertinent to this discussion of *Truth*, I argue that race cognizance[3] plays a crucial role in black fans' interpretation of superhero comics and accounts for their desire for nonwhite heroes to fight alongside existing heroes. The idealized fantasy that Brown describes is, even if readers and creators read it as nonraced, the very antithesis of popular conceptions of blackness. Black men, in the popular American imagination, are often read as hypersexual, criminal, and dishonest, and their excessive masculinity is read as transgressive rather than heroic. (Think of popular rap artists or athletes who would be decidedly out of place in a superhero's costume for just these reasons.) The ways that the idealized fantasy of the superhero reinforces particular racist constructions of blackness may be invisible, and thereby irrelevant, to nonblack readers because race cognizance is not one of the interpretive frames they use when reading comic books. For many black readers, as the repeated desire for black superheroes suggests, race cognizance is always at play in reading, and when a superhero story such as *Truth* employs race cognizance, that is, a black point of view, it is hard for fans to maintain the raceless fantasy that the genre depends on.

Red, White, and Black

The plot of *Truth* follows a group of black soldiers as they are subjected to the cruel and inhumane experiments of the U.S. government's Super Soldier program. They go out on several missions in the European theater of World War II, though their existence is never acknowledged by the government, which prefers the all-American Steve Rogers to be the face of the American fighting man. In the end, only one of the black soldiers, Isaiah Bradley, survives. His last mission finds him deep inside Nazi Germany in a stolen Captain America uniform.

It is important to note that the primary creators involved in this story—writer Robert Morales, artist Kyle Baker, and editor Axel Alonso—were not necessarily attempting to write a story with a black point of view. They were, however, attempting to tell a different kind of superhero story. The cover of the first issue, which features the silhouetted profile of a black man with a bandanna tied around his head and a large white star on his chest against a background of red and white stripes (no action shot here), announces its difference right away. *Truth* is a superhero origin story of a hero who no longer exists by the book's end. It is the story of a group of men rather than a lone individual. And it is a story firmly rooted in American racial history. Alonso told an interviewer, "I thought it would be a really interesting way to use the character to tell a larger story, a chapter of American history. [We used] *Captain America* as a metaphor for America itself" (Carpenter 54). Much of the World War II backdrop of the story is informed by Morales's black-history research at the Schomburg Center in New York. This research is particularly important because of the editorial decision to have the story adhere as closely to the Tuskegee experiments as possible (Carpenter 55).

As a result of this historical research, *Truth* opens in July 1940 with newly-weds Isaiah and Faith Bradley enjoying Negro Week at the World's Fair in New York and having their picture taken in front of Augusta Savage's 1939 sculpture *The Harp*. The effect of this opening is twofold. First, it places the story in a world and a historical moment that we recognize as real and as relevant to the Captain America mythos. We are in Marvel's New York, and we are positioned in time just before a scrawny fine-arts student named Steve Rogers will be turned away by army recruiters. These are facts that the narrative assumes readers know and facts that the creators employ to fulfill the contract of this Captain America story.

But there are other relevant facts in this opening. The sculpture the newly-weds are photographed in front of is not only a seminal work of African American art but also a reference to a very well-known African American poem/song. Savage's sculpture was inspired by James Weldon Johnson's 1900 "Lift Every Voice and Sing," popularly known as the "Negro National Anthem." The song/poem has been associated with black social and political activism throughout the twentieth century. To reinforce the characterization of the Bradleys as activists, or at least as living in a world informed by black activism, the first words that Faith speaks are to inform her husband of a speech being given by W.E.B. Du Bois at the fair. When Isaiah asks what he will talk about, Faith replies, "Oh, it's something about how Negroes have to learn their place, how we have to give up on our hopes to ourselves . . . you know how he is." (Morales and Baker 1:4) This is followed by two panels: the first shows Isaiah scowling down at a defiant Faith; the second shows them laughing uproariously at the idea of Du Bois counseling blacks to "learn their place." And then, as if to remind the Bradleys, and the readers, of exactly what their place is, the very next page shows them being barred from the "Amusement Area" of the fair because the white women dancing there do not like black men in the audience; they do not like "being looked at like they're animals" (1:6).

If Faith and Isaiah's presence at the 1940 World Fair places them firmly in Marvel's New York and Captain America's mythos, then Savage's sculpture, the allusions to Du Bois and Johnson's poem, and the segregated "Amusement Arena" places us firmly in a black point of view. The details lifted straight from black history are offered with no explanation, as if the readers would be as familiar with Du Bois's argument about civil rights as they would be with Captain America's World War II origins. From this point of view, a black point of view, race and American racial history are relevant to the story and produce, perhaps, a different vision of the United States than we might otherwise find in a main-stream superhero book.

As Christian Davenport points out in a 1998 article, "Cynicism, a lack of trust and belief in the efficacy of the existing political-economic system is pervasive in the African-American community." While we will meet characters who are more cynical and distrusting later in the series, that Faith and Isaiah, an otherwise happy and hopeful couple, are confronted so randomly with the cruelty of American racism makes this kind of cruelty part and parcel of lives and, consequently, part and parcel of the *Truth*. We will not be able to ignore race in this story.

Compelling, too, in this first issue is the diversity of black experience represented. While Isaiah and Faith are educated and middle class, the next character we meet, Maurice Canfield, is first seen addressing his parents' butler on the steps of his impressive Philadelphia home. Rather than a story of optimism tempered with the knowledge of racial injustice and threatened by racist practices that we see with Isaiah and Faith, Canfield's story of is one of a deep commitment to progressive politics masquerading as privileged indifference.

When Canfield arrives home in the middle of the night in December 1940, his suit is disheveled, and his face is bloodied, swollen, and bruised. We learn that Canfield, along with a Jewish colleague, has been attempting to organize stevedores in Newark. His mother, who describes her son as an "atheist" and a "socialist," wonders what his father will do when he sees Canfield. Canfield replies,

> I would expect Father to digest this with his usual stoic compassion. In any event, these fellows in Newark did not have Father's sturdy constitution. Listening to a Negro and a Jew give them counsel about their economic survival—let alone their social responsibilities—proved too much for the lads. And one of them brought the meeting to a swift conclusion with a stream of invective—much of it about you actually—culminating with "I never heard brotherhood meant I had to end my day of toil consorting with kikes and jigs." (1:14)

When his mother, with a defeated sigh, asks what he said in response, Canfield, mischievous smirk peeking through his swollen face, says that he "opined as the likelihood of such association throughout his lineage. Yes" (1:14).

The scene is comical and familiar to comic book readers. Maurice Canfield is exactly the kind of character whose hubris becomes his downfall in superhero books (think of the villains in Spider-Man's rogue gallery or Victor von Doom) or who will be able to use his privilege and wealth in his superhero cause (Bruce Wayne, Oliver Queen, Tony Stark). Indeed, Brent Staples, writing about the first issue of the series, places his bet on Maurice ultimately donning the Captain America uniform for precisely these reasons. Canfield, though, is also a black man who fears that this relative privilege has been bought with the suffering of other black people. "I don't want a fortune based on Negroes that are compelled to lighten their skins and straighten their hair. Especially when they turn around and take their self-hatred out on me" (1:17). As with Faith and Isaiah, Canfield feels the effects of America's racial hierarchy, though not in the same way.

The final character we are introduced to in the first issue is Sgt. Luke Evans. In June 1941 Evans tells an old friend, a pickpocket just back from a six-year stint in jail, the story of how he got demoted from captain. (He shoved an officer in an altercation over the wrongful death of a black MP.) The entire scene takes place in a smoky, run-down pool hall, complete with seemingly shady characters looking on. Evans is angry and frustrated but also resigned. He shoots pool in his uniform and gives no suggestion that he will leave the army. When his friend says, "That's a bad break man," Evans deadpans, "It is what is. Maybe I'll make Captain again in another seventeen years" (1:29). Evans possesses neither the Bradleys' optimism nor Canfield's desire to make it right. Evans has resigned himself to a racist world, believing that there is very little he can do to change it.

These three men anchor this story (it is through their experiences that we learn about the army experiment and its consequences) and give us a brief snapshot of the variety of ways black men found themselves enlisted in the U.S. military during World War II. Issue 1 ends with the December 1941 bombing of Pearl Harbor. Sgt. Evans hears the news being shouted from the street as he prepares to commit suicide. The news gives him a reason to live. "Well, all right," he says as he puts away his gun and pours himself a drink (33). Canfield, on trial for demonstrating against the war in January 1942, is given the choice, because he is from a respected family, of doing jail time or enlisting. And in February 1942 we see, against a backdrop of the New York harbor complete with the Statue of Liberty, Isaiah, in his army uniform, kissing a pregnant Faith good-bye (see fig. 6.1). Whether he has been drafted or enlisted is unclear; his grin, however, is full of optimism. The final words of the panel's voice-over, "That was the first of the worst days of my life," belie this optimism. While we know the voice (we will discover in issue 5 that the story's narrator is Faith) is referring to the army experiments that we know are coming, it could just as easily

6.1 *Truth*: Isaiah kissing his pregnant wife good-bye, complete with the Statue of Liberty in the background.

be referring to the harsh and sometimes cruel treatment experienced by black soldiers during World War II.[4]

Again, this is a superhero story with a black point of view that not only fulfills its "contract" by following the conventions of the genre and employing our knowledge of the Captain America canon but also employs American racial history to bring complexity and nuance to an otherwise formulaic genre. This is particularly true once the story moves to the experiments and the men's experiences in the army. The cover of the second issue features a medium shot of a large group of faceless black men dressed in army uniforms behind a set of red, vertical stripes that suggest both the American flag and prison bars. This cover highlights an important fact in this story: the men in *Truth* are subject to the Super Soldier program because they are part of an "inferior" race but also because they are soldiers. They are doubly expendable. By employing a black point of view, *Truth* revises the story we all know about Dr. Reinstein's efforts to create a supersoldier to fight the Nazis. Rather than the benign, brilliant scientist trying desperately to complete his formula before the Nazis find him, we instead have a morally ambiguous Reinstein who wants to test his early versions of the formula on a handful of black soldiers (precisely because they are black and, therefore, expendable) and who is willing to stand by while hundreds of other black soldiers are killed in cold blood to protect the secrecy of the program. Morales has this to say about the story:

> This is a story about people getting fucked and it's only incidental that they're getting fucked because they're Black. They're getting fucked because that's what happens in war. [Still], there's a racial reality to the way Blacks were [treated] during the war that people can forget now.
>
> People were sacrificed. Was it worth [it to sacrifice] a group of Blacks for the rest of society? [When] you get inducted into the Army, you're property whether you're Black or White, Italian [or] Irish. It doesn't matter. You're there for somebody to throw you at something. . . . And if you don't go, people will shoot you . . . that's the greater reality. (Carpenter 56)

Compare these soldiers' stories to that of Logan/Wolverine. While Wolverine's origins are too detailed and complex to get into here, the basic points are pertinent: the Canadian government, as part of the Weapon X program, subjected Logan, apparently a soldier, to brutal experiments that ultimately replaced his entire skeleton with adamantium. The cruelty of these experiments, and Logan's lack of memory of them, is central to Wolverine's mythos. The experiments in *Truth* are of the same sort; indeed, as we will discover as more and more is revealed about the Weapon X program, these experiments are exactly the same: attempts by governments to create supersoldiers. While I would argue with Morales that it is not at all incidental that these characters are black, I agree that they do not suffer because of their blackness alone. But again, here is where this superhero story with a black point of view does an excellent job of portraying the complexity of black experience. While race certainly does play a role in the way blacks experience the world, it is only one of the experiences. The black men in *Truth* are not simply black. They are also men, husbands, sons, lovers, soldiers, fathers, pool sharks, political activists, and superheroes. All of these roles are informed by race, but they are also, importantly, informed by all the others. This is to say, Isaiah's understanding of himself as a soldier is as much about his understanding of himself as a black man as it is about his understanding of himself as a husband.

Hitler discovers Isaiah's complex understanding of himself in issue 6 when he attempts to persuade a captured Isaiah, decked out in the red, white, and blue of Captain America, to join with the Nazis. Hitler compares himself to the wrongly accused Scottsboro Boys[5] and tells Isaiah that he has no quarrel with the Negro people. He asks Isaiah, "Why do your people fight for them?" and promises to help "free your people when the time comes" (6:20). This is a typical supervillain tactic, attempting to convince the hero to abandon his cause and join the ranks of the villainous. We know, of course, that the hero will never join because the cause for which he fights is righteous and true and superior to anything the villain might offer. What possible argument, for instance, could Lex Luthor make to convince Superman to abandon "truth, justice, and the American way"? Here, though, because *Truth* employs blackness to disrupt the superhero narrative, it would be perfectly reasonable, even if disappointing, if Isaiah, after all that has happened to him and his friends, joined Hitler. But Isaiah is not just an aggrieved black man and a soldier who has been treated cruelly. He is also Faith's husband. After Hitler's offer, Isaiah pauses a moment to think. The next panel is a close-up of his face, his head now bald and several times its original size because of the supersoldier serum. With something of the optimism and playfulness from issue 1 dancing in his eyes, he answers Hitler. "Guys, no," he says. "My wife would kill me" (6:20).

Can a Black Point of View Become Canonized?

Though *Truth* reads like a "What If ?" story (Marvel's noncontinuity, alternative-canon one-shots), it is in fact Marvel canon. Isaiah Bradley, the only one of the black soldiers still alive by the story's end, was an honored guest at Storm and T'Challa's wedding, and his grandson is a member of the Young Avengers. The experiments that he is subject to are an official part of the history of the Weapon X program. But what does it mean for this superhero story with a black point of view to become part of Marvel's regular continuity? Does it change the nature of the story? Is the idealized fantasy revised in any way? Do we come to think any differently about Steve Rogers / Captain America?

What happens, in fact, is that Isaiah Bradley's voice—and, I argue, his whole story—becomes marginal, and Steve Rogers is placed back at the narrative center. In issue 5, after all the members of Isaiah's unit have met various deaths, each related to the experiments they have all undergone, Isaiah, now in a Captain American uniform complete with a shield that features the Double V for Victory symbol[6] rather than the red, white, and blue flag theme, is sent on a suicide mission to liberate the prisoners in the Schwarzebitte concentration camp (see fig. 6.2). There he encounters Nazi experiments that very much resemble

6.2 Isaiah's Captain America uniform accompanied by a shield with the Double V for Victory symbol.

Reinstein's. When he tries to free the women from this camp, in a scene that echoes the earlier scene at the Amusement Area, they attack him as a monster come to rape them, which allows the camp guards to capture him. Throughout this issue, a voice-over tells the story. We assume it is Isaiah's voice until the very end, when it begins to encourage Isaiah to run away: "just think of me and our little girl" (5:24). The last page reveals Faith sitting at her kitchen table in present-day New York talking to Steve Rogers, in his Captain American uniform. Though the action in this issue suggests that Isaiah dies at Schwarzebitte, Faith assures Rogers that he is very much alive. The last two issues of the series, presumably, will reveal how Isaiah survived and answer the question of why he is no longer Captain America.

These questions are answered through Steve Rogers rather than Isaiah. We discover in issue 6 that Rogers had been completely ignorant of the Super Soldier program and its experiments before he became a test subject. He knew of no other soldier who had worn the Captain America uniform and certainly knew nothing of the incredible, murderous lengths to which the army and the U.S. government went to sweep all of this under the rug. Steve Rogers is an innocent in all of this, and he is allowed to remain innocent in the end because Isaiah is silenced, literally and figuratively.

After being smuggled out of Germany by the Red Ball Express,[7] Isaiah returns to the United States and is court-martialed for stealing Captain America's uniform. He serves seventeen years before being pardoned by President Eisenhower and sworn to secrecy. "Now here's the worst of it," Faith tells Rogers. "The early stages of what made you? It left my husband sterile, and after so many years of confined neglect, his brain slowly deteriorated. . . . He's a little boy now—he really can't even talk" (2:18). When Steve Rogers finally meets Isaiah, he does his "duty" and returns the now tattered and torn Captain America uniform that Isaiah wore during the war. Isaiah grins simply throughout the whole exchange, and the last image of the comic is the two of them standing shoulder to shoulder in their uniforms, posing for a picture.

That Alonso and Morales intended this ending to be an allusion to Muhammad Ali, because it represented a "greater tragedy than any of the other proposed endings," is telling (Carpenter 55). While Ali once represented virile, violent black hypermasculinity, the man we now see occasionally on television is none of these things. Parkinson's has stripped him of those traits that once made his blackness so threatening, and now he has become something of a national mascot. Rather than having to account for the ways in which the U.S. government and media at one time worked to harass and persecute Ali, we can instead sympathize with his plight and admire the strength it takes to get through it.

The same is true of Isaiah in *Truth*. He represents absolutely no threat to Steve Rogers, the status quo, or the superhero genre. He can never again be Captain America or any other hero. No one will really be punished for the havoc wreaked in this man's life. And Steve Rogers can remain the shining example of

American ideals because he is sufficiently appalled by this story and he does the right thing in the end. Rogers can now go back to the business of superheroing, the domain of the usual comic book superhero, because Isaiah will never be anything other than a mindless child.

Marc Singer notes that "the handling of race is forever caught between the [superhero] genre's most radical impulses and its most conservative ones" (110). I think this is especially true in *Truth*. Alonso wondered why "so many people have assumed the story will besmirch the integrity of Captain America. If Captain America is analogous to America itself, then why wouldn't a more complex understanding of his origin contribute to and deepen his mythology?" (Singer 110). It is to Alonso's credit that he perceives exploring American racial history through Captain America as an opportunity to "deepen" Captain America's mythology, despite the fact that an explicit treatment of race is often the death knell for a superhero comic. Here Marvel seems to give in to a radical impulse, the impulse to have Captain America be "analogous" not only to those parts of America we hold dear (democracy, rugged individualism, freedom) but also to those parts we would rather forget or ignore (systemic racism, violence, disregard for human life).

Yet it is the conservative impulse, the impulse to maintain the status quo, that ultimately wins out. If superheroes have been a way for us to "express popular longings to challenge and overcome the potentially atomizing, rationalizing, dehumanizing, and oppressive forces of urban industrial life," then the inability to attach a black face to these "longings" is a tremendous failure of imagination (Regalado 85). For it is not simply the demands of the story that makes it impossible for there to be two Captain Americas. It is also unwillingness to confront, for any length of time, our worse selves. As the readers in Brown's and Rockler's studies suggest, injecting race into comics disrupts the fantasy, inserts politics where politics ought not be, and makes comics too much like work and school and not enough like fun. The result of this failure of imagination? A neutered Isaiah Bradley and reification of an "idealized image of heroism that [is] explicitly honest, law abiding, chaste, excessively masculine, and above all, white" (Brown 3).

Because the conservative impulse wins out in *Truth*, black people, particularly black men, remain ideological pornographic objects. Patricia Williams defines pornography as a "habit of thinking" that has no necessary connection to sex but rather "permits the imagination of the voyeur to indulge in auto-sensation that obliterates the subjectivity of the observed. A habit of thinking that allows the self-generated sensation to substitute for interaction with a whole other human being, to substitute for listening or conversing or caring. . . . The object is pacified, a malleable 'thing' upon which to project" (123). This is exactly the state in which we find Isaiah at the end of *Truth*—a pacified figure on whom Steve Rogers and the reader can project innocence and absolution. The lifelong consequences of what Isaiah experiences are of little interest in the end because the story, ultimately, is not about Isaiah. The narrative satisfies us that none of this has been Captain America's (or our) fault and that we can get back to business as usual, namely, marginalizing the stories and voices of black characters and, I would argue, black readers.

While Marvel may have intended to deepen the mythology and complexity of Captain America by using race to disrupt the superhero narrative, it ultimately succeeds instead in demonstrating the genre's ideological limits.

Notes

1   There are, arguably, several successful second-string black superheroes in the Marvel and DC universes. Firestorm and Black Lightning are current members of the Justice League, and Steel acted as a Superman stand-in after that character's death. Storm is one of the more popular members of Marvel's X-Men (made more so by Halle Berry's portrayal in the movie franchise), and Luke Cage is currently experiencing a revival in the Marvel titles penned by Brian Michael Bendis. And Black Panther once again has his own title, for a time written by the director and BET entertainment head Reginald Hudlin. Despite the popularity and persistence of these characters, none of them command the visibility and following of marquee characters such as Spider-Man, Batman, Superman, or Wolverine.

2   It is difficult to write about Steve Rogers as the indestructible icon of American idealism without acknowledging the fact that Rogers, in current Marvel continuity, is dead. Indeed, his death comes in the wake of his defense of American ideals against people, in many cases, good friends, working as agents of the government. The evolution of Steve Rogers's Captain America post-9/11, from a symbol of American idealism, if not the American government, to someone almost always at intense ideological odds with that same government, would make an interesting study all on its own.

3   Naomi R. Rockler uses the concept of race cognizance to discuss readers who employ race in their interpretive strategies. The "terministic screen of race cognizance serves as a color filter that highlights or selects the ways race makes a difference in people's lives and challenges White privilege" (403).

4   For more on the experiences of black soldiers in World War II, see Astor; Morehouse.

5   In 1931 nine young black men, ranging in age from thirteen to twenty-one, were charged with the gang rape of two white women on a freight train. Tried and sentenced to death in Scottsboro, Alabama, they became a cause célèbre as many people believed they were framed and wrongfully convicted by an all-white jury.

6   In 1941 the *Pittsburgh Courier* began a "muckraking" campaign for black civil rights, seizing on the iconography of the Allies' "V" for victory. The "double V" for victory indicated a desire for an Allied victory and a desire for black liberation.

7   The Red Ball Express was an enormous convoy system created by Allied forces to supply their forces moving through Europe after the breakout from Normandy. Approximately 75 percent of the drivers in the Red Ball Express were black soldiers attached to American units but unable, because of racial discrimination, to serve on the front line.

Works Cited

Astor, Gerald. *Right to Fight: A History of African Americans in the Military*. Boston: Da Capo, 2001.

Brown, Jeffrey A. *Black Superheroes, Milestone Comics, and Their Fans*. Jackson: University Press of Mississippi, 2001.

Carpenter, Stanford W. "Truth Be Told: Authorship and the Creation of the Black Captain America." *Comics as Philosophy*. Ed. Jeff McLaughlin. Jackson: University Press of Mississippi, 2005. 46–62.

Davenport, Christian. "The Brother Might Be Made of Steel, but He Sure Ain't Super . . . Man." *Other Voices: The (e)Journal of Cultural Criticism* 1.2 (1998). Web. http://www.othervoices.org/1.2/cdavenport/steel.php. Accessed 31 Aug. 2012.

McCloud, Scott. *Understanding Comics*. Northampton, MA: Kitchen Sink, 1993.

Medved, Michael. "Captain America, Traitor? The Comic-Book Hero Goes Anti-American." *National Review Online* 4 Apr. 2003. Web. http://www.nationalreview.com/articles/206451/captain-america-traitor/michael-medved. Accessed 12 Nov. 2009.

Morales, Robert (writer), and Kyle Baker (artist). *Truth: Red, White, & Black*. Nos. 1–7. New York: Marvel Comics, 2002–2003.

Morehouse, Maggi M. *Fighting in the Jim Crow Army: Black Men and Women Remember World War II*. Lanham, MD: Rowman and Littlefield, 2006.

Regalado, Aldo. "Modernity, Race, and the American Superhero." *Comics as Philosophy*. Ed. Jeff McLaughlin. Jackson: University Press of Mississippi, 2005. 84–99.

Rockler, Naomi R. "Race, Whiteness, 'Lightness,' and Relevance: African American and European American Interpretations of *Jump Start* and *The Boondocks*." *Critical Studies in Media Communication* 19.4 (Dec. 2002): 399–418.

Sinclair, Tom. "Black in Action." *Entertainment Weekly* 22 Nov. 2002. Web. http://www.ew.com/ew/article/0,,390672,00.html. Accessed 12 Jan. 2009

Singer, Marc. "'Black Skins' and White Masks: Comic Books and the Secret of Race." *African American Review* 36.1 (2002): 107–119.

Staples, Brent. "Reliving World War II with a Captain America of a Different Color." *New York Times* 1 Dec. 2002. Web. http://www.nytimes.com/2002/12/01/opinion/editorial-observer-reliving-world-war-ii-with-captain-america-different-color.html. Accessed 12 Nov. 2009.

Williams, Patricia. *The Rooster's Egg: On the Persistence of Prejudice*. Cambridge, MA: Harvard University Press, 1995.

Chapter 7

Drawn into Dialogue

• • • • • • • • • • • • • • • • • • • •

Comic Book Culture and
the Scene of Controversy in
Milestone Media's *Icon*

ANDRE CARRINGTON

Comic books occupy a vexed position in the popular culture of the United States. In a century that saw the popularization and critical veneration of emerging forms such as film and television, the awkward situation of comics as both print and visual media often left their innovations and their retrograde elements alike on the shelf. Numerous academic studies have brought the political and economic dimensions of comic book publishing to critical attention in recent years, while trend-setting works including Scott McCloud's comic about comics, *Understanding Comics*, and the text to which it paid homage, Will Eisner's *Comics and Sequential Art*, considered comics as a visual form with the capacity to tell stories in unique ways. Among all the visual iconographies that comics contributed to popular culture in the twentieth-century United States, the most recognizable is the figure of the superhero. In the following pages, I examine a revision to the comic book superhero narrative that took place in the 1990s—Milestone Media's *Icon*.

Milestone's intervention was peculiar in many ways. It was a black-owned company publishing comics about multiracial superheroes, carrying the well-known imprint of DC Comics, emblematic of both mainstream and alternative currents in the comics industry. Though Milestone has now ceased publishing ongoing series, its inimitable blend of strategies to satisfy the audience while challenging their racial, sexual, and class mores provides a generous archive for scholars of the recent history of popular media. From mid-1993 to early 1994, *Icon* posed a mounting controversy for the reading public with the revelation that the eponymous hero's fifteen-year-old sidekick, Raquel Ervin, known as Rocket, was pregnant and contemplating an abortion. In the particular sequence from *Icon* that I call "Rocket's Decision," Milestone's publishers and fans explored the form of superhero comics to greater depths while they called the normative conventions of the genre into question. This chapter focuses on the interests that readers and commentators voiced about the way *Icon* reconciled the figure of the superhero with the concerns of black women, youth, and other denizens of the urban United States represented by characters such as Icon and the Rocket. My reading of Rocket's Decision emphasizes the venues in which commentators weighed in on the story's political implications. In the fan correspondence printed in *Icon*, readers aired dissenting opinions over a story line that brought into comics a heightened awareness of the way that race complicates notions of sexuality and the conceptualization of setting. I argue that this correspondence documents the attempts of comic book publishers and readers to reconcile their varying political interests with the shared economic and aesthetic aims they bring to their consideration of the medium.

I argue that the serial, visual form in which the controversy of Rocket's Decision unfolds is paramount to *Icon*'s ability to make an impact on its fans. Through strategies inherent to the medium of comics, especially the letters page, *Icon* also lends credence to the notion that audiences play an active role in the interpretation of popular media. By considering a broad range of formal elements at work in *Icon*—the layout of pages, the content of panels, the rhetoric of dialogue, and the representation of fan correspondence on letters pages—I argue that Milestone's comics elucidate their commercial and political strategies for readers, rather than conveying them surreptitiously. The artful execution of Rocket's Decision outlines the central drama of *Icon*, as the protagonist, a budding writer, struggles to drive her own narrative. Rocket offers the rare example in popular culture of a black female character whose political consciousness takes shape in and through her literacy. Rocket's Decision inspires readers to criticize the politics of *Icon* as a text, portraying comics in particular and textuality in general as integral, rather than exceptional, to the cultural repertoire of black Americans in the 1990s.

Four-Color Americans

Black characters have existed in comics longer than superheroes have, appearing early and often as racist caricatures. Long before black characters began to show up with "black" in their names (Black Lightning, Black Manta), their titles referenced their subordinate relationship to whiteness in comics. A blackface caricature named Whitewash was the comic relief in a propagandist comic called *Young Allies* during World War II, and the sidekick of Will Eisner's brainchild, The Spirit, was a broad-lipped, dialect-spouting kid named Ebony White. A more enduring example of the loyal black ally is Captain America's erstwhile sidekick, The Falcon. Trina Robbins's study *The Great Women Superheroes* documents a trend in which female characters have usually appeared as the sole representatives of their gender in superhero teams. This is often the case for black characters as well, and thus black female characters have almost invariably been cast in supporting roles. Jackie Ormes's plucky heroine Torchy Brown, the first black female protagonist of a comic strip, was a notable exception. Marvel Comics' African heroine Storm, on the other hand, is a telling example of the dominant tendencies of ensemble casting in comics. During a revision of the familiar series *X-Men* in 1975, she became the single black female member of a new group featuring Canadian, Russian, German, Japanese, and Native American men.

Narratives of the black and/or female superhero as a team player promulgate a reductive politics of representation that puts minoritized characters on the page in order to support white male characters' claims to iconic status. Black and female characters frequently appear to buttress the notion that the white male superhero is the sine qua non of the idealism that white Americans spread throughout the globe. When Milestone Media's creators began to alter this trend, one of the ways they lent meaning to the role of a black female protagonist was to present her as an idealist in her own right, with her concerns at the center of the series. Thus *Icon* became known, by fans and publishers alike, as "Rocket's book." Jeffrey Brown's influential study *Black Superheroes, Milestone Comics, and Their Fans* notes that comics such as *Icon* presented alternative representations of masculinity in comics. Situating the Rocket in relation to an alternative representation of black masculinity while, at the same time, placing her in a relationship conventional to the superhero narrative meant that the series would foreground the problems germane to the representation of black and female comics characters in a familiar context: from the purview of the sidekick.

Icon was one of the first four titles released by Milestone Media in 1993. The company was founded by black comics innovators and a business leader, Derek Dingle, the once and future editor of *Black Enterprise*. Milestone enjoyed a unique distribution arrangement with DC Comics that made the smaller company's comics available to as many retailers as those of the larger one. Over the years that Milestone published comics regularly, it added additional titles and miniseries, maintained a presence on the comics convention circuit, marketed itself on the Internet, and solicited a low level of buzz throughout comics fandom for its comics portraying characters with different racial backgrounds, gender identities, and sexualities in a fictional East Coast city called Dakota.

Icon chronicles the adventures of young Raquel Ervin, a teenager who meets the wealthy black conservative Augustus Freeman IV when her friends attempt to rob his mansion. Raquel is astounded to see the knowledge in Augustus's library and nearly steals his computer, but her cohorts are deterred from the burglary attempt by Freeman's bulletproof skin and ability to fly. Little does she know that Augustus is an alien, marooned on Earth for over 150 years in disguise as an African American.

Raquel's estimable wit matches Augustus's power and influence. When she returns to Freeman's home in daylight, awestruck and inspired, she proposes that he become a superhero and a symbol to the people of Dakota and that he take her on as a sidekick. When Augustus queries the superhero name that Raquel has chosen for him ("Icon? What's that?"), she says, "It means like an example, or an ideal." Augustus responds, perhaps indicating that his question was about the connotations rather than the literal meaning of his ascribed role, "Actually, it's a symbol, something that stands for something else." The allocation of moments in the narrative to different panels on the comics page, like the

7.1 Augustus's eyes narrow after Raquel's clever retort in *Icon*.

editing of film footage from multiple camera angles into one scene, directs the reader to observe Augustus's eyes narrowing at Raquel's clever retort: "Oh yeah? What do you stand for?" (McDuffie, Helene, and Bright, *Icon* #1, 24).[1]

In this first issue, the series recounts Augustus's background in space and his time on Earth as the child of an enslaved woman in the southern United States. His experiences as a freedman made him a Republican in the nineteenth century, and his accumulated advantages have kept him a political conservative in the present. For the most part, however, *Icon* foregrounds Raquel's journey: in her words, to become a writer "like Toni Morrison" (McDuffie, Helene, and Bright, *Icon* #1, 14). Tension constantly arises between the two heroes as they fight those who prey on the less fortunate and undertake the challenge that falls to superheroes in many of Milestone's stories: to save humanity from its shortcomings. *Icon* portrays an abiding faith that humanity is basically good, alongside an understanding that people in constrained circumstances often make less-than-ideal decisions. Augustus's ability to make the best of his considerable personal resources and Raquel's aspiration to do the same by securing expanded opportunities provide two differing but convergent perspectives on their common interests. This first scene demonstrates that it is Raquel, as the principal narrator, who conveys her perspective on Icon as well as Icon's perspective on her.

The Politics of Juxtaposition

The literal unfolding of the narrative of Raquel's pregnancy from one page to the next constantly reassures readers that, rather than airing a political critique whose mode of dissemination is a secondary concern, Rocket's Decision extends the range of what the medium of comics can do, formally. At the end of *Icon* #3, in a scene depicting the moments after Icon and Rocket have saved the city, Raquel has a startling revelation for Icon and the reader: she is pregnant. Icon jumps to several conclusions with this announcement. First, he assumes she will have to curtail her work as a superhero during her pregnancy, then he presupposes that she will carry the pregnancy to term, by making two parallel statements: "You're pregnant, Raquel. You're going to have a baby" (McDuffie, Helene, and Bright, *Icon* #3, 76). The ensuing controversy will undo that conflation of the Rocket's present state with her destiny, as Raquel takes exception to the notion that her fate is scripted by Icon rather than the other way around.

The page facing the aforementioned scene is the issue's letters column. The four letters printed in the column that month are excited responses to *Icon* #1. Readers have only now seen the events of this issue; it is too early, even via telecommunications, for their reactions to appear in printed, excerpted form under the editor's masthead. The only reference to Raquel's pregnancy in the column, and the only clue to what will happen next, is a picture in the bottom right corner of the page with the caption, "ROCKET learns the awful truth!" ("Iconoclasts," in *Icon* #3). That picture is a preview of the next issue's cover featuring Raquel, in her costume, holding what discerning readers will recognize as a home pregnancy test. On the letters page, the editor has room to back-announce the events of the issue at hand, like a radio DJ. But despite the sensational developments just one page away, this letters column redirects current readers' attention back to previous issues of the series.

The elementary logic of reading comics is juxtaposition. The seemingly dissonant but in fact complementary form of juxtaposition presented by facing pages of narrative content (the story) and editorial commentary (the letters page) provides an exemplary site to observe how writers, artists, editors, and fans take part in the interpretation of comics through the process of reading them. This holds true as Rocket's Decision unfolds. Raquel delivers on the promise of the next issue's tantalizing cover, through juxtaposition. On the front cover, under the subtitle "THE RESULTS ARE IN," Raquel is wearing her costume, alone, with the object she is holding identified by the box that reads, "E.P.I. HOME PREG" (the box is cut off by the cover's edge). The suggestive texts on the cover—the subtitle, the costume, and the test in progress—build suspense. The cover prompts uninitiated and loyal readers alike to wonder, how can a superhero comic, especially this one, portray a pregnant black teenager?

In an introduction to the letters column, editor Matt Wayne indulges in his opportunity to extend the suspense of this momentous issue. Even though the test has proven positive, lending credence to Icon's summary assessment of Raquel's fate, Wayne asks, "IS THIS NORMAL? Do superheroes get pregnant? At 15? Not until now, they didn't. There's a whole lot of reality out there, and we thought it might be nice to bring it into our pages. SOME 15 year-olds do get pregnant (usually 15-year old GIRLS)" ("Iconoclasts," in Duffie, Helene, and Bright, *Icon* #4). Wayne's intimations on the letters page suggest that Raquel's pregnancy is a break with the genre, and he associates it instead with "reality." On the cover, the confluence of superheroics and pregnancy is simultaneous, juxtaposing two distinct sets of imagery that are presumably recognizable by two distinct sets of readers. Though some readers might recognize superhero costumes (this one in particular, if they have seen *Icon* and the Rocket before), they might not recognize a home pregnancy test. On the other hand, readers might be intrigued by the image of a young black woman with a pregnancy test but might find it unusual to observe an *illustration*, rather than a photograph, of a black woman and even less familiar to see her wearing spandex on her neck and gloves on her hands under the masthead of a comic book. Wayne's introduction to his column informs the reader that *Icon* has strained the boundaries of normal comic book fare, but that begs the question, why does pregnancy occur to readers of superhero comics as something out of the ordinary?

To answer a question with a question, note Tony Norman's prompting in an interview with Milestone's founders, including Denys Cowan and Derek

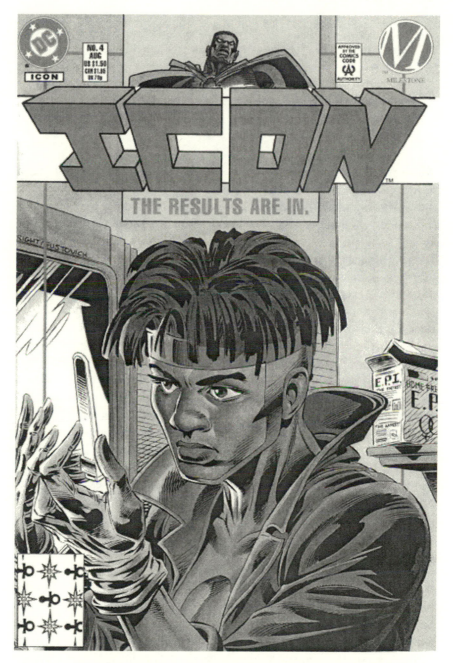

7.2 How can a superhero comic portray a pregnant black teenager?

Dingle, in the *Comics Journal*: "Is it possible that a comic book devoted to social realism, without the introduction of fantasmagoria or science fiction, can make it in the mainstream?"

> COWAN: I don't know. Somebody will do it if it can be done, but we're not doing that yet.
>
> NORMAN: Do you ever get the sense that people are looking towards you to do that, and, if they are disappointed, that might be the reason?
>
> DINGLE: I've certainly gotten that sense in this interview, but . . . [*laughter*]
> (Norman)

Wayne stated, "There's a whole lot of reality out there, and we thought it might be nice to bring it into our pages," implying that "reality" is normally foreign to the superhero genre. When Cowan insists that "we're not doing that" (a realistic comic book), he observes a measure of critical distance between Milestone comics and reality, in the same way that Wayne has indicated on the letters page. Dingle, Cowan, and Wayne all hold Milestone's comics to the standards of the superhero genre, and when the real world threatens to encroach on their pages, they frame it as an imposition the same way it appears to be throughout the rest of the comics industry. Dingle's reaction to Norman's line of questioning indicates that the notion that Milestone might not satisfy the genre expectations of superhero comics is a source of tension. The industry may well expect Milestone to eschew genre conventions for "reality" by setting and casting its comics in a less contrived fantasy world than other publishers do. Rather than the company undertaking the losing strategy of marketing nongenre comics, however, Milestone's characters, editors, and fans appear as surprised as the readers of other comics would be to see a diverse cast and setting in a superhero narrative. *Icon* meets their expectations but subtly revises them, by portraying Rocket's pregnancy in a series of installments, allowing the dissonance between the mundane and fantastic circumstances around her pregnancy to attenuate. Her centrality to the series makes it plausible for the topic of her pregnancy to follow the same gradual path to acceptance.

The Phantasmagoria of Choice

While the exposition of Rocket's Decision was aesthetically quite conventional for the medium, it was politically so novel that it required a conscientious editorial strategy. From issue #4 to issue #10, Matt Wayne's introductions to the letters page, "Iconoclasts," and the contents of the letters printed seem out of step with a plot that is nearing resolution. In *Icon* #7, the headline of "Iconoclasts" is, "ROCKET: *GREAT* WITH CHILD!" The off-color usage of "great," which promises a visibly pregnant rendition of Raquel's body, is intriguing. Its laudatory connotations yield a sense of excitement about Raquel's character development.

The headline leads to a diversion, however, indicating that Rocket's pregnancy is *great* for sales: "Y'know, if you only put a teenager with a home pregnancy test on the cover of a comic book, the letters will just pour in. The response to *ICON* #4 has got to be up there with the Silver Age gimmick of putting a really fat Superman or Lois Lane on the cover; the image is instantly intriguing. Don't be surprised if other companies start picking up on this, and twenty different pregnancy-test covers show up at once!" ("Iconoclasts," in Duffie, Helene, and Bright, *Icon* #7). As in issue #4, the letters column suspends consideration of the content of the current issue and refers to a past issue instead. Wayne's tongue-in-cheek comparison between pregnant Raquel and fat Superman becomes still more irreverent when he invokes the Silver Age, a term that describes a renaissance of superhero comics in the third quarter of the twentieth century. The reference draws readers' attention further away from the content of the issue that they have just read and back to the covers of comics past and present. The impertinence of this issue's "Iconoclasts" is all the more striking because under its own cover, which depicts Rocket in tears and promises "Rocket's Decision" with its subtitle, Raquel gets a decisive test at a doctor's office.

This scene portrays the tension between "reality" and genre cited by the men in charge of Milestone, but it was cowritten by one of the few women at the company, Erica Helene. It comes to light on this page that the topic of pregnancy is more amenable to the form of superhero comics than its readers had previously thought. Commentators such as Tony Norman and, according to the incredulous tone of Wayne's editorial introductions, *Icon*'s readers viewed "reality" as an imposition. If the line between "social realism" and "fantasmagoria or science fiction" is a matter of technical, scientific language, Raquel's conversation with her doctor upends traditional notions of what kind of words belong on either side of that line. The doctor utilizes medically appropriate terminology by first noting that the diagnostic Raquel has undergone detects an organ (the placenta) and not a viable fetus; on the following page, she names the specific procedure Raquel might undertake (aspiration) and advises Raquel that she is a matter of "weeks" pregnant, thereby eschewing the more colloquial and less diagnostically useful month-to-month chronology. A "real," nonscientific discussion of pregnancy might consist of ambiguous terminology, euphemisms, and category errors: using terms such as "baby" instead of "placenta," "kill" to refer to an individual life that had already begun instead of "terminate," referring to a process, and "months" instead of "weeks." "Fantasmagoria," on the other hand, invokes specific and unfamiliar terms. Writers and critics of science fiction would call this specialized rhetoric "hard science," if it were not also the language of women's health. The line between reality and fantasmagoria, then, is a matter of point of view, and Raquel's point of view in this scene is visibly perturbed but ultimately grounded in reality through her doctor's precision and care.

In fact, the way Norman invokes "fantasmagoria" in his interview with Milestone's founders, Anglicizing its spelling to indicate its close kinship with the

7.3 *Icon*: Raquel gets a decisive test at the doctor's office.

Anglo–North American lexicon of science fiction, the term loses its mystifying connotations and instead suggests its opposite: familiarity. If the paranormal is usually normal in superhero comics, but a frank discussion on a strange (and therefore welcome?) topic such as pregnancy seems so very abnormal as to be out of place even in such a credulous venue, we must ask, why are the dazed readers in the "real" world laboring under the illusion that pregnancy is a rare phenomenon while the sobered characters in the fictional one are aware of their situation? The state-sanctioned occlusion of information that this scene portrays suggests one reason that many readers have misconceptions about the decisions people in Raquel's circumstances face.

Reading Rocket's Decision

Icon's privileged misconception that he was in charge of telling Raquel's story, instead of the other way around, led him to jump to the conclusion that Raquel was going to give birth when her pregnancy had barely begun. In the situation at hand, however, the same privileged misconception, this time made by the state, structures Raquel's conversation with her doctor. When the doctor says, "This is a government-funded clinic. It's illegal for me to tell you what I'm going to," she is citing a prevailing interpretation of the Public Health Service Act, affirmed in the 1991 Supreme Court case *Rust v. Sullivan* (Duffie, Helene, and Bright, *Icon* #7, 160). Despite numerous challenges, it was illegal to dispense advice about abortion in federally funded family planning clinics in the United States prior to Bill Clinton's lifting the domestic gag rule by executive order in January 1993 (Pertman). Thus it appears that *Icon* #7, with a cover date of November 1993, was conceptualized and illustrated some time earlier. This anachronism renders Rocket's Decision a compelling departure from "reality" at the moment when the story is published, making it all the more precise to read this scene in its speculative genre context. For although the political subtext of Rocket's Decision has changed by the time we read about it, our ability to understand the story's implications historically reappears through the process of reading.

In the panel featuring a close-up on Raquel's face, her cartoonishly expressive eyes suggesting genuine curiosity, against a background comparatively warmed by the earth tones of the doctor's office, Raquel asks, "What if I don't want to have the baby?" (160) In the next "panel," however, it seems as though the doctor and Raquel have slipped out of place, without the other panels' clearly defined borders, with only a horizontal line at both characters' feet indicating that they are in the same plane. The statements they make occupy a veritable negative space, a space they move through in order for the doctor to offer her medical opinion on Raquel's query and to provoke her to further thought. Raquel confronts a new and difficult option, in the last panel on the page, in which both characters' faces appear in parallel planes against a small but fully illustrated background. What happened in the intervening "nonpanel," and why did it take place, on the page, in a way that seemed not to have taken place at all in the setting of the story, literally outside of its framing?

Raquel and her doctor recruit the reader in a new conversation at the moment when they appear out of panel, when they break with the legal framework around their situation. The impetus for their conversation is literally misplaced, according to its "government-funded" setting. But rather than bending *to* the rules of the setting in which it is represented, Rocket's Decision bends the rules regarding the representation of setting in this medium to make the significance of the ensuing conversation legible. The doctor and Raquel step out of the past, in which they occupied a space governed by certain conversational rules, in order to compose a narrative about the future, a veritable speculative fiction: "It's illegal for me to tell you what I'm going to." Because Raquel was never really in a government-funded clinic at all—she was in a comic book—she changes the setting. This change occurs in a fashion that it can only attain through comics: through a perceptible break with the moment portrayed in one panel and the rendition of a subsequent, different moment in the next panel. Thus Raquel draws the reader's attention to a new set of laws that bends the rules of comics ("Do superheroes get pregnant? At 15?") but does not break them ("Not until now they didn't").

The first letters in "Iconoclasts" to reference Raquel's pregnancy appear after Wayne's whimsical introduction to the column in *Icon* #7. As a representative example, Lara Hoffman of Ohio writes, "How many times do you see a superhero apologizing to somebody for breaking her windshield in the line of duty? Or a hero dealing with the concept that she might be pregnant?" Matt Wayne concludes the letters column with the note, "There are lots of different kinds of Milestone readers and I tear my heart out each week trying to make sure this page reflects that variety. I think that keeps the conversation more lively; am I right?" While the letters printed thus far indicate that comics presenting themes from "reality" excite and astonish fans, their responses display a uniform, generalized interest in the fact that the quantity of narratives about teen pregnancy in superhero comics has gone from zero to any at all ("How many times do you see . . ."). In the introduction and conclusion to this column, Wayne similarly focuses on the quantity of the readers' responses, rather than providing examples to buttress his assertion that there is "variety" among them. Although this edition of the column greets fans with a generic sense of amazement regarding the issue of Raquel's pregnancy, from both the editor and the letter writers, the specific ways in which the issue resonates with readers seem to hover below the surface of the letters page in the same way that Raquel and her doctor seem to stand in the background of their own story on the page in which they confront the possibility of Rocket's Decision. The missing piece to this quandary is, of course, what choice does Raquel make?

In *Icon* #7, Raquel asks Augustus, reluctantly, to loan her the money to get an abortion, but when he implores her to discuss her pregnancy, she balks.

Augustus subsequently tells Raquel about his late wife Estelle's decision to terminate her pregnancy. The circumstances were extraordinary in a story about abortion but are typical in a genre context. Augustus's alien genotype made their fetus a threat to Estelle's life, and abortions were dangerous, costly, illegal procedures in the early twentieth century, when this one took place. After relating his tale, Augustus says, "I cannot put myself in your place, I cannot tell you what to do. If you need the money, take it. It is a gift. Whatever you decide, I am your friend" (167). Then the Rocket slaps his glasses off his face (see fig. 7.4). This sequence forms the basis for the responses that the letters column will eventually print regarding the issue of Raquel's pregnancy. Once Rocket's Decision has taken place in *Icon*, the tone of "Iconoclasts" changes markedly. The various ways readers use Rocket's Decision to characterize *Icon* as a political intervention yield deeper insights into the way *Icon* represents itself as a comic book first and foremost, while acknowledging the politics on display in the broader media landscape.

7.4 The Rocket slaps Augustus's face in their discussion about her pregnancy in *Icon*.

Rocket's Decision as a Heroic Act

In the "Iconoclasts" column of *Icon* #10, a picture of *Icon* #7's cover precedes Wayne's introductory remarks. The editor writes, "We received a lot of mail after Rocket made her decision. The following is a good representation of the comments we got" ("Iconoclasts," in Duffie, Helene, and Bright, *Icon* #10). Three letters follow. The one recognized as the "Letter of the Month," rewarded with a signed copy of the issue in which it is printed, comes from a reader using the ominous pseudonym "King Solomon." The author of the letter of the month commends *Icon* #7 as "a well done exploration of the abortion issue, taking care not to be too slanted toward the pro-choicers or the anti-choicers." A further elaboration of Milestone's strategy for representing fandom comes in the next letter, from Kate Murray. Murray insists that "just by existing as a hero comic in an urban black setting," *Icon* sends a message: "You have presented, very effectively, all the reasons why she should not have this child. Now you show her choosing to do so as a quixotic, heroic thing. . . . I cannot tolerate your offering a 'hero' character who would make such a stupid, sentimental, short-sighted decision, which in real life would mean drudgery, poverty, and living death for two individuals." In the *Comics Journal* interview with Milestone's leadership, Denys Cowan addresses a problem brought to mind by Tony Norman's question, "Are there any particular books that you feel have a reason for being, other than the fact that it's great action and so forth? I mean, are there things in these books that you would say are purposefully written on the level of propaganda that is supposed to change people's minds?" Cowan replies, "These are not message comics. If there's any message, it's that they're good comics" (Norman).

There is nothing in *Icon* that its creators *would say* is purposefully written on the level of a polemic, nothing that makes their work "message comics" in a political sense. By conferring editorial recognition on King Solomon's letter, "Iconoclasts" has performed its function as a venue in which "a good representation" of fan opinion can occur. Within the hierarchy established under the appraisal that Wayne calls "comparably balanced," however, Murray's interpretation constitutes one extreme. The other contribution to this column's "good representation" and the other extreme contrast to King Solomon's letter comes from Michael Dlugozima, who complains, "A bias toward abortion permeates this entire issue," based on the doctor's and Icon's refusal to advise Raquel against terminating her pregnancy ("Iconoclasts," in Duffie, Helene, and Bright, *Icon* #10). The message that this column sends by valuing King Solomon's letter over the others is not about abortion per se. Rather, the critical stance in favor of "balance" articulated on the letters page validates the message in King Solomon's letter, that *Icon* is "good comics." The criterion the letters page establishes for that assessment is whether Rocket's Decision has achieved an aesthetic aim. Now, I do not mean to pull back the curtain and show *Icon*'s true colors as a "conservative" text, to argue that it refuses to take sides in portraying controversial issues, or to argue that it takes sides by pretending not to take a side. I mean to draw conclusions about precisely how, not why, *Icon* seems to take the politically controversial "how could she?" of Rocket's Decision off the table to foreground responses to the aesthetically provocative question of "how did she . . . ?" or "how did she do?" instead.

Murray's letter insists on a common enough notion that there is a message, a real-world import, to any "hero comic in an urban black setting." Lest we assume that this misconception is hers alone, we should take heed of where it comes from. Prevalent as it is in comics fandom, the misconception that black people are somehow more real or interesting than white people, even in situations where the two are equally fictitious, is a widespread problem in contemporary culture. Norman's discomfiting questions about whether Milestone comics would offer more "reality" than others recalls the limitations of the superhero genre, but it echoes the treatment of race in other fields of contemporary cultural criticism as well. Madhu Dubey, in her book *Signs and Cities: Black Literary Postmodernism*, comments on the selective ways black culture gets invoked to describe the present historical moment as postmodern:

> Even as black urban culture is exuberantly exploited to feed global commodity capitalism, mass-media and academic debates cast the black urban poor as the catalysts of social and cultural crisis. . . . A random but telling example is Scott Lash and John Urry's book *Economies of Signs and Space*, which argues the now-familiar thesis that 'economic and symbolic processes are more than ever interlaced' in the postmodern era. Lash and Urry assert that the 'real loser' in such a context is 'the single black mother in the Chicago ghetto,' who lacks the cultural capital that increasingly mediates access to economic and political power. (7–8, quoting Lash and Urry 149)

In other words, scholars take for granted that economically impoverished black people must be culturally impoverished as well, because economic and cultural exploitation work in tandem at this historical moment. Even though the cultural world is not identical to the economic world, in an age when they are increasingly imbricated, no person can prevail in one without securing a measure of success in the other. Yet the aching specificity of "the Chicago ghetto" in Lash and Urry's assertion underscores Dubey's critique of their line of reasoning. The single black mother in their example could just as well live in the city of Dakota, because she is *not real*. She is an artifact of the way academics, comics fans, journalists, politicians, and black authors alike think about blackness, class, and sexuality in a contemporary urban context. In an earlier letter to "Iconoclasts," Joey Marchese describes Raquel's pregnancy as a situation "which could happen to any inner-city teenage girl" ("Iconoclasts," in Duffie, Helene, and Bright, *Icon* #7). Even as he reserves judgment on whether black teenagers should become pregnant and what they should do in those circumstances, Marchese identifies Raquel's pregnancy with a consensus about the sex lives of black people in the urban United States on which cultural authorities, popular and academic alike, seem to agree.

Murray is dismayed at the way *Icon* #7 portrays Rocket's Decision as a "quixotic, heroic thing," and she chastises its creative team for presenting Rocket as "a 'hero' character." The implication, here, is that (super)hero and pregnant teenager are mutually exclusive categories, embodying different values, and that they are thus subject to different modes of representation. I find that Murray is upset with *Icon* #7 not because it fails to show what would happen in real life but because it fails to conform to her expectations about a black expressive culture, expectations formed under contemporary political and economic conditions, expectations she shares with readers of comics as well as other groups of commentators. By bringing "reality" into superhero comics, Rocket's Decision has bent the narrative of teen pregnancy to the rules of the superhero genre and the medium in which it takes place, including the delayed, narrowly framed responsiveness that governs the letters page. The panel wherein Raquel decides not to end the series at the edge of the real-life legal limitations on what can be said in a "government-funded" setting finally cracks the veneer over *Icon* as anything more than a commercial fiction narrowly bounded by its genre. Even within those limits, *Icon* forwards the notion that a black woman might attain the autonomy and resources to make her own decisions about her life—making a radical political departure without breaking its own aesthetic rules.

The stakes of portraying a black woman acting autonomously with regard to her sexual and economic life are high enough within the limits of a genre such as superhero comics without venturing into other cultural traditions to find even more constraints. Rocket's Decision demands that its readers think critically about race, sexuality, and genre, but it only requires them to utilize the reading strategies they normally bring to comics. Another set of formal techniques might address the political circumstances that Rocket's Decision represents differently from the way that *Icon* does. Raquel herself says as much, in her first words to the reader in *Icon* #1: "I've always wanted to be a writer, like Toni Morrison." When her boyfriend cajoles her into going to rob the house where she will meet Augustus Freeman for the first time by remarking, "we have a good night, maybe we'll make enough money for you to get yourself a typewriter," Raquel thinks, "I'll bet Toni Morrison has a typewriter" (15).

Morrison is an icon for Raquel and for Dubey as well. For Dubey, Morrison typifies the way contemporary black literature negotiates the problems wrought by readers' appetite for documents that reflect expressive culture instead of established forms of literary creativity:

Indeed, one of the paradoxes of the postmodern moment is that it witnesses the greatest effusion ever of print literature by African-Americans, along with a disavowal of their chosen medium by some of the most celebrated of these authors. Toni Morrison, for example, has said that she imagines her ideal audience to be "an illiterate or preliterate reader." One of my aims in writing *Signs and Cities* is to account for this paradox whereby the most prolific African-American authors feel compelled to present their works as something other than print literature. (6, quoting Morrison 387)

Raquel Ervin's relationship to Toni Morrison is constructed, in part, by her strivings to become a writer. But she is not so ideally situated with respect to Morrison's genre as to be part of her imagined audience. One of the ways *Icon* functions differently from the literary texts for which Morrison is iconic is that Raquel's narrative evidences no compunction about representing itself "as something other than print literature." In fact, in her own writings as conveyed in *Icon*, Raquel strives to compare her own writing within the text to print literature, while noting poignantly her lack of access to the technology that would make her dream come true.

The imagery used to portray Raquel's distinguishing feature, her literacy, demonstrates that her idealization of Morrison works precisely contrary to Morrison's idealization of her audience. Readers only learn the definitive story of Augustus's extraterrestrial origin when Raquel writes about discovering it. At the beginning of the issue in which that discovery takes place, Raquel is depicted writing these words: "I'm writing a book. I call it *Icon*. But the truth of the matter is, I don't know Icon's real story. It don't matter, though. This book is about me" (Duffie, Helene, and Bright, *Icon* #8, 172). And the first time she sees Augustus fly, what does Raquel do? She compares it to reading *Song of Solomon* (Duffie, Helene, and Bright, *Icon* #1, 19). An illiterate or preliterate reader could not be portrayed writing about such an incident for her manuscript through such a studied allusion. No, Raquel Ervin is not the ideal reader Toni Morrison's fiction imagines. She is the ideal reader *Icon* imagines.

The book-within-a-book that Raquel is writing positions the Rocket as an idealist—aspiring writer, not preliterate reader. Rocket's decision to convey her story through the form we see in *Icon*, a superhero narrative in dialogue with print literature, much like her decision to carry her pregnancy to term, criticizes the prevailing notion that a woman in her position is only and always *constrained* by economic, political, and cultural norms; rather, by giving form to her decisions on the panels of the comics and in the space between them, Raquel becomes free to articulate her interests in the manner of her choosing. Her writing implies that a literate, black, urban, young, working-class, pregnant woman can participate in the superhero genre and identify with print literature at the same time. As *Icon* diverges from the precedents set by previous black and female sidekicks, its representation of dialogue with its readers, its serial structure, and its visual methods of development makes it hard to question what on earth a character like the Rocket is doing in a superhero narrative.

Instead, particularly on the letters page, *Icon* presents thoughtful questions about *how* she was doing: where would Rocket's Decision(s) lead her, and the reader, next? "Iconoclasts" underscores the ways that *Icon* concerns itself with Raquel's aspirations as a black woman and a writer, affording a central role to the controversial but critically informed decisions of its protagonist. On the whole, the series portrays Raquel as a hero. After all, *Icon* always was Rocket's book.

Note

1   Page numbers in *Icon* cites refer to the reprinted compilation *Icon: A Hero's Welcome*; cites without page numbers refer to the original, unpaginated editions.

Works Cited

Brown, Jeffrey. *Black Superheroes, Milestone Comics, and Their Fans.* Jackson: University Press of Mississippi, 2001.

Dubey, Madhu. *Signs and Cities: Black Literary Postmodernism.* Chicago: University of Chicago Press, 2003.

Eisner, Will. *Comics and Sequential Art.* Tamarac, FL: Poorhouse, 1985.

Lash, Scott, and John Urry. *Economies of Signs and Space.* London: Sage, 1994.

McDuffie, Dwayne, and Erica Helene (writers), and M. D. Bright (artist). *Icon* #1. New York: Milestone/DC Comics, May 1993.

———. *Icon* #3. New York: Milestone/DC Comics, July 1993.

———. *Icon* #4. New York: Milestone/DC Comics, August 1993.

———. *Icon* #7. New York: Milestone/DC Comics, November 1993.

———. *Icon* #8. New York: Milestone/DC Comics, December 1993.

———. *Icon* #10. New York: Milestone/DC Comics, February 1994.

———. *Icon: A Hero's Welcome.* Reprint of issues 1–8. New York: DC Comics, 2009.

McCloud, Scott. *Understanding Comics: The Invisible Art.* New York: HarperCollins, 1993.

Morrison, Toni. "Memory, Creation, and Writing." *Thought* 59.4 (1984): 385–390.

Norman, Tony. "Milestone Interview." *Comics Journal* 160 (July 1993).

Pertman, Adam. "Clinton Eases Abortion Limits." *Boston Globe* 23 January 1993.

Robbins, Trina. *The Great Women Superheroes.* Northampton, MA: Kitchen Sink, 1996.

Chapter 8

Critical Afrofuturism

• •

A Case Study in Visual
Rhetoric, Sequential Art, and
Postapocalyptic Black Identity

REYNALDO ANDERSON

The comics medium provides examples of the links among gender, race, sexuality, technology, and the future in the production of science fiction. Previous scholarship by Edward Said and Toni Morrison has explored the novel as an artifact of bourgeois society, imperialism, and white racial identification with conquering the "wilderness." By extension and production, the comic magazine, a historically low-brow literary cultural product, projects the utopian tendencies of the Eurocentric Enlightenment phenomenon into the future, extending white psychological spaces, political influence, and economic control. The comic productions of *Watchmen*, *Crisis on Infinite Earths*, and *Guardians of the Galaxy*, to name a few, are manifestations of this phenomenon. In this chapter, I use critical Afrofuturistic theory as a tool to analyze and critique themes in the comic book *Ramzees: Prince of Planet Heru*, issue #1 (1997), a publication of Ghettostone publications of Kansas City, Missouri, which attempts to promote African cultural motifs in a postapocalyptic future America. *Ramzees* represents an attempt by the publisher to draw on African motifs that represent ancient Egyptian symbolism and Nile Valley theology in the context of the future. The literary production of *Ramzees* is emblematic of the political/cultural period of the mid-1990s in the United States, in which emerged the neosoul genre, globalization, and African-diasporic mobilization in the Million Man and Million Woman Marches. In this chapter, I critique the Eurocentrist paradigm embedded within the genre of comic science fiction and examine the themes of black identity within the text as it attempts to reimagine and redevelop a humanistic African image in the future. However, contemporary black identity across the African diaspora has been impacted by the values and politics of the European Enlightenment project.

Eurocentrism

Eurocentrism is not a social theory that integrates several different elements into a universal/global "coherent vision of society and history" (Amin 90). Rather, it is an active "prejudice that distorts social theories. It draws from its storehouse of components, retaining one or rejecting another according to the ideological needs of the moment" (Amin 90). Eurocentrism is composed of an annexed Hellenism that removes Greece from its historical relationship to the Near East and Africa, in particular, during the Romantic movement of the nineteenth century—a racism necessary for European cultural unity; it reinterprets a Near East– and African-imported version of Christianity to maintain cultural unity and constructs "a vision . . . on the same racist foundation, again employing an immutable vision of religion" (Amin 90). Therefore, due to the current influence of the European West and its contemporary position as the arbiter of science, rationality, efficiency, and so on, "it becomes impossible to contemplate any other future for the world than progressive Europeanization" (Amin 107).

Historically, there was no single coherent body or unity of cultures that represented the European Enlightenment; cultural differences existed (MacIntyre). The Enlightenment in northern Europe differed from that in France in three ways: northern Europe had (1) a secular Protestant background, (2) an educated class of clergy and government, and (3) new types of universities in England, Scotland, and Germany (MacIntyre). Therefore, as Alasdair MacIntyre asserts, what was occurring was primarily a northern European phenomenon. However, the Enlightenment project, which was an attempt to justify morality, was doomed to collapse because of internal inconsistencies (MacIntyre). For example, in the area of the arts and humanities, intellectuals such as Johan Joachim Winkleman (1717–1768) in his work *Geschichte der Kunst des Altertums* (History of the Art of Antiquity), followed by Johann Wolfgang Goethe (1749–1832), Petrus Camper (1722–1789), and Kaspar Lavatar (1741–1801), completed the mythological fetishizing of whiteness in relation to African features on the basis of imaginary Greco-Roman traits, although Greece was publicly seen as more Turkish due to its domination by the Ottoman Empire (Painter).

However, it can be argued that the project was continued in the New World by those Europeans fleeing oppression. Toni Morrison notes in her work *Playing in the Dark* (1993) the beliefs and philosophies of those European settlers by analyzing the literature of their foremost writers. Morrison asserts that even though Europeans were fleeing oppression, there was a need to establish their sense of freedom with control of the wilderness or the Other. The historian Bernard Bailyn, quoted by Morrison, describes William Dunbar, who "was a Scot by birth. . . . This well-educated product of the Scottish enlightenment . . . suppress[ed] . . . an alleged conspiracy for freedom by slaves on his own plantation. . . . Enterprising and resourceful, . . . and feeling within himself a sense of authority and autonomy he had not known before, a force that flowed from his absolute control over the lives of others, he emerged a distinctive new man, . . . a man of property in a raw, half-savage world" (Bailyn 488–492, qtd. in Morrison 42).

African Resistance and Counternarratives

It was here in the New World where Europeans' need or hunger to redefine themselves in relation to an *African* Other was established. This curious phenomenon of the presence of the Africanist Other existed in writings of other white writers such as Edgar Allan Poe, Mark Twain, and Willa Cather. Morrison asserts that this reflexive need for white writers to present their Africanist figures as alter egos of themselves that need to be "contained" arises from the need for whites to define themselves. According to Morrison, because of the formation of a country that necessitated speech and language codes structured to deal with the moral frailty and racial disingenuousness of the society, a real fabricated African presence was needed for the Europeans to feel like Americans. However, African American women were especially rendered voiceless under this projection of alter ego. According to Darlene Clark Hine, for black women, racism and sexism should be viewed as combining in such a way that they create a distinct social location, and black women's collective historical experiences powerfully shape their gender/identity and attitudes. In the narrative *Sapphira and the Slave Girl*, Cather writes about the power of a white woman who gathers identity to herself from the servile lives of Africanist presence and describes how her social pedestal rests on the spine of racial oppression. However, the two Africana characters in the novel, Till and Nancy, represent the stereotype of black women who are contained to a certain extent yet permitted to navigate in spaces where black men could not go.

Cheryl Thurber asserts that there were two primary images of black women that were constructed by white society: the mammy and the loose woman. The mammy represented the loyal, sexless slave who was permitted close contact with the mistress and the rest of the family, while the other image was that of the loose, sluttish slave who existed for the use of the slave master (Thurber). However, the mammy, because she could safely navigate certain spaces, could be a spokesperson for the interest of the black slaves (Thurber). Also, there existed a secondary code of motherhood and womanhood that assigned particular characteristics depending on certain roles that black women had to fulfill, making it harder for black women to establish their own credibility or identity (Etter-Lewis).

The fight for African Americans collectively to establish a distinctive identity has been a difficult struggle. The "double consciousness" articulated by W.E.B. Du Bois in his seminal work *The Souls of Black Folk* (1903) discusses the struggle to reconcile the self as African and American (Etter-Lewis). Yet even Du Bois neglected the possibility that gender may be a factor in consciousness. For example, African American women may have multiple consciousnesses available due to the intersection of race and gender (Hine). However, with these multiple consciousnesses, African Americans have been able to establish identity primarily within the context of community; community precedes autonomy (Etter-Lewis).

It is within these communities—with a collective ethos of caring and the ability to establish identity and resistance—that African American women found strength (Etter-Lewis). Historically, although not exclusively, the African American culture has been and continues to be to a certain extent an oral culture; blacks have a musical theology contained in the gospel tradition that speaks to and describes every chapter of the African experience in America, and this tradition began in the "Hush Harbors," where slaves would secretly hold their religious meetings and steal away from the gaze of their masters. Creating their own classical music in the form of the sound of jazz, the memory of an African worldview was expressed in a synthesis of thought and motion. The other half of the oral tradition that spawned intellectual development was in the person of the minister. Utilizing pulpit oratory, the black minister was able to tell the story or through narrative discourse powerfully move the congregation in a call-and-response give-and-take that would enrapture the participants.

This oral tradition, which included behaviors that originated in western Africa, contains creativity and constraint. Oba T'Shaka notes that in some of these societies from which the African slaves had come, there existed mutual respect between men and women; all just males and females were equally empowered to govern the society. Within these societies, a philosophy existed that to be a human being, an individual should possess both masculine and feminine principles (protector-nurturer) in order to have a healthy community (T'Shaka). This *twinness* also can be and was interchangeable as a survival mechanism for the slaves while in captivity as a necessary mechanism to develop resistance to domination in their minds, although they were physically in bondage. For African American women, this twinness has enabled them to shield themselves psychologically and to create a culture of dissemblance, an appearance of openness and disclosure, or hiding the self in plain sight of the oppressor (Hine). However, these diasporic epistemological strategies have created a distinct rhetorical tradition that interfaces with several artistic, technological, and spiritual dimensions. Maulana Karenga notes the existence of classical Nubian rhetorical practices that predate the Western Greco-Roman tradition by millennia. Also, rhetorical strategies include signifying, call-and-response, narrative sequencing, tonal semantics, technological rhetoric, agitation or nationalism, jeremiads, nommo, Africana womanist or black feminist epistemologies, black queer studies, time and space, and visual rhetoric and culture.

For example, the European Holocaust is used in a contemporary political project to raise huge amounts of money, to influence markets, and to sustain a "fear of annihilation"; "the specter of European fascism becomes the index of all political horror and its consequences, imposing once again a Eurocentric index of measure and political identity on the very concept of political horror" (Rogoff 25). Conversely, the unintended consequence of this posture assumes a "re-whitening" of the immigrant multicultural legacy of the United States and marginalizes or creates unnecessary contestations with the horror of the North American, South American, and Caribbean-basin legacies of the Maafa, the African holocaust or transatlantic slave trade, and the genocide of the indigenous American populations. Therefore, one of the challenges for Afrofuturist practice in relation to visual rhetoric is how to explore dimensions of *dehierarchization* in visual culture to determine meaning or multiple interpretations in the medium of sequential art.

Comics and Black Images

Since the late nineteenth century, there has been a dichotomy in how African Americans and the rest of society are portrayed in comic strips (White and Fuentez). The frequently negative images in comic strips were in opposition to modern expressions of African American masculinity emerging in the eighteenth century in the formation of Masonic fraternal organizations and independent black churches such as the African Methodist Episcopal Church and, following the Civil War, mutual-aid societies (Newton). These institutions encouraged black males to transform their labor and themselves in relation to the new industrialized American society that was taking shape in contrast to the agrarian society that was influenced by racism and white agricultural interests that discouraged black men from participating in self-made masculinity (Newton). By the 1920s, African American characters were featured as either working-class people or more minstrel-like characters that would later be associated with the show *Amos 'n' Andy* (White and Fuentez). However, by the 1930s, especially in black newspapers, comics tended to show African Americans in a more positive light, featuring characters such as Bootsie, first portrayed in the

Dark Laughter comic strip in a black-owned New York newspaper, the *Amsterdam News* (White and Fuentez). During the Cold War era, black masculinity was undergoing a transformation influenced by the civil rights movement, the Black Power movement, and the Black Arts movement. For example, according to Martin Gilens, two derogatory images that were fought against were the white-created images of Sambo and Mammy. Gilens notes, "More importantly, perhaps, the desire to maintain the . . . system created material incentives for whites to view blacks in particular derogatory ways" (195).

According to Judith Newton, in the case of the Black Panther Party for Self-Defense, there was a particular emphasis on addressing the masculine question in the form of survival programs that encouraged a nurturing form of masculinity, although a more violent form was also promulgated within the organization. However, by the early 1970s, a more aggressive, apolitical type of black masculinity was generated in popular entertainment, with figures in the movies *Shaft* (1971) and *Super Fly* (1972) representing the Hollywood establishment's effort to make money off the black urban market (Newton). Therefore, in the 1960s and 1970s, race relations had become a theme of comics, which portrayed blacks and whites on equal terms or used the white-hero/black-sidekick formula, with comics such as *Dateline Danger* and characters such as Friday Foster (White and Fuentez). Finally, by the 1980s, comics began to feature black families, showing the activities of young people and providing monologues and dialogues of black women (White and Fuentez).

Scholarship on comics by critical scholars of various ideological influences in the last decade of the twentieth century increasingly focused on the role of masculinity in relation to comic book production (Brown). However, in the 1990s, independent black comics publishers such as Milestone Media published comics with artistic representations of black masculinity that appealed to a diverse audience (Brown).

For example, contemporary black masculinity in corporate-driven media is currently generated and created within a context of the commodification of hip hop culture and societal nihilism and packaged within 'hood films and videomercials that sell the images (Henry). In relation to the comic book medium, masculinity is prized in the representation of muscles and the projection of physical strength, and unlike other masculinities, black masculinity is paradoxical in relation to the broader society's ideas about gender (Brown). For example, while black men are expected to meet the expectations of the larger society, they are denied legitimate processes to achieve these goals and therefore are emasculated yet feared and become grounded in the African American tradition of resistance and subjugation (Brown 28). Compounding this fact is the historical fear of black masculine behavior and sexuality, with its accompanying biases in relation to class, race, sex, and implied deviancy bordering on animalistic expression, all of which lead to destructive consequences (Brown).

There were modern expressions of black males in comics during the Blaxploitation era of the 1970s, represented by characters including Luke Cage, Black Panther, Black Lightning, and others, despite their antiestablishment and macho behavior (Brown). By the 1990s, black superheroes were represented in such a way that they were not taken seriously, with buffoonish performance by the Wayanses in the movies *Meteor Man* and *Blank Man* (Brown). Recent scholarship on the role of African Americans and African images in comics has been done by Nancy Goldstein and Lysa Rivera, who explore, respectively, the impacts of black women on the comics medium and the advent of the posthuman perspective through the persona of the black cyborg; yet a further critique of the ideological and cultural impulses of black masculinity is necessary to fully appreciate the extent of paradigmatic influences within the comic book medium.

Critical Theory Framework

The historical development of critical theory is an important one for scholars across disciplines. With an increasing critique of preexisting notions of knowledge, built primarily on Eurocentric, male bastions of knowledge, scholars are now reassessing the existing social milieu. Before a researcher can proceed, it must be determined (1) what are critical theory and interpretive theory? (2) when are they appropriate? and (3) how do they differ and how are they similar? According to John Cresswell, critical theory developed under the auspices of German scholars who are loosely referred to as the Frankfurt School.

Central themes that can be subsumed under critical theory include, but are not limited to, the interpretation of the context of social interaction, historical problems of domination and alienation, societal struggle, and critical analysis of society (Cresswell). Finally, critical theory can "be defined by the particular configuration of methodological postures it embraces" (Cresswell 81). The scholar working from this perspective seeks to conduct studies that help people examine and critique the everyday social conditions that they (the people) have to live with. According to Cresswell, research design within critical theory can be organized into two broad categories: methodological and substantive. Methodological research affects the ways in which individuals write and read. Substantive research affects the theories and focus of the researcher (e.g., theorizing about the role of global capital and its effect on culture [Cresswell]).

According to Cresswell, in critical action research, the following steps are observed: (1) philosophical guidance emerges from various perspectives of critical theory, such as queer epistemology, feminist theory, postmodern theory, and Marxism, (2) "assumptions of existing paradigms" are exposed in an evaluation of the knowledge base, revealing in whose interest knowledge is being transmitted, (3) the artifact to be studied is selected, to examine institutions from particular locations, (4) the collected information is interpreted, with an awareness on the part of the researcher of the guiding assumptions and an understanding that he or she is a part of wider culture, and (5) the research results in pedagogical transformation involving institutions and individuals. However, these largely Eurocentric, neo-Hegelian philosophical perspectives, developed during the multicultural moment of late twentieth-century America, are too limited in their utility because of their inherent cultural prejudices and the theoretical project of locating African peoples in the future. For example, the definition by Darko Suvin of *science fiction* as a dialectical tension between estrangement and cognition suffers from the problem of making generic distinctions on the basis of matters far removed from literature and genre (Freedman 17). Therefore, the utilization of a different theoretical framework to situate African people's futures is necessary to gain more insight into artifacts of the Africana unconscious and conscious.

To begin a theoretical assessment of African peoples, the future, and sequential art, I adopt the approach of critical race theory (CRT), which draws from its roots in black studies, a broad base in law, sociology, women's studies, ethnic studies, and Afrofuturism. According to Derrick Bell, the primary theoretical focus of CRT regarding the concept of interest convergence was to suggest that laws in the United States change to benefit African Americans if white Americans see that their interests are furthered. In this chapter, I introduce some tenets of CRT and Afrofuturism to the critique of race, masculinity, sexuality, technology, the future, and comics literature. CRT focuses on (a) race as a social construction, racism, and their intersection with other forms of oppression, (b) challenging hegemony and ideology, (c) a commitment to social justice, (d) the role of experiential knowledge and storytelling and counterstorytelling, and (e) a transdisciplinary perspective (Hartlep; Solozorno and Yosso).

The Genesis of Afrofuturism

African and African-diasporic art forms were tributary contributors to the emergence of modern art, music, and futurism. For example, the artwork of the Fang people of Gabon, in western Africa, influenced the emergence of cubism and artists such as Henri Matisse, Amedeo Modigliani, and Pablo Picasso (Ocvirk et al.). In particular, the style developed by Picasso, borrowed from traditional African sculpture and influenced by Paul Cezanne and Greek art, embraced a principle referred to as *simultaneity*, a practice of portraying multiple facets of objects in space (Ocvirk et al.). However, following the horror of World War I, art movements such as dadaism, futurism, and surrealism expressed various sentiments ranging from disillusionment with reason and rationality to the triumph of technology and science and a revolt against European civilization (Ocvirk et al.).

Futurism was an artistic and literary movement formed between 1909 and World War I by Italian artists, and principal luminaries of the art form were Gino Severini, Giacomo Balla, and Umberto Boccioni and the poet-critic Filippo Tommaso Marinetti (Ocvirk et al.). Italian futurism and the French-inspired literary/artistic movement surrealism were influenced by the African-diaspora art form of jazz. Italian futurists saw jazz as compatible with their philosophy of technological triumphalism; whereas the French surrealists, ideologically anti-imperialist, viewed jazz as an expression of the black working class and influenced the belief that non-Western cultures had communications and methods "that transcended the conscious" (Kelley 160).

Futurism in the United States originated during World War I and national planning projects following the Great Depression and partly as a response to social engineering in the Soviet Union, fascism in Italy, and Nazism in Germany (Bell). According to Michael Bennett, the very term *Afrofuturism* should give scholars pause due to similar terminology used by Russian and Italian futurists, who were fascistic in their politics, and the influence of the philosophy of Friedrich Nietzsche. However, this is where the appropriation of the tools of futurism is distinct between the European futurists and their Euro-American colleagues.

Many modern Eurocentric futurists focused primarily on the Nietzschean ideas of *will to power* and *Übermenschen*, or *over-mind*, and some Afrofuturists appropriate Eurocentric theoretical constructs to explore the semiotics of some artifacts. However, Afrofuturism differs from Eurocentric futurism in two important aspects. First, futurism and fascism in Europe emerged out of the cultural hegemony that was imposed on non-Western peoples in the late nineteenth and early twentieth centuries. For example, the roots of modern fascism in Germany can be traced back to the Vril society, a cult started in the nineteenth century that was steeped in Nordic folklore, metaphysics, and occultism and that influenced the development of white Aryan supremacist Nazi ideology and the pursuit of the study of new physics, extradimensionalism, and odic force. In contrast, Afrofuturism emerged in response to the transformation of African peoples through the oppressive forces of various forms of discrimination, urban life, and modernity; specifically, modern Afrofuturism emerged out of a nexus of migration, international and domestic social movements and conflict, influences of technology, and black music, religion, and literature. Second, and more importantly, the Afrofuturist location can establish a counternarrative and undermine or delegitimize the power of the *Leviathan*, the Eurocentric social contract that institutionalizes and maintains the power of the elite and the *people's* ability to collectively imagine or organize for an alternative future (Nurrudin). Correspondingly, the Afrofuturist location is a compass in relation to other futurisms. For example, the theoretical positions of Chicanafuturism and Rastafuturism exist along with Afrofuturism as a reflection of the cosmology of histories of survival, hegemony, *indigenismo*, and *mestizaje* (Nurrudin; Ramirez).

Finally, Afrofuturism serves as a philosophical compass in relation not only to Eurocentric futurism but also to the Arab-centric, Islam-influenced perspective in science fiction motifs. For example, the religious orthodoxy of Islam in Sunni and Shi'a systems possesses limited cosmology for the creation of Islamic science fiction; yet the proto-science-fiction works of *A Thousand and One Arabian Nights* are a valuable example of classic literature of the Arab world, and works by Mustafa Mahmoud and Imran Talib are major contributions in the genre of Arab science fiction (Nurrudin). However, the antiblack, anti-African features of pan-Islamic Wahhabism are parallel to the antiblack, anti-African cosmologies of Eurocentric Christianity. Therefore, the heterodox nature of African American–based Islam becomes important to the emergence of Afrofuturism in the African diaspora. Finally, key to the emergence of what can be referred to as a black consciousness / Black Power phase of Afrofuturism were Sun Ra, Elijah Muhammad, and several black literary writers.

The religious expression of Afrofuturism and its roots in urban science fiction cosmology emerged as a result of the migration of African Americans from the South to northern cities in the early twentieth century, the Marcus Garvey movement during the age of imperialism, and Jim Crow segregation (Nurrudin). In particular, four organizations—the Moorish Science Temple (est. Newark, 1913), the Nation of Islam (NOI; est. Detroit, 1930), the Five Percenters or Nation of Gods and Earths (est. New York, 1964), and the Nuwaubian Moors (est. New York, circa 1970)—influenced the urban flowering of the belief in extraterrestrial jihads and intergalactic black astronauts (Nurrudin). However, the key figure in this eschatological narrative development was the leader of the Nation of Islam, Elijah Muhammad.

Elijah Muhammad's exposure to the teachings of Noble Drew Ali, leader of the Moorish Science Temple, his personal presence, and that of his pupil Malcolm X were pivotal to the emergence of the Five Percenters and Nuwaubian Moors. Elijah Muhammad and the NOI's cosmological account of the beginning of white oppression over people of color, which begins with the evil scientist Yacub and the subsequent creation of a mutant white population that causes the downfall of a black utopian society, serves as a cornerstone for NOI theology (Nurrudin). Subsequently, the Five Percenters and Nuwaubian Moors formed rival sects in urban America and offered their own cosmologies in relation to science, the future, and race (Nurrudin). In addition to the religious cosmologies of the heterodox African American Muslim organizations was the attempt by black avant-garde jazz artists to transform the consciousness of the society.

The emergence of the avant-garde musician Sun Ra during the post–World War II, Cold War era represents a modern emergence, reconceptualization, redeployment, and technological re-creation in relation to political activity and black vernacular creative technological expression (Kreiss). Sun Ra and his band, the Arkestra, utilized metaphors in their performances to transform the minds of their African American audiences through the use of mythic technologically empowered consciousness and to develop black utopias, reconceptualizing African Egyptian legacies, reimagining outer space, and engaging with energy (Kreiss). Although avant-garde musicians such as Albert Ayler, Ornette Coleman, Cecil Taylor, and Sun Ra may have been affiliated with psychological liberation of the individual and the aesthetic of spontaneity that emerged in response to the alienation cased by a bureaucratic, technocratic corporate liberalism, by the mid-1960s, black artists were reconsidering their positions in the wake of the emergence of the Black Power movement (Kreiss).

However, the black consciousness position adopted by Sun Ra and others was only one of many competing articulations of the politics of black identity during the period in question. For example, the futuristic stance taken by Sun Ra represented a rejection of Christianity and a turn toward cultural regeneration, and it foreshadowed a move away from the politics of the civil rights struggle and toward the emerging black consciousness / Black Power movement (Kreiss). Yet organizations such as the Black Panther Party, under the leadership of Huey Newton, influenced by the works of Franz Fanon, believed that the transformation of consciousness must be accompanied by a revolutionary act of violence, and this division between Sun Ra and the Black Panthers was emblematic of future ideological discussion surrounding the transformation of the psyche and the African/African-diaspora community (Kreiss). Finally, the artistic arm of the Black Power movement, the Black Arts movement, also made a literary contribution to the emergence of Afrofuturism.

Although historically indebted to earlier works by writers such as George Schulyer and others, in the literary field, novels during the Black Power and Black Arts movements of the 1960s were part of the cultural atmosphere that contributed to the emergence of the black consciousness / Black Power period of Afrofuturism. For example, John A. Williams's *Sons of Darkness, Sons of Light* (1969) and Sam Greenlee's *The Spook Who Sat by the Door* were considered black revolutionary novels. And under the nom de plume Julian Moreau, J. Denis Jackson published *The Black Commandos* (1967), which represented the first attempt at using pop-culture idioms of comics, spy thrillers, and science fiction in a black revolutionary framework to influence the consciousness of the African American population.

Critical Afrofuturist Theory

Contemporary Afrofuturism is an intellectual and artistic movement that emerged in the late 1960s and early 1970s with musicians, including Miles Davis, John Coltrane, George Clinton & Parliament Funkadelic, R&B entertainers, and rap artists. The term *Afrofuturism* was described by Mark Dery in

1993 in relation to speculative fiction, technoculture, and its appropriation by African Americans. Afrofuturism examines the aesthetics and intellectual terrain of the so-called posthuman/postracial future posited by mostly white futurists and remains connected to an African humanistic past. It reinvents a visionary discourse relating to the diasporic experience and impacted by technological transformation, and it maintains a counternarrative that intersects history, progress, tradition, innovation, memory, the authentic and the engineered, and analogue and digital within spaces of African-diasporic culture (Eglash; David). Furthermore, Marlo David notes, "Afrofuturist thought posits a reconciliation between an imagined disembodied identity-free future and the embodied identity-specific past and present, which can provide a critical link through which post-soul artists can express a radical black subjectivity" (697).

An Afrofuturist is consciously or unconsciously writing, painting, or artistically expressing the lives of African peoples in relation to other sentient beings in the past, present, or future(s) and is released from a static representation of a *particularist* form of identity that is free and remains politically or artistically engaged. However, Afrofuturism is not a subgenre of science fiction but a larger aesthetic mode connecting artists and scholars with an interest in "projecting black futures derived from Afrodiasporic experiences" (Yaszek 42). Paul Gilroy's *The Black Atlantic* juxtaposes the primary ideological difference between the eschatologies of Western Eurocentric writers and the Afrodiasporic tradition, arguing that within the framework of European modernity, the theme of *Utopia* projects the idea that society progresses through rationalism, technological advance, complexity, and materialism, whereas conversely, the Africana tradition projects the idea of the *Jubilee*, or striving for perfection regardless of the destination (68). The Afrodiasporic worldview can be demonstrated by the fact that in religion, history, art, politics, and literature, Africans and their diaspora have repeatedly chosen to find a way to *resist or transform* their circumstances rather than to *rationally* accept their condition.

Early leaders in the contemporary Afrofuturist speculative-fiction genre were Samuel R. Delany, Octavia Butler, and Ishmael Reed; a newer generation includes the writers Alondra Nelson, Nalo Hopkinson, and many other members of the African diaspora. Kodwo Eshun asserts that Afrofuturism is "concerned with the possibilities for intervention within the dimension of the predictive, the projected, . . . the virtual, . . . the future" (293). Historically, much of African American literature has been regarded in terms of resistance and redemption; however, Mark Bould notes, "It would be easy to fall into the trap of merely celebrating Afrofuturism as 'resistance' when the still emerging theory of Afrofuturism parallels other futurisms in its lack of a *critical* standpoint in relation to future forces of production and social reality" (181).

Therefore, despite the creative possibilities of Afrofuturism, the continued threat posed by white supremacy in relation to biological processes and technology and a potential future for Africana peoples shows that a critical assessment related to struggle and the collective survival of the community cannot be neglected (David). Critical Afrofuturist theory operates from a standpoint that intersects theories of time and space, technology, class, race, gender, and sexuality and delineates a general economy of racialization in relation to forces of production and apocalyptic, dystopian, and utopian futures. In the remainder of this chapter, I address race, gender, sexuality, technology, and the expression of black masculinity in a futuristic setting, with consideration of the comics character Ramzees and the way black masculinity is constructed for consumers of the Ghettostone publication *Ramzees: Prince of Planet Heru*, issue #1.

Comics have proven a fertile territory for the depictions of race and "visually codified representations in which characters are reduced to their appearances, . . . and this reduction is especially prevalent in superhero comics" (Singer 107). Previous research has demonstrated that African Americans are attracted to covers or other artistic media with an African image (Gray). On the cover of *Ramzees*, an overly muscular black man with distinctly African features is flying with a red cape and what appear to be cosmic fields of power emanating from his fist. Although the portrayal of *Ramzees* is loosely based on Egyptology and African myth in a futuristic setting, the publisher attempts to promote a positive African image via the comics medium, and the text and visual art are closely structured after the patterns used in the West. According to Thomas Inge, "Comic book heroes also tend to fit most of the classic patterns of heroism in Western culture" (142). For example, the character Prince Ramzees, during his exile on Earth, saves the white daughter of an executive of Ameritex, a postapocalyptic domed city on the North American continent, and is asked by the business owner to play for his football team. Although Ramzees is not a human being and is clearly a more developed life form, he is cast into the stereotypical position of a black jock or athlete to fit into the predominantly white Ameritex society. However, the plot of *Ramzees* is extended further with the realization that in the future race, racism, and miscegenation are still major issues. For example, following Ramzees's successful exploits on the football field, and walking with his new white girlfriend, Ms. McKenna, whom he refers to as his "Flower," Ramzees experiences racism in the form of a white male who is angry with him for being an "Ashanti," a member of an African population inhabiting the city of Atlantaplex (5). The white male is angry about Ramzees's "Ashanti" appearance and accuses Ramzees of the death of his brother during a war with Atlantaplex, referring to him as "Ashanti Boy" (6). The rival city of Atlantaplex is ruled by Queen Shakur. Shakur is enraged that her daughter Sharazade is missing; unbeknownst to Shakur, Sharazade is sleeping with the son of Shakur's rival Ameritex ruler and has become pregnant. The text indicates that their relationship is illegal; however, Brett McKenna and Princess Sharazade believe that their love will be enough to continue the relationship (6). Yet, following an attack of mutated spiders on the city of Ameritex, the scene describes a fleeing Sharazade, who has apparently been betrayed by Brett

(10). The scene concludes with Prince Ramzees saving Princess Sharazade from her pursuers, and she verbally concludes, "It's because I'm Ashanti and I never should've learned to love an Ameritex man" (10). However, miscegenation also becomes an issue when Sharazade notes, "They will not destroy my child. It does not matter if he's only half Ashanti . . . we will stay with this man Ramzees . . . he will protect us" (10).

The construction of gender in the comics medium is prominent in textual and visual representation. In particular, the construction of the female body juxtaposed to the male form in the comics medium is frequently a result of nationalist mythology (Emad). The comics medium, as well as other literary media, has been influenced by nationalist impulses. For example, images and myths of the United States are told and retold through the comics medium (Emad). In relation to nationalism and the woman's body, Mitra Emad notes, "her body serves as a site of constantly oppositional encounters between gender and nation, private and public, and bondage and power" (956). The influence of nationalism, black speculative fiction, desire, and the body are also demonstrated in the pre–World War II works of George Schuyler (*Black Empire*) and in the postwar literature of nationalist writers (Ongiri). A cultural product of the 1990s, nationalist impulses, as well as the tension between black subjectivity and wholeness and the woman's body as a site of contestation, are present as well in the text and visual art of *Ramzees*.

For example, Prince Ramzees, upon his arrival, when he saves Ms. McKenna, becomes the object of female desire despite his Ashanti-like features. Ms. McKenna is portrayed as a single white female, daughter of a powerful leader in Ameritex, with sexual attraction to and control over the fate of Ramzees, despite the laws against interracial relationships. The tension between desire and control is present in an argument between two women, when Ms. McKenna asserts, "And besides, I found him first! He's mine! Now how can I apologize for fainting when I first caught sight of him? I don't know what came over me" (5). The tension between masculinity and sexuality is apparent in *Ramzees* when Queen Shakur is portrayed as a powerful woman with masculine characteristics, although her hypersexualized attire and visage is revealing much of her body, with cloth covering only her groin area and breasts (6). However, the body of Shakur's daughter Sharazade becomes a point of contestation between nation and desire. For example, when notified of Sharazade's absence, Queen Shakur asserts, "What if she's been captured by Ameritex? They could hold Atlantaplex hostage" (6). The fear of miscegenation by the Atlantaplex monarch is confirmed in the following scene when Sharazade, in the bed of Brett McKenna, says, "I know our families hate each other . . . once they know I'm carrying their only grandchild there will be nothing they can do about it" (6). However, Sharazade later changes her position after fleeing the city to save her unborn child and is saved by Ramzees; she is betrayed by Brett and reconsiders her relationship to a white Ameritex man.

Technologies and their link to control and subjugation and their implication in the maintenance of racial hierarchies in American society are part of the country's history (Banks). Following the end of World War II, American and Japanese comics/manga writers impacted the popular culture of their societies with stories of tragedy and atomic-related stories with characters such as Godzilla and Atomic Mouse (Szasz and Takechi). By the 1960s and during the Cold War era, the culture of American individualism and military technology glamorized the exploits of "total war" and destruction involving the invasion by aliens and an apocalyptic destruction (Witek). By the late twentieth century, with the rapid diffusion of technology, communications, and biotechnology, Patricia Clough notes, "Along with the high-powered mathematical technologies that allow us to see matter as inherently dynamic, operating as a complex, open system under far-from-equilibrium conditions, and the biotechnologies that mass produce genetic materials outside the organism, there has been a development of information technologies, . . . entertainment and surveillance . . . less about representation and the narrative construction of subject identities and more about affecting bodies, human and nonhuman, directly" (3).

In the comics medium, there is still a struggle to avoid the "visually codified representations in which characters are reduced to their appearances, and this reductionism is especially prevalent in superhero comics" (Singer 107). Yet in *Ramzees*, a counternarrative is constructed focusing on the fact that Ramzees is an African-featured interplanetary extraterrestrial that is a descendant of a race that has influenced the advancement of "mankind" for almost three millennia. Although Ramzees arrives in a postapocalyptic North America that has apparently misused technology and destroyed much of the environment, he still considers the humans "kindred" (3). After his arrival, Ramzees becomes aware of the fact that the European-appearing Ameritex people are frequently at war over technology with the African-featured Ashanti citizens of Atlantaplex. Ramzees becomes aware of the technological superiority that he possesses shortly after his arrival on Earth, when he notices that gravity has the effect of increasing his strength and his ability to save an Earth woman from an attack by spiders the size of horses. However, the drawbacks of technology's misuse are demonstrated when the same spiders grow to monstrous proportions and threaten the safety of the domed city Ameritex. Ramzees, aware that the Ameritex population would panic if alerted to his powers, destroys satellite capability to hide "visuals" of his actions and proceeds to destroy the spiders with his "impulse beam" technology (6).

The "morphing" state of masculinity in relation to gender, race, and heteronormative behavior has been interrogated since the 1970s (Palmer-Mehta and Hay 391). Also, there is a growing body of scholarship in relation to popular culture, masculinity, ethnicity, and comics as a socializing influence on young males (Palmer-Mehta and Hay). For example, in 2001, the long-running *Green Lantern* comic book in issue #137 focused on a character named Terry Berg, who is the victim of antigay violence (Palmer-Mehta and Hay). Beginning in the 1990s, black males in comics began to demonstrate multidimensional characteristics (Brown). Yet in *Ramzees*, this multidimensionality is missing. In a nod to traditional visual representations of black superheroes, Ramzees is constructed as a physical he-man type, which typifies the comics medium of the 1990s. For example, although there is no sexual intercourse between Ramzees and the woman he has saved, Ms. McKenna, the visual representation of the women fawning over Ramzees and the feelings displayed by Ramzees and other male characters reinforce a heteronormative narrative within the text.

Black males within the pages of *Ramzees* are also constructed in a particular way. Cultural and literary historians have noted the role of the black servant figure in relation to white families in various texts and settings, including film and other media (Foertsch). This framework is also present in postapocalyptic literature and media and is expanded into the savior-servant-savant (Foertsch). For example, in *Ramzees*, the character Prince Ramzees of Heru is thrust into the savior-servant-savant role immediately upon his arrival on Earth. Ramzees rescues the helpless white maiden from the mutant spiders and is rewarded by the white father with a job working for his family and later using his advanced technology and philosophical insight to build homes for minorities and the poor; he then saves the city from another attack from the mutant spiders. The role of Ramzees is also constrained by the artistic construction of his masculinity in relation to the other characters.

According to Jeffrey Brown, "The male identity in the twentieth century is perceived in extremes: man or mouse, He-man or 98-pound weakling. At one end is the hyper-masculine ideal with muscles, sex appeal and social competence; at the other is the skinny, socially inept failure" (25). In similar fashion, *Ramzees* seemingly constructs the black male characters as dangerous or aggressive and other males as less dangerous. This may have important ramifications considering the self-image of the consumers who read *Ramzees*. For example, "previous research suggested that African American consumers tend to be more receptive to advertising in general and more responsive to advertising featuring African Americans" (Lee and Browne 525). According to Maclan Saroup, identities are influenced by what we consume, what we wear, the commodities we buy, what we read, how we conceive our sexuality, and how we feel about the society.

The positioning of the bodies of the black males in the text frequently has them in suggestive positions to draw more of the consumer's eye contact to body parts, particularly in the area of the crotch, buttocks, and chest. The pictures project a sense of machismo that would be difficult to emulate for males who do not have a particular body structure. White males pictured in the text may be in some of the same positions but seem to appear less threatening. This tension is also exhibited throughout the comic by the limited subjectivity of women, with the exception of Queen Shakur, or the fawning adulation that the women exhibit toward male characters. When women are heard, they are

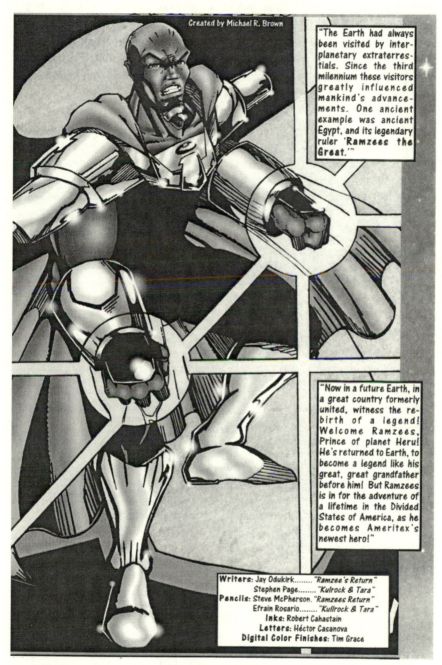

Created by Michael R. Brown

"The Earth had always been visited by interplanetary extraterrestials. Since the third milennium these visitors greatly influenced mankind's advancements. One ancient example was ancient Egypt, and its legendary ruler 'Ramzees the Great.'"

"Now in a future Earth, in a great country formerly united, witness the rebirth of a legend! Welcome Ramzees, Prince of planet Heru! He's returned to Earth, to become a legend like his great, great grandfather before him! But Ramzees is in for the adventure of a lifetime in the Divided States of America, as he becomes Ameritex's newest hero!"

Writers: Jay Odukirk........ "Ramzee's Return"
        Stephen Page........ "Kulrock & Tara"
Pencils: Steve McPherson. "Ramzees Return"
        Efrain Rosario........ "Kullrock & Tara"
Inks: Robert Cahastain
Letters: Héctor Casanova
Digital Color Finishes: Tim Grace

8.1 Prince Ramzees may be seen as a variation on the black servant figure that has been so common in various popular cultural texts.

seldom critical of any of the male characters. The overwhelming majority of women are constructed in the comic as passive sexual objects or subject to the control of men. This construction of a totalizing he-man male text in the comic automatically places female characters in uncomplimentary roles, and because the values of comics are frequently communicated in a dominant discursive mode, female characters are represented either as controlled, as silenced, or as sexualized objects.

The characters of *Ramzees*, issue #1, can easily be located within the Eurocentric tradition of the comics medium. In particular, the plot does little to examine or dismantle simplistic or binary notions of race, gender, sexuality, or masculinity; specific examples of this behavior are in the area of interracial sexual relations, gendered power, and identities.

First, regarding the portrayal of interracial sexual relations, the outcome in *Ramzees* makes the women characters solely responsible for the choices related to potential miscegenation: Ms. McKenna's desire and control in regard to Ramzees, Sharazade's desire for Brett, followed by Brett's betrayal of the relationship upon discovery of the pregnancy. The behaviors of the upper-class male members of the mostly white Ameritex population demonstrate a fear of miscegenation that operates in the interests of white supremacy and seemingly gives credence to the psychic fear of a disavowal of a common humanity and a contradictory desire for equality that could undermine Ameritex's racial hierarchy. However, the representation of "blackness" in the extraterrestrial form of Ramzees or in the personage of Sharazade implicitly reinforces the promotion of a kind of miscegenation that on its surface seems to be promoting a multiracial discourse but ultimately reinforces the ideologically reactionary, white-supremacist hierarchy of Ameritex. As long as Ramzees is potentially "knockin' boots" with Ms. McKenna, plays football, and has something to eat, he is not trying to figure out how to return home to Heru, and Sharazade, a leader of her people, engages in immature relations with an enemy of her community and risks the safety of the city of Atlantaplex and the Ashanti population.

The central contradiction of *Ramzees* is that in attempting to promote a positive African image, the text and imagery undermines the hero's potential to establish a truly alternative African presence. Therefore, in a postapocalyptic future America, Ramzees ultimately re-creates and reifies Eurocentric notions of the Africans and their gods.

Although *Ramzees* may not be ready to confront a genuinely Afrofuturist vision, other authors have made the attempt, in particular, in the work of W.E.B. Du Bois, George Schuyler, Samuel R. Delany, and Octavia Butler. For example, Du Bois's short story "The Comet," published in the collection of essays *Darkwater: Voices from within the Veil* and republished more recently in *Dark Matter: A Century of Speculative Fiction from the African Diaspora*, expresses fear and desire in an industrially advanced racist society that experiences natural disaster in the form of a comet that passes through the atmosphere and kills almost everyone in New York City. Two survivors, a black man and a white woman, for a time discard old prejudices to form a relationship, until the arrival of a rescue party from outside the city reinforces the racial and sexual paradigm that in the absence of other people had been forgotten and ignored. The story suggests that it will take a natural disaster to alter the nature of race relations in America. Significantly, "The Comet" echoes the experiences of the survivors and victims of Hurricane Katrina who were sharing the same fate in the New Orleans Superdome yet resumed previous hierarchical racialized relationships once the government ostensibly rescued them from their fate.

The pursuit of Utopian tendencies has also been addressed by black scholars such as George Schuyler in his works *Black Internationale* and *Black Empire*. Schuyler's work describes the formation of an international network organized to work for African liberation by utilizing biological warfare, weakening the West to the point that a powerful African empire can be built; oppression in the form of segregation, the transatlantic slave trade, and colonialism have psychologically prepared the black race for world domination. However, *Black Empire* points out that history frequently is the result of the nexus of accident and other events that give rise to power, and not simply race. For example, if race were the sole determining factor, the Republic of South Africa—with its black-elected government, representing citizens who are overwhelmingly people of African descent, after suffering humiliation, death, and worse under apartheid—would be able to transform the lives of its black citizens and become an African super-power, yet it remains unable or unwilling to do so.

The pursuit of *difference* has also been addressed within the black science fiction medium. For example, Samuel Delany's *Stars in My Pocket Like Grains of Sand* (1984) engages and explores a vast range of otherness or difference and conceptually explores a creation of worlds, societies, and species politically in contrast to contemporary society. The novel explores a broader system that comprises several thousand planets and sentient life forms, forming a federation that sponsors a computerized project called GI, or General Information, an encyclopedia construct that can download information into a sentient being's brain in nanoseconds and is part of managing the enormous complexity of life in the text's construction of the universe. Characters range from a survivor of a planetary holocaust, a person with brain damage, those who engage in interspecies sexual relations, and beings who are fluidly identified as either *him* or *her* depending on their sexual excitement levels. An Afrofuturistic, Afrodiasporic parallel to Delany's work may be in reimagining the past, present, and future of the African-Brazilian culture, with its range of color codes, dance as a repository of tradition, politics, and syncretism, contrasted with its links to Amazonian conquest, Yoruba culture, the transatlantic slave trade, and the intersexual intensity of its religious and cultural festival celebrations.

There are several reasons authors incorporate the Afrofuturist tradition into the comics medium. The first is an understanding of the cultural history and literary tradition and its relationship to the technocratic changes that have impacted Afrodiasporic communities and peoples. Second, the Afrofuturist tradition can interrogate the fallacies, hypocrisies, and conceits of the so-called postracial moment, exploring the paradox of black presidential representation and real black misery. Finally, the Afrofuturist tradition provides an indispensable framework for analysis of the current historical moment with its apocalyptic tragedies of genocide, natural disaster, and plutocratic control of resources necessary for human development and survival.

Works Cited

Amin, Samir. *Eurocentrism*. New York: Monthly Review Press, 1989.

Bailyn, Bernard. *The Peopling of British North America: An Introduction*. New York: Random House, 1986.

Banks, Adam J. *Race, Rhetoric, and Technology: Searching for Higher Ground*. Mahwah, NJ: Lawrence Erlbaum, 2006.

Bell, Derrick. "*Brown v. Board of Education* and the Interest-Convergence Dilemma." *Harvard Law Review* 93 (1980).

Bell, Wendell. "An Overview of Future Studies." *The Knowledge Base of Futures Studies, Vol. 1: Foundations*. Ed. Richard A. Slaughter. Melbourne, Australia: DDM, 1996. 28–56.

Bennett, Michael G. "The Adoxic Adventures of John Henry in the 21st Century." *Socialism and Democracy* 20.3 (2006): 245–258.

Bould, Mark. "The Ships Landed Long Ago: Afrofuturism and Black SF." *Science Fiction Studies* 34.2 (2007): 177–186.

Brown, Jeffrey A. "Comic Book Masculinity and the New Black Superhero." *African American Review* 33.1 (1999): 25–42.

Brown, Michael. *Ramzees*. Kansas City, MO: Ghettostone, 1997.

Cather, Willa. *Sapphira and the Slave Girl*. New York: Knopf, 1940.

Clough, Patricia Ticineto. "Technoscience, Global Politics, and Cultural Criticism." *Social Text* 22.3 (2004): 1–23.

Creswell, John W. *Research Design: Qualitative and Quantitative Approaches*. Thousand Oaks, CA: Sage, 1998.

David, Marlo. "Afrofuturism and Post-Soul Possibility in Black Popular Music." *African American Review* 41.4 (2007): 695–707.

Delany, Samuel R. *Stars in My Pocket Like Grains of Sand*. 1984. Middletown, CT: Wesleyan University Press, 2004.

Dery, Mark. *Flame Wars: The Discourse of Cyberculture*. Durham, NC: Duke University Press, 1994.

Du Bois, W.E.B. "The Comet." 1920. *Dark Matter: A Century of Speculative Fiction from the African Diaspora*. Ed. Sheree Renee Thomas. New York: Aspect, 2000. 5–18.

———. *The Souls of Black Folk*. 1903. New York: Penguin, 1989.

Eglash, Ron. "Race, Sex, and Nerds: From Black Geeks to Asian American Hipsters." *Social Text* 20.2 (2002): 49–64.

Emad, Mitra C. "Reading Wonder Woman's Body: Mythologies of Gender and Nation." *Journal of Popular Culture* 39.6. (2006): 954–984.

Eshun, Kodwo. *More Brilliant than the Sun: Adventures in Sonic Fiction*. London: Quartet Books, 1998.

Etter-Lewis, Gwendolyn. *My Soul Is My Own: Oral Narratives of African American Women in the Professions*. New York: Routledge, 1993.

Foertsch, Jacqueline. *Enemies Within: The Cold War and the AIDS Crisis in Literature, Film, and Culture*. Urbana: University of Illinois Press, 2001.

Freedman, Carl. *Critical Theory and Science Fiction*. Middletown, CT: Wesleyan University Press, 2000.

Gilens, Martin. *Why Americans Hate Welfare: Race, Media, and the Politics of Antipoverty Policy*. Chicago: University of Chicago Press, 1999.

Gilroy, Paul. *The Black Atlantic: Modernity and Double Consciousness*. Cambridge, MA: Harvard University Press, 1992.

Goldstein, Nancy. *Jackie Ormes: The First African American Woman Cartoonist*. Ann Arbor: University of Michigan Press, 2008.

Gray, Herman. "Television, Black Americans and the American Dream." *Critical Studies in Mass Communication* 6 (1989): 376–386.

Greenlee, Sam. *The Spook Who Sat by the Door*. New York: Richard W. Baron, 1969

Hartlep, Nicholas D. "Review of *Critical Multiculturalism: From Theory to Practice* by Stephen May & Christine E. Sleeter (Eds.)." *Education Review* 13 (2010). Web. http://www.edrev.info/reviews/rev941.pdf.

Henry, Matthew. "He Is a 'Bad Mother*$%@!#': *Shaft* and Contemporary Black Masculinity." *African American Review* 38.1 (2004): 119–126.

Hine, Darlene Clark. *Hine Sight: Black Women and the Reconstruction of American History*. Bloomington: Indiana University Press, 1996.

Inge, Thomas. *Comics as Culture*. Jackson: University Press of Mississippi, 1990.

Karenga, Maulana. *Maat, the Moral Ideal in Ancient Egypt: A Study in Classical African Ethics*. New York: Routledge, 2004.

Kelley, Robin D. G. *Freedom Dreams: The Black Radical Imagination*. Boston: Beacon, 2003.

Kreiss, Daniel. "Appropriating the Master's Tools: Sun Ra, the Black Panthers, and Black Consciousness, 1952–1973." *Black Music Research Journal* 28.1 (2008): 57–81.

Lee, E. Bun, and Louis A. Browne. "Effects of Television Advertising on African American Teenagers." *Journal of Black Studies* 25.5 (1995): 523–536.

MacIntyre, Alasdair. *After Virtue: A Study in Moral Theory*. South Bend, IN: University of Notre Dame Press, 1984.

Moreau, Julian. *The Black Commandos*. Atlanta: The Cultural Institute Press, 1967.

Morrison, Toni. *Playing in the Dark: Whiteness and the Literary Imagination*. New York: Vintage Books, 1993.

Newton, Judith. *From Panthers to Promise Keepers: Rethinking the Men's Movement*. Lanham, MD: Rowman and Littlefield, 2005.

Nurrudin, Yusuf. "Ancient Black Astronauts and Extraterrestrial Jihads: Islamic Science Fiction as Urban Mythology." *Socialism and Democracy* 20.3 (2006): 127–165.

Ongiri, Amy Abugo. "We Are Family: Black Nationalism, Black Masculinity, and the Black Gay Cultural Imagination." *College Literature* 24.1 (1997): 280–294.

Ocvirk, Otto, Robert Bone, Robert Stinson, and Philip Wigg. *Art Fundamentals: Theory and Practice*. 11th ed. New York: McGraw-Hill, 2002.

Painter, Neil Irvin. *The History of White People*. New York: Norton, 2010.

Palmer-Mehta, Valerie, and Kellie Hay. "A Superhero for Gays? Gay Masculinity and Green Lantern." *Journal of American Culture* 28.4 (2005): 390–404.

Ramirez, Catherine S. "Afrofuturism/Chicanafuturism: Fictive Kin." *Aztlan: A Journal of Chicano Studies* 33.1 (2008): 185–194.

Rivera, Lysa. "Appropriate(d) Cyborgs: Diasporic Identities in Dwayne McDuffie's 'Deathlok' Comic Book Series." *MELUS* 32.3 (2007): 103–127.

Rogoff, Irit. "Studying Visual Culture." *The Visual Culture Reader*. Ed. Nicholas Mirzoeff. New York: Routledge, 1998. 14–26.

Said, Edward. *Orientalism*. New York. Vintage, 1978.

Saroup, Maclan. *Identity, Culture, and the Postmodern World*. Athens: University of Georgia Press, 1996.

Schuyler, George Samuel. *Black Empire*. Boston: Northeastern University Press, 1993.

Singer, Marc. "'Black Skins' and White Masks: Comic Books and the Secret of Race." *African American Review* 36.1 (2002): 107–119.

Solorzano, Daniel G., and Tara J. Yosso. "Toward a Critical Race Theory of Chicana and Chicano Education." *Charting New Terrains of Chicana(o)/Latina(o) Education*. Ed. Carlos Tejeda, Corinne Martinez, and Zeus Leonardo. Cresskill, NJ: Hampton, 2000.

Suvin, Darko. *Metamorphoses of Science Fiction*. New Haven, CT: Yale University Press, 1979.

Szasz, Ferenc M., and Issei Takechi. "Atomic Heroes and Atomic Monsters: American and Japanese Cartoonists Confront the Onset of the Nuclear Age, 1945–1980." *Historian* 69.4 (2007): 728–752.

Thurber, Cheryl. "The Development of the Mammy Image and Mythology." *Southern Women: Histories and Identities*. Ed. Virginia Bernhard. Columbia: University of Missouri Press, 1992. 87–108.

T'Shaka, Oba. *The Art of Leadership*. Richmond, CA: Pan Afrikan, 1990.

White, Sylvia, and Tania Fuentez. "Analysis of Black Images in Comic Strips, 1915–1995." *Newspaper Research Journal* 18.1–2 (1997): 72–85.

Williams, John A. *Sons of Darkness, Sons of Light: A Novel of Some Probability*. Boston: Northeastern University Press, 1999.

Witek, Joseph. "The Dream of Total War: The Limits of a Genre." *Journal of Popular Culture* 30.2 (1996): 37–46.

Yaszek, Lisa. "Afrofuturism, Science Fiction and the History of the Future." *Socialism and Democracy* 20.3 (2006): 41–60.

Chapter 9

Bare Chests, Silver Tiaras, and Removable Afros

• •

The Visual Design of Black
Comic Book Superheroes

BLAIR DAVIS

Superman, Spider-Man, Batman, Captain America, Wonder Woman—these characters rank among the most immediately recognizable superheroes by comic fans and nonfans alike worldwide, having secured an enduring role in popular culture. Each embodies distinctive visual elements: colorful costumes, memorable masks and/or capes, unique symbols and adornments. All five heroes have been well represented in media outside comics, with Superman, Spider-Man, and Batman all enjoying successful film franchises, Wonder Woman appearing in the fondly remembered 1970s television series, and Captain America receiving his first big-budget Hollywood movie in 2011.

While Spider-Man was created in 1962, the other four date back to the late 1930s and early 1940s. As such, all of these characters predate the U.S. Civil Rights Act of 1964 that brought an end to segregation. Coincidentally, these characters all happen to be white, which is not to say that they necessarily contributed to the entrenched racism that the civil rights movement fought against; rather, it is to point out that black superheroes were not prevalent prior to the mid-1960s and were only beginning to gain prominence in the 1970s—the same era that also saw cinema audiences embrace Blaxploitation films such as *Shaft* (1971), *Super Fly* (1972), and *Dolemite* (1975).

Even now in the twenty-first century, few black superheroes have appeared thus far on television and in films, the only significant example being Blade. A vampire hunter who is in fact half vampire himself, Blade appeared in a trilogy of films starring Wesley Snipes between 1998 and 2004, as well as a short-lived television series in 2006. Audiences can be forgiven if they do not know that Blade's origins lie in the comic book medium, given that he forgoes all of the usual visual attributes of superheroes: he does not wear a colorful costume, being garbed mostly in black leather; he lacks a mask, instead wearing a pair of dark glasses; he does not wear a cape, choosing a dark trench coat in its place.

The larger question behind these costume choices is this: if popular culture's most prominent black superhero does not *look* like a superhero, what are the implications for our understanding of those characters that do adhere to the traditional iconography of costumes, masks, capes, and emblems? How are we to "read" the visual design of black superheroes when they are a relative afterthought in the comics industry? White costumed heroes had appeared in comic books for several decades before black superheroes began to appear with any kind of regularity in the industry. How, then, did (predominantly white) comic book creators approach the issue of visual design in creating these new characters?

Many previous studies of black comic book characters have focused primarily on issues of characterization and the stereotypes prevalent therein. What often goes missing in such approaches, however, is an extensive consideration of the visual qualities of such characters. In reviewing Geoff Klock's *How to Read Superhero Comics and Why*, Bart Beaty critiques Klock's approach to analyzing comics as being "entirely literary." "Indeed," writes Beaty, "one could read this book without any sense that comic books are a visual medium" due to the fact that Klock "discusses superhero comics merely as stories with no context and no formal qualities beyond their own self-referentiality" (405–406).

As such, my analysis of black superheroes largely sets aside issues of characterization and narrative in favor of examining visual design, a typically neglected but key element of comics scholarship. The focus here is on the visual elements that have proven common in the design of black superheroes, how these particular elements function as signs that have larger symbolic meanings, the kinds of signifiers that are present in these designs, and the (often hidden) cultural significances therein. Such an analysis will allow for a better understanding of how issues such as race, ethnicity, gender, and sexuality are both explicitly and implicitly embedded within the visual design of such characters and, in turn, how comic books starring black characters create complex meanings solely through their visual elements.

This approach draws on the scholarly tradition of semiotics, generally defined as the study of signs. Semiotics is understood as a technique "for studying meaning in human systems of representation," given that human beings "have the capacity to represent the world in any way we desire through signs" (Danesi 205) As such, the various depictions of black characters created by comic book writers and artists—especially such elements as dress, accessories, weaponry, and the like—become signs that convey particular representations of black culture, identity, and/or history. In other words, the various elements of visual design ascribed to black superheroes become "signs of blackness" that convey certain meanings (either intentional or unintentional) to audiences.

These meanings might be positive or negative—the reception depends on a combination of the images communicated by the comic's creators and the mental concept that is in turn understood by those who are reading the comic and engaging with its images. In semiotics, this is the distinction between the *signifier*, the sign's physical aspect, "which can be seen, heard, felt, etc.," and the *signified*, that which a sign "refers or calls attention to" (Danesi 210). Since readers can be different when it comes to age, gender, cultural background, and other factors, any given signifier/image can create numerous signified meanings—it can stand for numerous different things depending on who engages with it. In this way, signs can become complex sites of meaning, carrying information perhaps unintended by the sender and/or unknown by the receiver.

My efforts here specifically draw inspiration from the work of Roland Barthes in his book *Mythologies*, one of the central texts of cultural studies in general and semiotics in particular. Barthes analyzes such elements of visual culture as professional wrestling and Greta Garbo's face, showing how the cultural meanings behind each are intricately constructed. Barthes describes the inspiration for various essays in his book: "The starting point of these reflections was usually a feeling of impatience at the sight of the 'naturalness' with which newspapers, art and common sense constantly dress up a reality which, even though it is the one we live in, is undoubtedly determined by history. In short, in the account given of our contemporary circumstances, I resented seeing Nature and History confused at every turn, and I wanted to track down, in the decorative display of *what-goes-without-saying*, the ideological abuse which, in my view, is hidden there" (11).

In turn, this chapter was also inspired by a similar restlessness concerning some of the visual qualities of black superheroes, their seeming naturalness within comic book culture, and the resultant ideological implications that often go unstated. Focus will be placed on five characters—Luke Cage, Black Lightning, Storm, Vixen, and Cyborg—from the two major comic book publishers, DC and Marvel. Given both these publishers' overall marketplace dominance and long-standing presence in the industry, characters that were created in the 1960s and 1970s are still prominent in modern comic titles and have often been redesigned multiple times over the years. This examination centers in particular around black characters that were created as "original" superheroes, rather than characters that were created to serve as replacement versions of preexisting white heroes. Examples of the latter include John Stewart, who was initially a substitute for the Green Lantern, and Jason Rusch, who became Firestorm after the death of the previous incarnation, Ronald Raymond.[1] DC often refers to such replacements as "legacy characters," whereby the originals give way to newer and often younger versions of the same character; these replacements are often short-lived, however, and the pattern of original characters returning to glory after a period of absence has become a well-entrenched one in modern comics.

Luke Cage, Power Man

Given the unique way in which comic books combine image and text, the medium is well suited to semiotic analysis, a fact that is underscored in the debut of the superhero Luke Cage (who usually goes by his real name rather than his superhero moniker, Power Man). He first appeared in 1972 in the first issue of Marvel's *Luke Cage, Hero for Hire*, a monthly series in which he starred until 1986.[2] The first page of this debut issue serves as a kind of manifesto for the semiotic study of black superheroes, with narration that declares, "Look closely at the figure before you. Study *him*, study his *costume*. This is Luke Cage *now*. A super-hero . . . yet *unlike* any other before him. But he was not *always* as you see him. Before the super-hero, there was the *man*."

As such, readers are invited, even commanded, to reflect on the visual design of a character whose adventures they have not yet even begun to experience. In short, readers know nothing about Luke Cage beyond what they can observe; the standard process of introducing a hero via narrative-based characterization is forgone here, replaced with imagery that has no substantial narrative context thus far. This introductory text appears among a full-page image of Cage, surrounded by several smaller images establishing the world he inhabits—an alleyway shootout, an attractive female at a nightclub, cards and dice (gambling paraphernalia), a police officer and a police car with sirens wailing, signs for various bars, and the word "Harlem" in large block letters (*Luke Cage* #1, 1) Readers must interpret this amalgam of lurid imagery as they simultaneously form an opinion of a character to whom they are being introduced. Cage (and his costume) therefore assumes the very nature of all of the images that surround him, being linked in the reader's mind with scenes that are implied as being criminal and/or morally questionable given the entrenched presence of the law among this visual milieu.

An escaped-yet-reformed convict given superpowers who decides to make a difference in his community, Cage selects his costume from a costume shop; it features a distinctive yellow shirt that opens to reveal his bare chest, a silver headband, and steel bracelets, all of which formerly belonged to an escape artist. "Escape artist, huh? Kinda tried something like that myself," he says in reference to his prison breakout. "Kinda like this headband," says Cage, "'specially with my hair getting longer." As he tries the costume on, he asks the owner, "Not bad,

9.1 Luke Cage is linked to criminality and morally questionable pursuits through the visual design that contains images of the police and sexuality.

but pretty quiet . . . anything left in that trunk with a little flash?" The answer comes in a thick length of steel chain, which is used to make a belt (*Luke Cage* #2 [August 1972]: 7) Cage states how he can relate to the chain, which he says will serve "as a kind of reminder" (7). While not explicitly stated, it may be assumed that this chain is meant as a reminder of his recent incarceration and any questionable activities in his past life. By extension, the steel chain (along with his bracelets, which resemble shackles) also serves as a reminder of the heritage of slavery that Cage carries with him as a black male, signifying the chains that bound those who were loaded onto slave ships to make the forced journey from Africa to foreign lands. Though his chain binds him (given that it is used as a belt around his waist), Cage has the ability to use it as a weapon if desired and to use it against those who might oppress him in ways that his ancestors could only dream of.

As Cage puts his costume on at home for the first time, he declares (with some buyer's remorse?), "Yeah! Outfit's kinda hokey . . . but so what? All part of the super-hero scene. And this way when I use my powers it's gonna seem natural" (*Luke Cage* #1, 22). Being a superhero apparently connotes a certain sense of the ridiculous, perhaps given the colorful flamboyance of many heroes' costumes (with their capes, tights, masks, and exterior underwear, etc.). Yet such lavishness is apparently to be excused if accompanied by a display of one's powers, as if superheroes need to be made visually distinct from the general public so as to avoid the shock of an ordinary man or woman performing incredible, seemingly inhuman feats of strength or other such abilities. Cage therefore intends his costume to serve as a sort of uniform, one that identifies him as a protector, rather than an offender, and as a member of a higher rank that typically carries with it a certain amount of social status, respect, and/or fear—much as the uniform of a police officer does.

What has often greeted Cage in the comic book community, however, is not admiration, at least not fully. Discussions among comic book fans and creators surrounding Cage in recent decades have routinely focused on one item of his costume: his headpiece. Though it is not referred to as such in his earliest appearances, the headband has since become known as a tiara—an item commonly worn by brides and princesses and therefore representing intense femininity. In an issue of the Marvel series *New Avengers*, a superhero group to which Cage currently belongs, his wife jokingly tells him with regard to a failed reunion with his father, "What do you want from the man? You used to wear a metal tiara. In public" (*New Avengers* 1, #47 [January 2009]: 27). Furthermore, his steel wristbands appear strikingly similar to those worn by Wonder Woman, further aligning him with historically feminine costume patterns. The joke can also be found in pop-culture examples outside the comics medium; in an episode of the animated television show *The Boondocks*, a young character states that he would not want to have a superhero based on him because "all the black superheroes are corny": "They'd probably give me a metal headband and a yellow disco shirt or something stupid" (*The Boondocks*, Cartoon Network, 4 January 2006).

Given the perceived absurdity of Cage's costume, the character was redesigned in a 2002 Marvel miniseries, in which he wore street clothes instead of a costume. Gone were the silver tiara and steel chain belt, accessories that were replaced with a long gold chain around his neck with the word "Cage" attached, along with a gold watch, sunglasses, and headphones attached to a portable music device. Garbed in blue jeans, sneakers, a denim vest, and a skull cap, Cage is reintroduced to the reader as he sits watching a stripper in a topless bar, albeit via a full-length mirror, with his back turned to the room (*Cage* #1 [April 2003]: 3). Whereas the opening montage of images in his 1972 debut places him in a world of crime, gambling, and nightclubs, with the narrator implying that he is no longer prone to such vices ("Before the super-hero, there was the man"), in 2002 Cage's appearance gives the impression that he is once again part of an illicit subculture that he had formerly renounced. The flashy jewelry and baggy jeans serve to align him with the countless drug dealers who undoubtedly wear the same attire in the story's inner-city setting, while the fact that he wears sunglasses and headphones in a bar suggests a sense of disconnect with his surroundings, a barrier that prevents others from fully knowing what he might be thinking or feeling.

The mirror that Cage uses to observe his surroundings involves a literal process of reflection, but on a larger symbolic level, it also invites the reader to reflect on the new character design and its stark differences from past iterations. The reader is compelled to (just as the 1972 narrator states) "look closely" at Cage and "study him," something that Cage may well be doing himself as he stares into the mirror. Here, as with Cage's debut appearance, the black superhero is presented to the reader as an object of study to be visually scrutinized, to be looked at and considered closely, to be deliberately gazed upon. In film studies, the concept of the gaze refers to the relationship between spectator and screen and the somewhat voyeuristic implications involved in how the viewer derives pleasure from watching (usually while in a darkened theater) people/characters who are unaware that they are being observed (Hayward 156–159). Many feminist film scholars see the cinematic gaze as being "male," with Laura Mulvey describing how "the unconscious of patriarchal society has structured film form" (746). "Going beyond highlighting a woman's to-be-looked-at-ness," she argues, "cinema builds the way she is to be looked at into the spectacle itself" (756). In turn, then, it is worth asking if a "comic book gaze" exists, and if so, whether this gaze is a "white" one, particularly regarding depictions of ethnic diversity.

Most recently, in 2004, Cage became a member of the Avengers, Marvel's premier superhero team. His visual design has been made even more minimalist, however, as he sports a shaved head and typically wears only jeans and a T-shirt or undershirt (his jewelry and headphones perhaps a hindrance in battle). As such, Cage stands out as the only member without a costume on a team consisting of such colorfully costumed characters as Spider-Man, Wolverine,

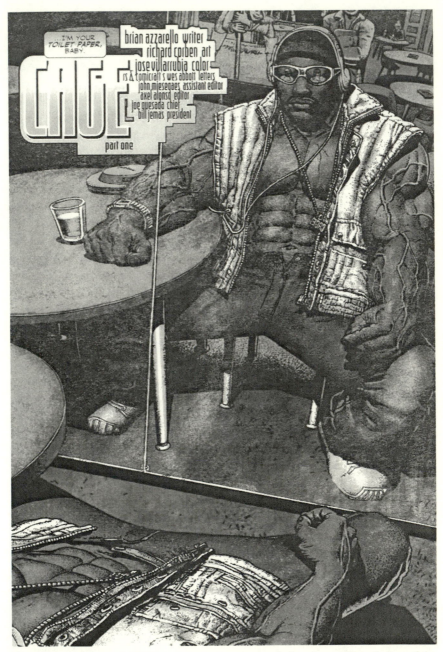

9.2 The flashy jewelry and baggy jeans align Luke Cage with the culture of drug dealers, while the sunglasses and headphones he wears suggests a sense of disconnect with his surroundings.

and Captain America. In this sense, Cage's clothing suggests a kind of negative presence: for all but the very newest of readers, Cage's current noncostume constantly invokes his old 1970s costume/visual design because all of its elements have been stripped away—his clothing, accessories, and even his Afro hairstyle have all been eliminated, leaving no trace of his former appearance.

To perceive the modern Luke Cage is therefore to view him through the filter of his past incarnations. We recognize him as a superhero even though his outfit lacks any such symbolism because we know which visual elements are missing and have been abandoned. Just as his 1972 debut sought to chronicle his rise from "man" to "super-hero," it can be argued that modern writers apparently desire to return his "manhood" to him after several emasculating years of "silver tiara" jokes (although those occasionally still persist) and to distinguish him visually from all of the "hokey" costumes that constitute the "super-hero scene." In so doing, however, Cage's status as a superhero becomes relatively more limited outside the context of comic book fans, given that he currently lacks the iconographic imagery that the costumes of such internationally recognizable heroes as Superman and Spider-Man provide to audiences.

To unfamiliar readers, Cage appears to be just an average man; perhaps this is exactly the point: that the average person can indeed be a hero and make a difference in his or her community, an ideal that Cage has sought to uphold since his debut. There still remains an unsettling factor in this explanation, however. Given the minuscule number of black superheroes in existence, perhaps the fact that Cage is a black man is meant to be a "costume" in and of itself—his skin color alone is enough to distinguish him visually from the overwhelming number of white heroes that surround him.

Black Lightning

A similar pattern to Luke Cage's can be found in the evolution of the character design of Black Lightning—a high school teacher and Olympic gold-medal decathlete named Jefferson Pierce who moonlights as a superhero with the power to generate electrical blasts. Created in 1977 and the first African American superhero to receive his own series at DC Comics, he wears a costume that reflects his powers, in that it has yellow lightning bolts adorning the length of both his sleeves and chest. While readily conveying the nature of his superhuman abilities, the outfit is not the most visually distinctive element of Black Lightning's costume. As a way of protecting his secret identity, Pierce wears a white mask covering his eyes and forehead—a mask that is attached to an Afro wig. Although he already has a full head of hair (which he keeps relatively close cropped), the use of the wig serves to render Pierce practically unrecognizable in his civilian life.

Various entries of Black Lightning's short-lived 1970s series depict the process of putting on and/or removing the mask/wig, an image that is somehow mildly disturbing despite the seeming ordinariness with which this action is

9.3 While readily conveying the nature of Black Lightning's superhuman abilities, the outfit is not the most visually distinctive element of his costume.

typically presented (as a simple costume change while the hero talks or thinks about his adventures, motivations, etc.). As opposed to the ability of film, photography, and television to capture images in a realistic manner, comic book art is a much more abstract representation of reality that renders human bodies and faces as icons—that is, as visual signs that distinctly resemble a particular subject. Even though they are simply lines drawn on paper, we still recognize Luke Cage and Jefferson Pierce as black men, since the sum of these lines clearly conveys their ethnicity. In Black Lightning's case, his Afro is a distinct signifier of his ethnicity, albeit one chosen for the purposes of disguise. For those readers unaware of the fact that this Afro is part of a removable mask, however, his hair style would appear to be a natural one, until such time as he is seen removing it. Given the relative lack of realism found in comic book art, the reader is therefore unable to discern that Black Lightning is wearing a wig (unlike in film and television, where astute viewers might be able to recognize the wig for what it is, given that many use synthetic hair, are poorly constructed, etc.). A comic book wig, on the other hand, will largely appear indistinguishable from real hair precisely because we are *not* seeing real hair but rather an iconic hand-drawn representation of human hair, one that need only give the *impression* of being hair rather than re-create it in completely authentic detail.

As such, when Black Lightning removes his mask and wig, the hair that he sheds appears virtually identical to the hair that is revealed to be underneath, given that it is typically drawn in the same way; the hairstyles themselves may be different (Afro versus shorter cut), but the actual hair itself appears identical given that relatively few lines are required to draw it. On a visual level, Black Lightning's Afro therefore appears to be a sort of second skin; it is ultimately artificial in nature but attains a certain naturalness in the way that it is depicted given how the comic book medium encodes reality through images that are composed of degrees of abstraction. Connected to the mask as the Afro is, it consequently appears somewhat similar to a severed or scalped head upon removal—an image that unwittingly becomes more unnerving given how individual panels of the 1970s series often seem to show Pierce holding it aloft like a kind of trophy, deliberately showing it to the reader in order to clearly demonstrate the very nature of the disguise itself.

The Afro-mask also serves to make an ethnic minority character "more ethnic" by giving him a hairstyle that was viewed not only as a fashion statement but also as a form of political expression in the 1970s. The Afro became closely connected to the "black is beautiful" movement that emerged out of the civil rights struggles of the 1960s. "African Americans have long had a seriously vexed relationship with the very notion of beauty," states Kendra Hamilton, with the Afro therefore becoming a way of reclaiming and celebrating an African identity that American society had long sought to alter and repress (34). Pierce's ability to affix and remove his Afro as desired signifies a paradoxical acceptance and rejection of the Afro's beauty: with his superhero persona striving to be a symbol of justice and power, the Afro in turn becomes a sign of strength and virility. When he removes it to assume his civilian identity, the Afro sits impotently on the shelf while Pierce teaches the youth of a neighborhood known as "Suicide Slum"—children whose socioeconomic status often presents them with struggles in arriving at the kind of identity construction that the "black is beautiful" movement attempts to foster. This begs the question as to whether Pierce is using the Black Lightning persona and its Afro-mask to construct his own sense of identity, one that potentially goes beyond expressions of ethnic pride and masculinity that are possible within the institutional confines of his role as a high school teacher.

While Black Lightning's series was canceled in 1978, the character endured in both guest appearances and as part of a team of superheroes called the Outsiders throughout most of the 1980s. Black Lightning was given a second solo series in 1995, which allowed the opportunity for a visual redesign. Gone was his original costume, mask, and wig, his true face now exposed. In place of his old outfit, he now wore a leather jacket adorned with lightning bolts—still somewhat visually distinctive, although similar enough in style to the colorful "8-ball" leather jackets that were popular among some hip-hop enthusiasts in the early 1990s so as to go unnoticed. As such, the jacket serves to connect Black Lightning with his urban environment more directly than his former costume did (as "street wear" rather than seeming traditional or "hokey"), especially given that some of the villains that he faces in this new series also wear leather jackets.

In this way, the jacket serves as a symbol of what was considered to be masculine in the 1990s within the context of an inner-city culture. Whereas in the 1970s this context would have included the Afro as a symbol of black masculine identity, as cultures change over time, so too does the symbolism through which gender identity is constructed. The Afro eventually gave way to other hairstyles, including the shaved head (as popularized by athletes such as Michael Jordan and rappers such as Tupac Shakur). By the late 1990s, the shaved head became a new standard for black masculine identity (particularly in urban settings), perhaps for its perceived athleticism and/or toughness.

It is therefore no surprise that characters such as Black Lightning and Luke Cage were redesigned in the early 2000s to include the shaved head as a part of their visual design. With Pierce a member of DC's Justice League of America since 2006, his new costume, a spandex one-piece yet again adorned with lightning bolts, clearly distinguishes him as a superhero in a way that his 1990s leather jacket did not—which is only fitting given that the character has never been more prominent in the DC Comics universe.[3] Much like Cage's visual redesign, Black Lightning's shaved head also suggests a negative presence given how central his Afro was to his original costume; his shaved head serves as a denial of the Afro-wig's symbolism and possibly an attempt by modern comics creators to undo any perceived symbolic damage caused by the wig's artificiality. He still wears a mask in his modern incarnation, suggesting the same need to protect his civilian identity, yet the Afro-wig has been replaced by a new set of signifying practices. Each era defines masculinity differently, with such definitions also being subject to variations based on such factors as ethnicity. With many superheroes serving as conspicuous symbols of masculinity (e.g., the strength of Superman, the Hulk's rage, etc.), it is natural for black male superheroes to reflect, consciously or not, the dominant societal values that construct black masculinity in any given period.

Storm and Vixen

While black masculine identity is frequently constructed in comic books through the use of hairstyles and distinct costume accessories, so too are black female superheroes often designed with similar elements in mind. Unlike Cage and Pierce, both Storm of Marvel's X-Men and Vixen of DC's Justice League are from Africa, later migrating to America and joining their respective teams. As such, their costumes include design elements that reflect this African culture. The question becomes whether such imagery is used to celebrate their heritage or whether it is used for the purposes of mere exploitation.

Storm (whose real name is Ororo Iqadi Munroe) has gone through many different changes in costume and hairstyle throughout her history. Her first appearance finds her initially portrayed not as a superhero, however, but as a kind of deity. Her debut in 1975 sees her living as a self-proclaimed goddess in Kenya, using her power of weather control to aid the drought-induced suffering of the local villagers, whom she repeatedly refers to as "my children." She stands before a large stone portal atop a hillside as the locals cry, "Ororo, great goddess of the storm . . . come ease us of our burden!" (*Giant Size X-Men* #1 [Summer 1975]: 7). She wears only a skirt and a headdress, and her long white hair covers her breasts—her seminude body is in keeping with those of the villagers who pray before her. An apparent part of her culture, such nudity therefore becomes naturalized within the context of the scene, with only her headdress setting her apart from the others.

In this way, the headdress becomes a focal point, a symbol of her role as a religious figure in this community, becoming imbued with ceremonial power. As an American superhero using powers that were initially honed in Africa through religious ritual and at the behest of humbled villagers, Storm's initial displays of such power while in battle therefore take on this religious context since she is using abilities typically meant to aid her flock of worshippers. Her headdress therefore serves as the only connection between her role as goddess and her new role as superhero—which requires a costume to cover the nudity that was permissible in her former cultural context. Yet rather than embrace this new role and look, Storm was often portrayed in the 1970s as feeling more comfortable in her Kenyan attire. "Gods, this feels marvelous!" she says as she strips her costume off entirely, her long hair once again covering her breasts and midsection. "We X-men have been fighting so hard, for so long. . . I'd almost forgotten what it's like to relax." Later, as the team swims and sunbathes, a bikini-clad Ororo comments on Western traditions concerning beach attire. "The sun feels so good, it reminds me of home. Gods, I wish I didn't have to wear these absurd scraps of cloth . . . it is only for the Professor's sake that I endure this land's strange taboos" (*Uncanny X-Men* #109 [February 1977]: 3, 13).

As such, Storm becomes an ethnic fish out of water, whose comments on the strangeness of American clothing customs undoubtedly serve to make the nudity and tribal attire from her life in Kenya appear themselves unusual and questionable to many readers in turn. In any case, it is clear that Storm does not feel that her costume reflects her true identity; rather, it is only a trapping that she endures in order to fulfill her role on the team. It is not surprising, then, that she underwent a kind of visual identity crisis in the 1980s, with her initial costume and hairstyle eventually replaced by a leather punk outfit and Mohawk hairdo. The headdress that had served as her only visual link to the past and her African culture was now gone, a relic of her former self; the Mohawk literally does not provide enough hair to support such a headpiece, just as there is apparently no room for African cultural identity within this punk wardrobe. *X-Men* artist Paul Smith recently admitted that Storm's punk look was "a bad joke gone too far": "I knew that they were going to cut the hair, so as a joke I put a Mr. T mohawk on her. . . . But once you get into the whole leather and stud thing it was a bad joke that got way out of hand" (*Marvel Spotlight: Uncanny X-Men 500 Issues Celebration*, June 2008, 20).

In other words, this new redesign did not reflect Storm's true character or her cultural heritage, which is why it seemed so absurd and was abandoned before long. In recent years, Storm has been returned to Africa through her marriage to T'Challa, a character who goes by the moniker Black Panther and is king of the fictional African nation Wakanda. In her new role as an African queen, Storm has been returned to her initial elevated status in her homeland, only this time as royalty rather than as a goddess. Her character design reflects this change, as she now often wears luxurious dresses and other such garments befitting an African queen rather than always wearing her superhero costume. She now also regularly wears her original headpiece again, a symbol of the fact that modern creators have returned the character to her cultural roots, whereby her identity is constructed through ethnic pride rather than by way of her flagrant otherness in American society.

In contrast to this modern reclaiming of Storm's original visual design, the original look of DC's Vixen (whose real name is Mari Jiwe McCabe) was almost immediately abandoned and remains little known in modern comics culture. With Vixen first set to star in her own ongoing series in 1978, the book was canceled before it was ever released due to a company-wide reduction in its total output of titles. The first issue was written and drawn, however, and reproductions are available through private collectors. Vixen, also known in an early nickname as the Lady Fox, has the power to draw on the abilities of any animal through the use of her "Tantu Totem"—supposedly a powerful object in African mythology.

Her first outfit, a leftover Halloween costume found in her closet, included a gold mask with fox ears, along with the golden totem necklace. As she puts the necklace on for the first time, she draws on the power of a lion, a fox, and antelopes (whose "spirits" we see the outline of), while the narrator describes the "slow opening of eyes that are no longer human . . . Suddenly her head lifts, and as a jungle cat, she senses something in the air." The canceled issue concludes with Mari describing her first efforts as a superhero: "Last night I felt something I'd never known before . . . a totality . . . a completeness . . . so primitive it was almost a rebirth" (*Cancelled Comics Cavalcade*, 240–241, 253). Such rhetoric (inhuman, cat-like, primitive), combined with the fox mask and animal-based powers, becomes problematic given Vixen's African heritage. Numerous writers from the nineteenth and early twentieth centuries drew parallels between the "negro" and the "animal": Robert Wilson Shufeldt states that "negroes are grossly animal" in his 1915 book *America's Greatest Problem: The Negro* (145), while John H. Van Evrie describes "the negro child" as possessing a "vastly greater approximation to the animal" than white children in his 1870 book *White Supremacy and Negro Subordination* (227). Examples such as these are commonly found throughout this period, with this negro-as-animal discourse still persistent among white supremacists today—even turning up in a February 18, 2009, *New York Post* cartoon that seemingly compares President Barack Obama to a chimpanzee (Reuters).

Vixen's first published appearance came in 1981 alongside Superman in an issue of *Action Comics*, with the narrator describing her as "a She-Fox on the prowl" (*Action Comics* 1, #521 [July 1981]: 1). Wearing the same costume as she did in her canceled book, she is also seen in her civilian identity wearing

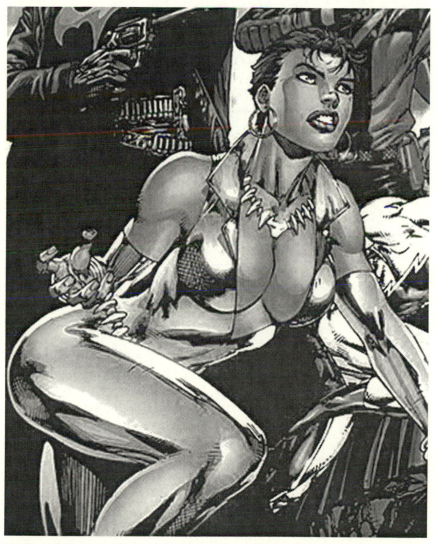

9.4 Through costume and hairstyle, Vixen is made to look more feral, savage, and animalistic than most female superheroes.

a dress with white, jagged edging around the neckline, therefore resembling teeth to extend the animal imagery even further. She appeared in only one other issue with Superman in her original costume, before joining the Justice League of America in 1984. With only two appearances in the period 2011–2014, she was relatively unknown enough to warrant a new costume, since her original look was known by few. The Tantu Totem necklace, initially an abstract-shaped figure, was changed to resemble a wolf's head. The same wolf's-head pattern also appears on the lower back of her costume, further reinforcing her connection to the animal world. Her mask now discarded, in its place stands a distinct hairstyle—long hair entirely covered with beads in the back, with shorter hair on top that sweeps up into two sharp points. Beads are often worn in the hair of African chiefs and warriors as a sign of prestige (Hoffman), yet the fact that the sweeping points in her hair are reminiscent of horns once again makes her look more feral, savage, and animalistic than most female superheroes.

Any sexuality that Vixen embodies, therefore, becomes closely tied to the "wild" and "savage" nature of her costume as based on her animal-drawn powers. This sexuality, much like Ororo's nudity, is distinctly nonurban in nature; unlike the urban masculinity of Luke Cage and Black Lightning, black female sexuality as embodied by Storm and Vixen is connected to the natural environment of Africa. Vixen's new visual design may therefore be seen as either constructed to honor her African heritage or else in exploitation of it. Those who are inclined to argue the latter might cite as evidence the DC character Animal Man, a white superhero with extremely similar animal-based powers whose costume betrays none of the animalistic symbolism that Vixen embodies. The only thing relatively distinct about his costume (consisting of an orange spandex bodysuit, goggles, and a blue jacket and boots) is the large "A" on his chest—none of which gives any indication of his powers or his heritage.

Cyborg

DC's Cyborg (whose real name is Victor Stone) is a member of the Teen Titans whose body was almost entirely rebuilt using enhanced cybernetic prosthetics. The result left him a combination of man and machine, with nearly half of his skull and all of his extremities now made of metal, giving him enhanced speed, strength, and other abilities. Cyborg's altered appearance drove him into deep despair as he "found himself the victim of frightened stares and the rejection of former friends" (Wein, Wolfman, and Greenberger 31). This notion of duality and the anguish that it can provoke is echoed in W.E.B. Du Bois's 1903 examination of the African American condition, *The Souls of Black Folk*:

> It is a peculiar sensation, this double-consciousness, this sense of always looking at one's self through the eyes of others, of measuring one's soul by the tape of a world that looks on in amused contempt and pity. One ever feels his

twoness,—an American, a Negro; two warring souls, two thoughts, two unreconciled strivings; two warring ideals in one dark body, whose dogged strength alone keeps it from being torn asunder. The history of the American Negro is the history of this strife,—this longing to attain self-conscious manhood, to merge his double self into a better and truer self. (3)

The awkwardness and unease that Cyborg's artificial body inspires therefore becomes a metaphor for the "contempt and pity" that Du Bois describes. While it is Cyborg's mechanical appearance rather than his race that serves to differentiate him, the character serves as a kind of allegory about judgment based on physical appearance. This notion was likely a factor in the decision to use Cyborg as a member of the Justice League in the final season of the popular children's television cartoon *Superfriends*, in which his origin was retold. In a 1985 episode titled "Seeds of Doom," viewers are told how Cyborg was "so distraught over his robotic appearance that he became reclusive and shunned all publicity." He initially declines an offer to join the group, stating, "I want to have a regular life. . . . Look at me, take a good look. I'll never have a secret identity. I can't hide this face and pretend I'm somebody else. . . . It's tough enough getting people to accept me as normal. Imagine what life would be like if I joined."

Once again, viewers are directly invited to "look" at a black character, echoing Du Bois's rhetoric as he describes a world that is forever "looking on." Just as Luke Cage's narrator compels the reader to "look closely" and "study" him, Cyborg too becomes an object of scrutiny—the black superhero subjected to the gaze. What makes this compulsive gazing even more problematic, however, is the fact that varying degrees of exposed flesh factor into the visual design of all five characters examined herein. In addition to Vixen's backless costumes, Storm's costumes regularly display her bare thighs and/or shoulders, while both Luke Cage's and Black Lightning's original costumes feature shirts that open up to display their bare chests (the latter trend also seen in the exposed chests of other black male heroes of the 1970s, such as The Falcon, Black Goliath, and Brother Voodoo). This pattern is taken to further extremes with Cyborg, whose mechanized body features exposed areas of skin throughout. His chest, shoulders, and thighs are all prominent to varying degrees, as if to remind the reader that he is more than just a mere robot (and in turn persistently reinforcing the double consciousness that he embodies).

Michael Eric Dyson argues that for white Christians in the era of slavery, "the black body was a savage body" (240). Slavery therefore became rationalized along theological lines, "which introduced into our culture some vicious beliefs that have negatively impacted our racial self-perceptions," not the least of which, says Dyson, has to do with black men and women "as the subjects of our own sexuality" (240). When slaves were sold at auction, their bodies became subject to close scrutiny by white bidders who sought to determine the strength of potential male slaves, who would be put to work, and the desirability

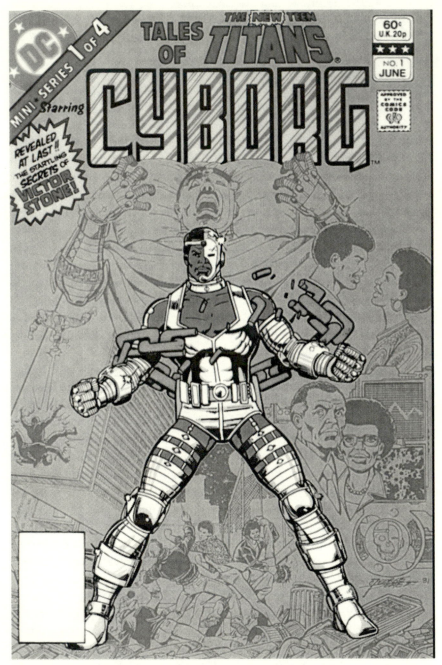

9.5 Cyborg echoes Du Bois's idea of contempt and pity; the character serves as an allegory about judgment based on physical appearance.

of female slaves, who were often subjected to rape by their masters. Jay Grossman describes how the slave auction "represents one of the relatively few arenas for the public display and the literal commodification of the human body" in pre–Civil War American culture (183). The need to "look closely" at the chest, arms, and thighs of such slaves becomes uncannily paralleled in the visual design of many black comic book superheroes, particularly when readers are spurred by a narrator to scrutinize the black flesh that has been so blatantly put on display.

Representations and Revelations: Cultural Evolutions

Asked what the state of ethnic characters in the comic book industry was in the early 1990s, Michael Davis (a founder of Milestone comics, an imprint of DC from 1993 to 1997 featuring African American superheroes that were brought back again in 2009) replied, "As far as I'm concerned, if [a] state did exist, it wasn't much of a state. It was a smattering of black characters here and there from DC and Marvel." Milestone cofounder Denys Cowan added that by 1993, "there were black characters like the Luke Cages and the Black Panthers and the Falcons. But . . . it didn't seem like there were any characters of color that had a prominent place in [any] comic book company's pantheon. They weren't the same as—and very few characters are—the Batmans, the Supermans, the Captain Americas" (Powell 26).

A major factor in what sets such heroes as Luke Cage and Black Lightning apart from Superman, Batman, and Captain America is the role of their costume design and the deployment of vague or temporally specific iconography. Superman's cape, Batman's cowl, and their respective chest symbols, as well as Captain America's American-flag color scheme and shield, are so visually distinct that they prove highly memorable, along with the fact that such imagery plays an ongoing role in the characterization of each hero. By comparison, the costumes of many black superheroes tell us little about the characters—perhaps explaining why such costumes seem to get redesigned every decade or so. At best, many of the accessories that make up these costumes are somewhat oddly developed, a little "hokey," but perhaps simply a product of their time, such as the removable Afro and the silver tiara; at their worst, they can be construed as the bizarre fetish objects of white mainstream representations of black identities that soon became objects of ridicule within the comic book community.

Du Bois describes how "the Negro is a sort of seventh-son, born with a veil and gifted with a second-sight in this American world,—a world which yields him no true self-consciousness, but only lets him see himself through the revelation of the other world" (3). Given that white writers and artists created the majority of black superheroes, these characters, and their reception among audiences, can therefore be seen as touchstones for how white American society regards black identity (including such concerns as ethnicity, gender, and sexuality, among others) in any given period. Since cultural beliefs typically change over time, so too does the visual design of these characters evolve, with specific costumes, hairstyles, and the like becoming closely connected to specific eras in American history, along with their respective dominant discourses surrounding race and culture. As we move into the future, how, then, will both current and future characters reflect the cultural changes that are to come?

Notes

1 Legacy characters at DC typically wear the original costume of the original hero that they are replacing or filling in for, although minor design modifications are often made.
2 The series underwent two title changes, the first to *Power Man* in 1974 and then to *Power Man and Iron Fist* in 1977 with the addition of a new partner.
3 For instance, Black Lightning was featured in a tie-in issue of DC's *Final Crisis* mini-series, the company's highest selling books of 2008.

Works Cited

Barthes, Roland. *Mythologies*. Trans. Annette Lavers. London: Granada, 1973.

Beaty, Bart. "Review Essay: Assessing Contemporary Comics Scholarship." *Canadian Journal of Communication* 29.3–4 (2004): 403–409.

Danesi, Marcel. *Encyclopedic Dictionary of Semiotics, Media and Communications*. Toronto: University of Toronto Press, 2000.

Du Bois, W.E.B. *The Souls of Black Folk*. 1903. New York: Oxford University Press, 2009.

Dyson, Michael Eric. "Homotextualities: The Bible, Sexual Ethics, and the Theology of Homoeroticism." *The Michael Eric Dyson Reader*. New York: Basic Civitas Books, 2004. 238–257.

Grossman, Jay. *Reconstituting the American Renaissance*. Durham, NC: Duke University Press, 2003.

Hamilton, Kendra. "Embracing 'Black Is Beautiful.'" *Black Issues in Higher Education* 17.23 (2001): 34–35.

Hayward Susan. *Cinema Studies: The Key Concepts*. 2nd ed. New York: Routledge, 2000.

Hoffman, Deborah. "Fashion; Out of Africa: Beads with a History." *New York Times* 17 June 1990. Web. http://www.nytimes.com/1990/06/17/style/fashion-out-of-africa-beads-with-a-history.html. Accessed 27 August 2012.

Klock, Geoff. *How to Read Superhero Comics and Why*. London: Bloomsbury Academic, 2002.

Mulvey, Laura. "Visual Pleasure and Narrative Cinema." *Film Theory and Criticism*. 4th ed. Ed. Gerald Mast, Marshall Cohen, and Leo Braudy. New York: Oxford University Press, 1992. 746–757.

Powell, Matt. "The Milestone Retrospective." *Wizard* 209 (March 2009): 25-27

Reuters. "New Yorkers to Boycott *NY Post* over 'Racist' Cartoon." 19 February 2009. Web. http://uk.reuters.com/article/mediaNews/idUKN1949241020090219. Accessed 27 August 2012.

Shufeldt, Robert Wilson. *America's Greatest Problem: The Negro*. Philadelphia: F. A. Davis, 1915.

Van Evrie, John H. *White Supremacy and Negro Subordination*. New York: Van Evrie, Horton, 1870.

Wein, Len, Marv Wolfman, and Robert Greenberger, eds. *Who's Who: The Definitive Directory of the DC Universe*. Vol. 1, no. 5. New York: DC Comics, July 1985.

Panel IV

Graphic Blackness

• •

Chapter 10

Daddy Cool

● ●

Donald Goines's "Visual Novel"

KINOHI NISHIKAWA

Visual stereotypes have played a critical if sometimes troubling role in the development of comics art in the twentieth century. To the extent that the medium grew out of a need to satisfy popular tastes, ready-made signifiers of racial and ethnic difference have served as modes of shorthand to establish or prop up white characters' wit, integrity, physique, and even superhero status. Early comic-strip artists drew African American characters in particular as outsized yet somehow "representative" figures of laziness, servility, and a primitivism born of Africanist origins or basic human naiveté. Much like their cinematic counterparts in Hollywood, who would have been played by typecast blacks or whites in blackface, these characters were also given bits of dialogue that underlined their essential otherness with literal-minded, heavily accented, and otherwise "improper" speech.[1] In a survey of comics' extensive use of visual stereotypes over the course of the medium's development, Christian Davenport has aptly reflected, "Even within a medium usually associated with fantasy and escape, [blacks] were not allowed to get away from American racism" (22).

The rise of black male superheroes in the post-civil-rights era seemed to augur a shift in dominant representations of race in comics art. Characters featured in mainstream series, such as Luke Cage, Black Goliath, and Black Lightning, shed the docile disposition and clunky speech of previous generations' figures and embodied strong, self-aware, and ostensibly race-positive images of black

215

derring-do. These images no doubt constituted the industry's way of responding to the liberalizing terrain of American racial politics in the 1960s. Even here, though, critics have pointed out the limiting conditions of African Americans' visibility as superheroes. Davenport, for one, has suggested that these characters were confined to scenarios that only served to index their racial particularity. The black superhero, then, often was cast in "local" or neighborhood story lines "that do not [a]ffect (or have limited implications for) the greater society" (23). This burden of particularity found its complement in what Jeffrey A. Brown has referred to as the "one-dimensional masculine ideal" of black superheroes. For him, the terms of hypermasculinity—"being *too* hard, *too* physical, *too* bodily"— that had previously been used by whites to restrict black men's civil rights were unduly reanimated in characters who are "more overtly macho than their white-bread counterparts" (26, 28, 34).

If post-civil-rights visibility in comics art demanded that black superheroes be restricted to urban scenarios that lauded hypermasculine traits, one might conclude that the racialized characters who did come out during this time were no less typecast than earlier figures had been. These characters simply followed a different, equally limiting, script. While such a conclusion has ensued from criticism of white-authored comics, it may well apply to an overlooked text in black comics art: *Daddy Cool* (1984), which listed Donald Goines as the author. As the first graphic novel to have appeared under an African American author's name, *Daddy Cool* draws from the same arsenal of Blaxploitation stereotypes that Brown has linked to post-civil-rights superheroes' essentializing hyper-masculinity (31). And because the text's script revolves around an urban crime scenario, it would appear to succumb to the kind of ideological particularity that has yoked visual stereotypes of race to notions of inner-city violence and crimi-nality. That these elements may be found in a graphic novel attributed to Goines is troubling, given the genre's presumed superiority in meaning and message over traditional comics. Indeed standard surveys of African American graphic novels, which usually begin in the 2000s with texts that consciously refigure and critique racial stereotypes, would seem to have no place in the young tradition for *Daddy Cool* (see Chaney).

In keeping with the pulp fiction writer's series of hard-boiled novels pub-lished in the early 1970s, *Daddy Cool* is an adaptation that traffics in stereotypes, and particularly images of tough black masculinity and sexually available black femininity. Like its pulp predecessors, the book was marketed to a predomi-nantly black audience. Yet despite the attribution to Goines, *Daddy Cool* was written by Don Glut, a comics veteran and fringe Hollywood scriptwriter, and illustrated by Alfredo Alcala, a Filipino comics artist who specialized in spectac-ular images of masculine brawn and female eroticism. Neither man had known Goines, and each only had his 1974 novel of the same name on which to base his adaptation. Still, there is a case to be made for claiming *Daddy Cool* as the first black graphic novel.[2] Historically, Holloway House, the independent Los

Angeles publisher that had discovered Goines and published all of his work, was the country's leading source of African American popular literature by the 1980s. *Daddy Cool* represented the firm's latest foray into a genre that had the potential for widespread appeal among black readers themselves. Equally significant, on the level of form, *Daddy Cool* demonstrates a certain reflexivity in its use of stereotypes, playing word and image off each other in a way that complicates any straightforward reading of the novel as yet another turn on the wheel of racist stereotyping in American visual culture. Glut and Alcala's formal collaboration in fact yields complex negotiations of racial type and nontype—what I refer to as *black surface* and *black depth*, respectively—that subsequent comics artists have implicitly invoked in their own work.

The analysis that follows not only uncovers the history behind a "lost" text in the black comics tradition but also theorizes a tension between surface and depth that is itself a function of the "skin," or surface appeal, of the visual work. *Daddy Cool*'s use of visual stereotypes, I argue, is mitigated to some degree by the large amount of text devoted to characters' interior monologues. Between the third-person narrative and these thought bubbles, we literally see how *Daddy Cool* weds racial and gendered stereotypes to a shifting terrain of black psychological depth. Crucially, such depth is predicated not simply on words-as-text (that is, prioritizing word over image in expressing psychology) but on the critical interplay between words and images in discrete, medium-specific units (panels, pages, and so forth). As such, *Daddy Cool* combines traditional comics' recourse to type (black surface) with a narrative commitment to characterological interiority (black depth) precisely through the visual field.

Visualizing Blackness

Daddy Cool's narrative is the stuff of hard-boiled pulp fiction. The titular character is a middle-aged black man whose real name is Larry Jackson. Under the cover of running a pool hall in Detroit, Larry works as a hit man for bosses in the black underworld. Despite his fearsome demeanor and preference for homemade knives to do his killing, Larry is quite the family man: he uses income from contracts to provide a comfortable life in the suburbs for his wife, Shirley; their teenage daughter, Janet; and his stepsons, Jimmy and Buddy. Yet the underworld from which Larry seeks to protect his family (while working in it on the sly) proves too alluring for his children, with tragic consequences. Jimmy and Buddy get caught up in the fast life with a local hoodlum, Tiny. After the trio robs a local numbers house, Larry must hold Jimmy and Tiny to account for the rape of the boss's thirteen-year-old daughter. Larry dispatches the guilty parties with ease and forces Buddy to leave town. But Janet, too, poses tremendous problems for Larry when she runs away from home to follow Ronald, an up-and-coming pimp who she thinks will become her boyfriend and then husband. Ronald has nothing of the sort in mind, of course, and he leads

Janet on until she starts working as a prostitute herself. Despite the downturn in her fortunes, Janet continues to choose Ronald over Larry. When the former is killed by one of her father's associates, she gains revenge with the very instrument her father taught her to use: a knife. In the end, Larry is slain by his own daughter, and the story concludes with his middle-class, nuclear-family dream in ruins.

Daddy Cool was originally published by Holloway House at what was the peak and terminus of Donald Goines's literary career. No fewer than half of his sixteen pulp novels appeared in 1974. However, in October of that year, Goines and his live-in partner, Shirley Sailor, were brutally gunned down in their Detroit home by unknown assailants. Although the double homicide is unsolved to this day, relatives, acquaintances, and authorities alike have speculated that some aspect of Goines's criminal past—drug contacts from his time abusing heroin, underworld figures who had not appreciated making (veiled) appearances in his novels, and so forth—caught up with him (Allen 173–200). Whatever the case may be, a sad irony pervades the fact that one of Goines's final literary creations, Larry Jackson, should come to mirror his own position as a father and breadwinner, shuttling uncomfortably between the middle class and the underworld, with the real-life Shirley sharing his deplorable fate. The undoing of patriarchal authority by false idols or father figures from the underworld is the subject of *Daddy Cool*, and Goines's enduring popularity among African American readers owes no small part to the impression that he actually experienced this and similar trials throughout his troubled life.

Adapting *Daddy Cool* into a graphic novel ten years after its publication would have been greatly facilitated by the fact that Goines's prose possesses the snap and zing of an action-packed Hollywood movie. In fact, he had spent a part of the year before his death living with Shirley in Los Angeles, where he could be closer to his publisher and explore the possibility of becoming a scriptwriter for Blaxploitation movies. Goines did not manage to break into the industry, but he did learn to emulate narrative templates in which urban black men on both sides of the law—the likes of John Shaft, Youngblood Priest, and the anonymous fugitive otherwise known as Sweetback—achieved renown for their streetwise cunning and sexual virility. The pulp fiction writer in turn rarely bothered with narrative detail or long-form description in his later novels: what mattered above all was propelling the protagonist's action forward, much like how one storyboards a movie by homing in on its most arresting scenes. Larry Jackson, a.k.a. Daddy Cool, would vie with the gangster-revolutionary Kenyatta as Goines's most recognizable character culled from spectacular images of urban black masculinity.

In keeping with Goines's vision, the graphic novel of *Daddy Cool* debuted in a sturdy eight-by-eleven edition with a cover that harked back to the classic hard-boiled detective of an earlier age (see fig. 10.1). Goines's name is emblazoned over the red-colored title, under which is a malapropistic but nonetheless evocative subtitle reading, "The story of a hit man's fearful vengeance in defense of his teenage daughter's honor." To the left of the text, Larry Jackson is prominently displayed as a lone, well-clad figure incongruously positioned in what appears to be a trash-strewn alleyway. If the dirty, cast-off setting is meant to conjure the image of urban decline, then Larry stands tall as the rugged, calm, and collected—that is, "cool"—black man who metaphorically transcends such

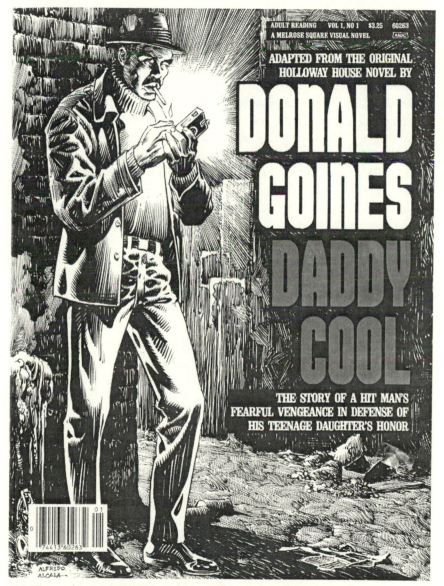

10.1 The graphic novel of *Daddy Cool* debuted in a sturdy eight-by-eleven edition with a cover that harked back to the classic hard-boiled detective of an earlier age.

poverty of place and spirit. Accordingly, the match that Larry has just lit to touch against the cigarette casually dangling from his lips shines a beacon of light on his face, as well as on the wall behind him. The starkly vertical figure thus embodies what Goines imagined as his own urban masculine ideal, a figure who, like countless Blaxploitation (anti)heroes before him, occupies an unusually powerful position on the street: in that space yet singularly not of its filthy, soul-crushing milieu.

As striking as the cover is, the graphic novel's publication undeniably signaled Holloway House's attempt to capitalize on another emerging market in American print culture. Ever the opportunistic publisher, the firm had previously dipped into true crime, erotica, tell-all biography, black pulp fiction, and similarly lowbrow paperback genres while being linked to periodical ventures, controlled by the same owners, that ran the gamut from pinup magazines to *Mankind*, a cheap imitation of *National Geographic*. Nonetheless, *Daddy Cool* was a legitimate entry into the nascent graphic novel market, appearing as it did under Holloway House's imprint Melrose Square as the first "visual novel" in its proposed series of the genre. Will Eisner's *A Contract with God, and Other Tenement Stories* had popularized the term *graphic novel* in the trade market upon its publication in 1978. As Charles Hatfield has noted, Eisner's intention in using the term "was to break into bookstores, not comic shops," to fashion "a way of promoting serious comics to . . . a general readership" (29). Like *A Contract with God*, *Daddy Cool* had not been previously serialized, and while the marketing term differed in name, the book's length, design, and cost ($3.25) would have made it immediately recognizable as part of the genre. But unlike Eisner's work, *Daddy Cool*'s veering away from traditional comics fans led it not to the general market but to the places where black pulp fiction was already being sold: newsstands, bookstores, and corner shops in the black community.

With Goines's popularity already well established in the black community, the graphic novel likely proved to be a tempting investment for the intrepid publisher. To capture the essence of Goines's fast-paced narrative in comics form, Holloway House enlisted the Los Angeles–based Don Glut to adapt and write the script and Alfredo Alcala to compose the artwork for *Daddy Cool*. Born in Pecos, Texas, in 1944, Glut had been raised in Chicago and made his name as a young director of homemade amateur movies featuring monsters, dinosaurs, and superheroes. Glut's precocious filmmaking brought him to the attention of comics artists, B-movie producers, and fellow genre buffs at various fan conventions. He eventually moved to Los Angeles, where, after a brief spell at the University of Southern California, he edited prominent fanzines and became a scriptwriter for movies, television, and comic books (Glut, *Teenage*; Glut, home page). Alcala shared Glut's bottom-up entrée into the comics scene, but he had made his name on the other side of the world. Born in 1925 in Talisay, Philippines, Alcala was a self-taught illustrator who began cartooning in earnest during the Japanese occupation in World War II. His reputation took off after the war, drawing as he did for the country's biggest komiks publishers, and in 1963 he created what is considered to be his greatest work: the fantasy serial *Voltar*. In that entirely self-produced comic, Alcala's intricately lined, lavishly detailed aesthetic brought to life the chiseled titular protagonist, his beastly antagonists, and a bevy of buxom female characters. The popular strip caught the attention of American comics publishers, and in 1972 Alcala permanently moved to the United States, where over the next two decades he worked on numerous fantasy, horror, and superhero serials for DC and Marvel. Of these, Alcala's influential renderings in *Conan the Barbarian* not only drew inspiration from *Voltar* but critically determined how American popular culture forever envisioned the sword-and-sorcery hero (see MacDonald and Yeh; Spurgeon).

Glut and Alcala brought their respective experiences to bear on *Daddy Cool*. Each had established himself as an accomplished practitioner of the popular sequential arts, yet neither could be said to have challenged the medium's reliance on digestible narrative or recognizable stereotype. Their collaboration did not yield a graphic novel that completely reworked previous efforts to visualize blackness in the post-civil-rights era. Their sixty-four-page end product also left no time or space for a self-conscious "break" in the chain of events that plummet characters ever further into the criminal underworld. For all that, Glut and Alcala's mastery of medium-specific conventions was the very thing that allowed them—again, with only Goines's novel to go on—to shape *Daddy Cool* into a complex reflection of racial type and nontype. Glut and Alcala worked purely on the surface of the comics text—what I earlier called its skin—and it was on that plane that they sought to keep word and image in tense relation throughout the book. By doing so, they remained true to Goines's urban masculine ideal while mining the narrative motivations and visual paradoxes that lay behind such an ideal. Their efforts yielded a groundbreaking work that aims to visualize blackness's surfaces and depths not through what is "said" or implied but precisely (and only) in what is seen.

Hard-Boiled Men

Larry Jackson embodies hypermasculine traits that underscore his racial particularity and thereby threaten to obstruct nuanced perspectives on post-civil-rights African American subjectivity. Yet as Dennis Chester has argued, Donald Goines made the most of working within "generic pulp-fiction structures" and created in Larry a character who is "primarily concerned with family issues" (99). For all of *Daddy Cool*'s validation of Larry's toughness, his steely-eyed determination, and even his uncompromising view of death as a job to be carried out with professional indifference, its narrative ultimately amounts to a father's efforts to save his children, and particularly Janet, from the streets. This conceit, it turns out, has a long pedigree in the hard-boiled tradition. Leonard

Cassuto, in outlining the cultural politics of an ideology he terms "hard-boiled sentimentality," has ventured the rather counterintuitive claim that male-authored crime fiction of the twentieth century embraced and put a new spin on themes that had their origins in female-authored sentimental fiction from the nineteenth century. His suggestion is that insofar as hard-boiled novels have dwelled on the corruption and alienation of (post)industrial society, what we see is the famously lone hard-boiled protagonist finding his true cause or purpose in protecting communal ties and family values, just as sentimental heroines had done in the past. These typically opposed genres thus share a deep investment in "the home as a center of value against the public market economy" or, in Goines's case, the inner city's black market (Cassuto 11).

A complex narrative of wayward youth, patriarchal concern, and female sexual exploitation undergirds *Daddy Cool*'s lattice of racial type. Chester has reminded us that the key to unlocking this story line is to attend to Goines's "focus on Larry's innermost thoughts," which in its very interiority "reveals his personal struggles and complicated relationship with mainstream society" (99). Of course, Don Glut and Alfredo Alcala could not draw from the exact set of resources available to Goines in composing their version of *Daddy Cool*. Their basic unit of representation—a flat visual surface—by definition could not access the "private" or reflective space of Larry's thoughts to the degree that even the stripped-down, word-based narrative did. So Glut and Alcala, mindful of the need to keep up the tempo of action in sequential art, worked around this obstacle by composing finely calibrated page layouts that played type and nontype, movement and thought, off each other. With this dance of visual contradictions, they managed to capture the illusion of depth on the projected screen of the urban masculine ideal.

The extraordinary compactness of *Daddy Cool*'s visual storytelling informs the terms by which Glut and Alcala achieve the illusion of depth. Alcala's comics generally evince a preference for the six-panel layout over the standard nine panels because having too many images on a single page, he once said, can "lead to confusion on the part of the reader" (qtd. in MacDonald and Yeh 36). In one illustrative set piece composed on a single page, three panels show Larry lost in thought, worrying over Janet while surveying a target in Los Angeles. What is particularly striking about the first two images is how Larry's calm, collected stride and fixed gaze are put in tension with thought bubbles that bespeak his anxiety. The close-up of his face is particularly telling as he realizes the extent to which Janet intrudes on his professional indifference: "At this rate, I might end up payin' the dues I owe too!" (Glut and Alcala 23). With that piece of insight, one is almost forced to recast his gaze not as hard or self-assured but as blank—that is, unfocused on the job at hand. The façade of toughness that this image displays on one level is further complicated by the fact that, just two pages earlier, Glut and Alcala devote two purely pictorial panels to the Afro wig and "black face makeup" that Larry dons in order to complete his hit-man disguise. Larry's cool exterior, then, is quite clearly just that: an artificially "dark-ened" mask that conceals a welter of personal and family strife.

The decisive third panel zooms out to reveal the potential cost of Larry's brooding distraction: a gang of young men is now tracking the tracker. From here to the end of the page, it is the muggers who are endowed with forward momentum, with Larry cutting an almost static figure. The fourth panel breaks completely from his interior state to intone, "But now, his mind 2,000 miles away, he never even hears the hurrying footsteps" (23). The muggers succeed in overtaking Larry, whose only utterances on this page are words of shock and an onomatopoetic cry of pain. Interiority has betrayed him here, and while Larry eventually musters the concentration to kill his mark several days later, this epi-sode forces him to concede his wallet and dignity to the young criminals. To be sure, Larry's victimization is precisely orchestrated to convey a set of concerns that run deeper than his fearsome persona would otherwise suggest. Glut and Alcala's combination of narrative, thought, and speech—all on the surface of the page—propel Larry to his comeuppance at the same time that it reveals the urban masculine ideal's fatherly soft spot.

That soft spot's appearance in *Daddy Cool* is by no means an inherent expres-sion of weakness on Larry's part. In fact, the representational possibilities of his sentiment are all relative to Alcala's set pieces, as two earlier pages demonstrate. The first has a five-panel grid that begins with a wide image of the cozy suburban street on which Larry has worked tirelessly to situate his family (see fig. 10.2). The next panel interrupts the expansive serenity of the scene as Larry espies Ronald's "pimpmobile" parked in front of his house (6). His interior mono-logue provides useful exposition that establishes Ronald's perfidy. Yet the fourth panel alternates between thought and speech in a way that exceeds a rote state-ment of facts. Lacking an iconic cigarette dangling casually from his lips (as it is in the middle panels), the increasingly agitated Larry moves from thinking about Janet's folly to blurting out "Gotta keep cool" to fretting inwardly that he must not let his family see him "get really mad!" (6). This panel shows Larry's inner turmoil to great effect, and the sixth panel—wherein he recalls his "only close friend" Earl's offer to "handle [the] young disrespectful punk" (6)—adds to such turmoil with a frame that implies a state of dark reverie.

Whereas the mugging episode attributes stasis and distraction to Larry's untimely consideration of Janet's predicament, here being in close proximity to his rival for Janet's love transforms his troubled thoughts into a course of action. On the next page, a six-panel layout, the perspective shifts from Larry's car to Ronald's, in which Ronald and Janet are caught being intimately involved. The young man looks the antithesis of Larry at first blush, sporting a conservative suit and well-coiffed hair. But Glut and Alcala lend Ronald his own illusion of depth once Larry's blinding headlights shine into the vehicle. The middle pan-els show Ronald forcing Janet out of his car while executing his exit so as not to seem scared: "Don't want to start the engine too fast," he pauses to reflect,

10.2 The representational possibilities of Larry's sentiment are all relative to Alcala's set pieces. Note this five-panel grid that begins with a wide image of the cozy suburban street on which Larry has worked tirelessly to situate his family.

"when I got enough time to just cruise out of here and show Daddy Fool I ain't that shook by the motherfucker" (7). In just four panels, Glut and Alcala envision Ronald first as a middle-class man about town, then as a tough guy, and finally as a figure who is playacting both roles to conceal his true identity as a hustler and procurer. If Larry has a soft spot at the core of his hard-boiled persona, then Ronald has a hard heart that contrasts markedly with all of Janet's expectations for his character.

The final two panels in the set piece actualize Larry's inner turmoil in a way that may be motivated by sentiment but is most assuredly not sentimental. Janet has words for her father, the abundance of which takes up a fair amount of the fifth panel while spilling over into the sixth. In a moment of clarity, she acknowledges that Ronald drove off gradually only to appear unfazed by Larry's presence. That fleeting realization does not amount to much, however, as Janet chooses Ronald over Larry: "I mean, he's a man too—even if he is much younger than you!" (7). This comment provokes Larry to lash out at his daughter in a manner that conforms to the stereotypically ruthless behavior of the urban masculine ideal (see fig. 10.3). With a hit man's swiftness of movement, he slaps Janet across the face and shouts, "Hear this, littl' bitch! If you ever try speakin' to me in that tone of voice again, I'll kick your ass so hard you won't be able to sit sideways in that goddam Caddie!" (7). Larry's violent thrust forward is one of the most disturbing images in the book, highlighting as it does fleshly impact, whereas his professional targets are visually distanced by a throw of the knife. And while the previous page establishes an underlying motive for such an act, it is nonetheless telling that Larry's soft spot is expressed here in a denunciation that has a recognizably Blaxploitation ring to it.

That the clearest example of hypermasculine stereotype in *Daddy Cool* arrives at Janet's expense no doubt indexes the unchallenged status of patriarchy in the narrative. Larry's outburst takes the form of displaced aggression; the true object of his ire, Ronald, escapes unscathed, leaving Janet to suffer the blow of his pent-up rage. In such a competition between men for her love, it is ironically the case that the previous six-panel grid is the only one in which Ronald and Larry appear on the same page. Yet neither here nor anywhere else in the book do the men meet face to face. Instead, their battle is taken to be more symbolic than literal, with the ultimate goal of swaying Janet's affections one way or the other. Glut and Alcala emphasize this formal, symbolic link much later in the novel when Ronald slaps Janet out of the blue, echoing Larry's use of the term "bitch" in accusing her of holding back on prostitution income (49). By that stage, we have already seen Larry in his Los Angeles guise, and the resemblance between it and Ronald's image is both uncanny and deliberate.

In a final twist of irony, Glut and Alcala move beyond the patriarchy script and visualize Larry's erstwhile friend, the pool-hall tender Earl, as the most atypical figure of urban black masculinity in the graphic novel. Earl is a portrait of contradictions: hulking in physique yet sensitive in spirit, his heavily scarred face belying a personality that balks at swearing and being labeled a "freak" (12). It is Earl who, recognizing the turmoil that Larry tries to keep bottled up, takes it upon himself to do away with Ronald. His intention may be to help Janet, but in truth his reverence for Larry as his benefactor and friend is what drives Earl to take decisive action. The final chapter of the novel is revealing in that Earl, not Larry (whose death at the hands of Janet is rendered almost an afterthought),

10.3 Larry lashes out at his daughter in a manner that conforms to the stereotypically ruthless behavior of the urban masculine ideal.

occupies pride of place in Alcala's drawings. Larry's dark reverie from the car is literalized as Earl lies in wait for Roland outside his apartment. In a panel that takes up four of the usual panel slots, the chapter's first image has a hooded Earl, arms crossed and body shrouded in etched darkness, standing as the ultimate hard-boiled figure. Crucially, he is no Daddy Cool, and for good reason: Earl's decision to go against Larry's wishes—"Daddy Cools gonna be mad about this," he muses (59)—subordinates the stereotypical patriarchal script to the latent homosocial one. When he finally does strangle the life out of Ronald, thereby setting in motion events that lead to Larry's death as well as his own, we already understand that Earl operates on an order of cool different in kind from Larry's. Curious as it may seem, the narrator remarks in the opening panel of the page that Earl "hates . . . having to be out in the streets" (59).

Sexual Divisions

To be sure, there is nothing strictly latent about Earl's act at all: its homosocial motive is as apparent on the page as anything else. Perhaps, then, it is more accurate to say that it is only at the end of the book when Earl's embodiment of urban black masculinity visually emerges as the critical double to Larry's. Between these two characters, *Daddy Cool* ends on a note that binds homosociality to patriarchy in a manner that keeps both "alive" to the reader's sensibilities. Earl's centrality to the final chapter may not undo the martyr effect achieved by the death of Larry, but it certainly goes some way toward revealing fractures within, as well as paradoxical iterations of, the hard-boiled archetype. Gliding along the skin of the text, Earl—the only character who ever confronts Ronald face-to-face—adds layers of atypical meaning to those scenes in which *Daddy Cool* reverts to type.

The same is more difficult to argue when it comes to the graphic novel's female characters. Following Donald Goines's lead, Don Glut scripts and Alfredo Alcala draws black women who fit into one of two categories: mother figure or sexual object. Such a stereotypical division arguably orients *Daddy Cool*'s technique of characterization more around the axis of gender than it does race. This makes a certain amount of sense if one considers the fact that the underworld in which the characters conduct their business is an exclusively black space. Goines, moreover, never wrote for a "white" audience—a luxury that Holloway House afforded him as the king of black pulp fiction. The point, then, is that it is not particularly surprising that *Daddy Cool* should distribute visual difference as much intraracially as it does between blackness and a tacit, or implied, whiteness. Both the text and its reception context locate finer shades of racial community precisely in the assumed bedrock of gender difference. Of course, what this also means is that female characters in the graphic novel risk being ossified as gender types that lack any character depth whatsoever.

Let us consider how that risk is negotiated in Glut and Alcala's renderings of the two sides of black femininity in the narrative. First, middle-aged and older black women in *Daddy Cool* are invariably cast as buxom and asexual caregivers who are incidental to the progression of male action. For example, two respectable women come to Larry's aid after the mugging assault in Los Angeles. Their motives are pure, but Alcala's emphasis on their dark, heavyset bodies conjures the stereotype of the mammy or maid as the eternally servile black woman. If we recall the wig that Larry sports in the episode, it is perhaps significant to note that Alcala renders all three characters' hair indistinguishable. This detail seems to suggest that the do-gooders exist only to affirm the urban masculine ideal that is the focus of their attention. That the set piece concludes with an image of the sexualized Janet—who is still in Detroit—inviting the reader's gaze to survey her scantily clad body, makes demonstrably clear that Larry's rescuers are mere bystanders to *Daddy Cool*'s narrative development.

A more complex mother figure may be found in the character of Shirley. At first, Shirley is cast as a homely screwup whose ostensible permissiveness in parental matters is to blame for the children's waywardness. In the scene immediately following Larry's discovery of Ronald's car, Shirley receives a tongue-lashing from her incensed husband: "If you had taken care of your responsibilities like you should have this wouldn't have been necessary" (8). The next morning, Shirley, wearing the same low-cut nightgown as the night before, reveals that Janet ran away from home. Here Alcala's rendering of her ponderous breasts, which seem on the verge of spilling out of their support, indicates an untoward maternal influence. Larry says as much when he calls Shirley's sons— one of whom we soon realize is indeed in cahoots with Ronald—"spoiled littl' bastards, use to [sic] havin' their own fuckin' way" (11). Within this context of family turmoil, Shirley's literal figure seems to stand in for what Larry identifies as her motherly excess: babying the children to the point where they revolt against the law of the father.

Toward the end of *Daddy Cool*, however, Glut and Alcala impart the illusion of depth to Shirley's character in a manner that suggests that she, too, struggles under the weight of Larry's unreasonable expectations. Over three sequential panels that do not fit into the usual page layout, Larry sets off to gain revenge (for a paying client) against his stepsons and their partner in crime, Tiny. Just before he leaves, he kisses his wife passionately on the lips, and it is her thought bubble that punctuates the panel's visual organization: "Our first kiss in ten years" (55). The revelation comes as something of a surprise insofar as it is related from Shirley's perspective. Glut's words tentatively locate frustrated desire in the wife's consciousness, which here stands apart from the shortcomings that Larry has up to now projected onto her. The next two panels continue to track Shirley's musings as she sees her husband in a new light: not as a young lover or doting father but as an "old" man who looks as though he has the mark of "death on him" (56). One may well blush at such potboiler insight, but the fact that this, Shirley's final appearance, shows her thinking for herself and presaging Larry's demise is important. Not coincidentally, Alcala's rendering of her ample bosom in the second panel no longer appears ponderous but seems desirable in its own right. Informed by the interior monologue, the skin of the text here lends depth to Shirley's character precisely by sexualizing a previously cumbersome feature.

A modicum of interior agency is granted to Shirley through the interplay of word and image in this two-page sequence. But what of the female characters who are visually sexualized to begin with? These characters are teenagers and young black women, almost all of whom appear nude or at least scantily clad in the graphic novel. What is more, each girl or young woman is incongruously endowed with large, firm breasts and a voluptuous physique. Subtending that image, of course, is the pernicious stereotype of black female hypersexuality, and Holloway House, it turns out, had a long track record of promoting its visual representation. One of the company's more successful offshoot productions was *Players*, the world's first all-black pornographic magazine, which debuted in 1973. A sort of *Playboy*-cum-*Penthouse* for African American men, *Players* combined feature articles, consumer reporting, and literary fare (spanning black pulp fiction to Ishmael Reed) with photographs of explicit female nudity. Unsurprisingly, the idealized body type displayed in Alcala's drawings is the same one that had been celebrated, drooled over, and rendered completely available in the pages of *Players* for over a decade. *Daddy Cool* would have circulated right alongside copies of the magazine, as both were marketed to the public by Holloway House's own distribution company.

Along with this precedent, *Daddy Cool*'s investment in erotic imagery would have been loosely associated with Glut's work on the only other graphic novel released by the imprint Melrose Square. Likely a compendium of serials from one of Holloway House's pornographic magazines for white men, *Fanta* was also published in 1984 and called "A Fantasy in Visuals." Glut served as the scriptwriter, while Brian Forbes, a comics artist at *Penthouse*, provided the X-rated illustrations.[3] The sixty-five-page, all-color book underscores the extent to which Holloway House entered into the comics market aiming to capitalize on prurient rather than self-consciously "literary" interests. The book, in fact, may not meet the criteria for graphic novel status insofar as its twelve stand-alone episodes are brought together under the flimsy pretext of wandering through the titular character's "House of Pleasure" (see fig. 10.4). Although *Fanta* would have been distributed primarily to Holloway House's smaller audience of white readers—indeed its volume and issue numbers distinguish it as separate from the planned-for series after *Daddy Cool*—it nonetheless establishes Glut's association with the frankly pornographic in a way that should inform our assessment of his collaboration with Alcala.

Perhaps it is to Glut and Alcala's credit that *Daddy Cool* is actually quite different from *Fanta* in the way it visualizes sexual objects. Whereas the latter provides an almost seamless path toward the consummation of normative heterosexual fantasy, the former is constantly engaged in the process of granting and then short-circuiting male desire. To be more precise, Alcala's illustrations of young female bodies are undoubtedly linked to the aesthetic of black softcore pornography that *Players* helped to establish. Yet more often than not, spaces of sexual objectification in *Daddy Cool* lie in close proximity to images of perverse, exploitative, and theoretically "uncool" expressions of male lust. Examples that illustrate this point include one view of a completely naked Janet followed up by an image of her first john pinning her to the bed in an act, we are told, that "takes less than three minutes" (Glut and Alcala 36) and one view of the

10.4 *Fanta* was called "A Fantasy in Visuals" and was aimed at exploiting prurient rather than literary interests.

naked daughter of a local crime boss followed on the same page by images of Jimmy violently raping her. This self-conscious interplay of objectification and repulsion is most spectacularly achieved in a two-page set piece depicting Ronald's seduction of Janet. The first page makes the unique move of dissolving all panel borders in order to capture the otherworldly pleasure that Ronald visits on her body. The second page, however, reintroduces the six-panel grid in order to demarcate Ronald's thought bubbles, which emphasize his cold and calculating plan to exploit her body (see fig. 10.5). The contrast between the pages is great, and it intends to show how opposite Janet's ecstasy and Ronald's desire, her naiveté and his cunning, really are.

In these examples of Alcala's visual pairings, the compositional proximity of the second set of images to the first lends the illusion of depth not necessarily to the female characters or even to the males. Rather, the illusion makes available deeper reflection on the pornographic image itself: to desire it is, sequentially speaking, to wish to do violence to it. This structure of visualization is so pervasive in *Daddy Cool* that the only set piece in which exploitation is neither proximate to nor emergent from the image of the female nude has to introduce a new perversion to its logic. Like the enlarged panel featuring Earl in the final chapter, the panel featuring Janet at the beginning of chapter 3 has a decisive effect on how we see her character. Having run away to be with Ronald, Janet is shown alone and fully exposed while in the shower; Alcala ensures full access to her body by somehow excluding a curtain. The narrator relates how Janet regrets "no longer [being] a virgin," but it is the thought bubble, hovering just over to the left of her curvy figure, that immediately catches the eye: "Oh, Lord, why couldn't I've met a man like Daddy to take care of everything!" (27). So the citation of "Daddy" within the image raises the uncomfortable specter of incest in the narrative. Even here, then, where the sexual object is rendered voyeuristically

10.5 Ronald's seduction of Janet initially removes all panel borders in order to capture the pleasure Janet feels. The second page reintroduces the panel borders to emphasize Ronald's cold and calculating nature.

available to the male gaze, the incursion of a symbolic truth, and maybe a literal half truth, qualifies the fantasy that Janet's body is meant to foment.

Far from overreaching, this point reaches its logical outcome in the penultimate meeting between father and daughter. In that episode, Larry picks up Janet, now a full-time prostitute, off the street, and almost immediately two white policemen attempt to arrest him. On a narrative level, the accusation of paying money to sleep with his own daughter intrudes on what is supposed to be a warmhearted reunion. Larry stridently denies the misapprehension and eventually straightens things out. Yet the rest of the episode is devoted to laying out exactly how Larry pays for Janet's affection. Having showered her with $2,000 for her birthday, it becomes abundantly clear that Larry, not Shirley, is the spoiler between the two and that his soft spot is more determining of his actions than he could possibly acknowledge. As Alcala uses two panels to highlight the exchange of money from father to daughter, and when he then punctuates the scene with an image of Janet cutting a lone figure walking down the street in miniskirt and halter top, we come to visualize the Jacksons' demise before the fact: he hides under the mask of a self-possessed tough guy, and her desire is bought by Daddy Cool himself.

In a groundbreaking analysis of racial types in the superhero comics tradition, Jeffrey A. Brown has argued that one way of challenging the burden of hypermasculinity in our visual culture is to "incorporat[e] the associated properties of the mind (e.g., intelligence, control, wisdom) into the popular presentation of black male identity" (31). The uniqueness of *Daddy Cool* as the first graphic novel in the black comics tradition rests not only on its negotiation of stereotypes long associated with black hypermasculinity and black female hypersexuality but in its wager that the atypical aspects of post-civil-rights racial identity must always exceed the bounds of a prescripted interiority (that is, "intelligence, control, wisdom"). Indeed "seeing" characters' interiority in the graphic novel is but an effect of Don Glut and Alfredo Alcala's efforts to yield layered, contradictory, and paradoxical meanings in *Daddy Cool*'s surface narrative. Throughout this chapter, we have seen how those meanings do not conform to a singular method of complicating stereotypes. In fact, they are just as likely to bring to light hypocrisy, unconscious desire, and a troubling will to exploit as they are reason, sensitivity, and a faith in being fully human. And of course, why should it be otherwise? *Daddy Cool*'s pulp roots in Donald Goines's fiction teach us that the interior life of urban black characters is sufficiently complex to leave room for representing the gamut of human motive and interest.

It bears repeating, too, that the process of bringing to light this fraught interiority in *Daddy Cool* transpires entirely on the surface of the comics page. How we apprehend black depth in the graphic novel is, as this chapter has maintained, less an effect or function of narrative revelation as it is of visual composition. For this reason, the 2003 reprint of Goines's "visual novel" threatens to undo the very form by which the preceding analysis has staked its claims.

The reorganization of Alcala's panels and page layouts into a form conducive to the mass-market paperback not only distorts the relative meaning assigned to different panels; in the process, it also subordinates the interplay of word and image to the successive display of easily consumable types. Compositional parallels and contrasts that were essential to the first edition's artfulness are, lamentably, no longer available in print. Among other impressions, the imprint leaves us with undue emphasis on Larry's sanctimonious rants and subsequent death, the ill-timed plotting of Earl's intervention, and above all, the lingering, detached gaze of straightforward sexual objectification. It may well be prudent to assert in closing, then, that recovering the formal innovation of *Daddy Cool* to the black comics tradition needs to go hand in hand with the recovery of its original material form.

Notes

1 For a catalogue of early comics images in this vein, see Strömberg.
2 This statement could be qualified on a number of levels, not least its determination of race and its periodization of and geographical attribution for the term *graphic novel*. Don McGregor and Paul Gulacy's *Sabre: Slow Fade of an Endangered Species* (1978), for example, is regarded as one of the first modern graphic novels, but its postapocalyptic protagonist bears no creative connection to African American writers or artists. Georges Wolinski and Melvin Van Peebles's French-language comics adaptation of the first book in Chester Himes's Harlem series, *La reine des pommes* (1979), meanwhile, has much in common with *Daddy Cool*'s production history, but its generic status is arguably better suited by the Franco-Belgian term *bande dessinée*. Let us say, then, that the statement is heuristic in nature, put forth ultimately in the service of advocating a more robust and comprehensive historicization of African American graphic novels.
3 These points of textual history have been derived from the author's consultation of a personal copy of the exceedingly rare work. See Glut and Forbes.

Works Cited

Allen, Eddie B., Jr. *Low Road: The Life and Legacy of Donald Goines*. New York: St. Martin's, 2004.

Brown, Jeffrey A. "Comic Book Masculinity and the New Black Superhero." *African American Review* 33.1 (1999): 25–42.

Cassuto, Leonard. *Hard-Boiled Sentimentality: The Secret History of American Crime Stories*. New York: Columbia University Press, 2009.

Chaney, Michael A. "Drawing on History in Recent African American Graphic Novels." *MELUS* 32.3 (2007): 175–200.

Chester, Dennis. "By Certain Codes: Structures of Masculinity in Donald Goines's *Daddy Cool*." *Word Hustle: Critical Essays and Reflections on the Works of Donald Goines*. Ed. L. H. Stallings and Greg Thomas. Baltimore: Black Classic, 2011. 93–105.

Davenport, Christian. "Black Is the Color of My Comic Book Character: An Examination of Ethnic Stereotypes." *Inks* 4.1 (1997): 20–28.

Eisner, Will. *A Contract with God, and Other Tenement Stories*. 1978. *A Contract with God Trilogy*. New York: Norton, 2006.

Glut, Don. Home page. http://www.donaldfglut.com. Accessed 11 November 2013.

———. *I Was a Teenage Movie Maker: The Book*. Jefferson, NC: McFarland, 2007.

Glut, Don (writer), and Alfredo P. Alcala (illustrator). *Daddy Cool*. Los Angeles: Melrose Square, 1984.

Glut, Don (writer), and Brian Forbes (illustrator). *Fanta*. Los Angeles: Melrose Square, 1984.

Goines, Donald. *Daddy Cool*. Los Angeles: Holloway House, 1974.

Hatfield, Charles. *Alternative Comics: An Emerging Literature*. Jackson: University Press of Mississippi, 2005.

MacDonald, Heidi, and Phillip Dana Yeh. *Secret Teachings of a Comic Book Master: The Art of Alfredo Alcala*. Lompoc, CA: International Humor Advisory Council, 1994.

Spurgeon, Tom. "Obituary: Alfredo Alcala, 1925–2000." *Comics Reporter* 30 May 2000. Web. http://www.comicsreporter.com/index.php/resources/longbox/2073/.

Strömberg, Fredrik. *Black Images in the Comics: A Visual History*. Seattle: Fantagraphics, 2003.

Chapter 11

The Blues Tragicomic

· ·

Constructing the Black Folk
Subject in *Stagger Lee*

QIANA WHITTED

The graphic novel *Stagger Lee*, written by Derek McCulloch and illustrated by
Shepherd Hendrix, is at its core a villain's story of origins. The opening pages
seek to unmask the late-nineteenth-century African American outlaw figure,
immortalized in blues songs and prison toasts for killing a man in a St. Louis
saloon during an argument over his Stetson hat. McCulloch and Hendrix flesh
out the legend by moving in and out of history—backward across landscapes
of American racial segregation and political corruption; forward through the
cultural discourse of Stagger Lee blues from nearly every decade and popular
musical genre of the past century. Yet, even as a clearer portrait of "Stack Lee"
Shelton begins to materialize in the comic, the larger narrative tensions between
blackness, nation, and manhood coalesce to productively obscure and entangle
the meanings of "that bad man" in a society where difference of any kind is vili-
fied. What results is a comic that visually and verbally deconstructs the reality
from which Stagger Lees emerge, a worldview in which death and devastation
are inevitable and, as James Baldwin's poem suggests, the assurances of "truth,
justice, and the American Way" are not (14).

This chapter evaluates the emergence of black folk subjectivity in *Stagger
Lee* by situating it at the forefront of a developing trend in twenty-first-century

235

comics, one that integrates the formal and aesthetic structures of sequential art with the existential lament and the intertextual dialogue of African American blues music. Often these "blues comics" call forth the past through images of violence and racial terror, yet their storytelling processes are keenly dialogic, rewriting historical narratives and placing cultural artifacts under fresh scrutiny in a way that speaks to contemporary realities. Some focus explicitly on elements of blues performance, but most embody the blues *as a way of being*, combining the hard-edged wisdom of the singers Robert Johnson and Bessie Smith with a pastiche of trickster tales, pulp westerns, and the antiheroics of comics made popular by Alan Moore and Frank Miller. Blues comics, like all blues narratives, confront racial trauma with a sadness that is, to quote Langston Hughes, "not softened with tears, but hardened with laughter" (86). They deal with tragicomic figures that are not regarded as models of virtue, but are nevertheless valued for the manner in which they provide "a symbolic assault on the system" (Roberts 190).

The heroic badman whose misdeeds generate such vicarious triumph has been central to representations of black history in recent American comics. Rob Vollmar and Pablo G. Callejo's *Bluesman* (2006)—"a twelve bar graphic narrative in the key of life and death" (title page)—tells the story of a struggling black musician who is wanted for murder in the Jim Crow South, while the guitarist Robert Johnson suffers the loss of his soul for his uncommon musical talent in the manga series *Me and the Devil Blues* (2008) by Akira Hiramoto. The title character of Jeremy Love's *Bayou* (2009–2011) is a swamp monster that plays the Delta blues with a crafty Br'er Rabbit and lives in fear of a white bossman along the Mississippi River.[1] *The Original Johnson* (2010) by Trevor Von Eeden is a graphic novel biography of the controversial heavyweight-boxing champion Jack Johnson and the racial politics of his athleticism. Even Kyle Baker's *Nat Turner* (2008) draws on a blues aesthetic to memorialize the title character as a tragic "action hero" in his account of the 1831 Virginia slave uprising.

These works join *Stagger Lee* in an evolving subgenre that is particularly adept at probing the moral ambiguities of racial suffering and survival and that does so in a manner that exploits the visual and verbal codes that are unique to the comics form. Iconic figures such as Nat Turner and Stagger Lee are accused of murder, deception, or other forms of wrongdoing; some are demonized merely for defying the status quo. I argue, however, that blues comics are less interested in exonerating these men than they are in questioning notions of black deviance and uncovering the racialized networks of power that contribute to their actions. My reading of *Stagger Lee* demonstrates how McCulloch and Hendrix draw specifically on multivocal narratives, compensatory satire, and fragmented, metafictional structures to embody a participatory musical aesthetic, a kind of "call-and-response" sequencing that challenges Lee Shelton's hyperbolized status as villain. I further posit the adaptation of Old West comics as one interpretive model for the heroic black badman and conclude with an analysis of the ways in which *Stagger Lee* and other blues comics seek to develop new frames of reference—new origin stories—that more effectively contextualize acts of African American social and moral resistance.

The Stagger Lee Songbook as "Evidence"

In an analysis of the graphic novel *Watchmen* (1987), Iain Thomson asserts that writer Alan Moore and artist Dave Gibbons enact a "masterful deconstruction of the hero" through acts of *re*reading and retrospection (102). The suspenseful plot, which focuses on a group of retired superheroes who are being murdered amid the chaos of the 1980s nuclear standoff between Russia and the United States, upsets traditional representations of costumed heroes by depicting crusaders who are insecure, recklessly self-absorbed, and deeply human. In Thomson's reading, the psychoanalytic unraveling that distinguishes *Watchmen* is achieved through multiple layers of text and image that take advantage of the reader's assumptions and adhere to a moral logic that disintegrates upon reflection. As a result, the rereading that *Watchmen* initiates extends beyond visual cues and symbols to the larger questions that Moore and Gibbons raise about the unintended consequences of heroism in our modern world. Thomson explains: "When rereading uncanny works, we find ourselves no longer at home in our first reading; we realize that the first reading was not a 'reading' properly so-called, since (we now realize) we had not yet understood the text on that first reading, although we assumed, of course, that we did understand it, and so we learn (or at least are encouraged to learn) to become more reflective about the course that we had been following with unreflective self-assurance" (104). The task that Thomson refers to in his study as "retroactive defamiliarization" (103) also has its counterpart in the subversive practices of African American storytelling traditions. Among the array of rhetorical strategies that distinguish early folk tales, slave narratives, and black literary fiction is the syncretic mediation of African and Euro-American cultural forms and practices that use indirection, as well as intertextual revision and wordplay, to argue against white supremacy. Such strategies are commonly associated with Henry Louis Gates, Jr.'s formulation of "signifyin(g)" as the black vernacular processes of revision and repetition "with a signal difference" (xxiv). Consider how the autobiographies of Frederick Douglass, Henry Bibb, and Harriet Jacobs are crafted in the sentimental traditional to make an antislavery appeal or the ways in which the racial subversions of the post-Reconstruction writings of Paul Laurence Dunbar and Charles Chesnutt are cloaked in the vernacular language and archetypes of the local color genre. Modern African American literature further exploits this creative and political tension in texts by Zora Neale Hurston, Ralph Ellison, and Toni Morrison that, to use Thomson's phrase, "must be reread in order to be *read*" (104). Their works adapt and modify existing discursive models in order to argue for alternative modes of blackness, to fill in historical gaps and silences, and to upset flawed social and cultural standardizations that account only for the experiences of white Americans.

In *Stagger Lee*, multiple plots attempt to reconstruct and to retroactively defamiliarize the infamous story of "Stack Lee" Shelton, whose deadly quarrel with Billy Lyons in 1895 has become the subject of dozens of blues songs (as well as county, soul, and rock iterations) in which the badman is called Stagolee, Stack o' Lee, Stackalee, and Stagger Lee. Historians and cultural critics have investigated the details surrounding the incident and reveal, for instance, that the Stetson hat that is often cited as the impetus for the argument belies the criminal activity in which both were engaged through their political affiliations—with Shelton buying votes for the Democratic Party and Lyons, like most blacks at the time, supporting the party of Lincoln. Lost, too, in the larger-than-life image of Stagger Lee slugging it out with the devil is the fact that Shelton died of tuberculosis in prison in 1912.

What remains of the abridged version of Shelton's life, however, is what Cecil Brown describes as a countercultural paradigm of black masculine power, the "Stagolee paradigm" of violent racial and socioeconomic resistance that undermines an oppressive system (14). When this paradigm is placed within the framework of the comics medium, a form commonly associated with superheroes and the "myth of idealized masculinity," new cultural and ethical tensions begin to surface. Brown astutely articulates the questions that could be said to confront readers on the first page of McCulloch and Hendrix's comic: "We Americans love our folk heroes and the ballads made about their lives. Yet we are reluctant to admit that many of those heroes come from the lowest levels of society. Like the 'Frankie and Albert' ballad, 'Stagolee' may have originated with a pianist in a bordello. The 'hero' of the ballad was a pimp, and the 'heroic deed' was the murder of a defenseless black man. How much of this can we really applaud?" (12). As a result, the hero in *Stagger Lee* embodies more than just the superhero genre's familiar "wimp/warrior theme of duality" but emerges as a figure whose unapologetic brutality seems to reinforce problematic notions of blackness as inherently depraved and, as Jeffrey A. Brown states, who risks "being read as an overabundance, and potentially threatening, cluster of masculine signifiers" (32, 34). Yet it is the very assumptions fueling the hyperbolic villainy of the Stagolee paradigm that furnish McCulloch and Hendrix's graphic novel—and blues comics, more generally—with their compelling, signifying power. The complex narrative encourages the reader to go beyond the conjecture of a "first reading," while each iteration of the Stagger Lee blues suggests a rereading of what the folk hero can represent. This approach is what Michael Chaney, in his analysis of Ho Che Anderson's *King*, refers to as "visual signifyin'," which results in a recasting of the historical record "not as monolithic or monologic but as dynamic, dialogic units of communication available for recombination and interpretation" (199).

So while it is true, as the graphic novel's narrator explains, that "the Stagger Lee songbook was never called into evidence" during Shelton's 1896 trial, the countless songs that seek to imagine Stagger Lee and to re-create the incident that took place in Bill Curtis's saloon are the means through which readers are compelled to reevaluate their unreflective self-assurance about the black subject (McCulloch and Hendrix 76). We discover that "most of the time, Stag shoots Billy . . . but every once in a while, he gets shot. Sometimes he's brought to justice . . . sometimes not. Sometimes Stag dies and burns in hell . . . sometimes he decides the place could use new management" (25). Each variation of the song from Mississippi John Hurt, Floyd Price, Woody Guthrie, Bob Dylan, and others decenters our understanding of what Stagger Lee means across time and in relation to different audiences. Consider, for instance, the comic's instructive comparison between the accounts of Stagger Lee's death as performed by black and white singers: "When this verse is sung by a white artist, 'we' are all glad to see him die. When sung by an African-American, 'they' are glad" (47; see fig. 11.1). Feet dangle between the images of Hurt and Guthrie, edging over the panel borders like a bridge that connects the two realities. With this inclusion of the body on the surface of the page, the audience that circles around the

11.1 Stagger Lee's death is related by black and white singers; for the white singer, "we" are glad to see him die; for the black singer, "they" are glad.

blues and folk music performers become bystanders whose faces replicate the spectatorship of twentieth-century lynching photographs—the grim, mournful expressions of the black listeners are juxtaposed against the grinning white ones. In another example, McCulloch and Hendrix allow readers to draw their own conclusions about the song's somewhat interchangeable depictions of the devil and a Jim Crow sheriff (105).

Other versions of the tale emphasize the perspective of the women who love Stagger Lee (Ma Rainey), the badman's struggle to come to terms with the consequences of gambling and other losses (Furry Lewis), and the contemplation of guilt over the murder (Frank Hutchison). McCulloch's acknowledgments list these songs along with dozens more that he says served as his soundtrack during the writing and Hendrix's illustration of the graphic novel. *Stagger Lee* is, itself, a new addition to this playlist of blues songs, ballads, and toasts, not only by virtue of the comic's visual signifying but also through an original composition that McCulloch wrote for the fictitious piano player named Hercules Moffatt in the story. Romantic troubles move Hercules to give voice to the first versions of Stagger Lee blues during Shelton's trial (54–55, 83). In an interview, McCulloch explains, "I took lines and ideas from early versions, rearranged and reworded as necessary, and added whatever new lines I needed, . . . very much the same process as the early oral mutations of the song." So when McCulloch places his character at the piano to sing, "If your man come home, he'll have to pay. / Oh that bad man, cruel man, mean man, Stagolee," his words simultaneously initiate and revise the century-old Stagger Lee songbook (McCulloch and Hendrix 83). This new version enlarges what McCulloch refers to as the legend's "elasticity" in blending history and myth (McCulloch); it also encourages another rereading of the social contexts that mold Stagger Lee's iconic image.

The explications of the songs are further shaped by the irreverent and wry narrative voice of *Stagger Lee*, which suggests the same kind of dialogue with the reader that the bluesman does with his listeners. Invoking a conversational tone, the narrator raises rhetorical questions and educates the audience on the legend's instructive discrepancies. At times, the voice draws on amusing empirical data to offer a composite portrait of Stagger Lee (for example, a pie graph that charts the number of references to the Stetson hat [129]), and in other instances, it supports the nonlinear visual layers that symbolize Stagger Lee's many faces. One panel, for example, showcases the title character's dual identity with a sedate and realistically drawn Lee Shelton standing alongside a grimacing Stagger Lee, his imposing body brandishing a large phallic-shaped weapon in each hand (27; see fig. 11.2). The stark, "near-tragic, near-comic lyricism" of the visual pairing reveals the extent to which Shelton's hypermasculine physical frame becomes a projection of social fears about black men who have been "systematically denied full access to the socially constructed ideals of masculinity" (7, 149). Likewise, Hendrix is especially masterful in using the chaotic, swirling line pattern to denote Stagger Lee's presence, whether the figure with the hat is a white or black

11.2 Lee Shelton versus Stagger Lee: sedate and realistic compared to the imposing brandishing of large phallic-like weapons.

person, large or small, wielding a weapon or cowering in fear Lee's imprint even appears on his money (26) and the satchel in his hand (36). Billy Lyons, in contrast, is known by the even, grid line pattern on his hat and suit. And yet these distinctions are not uncomplicated. In response to the query "Who's the Bully?" the narrator notes the way Stagger Lee songs actually blend the exploits of Shelton Lee and his victim into a new archetype (74). So the visual coding that recasts the protagonist and antagonist from song to song also helps to ensure that the abstract connotations that are associated with Stagger Lee and Billy Lyons are reiterated even when the physical circumstances have changed.

However, the comic's representation of the different Stagger Lees are intended not merely to illustrate the legend's musical evolution but to foreground the fragmented, polyphonous quality of the reality surrounding Shelton Lee and his community. Multiple songs exploit the gaps, variations, and inconsistencies in the story in an effort to instruct readers about the social and historical context of black folk life in the late nineteenth and early twentieth centuries. In other words, the comic's participatory reading extends to stories of suffering and transcendence that go beyond the circumstances surrounding Billy Lyons's death. *Stagger Lee* fictionalizes the perspective of the Lyons family, the love story of a blues musician, the experiences of Shelton's attorney and law clerk, and even a glimpse into the title character himself as a child in the South. As the stories cut abruptly back and forth from scene to scene and across time, the comic generates a call-and-response sequencing through word and image, a dialogue between the narrator, reader, and the social construct known as "Stagger Lee" (whose artificiality is often reinforced by his intermittent appeals directly to the reader).

A similar strategy unfolds in comics such as *Nat Turner* and *Bluesman* that generate a verbal and visual conversation between the historical events and documentation of the period. Kyle Baker's *Nat Turner* contains virtually no dialogue but takes its narrative structure mainly from the lawyer Thomas Gray's 1831 account, "The Confessions of Nat Turner." In spite of the unbroken historical account that makes up the "Confessions," Baker's design and artwork furnish Turner's character with new dimension, refuting and rereading Gray's nefarious image of the rebel leader. Baker locates him within a larger community of enslaved men and women, emphasizing Turner's experience as a son, husband, and father. Deep shadows anchor the intensity of the black characters' facial expressions in the eyes of sharply angled faces. Their looks of outrage and vulnerability, the furtive glances, and the dawning realizations suggest a depth unacknowledged by the bland, indifferent gaze of the white enslavers. The tensions between Baker's and Gray's interpretations of the revolt helps to complicate what readers may initially assume is merely a straightforward adaptation of an authorized history.

Bluesman contains the original story of Lem Taylor, but in a manner similar to *Stagger Lee* and *Nat Turner*, Rob Vollmar and Pablo G. Callejo frame the first volume of this three-part series with excerpts from a scholarly article on itinerant bluesmen in the South. The narrative also uses music as a structural metaphor for telling Lem's tale, with the three volumes divided into twelve parts (or "bars" of a traditional blues song) and charcoal sketches that bring to mind woodcut illustrations of a folk past. The quoted excerpts quickly establish the context of the story as the traveling bluesmen are described as liminal figures that have escaped "a life of hard labor and uniform squalid poverty" of the South by making a living off their music (6). At the same time, their outsider status makes them "an easy target on whom to pin the negative attributes uniformly assigned to all members of their race by the Anglo dominated society which surrounded them" (6). And indeed, the plot is set in motion once Lem is falsely accused of murdering a white man and becomes the target of a lynch mob. As with *Stagger Lee*, the physical presence of historical documents and cultural artifacts in *Bluesman* help to frame the visual and verbal call of a "first reading" about blackness and masculinity, a call whose authority is challenged, revised, or affirmed in the comic's sequential response.

Comics, then, emerge as an art form that is well suited to the participatory demands of blues narratives. The complexity of these stories is also illustrative of a growing comics readership that, as Charles Hatfield maintains, is increasingly "experienced, playful, and tolerant of discontinuity" (66). In an interview, McCulloch cites Alan Moore and Eddie Campbell's *From Hell* as influencing his thinking about experimental narrative structures, specifically praising "their commitment to creating, as accurately as possible, a sense of time and place; their willingness to escape conventional narrative constraints and let, for example, each section of the story be as long or as short as it needed to be; and their trust in the sophistication of their audience and its ability to negotiate the complexities of the story." Such sophistication is further demonstrated by the way the story fragments in *Stagger Lee* appear to invoke the improvisational practice of musical performance and to mimic the interpretive process of decoding the subtext, symbolism, and depth of emotion in song. Furnished with this sequential songbook as evidence, the reader is better equipped to reconsider other blues moments in the comic: to evaluate Lee Shelton's social and political maneuvers in a system that favors his disenfranchisement; to sympathize with the sorrow of Hercules Moffatt, who is in love with a woman he cannot marry; or to see in the stories of Shelton's legal counsel, Nathan Dryden and Justin Troup, the struggle of a middle-class African American community to maintain its dignity and respect.

The Black "Heroic Badman" of Blues Comics

The blues aesthetic is manifested on the comics page in other ways that are central to the transgressions of the Stagger Lee legend, notably through the image of the defiant outsider "who represented forces that whites found disreputable or downright threatening" (C. Brown 207). Stagger Lee transforms the well-known trickster figure into what James C. Cobb refers to as the "heroic badman" through his association with murder, prostitution, gambling, and political corruption (169). Like Br'er Rabbit tales, the lore surrounding Stagger Lee is less concerned with the possession of material rewards than with empowerment, manipulation, and self-preservation (Levine 109). But as a heroic badman, Stagger Lee further symbolizes a modern "rejection of white values whether codified by law or sanctified by the church" through his ability to defy the sheriff and commandeer the devil's place in hell (Cobb 169). Also known as the "ba-ad nigger," this image of Stagger Lee models the public perception of black men such as the boxer Jack Johnson, the political activist Bobby Seale, and the rapper Tupac Shakur as well as fictional characters such as Sterling Brown's Slim Greer, Richard Wright's Bigger Thomas, and Marvel Comics' Luke Cage. Regardless of their status, these male figures "welcomed and often instigated direct confrontations with white society's stereotype of the Negro's role and place in American life" (William H. Wiggins, Jr., qtd. in C. Brown 150).

In *Stagger Lee*, McCulloch and Hendrix reconstitute this image and its social and cultural subversions, in part, through conventions commonly employed by comics about the American West. The relationship is evident in the title's use of an antique typeface associated with vintage newspaper print and Old West "Wanted" posters; the artwork's deep brown color is reminiscent of late-nineteenth-century sepia-toned photographs. The effect is not one that McCulloch had originally intended when scripting the graphic novel (St. Louis in 1895 was hardly a frontier town), but the impression results nevertheless from the collaboration of writing, illustration, coloring, and lettering on the comic. The Comicraft design and lettering team included John Roshell, who implemented the typeface and font styles, while Jimmy Betancourt and Richard

Starkings—whose previous work included Don Hudson's *Gunpowder Girl and the Outlaw Squaw*—helped make the case for the nuance and texture of the sepia color (McCulloch). With these design elements in place, the narrative's milieu of gunfights, saloons, hangings, and Stetson hats is, at times, more readily associated with the American frontier than with the industrialized cityscapes of St. Louis.

But the comic makes even more substantial choices that appear to align the Stagger Lee legend with cowboy motifs that developed as the song made its way through Oklahoma and Indian Territories out West (C. Brown 135). For one thing, McCulloch's account of Lee Shelton minimizes his primary occupation as an urban pimp who lived and worked in the red-light district of St. Louis on Sixth Street. While a secondary story in Sarah "Mama Babe" Connors's Castle Club foregrounds the fictional relationship between the former prostitute Evelyn Prescott and the bordello's pianist, Hercules Moffatt, Shelton's association with the commercial sex industry is merely implied, as is his own personal relationship with a woman who, "in some versions, works far beyond the call of love to raise his bail" (McCullogh and Hendrix 120). (In contrast, the Stagger Lee that appears in Jeremy Love's *Bayou* is an aloof northern "dandy" whose sexual exploits as a pimp are matched only by his cruelty and ruthlessness with a razor [170].) More prominently featured in *Stagger Lee*, however, is Shelton's involvement with the political rivalries of St. Louis's black social clubs during a transitional moment in history when black voters began shifting their allegiances from the Republicans to the Democratic Party in the interest of policy and profit (C. Brown 79–81). Shelton's affiliation with the Democrats further reinforces his dissatisfaction with the status quo, his refusal to be bound by tradition. McCulloch's creative choices, therefore, affirm the image of Stagger Lee as a loner, a vigilante who follows his own codes of respect and retributive justice on the margins of a law-abiding society.

On the surface, then, the comics and pulp magazines of the Old West contain a format that works well with Stagger Lee's tale. The American cowboy of western comics reached his popularity during the early 1950s, and to the extent that he was "among the most socially responsible of all comic-book types," this archetype even managed to survive many of the restrictions of the 1954 Comics Code (Savage 69). The most popular titles were drawn from family film and television personalities of the day, such as Roy Rogers, the Lone Ranger, Hopalong Cassidy, and Davy Crockett. These and other western comics feature incorruptible heroes who are often governed not by the military, law enforcement, or a federal agency but, as William Savage notes, by their own sense of duty to their country and its societal values (72). Ironically enough, the first African American character with his own comic book was a cowboy hero called Lobo, written and drawn by Tony Tallarico in 1965 for Dell Comics (Watson). Although *Lobo* was canceled after two issues, its opening pages reminded readers that "cowboys came in all shapes, sizes, and temperaments . . . and they created all sorts of legends. Some were good, some were bad and some were indifferent" (Tallarico 1). The social subtext of this former Union soldier traveling the American plains as "A Fugitive on the Side of the Law!" becomes even more provocative when the cowboy is a black man who declares, "I didn't kill the boss and I won't hang for it. If I'm a lobo, it was forced on me" (16). Indeed, the cowboy archetype is composed of variations that can extend beyond the genre's predilection for clear-cut moral distinctions to encompass characters such as the "masked Western hero," the "loveable rogue," and the noble or "reformed outlaw" (Horn 201–202). In the case of this last figure, the hero engages in acts that only *appear* to be criminal—such as killing to protect others—and the story often follows his attempts to escape or correct the record.

Against even the broadest standards of Old West comics, however, it is still quite easy to imagine Stagger Lee as the villain. Vanity and pride lead him to cold-blooded murder. He is uninterested in law or order. His crimes are neither "lovable" nor selflessly committed in the interest of people in need. But as McCulloch and Hendrix demonstrate, the songs that memorialize the legend of Stagger Lee are not meant to function as morality tales. Nearly every character in *Stagger Lee* is flawed and vulnerable, while national institutions and figures of established authority are corrupted by racial prejudice, greed, and abuses of power. (Baldwin's "Stagolee Wonders" boasts a similar rejection of American moral exceptionalism, saying, "I've *seen* some stars / I *got* some stripes" [16].) In this context, Lee Shelton's remorseless black badman is endowed with a unique kind of cultural heroism. John W. Roberts explains: "To be called a 'badman' simply meant that one was willing to act against established social, moral, and legal codes that restricted the lives of blacks with full awareness of the consequences of those actions. Certainly, his actions did not always elicit approval, but they were understandable under the circumstances which both his admirers and detractors probably shared" (190). The prologue of *Stagger Lee* visually articulates this moral tension with shocked silence; a hush falls over the crowd at Bill Curtis's saloon in the wake of the gunshot that sets the story in motion. In the two-page spread of startled faces, the reader sees only Lee Shelton's back, the smoke rising from his gun, and his hand breaking through the panel frame to retrieve his Stetson from the bleeding man's grasp (see fig. 11.3). Shelton's words, delivered coldly and without looking back, underscore the senseless nature of his crime: "Nigger, I told you. I told you not to touch my hat" (McCullough and Hendrix 11). Such a futile, reckless act hardly seems to demonstrate a full awareness of the consequences.

Yet in keeping with the graphic novel's adaptation of the western genre conventions, *Stagger Lee* returns repeatedly to this and other hats as a visual code, like the call-and-response sequences of blues songs, that helps to facilitate a reconsideration of the black badman. Cecil Brown notes that during the 1890s,

11.3 Lee shoots a man over an argument regarding his hat; his hand enters the panel to retrieve the Stetson from the bleeding man's grasp.

particularly in a large urban area such as St. Louis, "the Stetson was the archetypal western hat" (100). Although the one that Shelton may have worn would not have been a cowboy hat, the virility suggested by its wide brim was often juxtaposed with the smaller derby hat that Lyons wore. The act of knocking off another man's hat, Brown continues, compromises this virility as a "a sign of castration" (101)—a sign well supported in *Stagger Lee* by the recurring images of the men's hats being snatched, slammed, and crushed amid insults (McCullough and Hendrix 43, 116, 133–134) and even by the slumped figure of Lyons, collapsed on the floor with his crumpled derby askew (10–11).

However, it is a secondary story line that takes place in Shelton's childhood home in Texas that generates an especially productive rereading of the hat's symbolic significance. The fictional account of a fishing trip between Shelton and an elderly black man named Zell Baxley is interspersed throughout the first section of the graphic novel in a setting that resembles the pastoral "Garden of the West" from Golden Age western comics (Horn 178). When Zell cautions the naïve youth that "everything goes away someday," the elder's wide-brimmed cowboy hat nearly fills the panel, obscuring everything except Shelton's eyes (McCullough and Hendrix 15). Later in the story, these same eyes watch in horror as two local white deputies humiliate Zell for using a restricted outhouse. They force the black man to remove his feces with his hands and place it into his "brand-new Stetson" (57).

McCulloch and Hendrix use the racialized emasculation of the story's only genuine cowboy, Zell Baxley, to visualize the sense of helplessness that an adult Lee Shelton rebuffs at any cost. So when Shelton divulges to his lawyer, Nathan Dryden, "Aw, I didn't kill him over no hat . . . the man didn't have no respect" (66), the deeper significance of his misdirected rage becomes clear. The Stetson hat, like the .44 Smith & Wesson, invokes a larger power struggle over dignity, manhood, and justice. For Dryden, a black military veteran and well-established attorney in the city, such indignities take shape in the way he holds his own hat in the presence of white men who will not even shake his hand (58), or when overcome by alcohol and drug addiction, he waves his gun and, recalling Lee Shelton, shouts, "I'm the man of the house! The man!" (102). All of these men are connected by the "fantastic tightrope" to which James Baldwin refers, by the kind of blues experience that transforms Lee Sheltons into Stagger Lees:

> You've seen these black men and women, these boys and girls; you've seen them in the streets. But I know what happened to them at the factory, at work, at home, on the subway, what they go through in a day, and the way they sort of ride with it. And it's very, very tricky. It's kind of a fantastic tightrope. They may be very self-controlled, very civilized; I like to think of myself as being very civilized and self-controlled, but I know that I'm not. And I know that some improbable Wednesday, for no reason whatever, the elevator man or the doorman, the policeman or the landlord, or some little boy from the Bronx will say something and it will be the wrong day to say it, the wrong moment to have it said to me; and God knows what will happen. I have seen it all. I have seen it all, I have seen that much. What the blues are describing comes out of all this. (Baldwin, "Uses" 59)

Stagger Lee, the heroic black badman, is the embodiment of this "improbable Wednesday." According to some versions of the legend, he was so *bad* that when confronted by the law, he declared, "You may be the sheriff, and you may be white, but you ain't Stagolee. Now deal with that." His direct challenge to moral authority may brand him as the antagonist in a Roy Rogers comic (or in a *Lobo* story line), but through the context that McCulloch and Hendrix establish—particularly through characters such as Zell Baxley and Nathan Dryden or visual codes such as the hat and gun—Stagger Lee and his blues songs emerge as the "manifestations of the feeling that, within the circumstances with which they operate, to assert any power at all is a triumph" (Levine 418).

It is important to note one final distinction between the black outlaw and his white counterpart that qualifies the impact of such triumphant assertions of power. Cobb clarifies: "For black audiences the outlaw story or song might prove cathartic and vicariously inspirational, but the pleasure, the sense of release, was wholly temporary, *and the return to reality was swift and inevitable*" (169, emphasis added). The same might be said of the slave trickster's vicarious rewards or of the catharsis evoked by the bluesman's performance, that the social transformations brought about by the heroic badman are generally short-lived. Roberts also notes that black outlaws are generally "limited by the folk perceptions of their own possibilities" (189). With this in mind, blues comics often favor the inspirational impact of the badman's transgressions over any material improvements. Nat Turner's rebellion, for instance, actually heightened whites' fears in its aftermath and brought about harsh legislative restrictions on the ability of enslaved blacks to read, travel, and assemble as a group. Yet Baker's comic closes on the promising image of a young black child who has found a copy of Turner's "Confessions," and holding it to her chest, she fades into the darkness in a series of reflective moment-to-moment panel transitions (94).

McCulloch and Hendrix take a different approach, one that affirms Cobbs's observations while being in accord with the "realistic, unsentimentalized portrait of Stackolee" from blues songs and ballads (Roberts 182). Behind the fantastic image of a badman with a Stetson hat, the social realities of Lee Shelton's life remain tragic and wretchedly mundane. In the graphic novel, Stagger Lee may laugh about the way singers and songwriters have portrayed him or acknowledge the irony of his rebirth as a hippie folk hero, a 1970s pimp, and a gangster thug. But behind bars, an unsmiling Lee Shelton is drawn with sober and contemplative expressions beneath heavy brows. As the Stagger Lee songbook flourishes, Lee Shelton's psyche begins to waste away. He is erased from the narrative of his own exploits until, in a nightmare, the ghost of Billy Lyons breaks the news: "Even your name ain't your own no more" (McCullough and Hendrix 166). This last section of the comic, appropriately titled "The Ghost," exposes Stagger Lee as a complete simulation, a construct that may well embody black social and judicial anxieties but offers little consolation to Lee Shelton behind bars. Curled up in anguish, he presses a pillow over his ears to deafen the sound of a bluesman singing in a nearby cell (fig. 11.4). In this last image of Shelton, the jagged word balloon above him reads, "Make him stop! MAKE HIM STOP! Make him stop! Make him stop!" (218).

Interestingly, Shelton's disintegration is juxtaposed with the woman who arguably serves as his female counterpart in the comic: Evelyn Prescott. In an effort to abandon a life of prostitution, she develops an elaborate ploy to marry

11.4 In jail, Lee Shelton presses a pillow over his head in anguish as a bluesman sings in a nearby cell.

into high society—with the help of Mama Babe Connors—by re-creating herself as different women named Thelma, Evelyn, and Jean-Alice (194). Fragments of these multiple identities surface in her unexpected relationship with Hercules, as she is associated with both the middle-class respectability of the church and the worldly experience of the red-light district. Yet, as with Shelton, the ease with which Evelyn might be judged for her crimes is hindered by a fuller reconsideration of the circumstances that shaped her condition—which Hercules discovers when he learns how Mama Babe rescued her as a child from a southern brothel. Her longing to "be whole again" (195) is paralleled in the fractured image of Lee Shelton that emerges in the comic; he too is haunted by names that have been broken "in little bits and pieces" (194). As a result, the verbal and visual rereading of characters such as Shelton and Evelyn Prescott effectively complicates the image of black deviance and cruelty that is assumed in the Stagger Lee legend, and just as importantly, it underscores the existential crisis that is central to blues comics.

Origin Stories: Blues Comics as "Usable History"

Perhaps one of the strangest scenes in *Stagger Lee* occurs after the attorney Nathan Dryden has died and his clerk, Justin Troup, is compelled to take over Shelton's defense. In a letter of instructions left behind, Dryden recounts a West African fable about the relative nature and responsibilities of power through the archdivinity of the Yoruba people, Obatala. Mistaken for a thief in the story, Obatala is imprisoned until another deity (or *orisha*), named Shango, realizes the error and releases him several weeks later. When Shango claims ignorance of the events that occurred, Obatala asserts, "Can a ruler be said to truly rule if he does not know what his servants do with the authority he has given them?"

(McCullough and Hendrix 164). When applied to Lee's situation, the ancestral tale reminds readers of how often and how flagrantly due process has been denied to the descendants of Africans in America; in seeking justice even for a man like Stagger Lee, the story affirms the rights of humanity in a broader sense. Dryden thoughtfully concludes the tale by telling his clerk, "Of course, Lee is not blameless as Obatala was, but Justin, please remember. He is being judged by men who have no understanding of the conditions that brought him to their prison" (164). Might these Yoruban deities be Lee Shelton's West African forefathers, providing yet another "version" of the Stagger Lee blues?

Covering less than four pages, the brief scene provides yet another instance in which the ancillary plots of *Stagger Lee* contribute to the narrative's larger message. Obatala's tale, like the account of Zell Baxley's fishing trip, deepens the reader's awareness of the people, places, and ideas that led to Stagger Lee's creation. And this variation of the character's origin story precedes even the twelve bars of a blues song. What is especially fascinating about the story Dryden tells is the manner in which Hendrix illustrates the telling, seamlessly connecting the plains of Oyo, Nigeria, to a St. Louis courtroom in an effort to provide a different perspective on Shelton's treatment and, by extension, the treatment of black people and other oppressed communities. Dryden, whose appearance in this scene is merely as a projection of his letter, speaks directly to Justin, yet his gaze extends outside the page to readers who may also benefit from his words. "I know you disapprove of Lee and strongly presume his guilt," he states, "I understand that, but hope that you can summon the professional dispassion necessary to give him a full and vigorous defense" (161). In the next panel, Dryden has been relocated across the Atlantic Ocean, outside of history, where Obatala's story takes place.

That Dryden's advice relies on a West African source is significant, of course, in affirming cultural continuity between black Americans and their African ancestry. Dryden is mindful of just how fragile this connection is when he prefaces the tale of the Yoruba people by telling Justin, "They may be your people and may be mine, but how are we to ever know?" (162). Through panels that bridge reality and myth as well as space and time, the figure of Obatala is portrayed with a large oval head shaped like an African mask, wide blank eyes, and fists swinging confidently by his side. Although the orisha who is the primary subject of the tale is known for representing a sense of moral authority as spotless as his white robes, Shango, the thunder god, is more readily associated with the power and virility suggested by the Stagger Lee paradigm. Yet questions of morality and justice, as shaped by hierarchies of power and societal norms and perceptions, are as essential to the Stagger Lee legend as they are to Obatala's story—a point that McCulloch highlights in his decision to include the story in his script. As Dryden makes clear, both figures are susceptible to the whims of the irrational and the absurd, whether through Eshu, the

11.5 Dryden relates a West African story to his clerk, Justin Troup, in order to affirm cultural continuity between black Americans and their African ancestry and to convince Justin to treat Lee with a full and vigorous defense.

trickster god, or through the arbitrary restrictions of the black codes in late-nineteenth-century America. While the Zell Baxley incident situates the heroic outlaw's origins within a singular moment of trauma—a familiar technique in a medium known for orphaned and wounded heroes—the myth of Obatala's imprisonment suggests a metaphor for understanding trauma and injustice in a systemic way.

An analogous strategy is utilized by Kyle Baker in the first section of *Nat Turner*, in which he departs from Thomas Gray's "Confessions" to imagine a richer and more detailed origin story that begins with Turner's mother being captured by enslavers in Africa and experiencing the horrors of the Middle Passage. Baker documents the wide-ranging, premeditated acts of violence that sustain the institution of slavery with as much detail as he does the 1831 insurrection—not only the transatlantic slave trade but the separation of families, grisly whippings, maiming, and rape. Alternatively, Love's *Bayou* places Baker's gritty realism in concert with realms of fantasy, retroactively defamiliarizing black folk culture through a parallel world that is inhabited by the characters of Uncle Remus tales and other magical creatures. Love's approach to remapping the South in *Bayou* relies on the same porous boundaries between myth, music, and history that allow an African American man from the nineteenth century to share the same page as a West African creation god in *Stagger Lee*. All of these comics imaginatively construct new sources of knowledge to counter the sanctioned presumptions and oversimplifications that impede a full understanding of the past.

The blues comic's deep fascination with black folk origins, with the formative traumas and tensions of black subjects, may also indicate an effort to challenge the manner in which such images have fared within the comics industry in years past. Chaney maintains that recent comic book writers and artists who represent African American experience are endeavoring "to discover or invent a usable history by repurposing inflexible items or images from an archive founded upon black exclusion and misrepresentation" (199). This assertion can also be expanded to include the "archive" of comic books that have tended to depict blackness as a sign of the aberrant Other. Often, in the industry's early years during the Great Depression and the Second World War, nonwhites were exploited to express the depths of depravity and malevolence and ridiculed as spectacles of difference. The comic book historian Bradford Wright observes, "Whatever the comic book industry generally implied about tolerance in its call for national unity was overwhelmed by its consistently demeaning portrayals of nonwhite races" (54). Mainstream genres of the 1940s and early 1950s, from jungle comics to detective serials, typically offered crude images and undecipherable dialogue to connote the physical appearance, speech, movement, culture, and identity of all people of African descent. The risks that *Stagger Lee* and other blues comics take in humanizing figures that are known for acts of villainy are compounded, then, by the extent to which all black men and women in comics are portrayed as having an inherent capacity for vice. Nevertheless, it is also a testament to the pliable and dynamic interplay of comics as an artistic medium that the form that once affirmed such stereotypes can also be used to dismantle them. Blues comics take advantage of the medium's flexibility to engender antiracist rereadings that extend not only to the social and cultural contexts in which the stories take place but also to the exclusionary comic book elements that the stories seek to displace.

Ultimately, what is being unmasked in *Stagger Lee* is more than just the ruthlessness and conceit of an outlaw but is also the mutually dependent consequences of his real and imagined crimes. Although Stagger Lee's life began as Lee Shelton, his story persists as an open signifier that mirrors the shared experience of those who continually sing him into existence in juke joints, in saloons, on street corners, and even on the pages of a graphic novel. As James Baldwin once stated, "People who have no experience supposed that if a man is a thief, he is a thief; but, in fact, that isn't the most important thing about him. The most important thing about him is that he is a man and, furthermore, that if he's a thief or a murderer or whatever he is, *you* could also be and you would know this, anyone would know this who had really dared to live" ("Uses" 64–65). Comics such as *Stagger Lee* explore this existential daring, often in ways that value the blues as a tragicomic ethos, as a cultural resource, and as a dynamic narrative framework for understanding black folk subjectivity.

Note

1 Love is drawing on the Br'er Rabbit folktales that came down from African culture and then slave stories. The character in the comic is referred to variously as "Rabbit," "Bruh Rabbit," "Brer Rabbit," and "Mistuh Rabbit."

Works Cited

Baker, Kyle. *Nat Turner*. New York: Abrams, 2008.

Baldwin, James. "Staggerlee Wonders." *Jimmy's Blues*. New York: St. Martin's, 1985. 7–23.

———. "The Uses of the Blues." 1964. *The Cross of Redemption: Uncollected Writings*. New York: Pantheon Books, 2010. 57–66.

Bibb, Henry. *Narrative of the Life and Adventures of Henry Bibb, an American Slave*. New York, 1849.

Brown, Cecil. *Stagolee Shot Billy*. Cambridge, MA: Harvard University Press, 2003.

Brown, Jeffrey A. "Comic Book Masculinity and the New Black Superhero." *African American Review* 33.1 (1999): 25–42.

Chaney, Michael. "Drawing on History in Recent African American Graphic Novels." *MELUS* 32.3 (2007): 175–200.

Chesnutt, Charles. *The Conjure Woman*. New York: Houghton Mifflin, 1899.

Cobb, James C. *The Most Southern Place on Earth: The Mississippi Delta and the Roots of Regional Identity*. New York: Oxford University Press, 1992.

Douglass, Frederick. *Narrative of the Life of Frederick Douglass, an American Slave*. Boston, 1845.

Dunbar, Paul Laurence. *The Collected Poetry of Paul Laurence Dunbar*. Ed. Joanne Braxton. Charlottesville: University of Virginia Press, 1993.

Ellison, Ralph. *Invisible Man*. New York: Random House, 1952.

———. "Richard Wright's Blues." 1945. *Shadow and Act*. New York: Random House, 1964. 77–94.

Gates, Henry Louis, Jr. *The Signifying Monkey*. New York: Oxford University Press, 1998.

Hatfield, Charles. *Alternative Comics: An Emerging Literature*. Jackson: University Press of Mississippi, 2005.

Hiramoto, Akira. *Me and the Devil Blues: The Unreal Life of Robert Johnson*. 2 vols. New York: Del Ray, 2008.

Horn, Maurice. *Comics of the American West*. New York: Winchester, 1977.

Hudson, Don. *Gunpowder Girl and the Outlaw Squaw*. N.p.: Active Images, 2005.

Hughes, Langston. "The Black Blues." *Vanity Fair* 24.6 (1925): 86.

Hurston, Zora Neale. *Their Eyes Were Watching God*. New York: Lippincott, 1937.

Jacobs, Harriet A. *Incidents in the Life of a Slave Girl*. Boston, 1861.

Levine, Lawrence W. *Black Culture and Black Consciousness: Afro-American Folk Thought from Slavery to Freedom*. New York: Oxford University Press, 1977.

Love, Jeremy. *Bayou*. 2 vols. New York: DC Comics, 2009–2011.

McCulloch, Derek. Personal interview. 31 January 2011.

McCulloch, Derek (writer), and Shepherd Hendrix (artist). *Stagger Lee*. New York: Image Comics, 2006.

Moore, Alan (writer), and Eddie Campbell (artist). *From Hell*. Marietta, GA: Top Shelf, 1999.

Moore, Alan (writer), and Dave Gibbons (artist). *Watchmen*. New York: DC Comics, 1987.

Morrison, Toni. *Beloved*. New York: Knopf, 1987.

Roberts, John W. *From Trickster to Badman: The Black Folk Hero in Slavery and Freedom*. Philadelphia: University of Pennsylvania Press, 1990.

Savage, William W., Jr. *Comic Books and America, 1945–1954.* Norman: University of Oklahoma Press, 1990.

Tallarico, Tony. *Lobo* #1. New York: Dell Comics, December 1965.

Thomson, Iain. "Deconstructing the Hero." *Comics as Philosophy.* Ed. Jeff MacLaughlin. Jackson: University Press of Mississippi, 2005. 100–129.

Turner, Nat, and Thomas Gray. *The Confessions of Nat Turner.* Baltimore: Thomas R. Gray, 1831.

Vollmar, Rob (writer), and Pablo G. Callejo (artist). *Bluesman.* New York: ComicsLit, 2006.

Von Eeden, Trevor. *The Original Johnson.* New York: IDW, 2010.

Watson, Rob. "For These Comics Creators, Not Just Funny Business: African American Gathering Will Teach Nature of the Industry." *Philadelphia Inquirer* 19 May 2006. Web.

Wright, Bradford. *Comic Book Nation.* Baltimore: Johns Hopkins University Press, 2001.

Wright, Richard. *Native Son.* New York: Harper, 1940.

Chapter 12

Provocation through Polyphony

● ●

Kyle Baker's *Nat Turner*

CRAIG FISCHER

The Question

When I think of Kyle Baker's graphic novel *Nat Turner* (2008), I immediately recall, in detail, the book's splash page of a big, bald slave named Will swinging his axe and beheading a cherubic white child. What does this image *mean*?

The Artist

Kyle Baker was born in 1965 in New York City. His father was a direct-mail advertiser—"He's the guy who makes the junk-mail envelopes that say 'You may have already won a million bucks'" (Worcester 40)—and his mother worked at a local high school after going to art school. Baker grew up reading newspaper comic strips (he remembers late-period *Pogo* and *Steve Canyon*) and comic books featuring Donald Duck, Dennis the Menace, and Archie Andrews—anything but superheroes. Baker notes that he was "never been a big superhero fan. It's just not my thing, that's all" (Worcester 40).

Baker drew voluminously as a child and teenager and interned at Marvel Comics in his senior year of high school (1982–1983). Despite his ambivalence

12.1 A powerful splash page of a big, bald slave beheading a cherubic white child challenges the reader in *Nat Turner*.

toward superheroes, Baker enjoyed his time as a Marvel staffer, especially the opportunities to hear stories about the comics business from lifers Vince Colletta and Jack Abel. After leaving Marvel to enroll in New York City's School of Visual Arts, Baker paid his tuition by working as a freelancer for Marvel and DC, penciling and inking pages for such comic books as *Codename: Danger*,

The New Mutants, and the comic book adaptation of the *Howard the Duck* movie.

After two years at the School of Visual Arts, Baker stopped showing up to classes and dove full-time into his art career. Baker produced spot illustrations for *Spy*, *Details*, *Esquire*, and other magazines, worked as an assistant to comic book artists, and developed his own newspaper strip, *The Cowboy Wally Show*. (*Wally* was never picked up by a syndicate for distribution, although a version of the material was published as a book by Doubleday in 1988.) His first high-profile jobs for a mainstream comics company were his pencils and inks for *The Shadow* (1988–1989) and *Justice Inc.* (1989), two irreverent reboots of pulp-magazine properties done in collaboration with the writer Andrew Helfer. At the time, neither was a success—*The Shadow* was canceled due to low sales—but their reputation has grown over time. In 2010, the critic Chris Mautner enthused over *The Shadow* thusly: "By refusing to be beholden to nostalgia or the then popular 'grim and gritty' ethos, [Baker and Helfer] were able to create a manic, inspired and downright hilarious comic that is quite unlike anything that was being published at the time or has come down the pike since."

Baker, during much of his career, has balanced working for DC and Marvel with personal projects. One of Baker's most popular books was *Why I Hate Saturn* (1990), a graphic novel about the tensions between a sarcastic, hard-drinking urbanite and her eccentric but better-adjusted sister. *Saturn* was initially released through Piranha Press, a short-lived (1989–1994) DC imprint designed to bring alternative sensibilities to the mainstream giant. After the collapse of Piranha, some of Baker's graphic novels (including *You Are There* [1998], *I Die at Midnight* [1998], *King David* [2002], and *Undercover Genie* [2003]) found a home at Vertigo, a DC subdivision less experimental than Piranha but also less mainstream than the company's typical superhero comics.

In addition to Baker's work for Piranha and Vertigo, he has occasionally drawn superheroes for DC and Marvel, although the results have been critics' darlings rather than sales blockbusters. With the writer Robert Morales, Baker produced the miniseries *Truth: Red, White and Black* (2003), a bold revision of the Captain America origin story; in its story of African Americans injected with an early, flawed version of the Super Solider serum that changed Steve Rogers into Captain America, *Truth* explicitly invokes the historical crime of the Tuskegee experiments. For DC, Baker wrote and drew the first twenty issues of a *Plastic Man* revival from 2004 to 2006, revisiting much of the ludic humor of the comics by the character's creator, Jack Cole. At least once, however, Baker's zany humor proved too controversial for the superhero genre. In 1999, Baker and cowriter (and wife) Elizabeth Glass did a ten-page story, "Letitia Lerner, Superman's Babysitter," for *Elseworlds 80-Page Giant* #1 (1999), but the copies of the comic printed for the North American market were destroyed when DC's then president Paul Levitz found a gag about a babysitter microwaving Superman as an infant to be in excessive bad taste for DC's readership (Kimball).

"Letitia Lerner, Superman's Babysitter" was eventually made available to U.S. fans in *Bizarro Comics* (2001), an anthology explicitly aimed at mature readers.

Simultaneous with Baker's work for big comics companies, he has published through prose book publishers, and he has also experimented with self-publishing. The film producer-director Reginald Hudlin (*House Party*, 1988) and the comic strip creator Aaron McGruder (*The Boondocks*, 1999–2006) wrote the script for the Crown graphic novel *Birth of a Nation* (2004), which borrows plot points from the British film *Passport to Pimlico* (1949) in its tale of East St. Louis's secession from the United States. Kyle Baker Publishing, the artist's own DIY company, has so far released the comic book *The New Baker* (2003) and several longer books of his art, including *The Bakers: Do These Toys Belong Somewhere?* (2006) and two volumes of *Kyle Baker: Cartoonist* (2004, 2005). (A common presence among these self-published books is "The Bakers," a semiautobiographical, humorous domestic strip that reads like a charming twenty-first-century updating of *Blondie*.) *Nat Turner*, Baker's adaptation of *The Confessions of Nat Turner* (1831) and the subject of this chapter, began as a self-published comic book (2005–2006), because, in Baker's words, "If you're doing a book about slavery, you sort of have to make sure you get all the money, because the whole definition of slavery is when one person does all the work and the other person gets the money [laughs]. So it's kind of important that the guy who does the book gets the money this time. So I'm self-publishing that one" (Farago). *Nat Turner* actually concluded in a comic coreleased by Baker and Image (2006) and was collected into a complete graphic novel by the art-book publisher Abrams (2008), aimed at an audience outside comic shops. Since the release of *Nat Turner*, Baker has worked on various projects, including the miniseries *Special Forces* (2009, and about which more later), Marvel's *Deadpool* character, and animation projects. (Much of this information about Baker has been culled from the interviews conducted by Worcester and Nolen-Weathington.)

The Dissonance

Baker is an African American cartoonist working for companies (Marvel, DC, and Image) that are overwhelmingly white. Baker's dual consciousness, however, seems less a Du Boisian straddling of white and Black culture than a vexed relationship with "commercial" comics across his entire career. According to Baker (and, I think, indisputably true), comic books are currently a "nostalgia business" catering to the narrow tastes of middle-aged males who grew up on superhero comics. By emphasizing superheroes to the virtual exclusion of all other genres, comics have lost touch with a larger, more inclusive audience, a point Baker makes when he talks about trying to create a "kiddy comic" for DC:

I said, "OK, that's the kiddy department, I'll call them up and say I've got an idea for a kiddy comic." And [editor Dana Kurtin] said, "Well, I'll tell you the truth. We would do it because we like you, we have a relationship with you; we would do it because it's you. But DC would not push it, because they don't sell those Cartoon Network books. The Cartoon Network and Bugs Bunny books, we do 'em because Warner Brothers makes us do 'em. They say, 'Push Bugs Bunny. We need you to make a Bugs Bunny comic,' but no one buys Bugs Bunny comic books." And again, if you can't sell Bugs Bunny, you should get out of town. (Worcester 74)

A fan of Bugs Bunny, Donald Duck, and humor comics, Baker has consequently been an uneasy fit at DC and Marvel. Even though *The Shadow* was "a manic, inspired and downright hilarious comic," it was such a radical reimaging of the character that it was rumored that Condé Nast, the copyright holder for the Shadow, asked for the title to be canceled. Baker's attempt to inject humor into the Superman mythos (with "Letitia Lerner, Superman's Babysitter") led to the pulping of thousands of comics, while the Captain America miniseries *Truth* prompted so much criticism that the Marvel editor Alex Alonzo spoke out against "outright racists who just don't like the idea of a Black man in the Cap uniform" (Sinclair). Baker is acutely aware of his status as odd man out; in an interview with Eric Nolen-Weathington, he described his intention to honor *Plastic Man* creator Jack Cole by treating the character with zany humor and then predicted the eventual fate of the title: "I guess I'm just going to write a book that nobody buys" (48).

The Book

The book that Baker is best known for, his chronicle of the life of the insurgent slave Nat Turner, piggybacks on and borrows from previous auto/biographies of Turner.

Nathaniel "Nat" Turner (October 2, 1800–November 11, 1831), the leader of a slave rebellion in Virginia on August 21, 1831, that resulted in fifty-five white deaths, was executed for his insurrection and quickly passed into cultural immortality. *The Confessions of Nat Turner: The Leader of the Late Insurrection in Southampton, Virginia* (1831) was an account published by the attorney Thomas Ruffin Gray, supposedly based on discussions between Gray and Turner while the ex-slave waited to die. (Most of the text in Baker's *Nat Turner* is quoted verbatim from the Turner/Gray *Confessions*.) One hundred and thirty-six years later, William Styron combined material from Gray's pamphlet with fictional extrapolation in *The Confessions of Nat Turner* (1967), a novel that received praise from Ralph Ellison and James Baldwin and criticism for its portrayal of Turner as an ineffectual warrior and its sympathetic treatment of certain slave owners. (For more information about the influence of these sources and others on Baker's treatment of Nat Turner, see Kunka.)

Baker's version of Nat Turner's story splits into four chapters. The first, "Home," shows Turner's mother kidnapped from her African village by slavers. Chained to other victims, she is forced to walk a vast distance to board the ships and sees atrocities (most sensationally, a baby fed by its mother to hungry sharks) during the Middle Passage. She is finally bought at a slave auction and brought to a plantation in Virginia. She then tells these stories of her horrific voyage to the other plantation slaves.

In chapter 2, "Education," Turner grows from boyhood to adulthood, with both the ability to read (gained from eavesdropping on classes for the master's children and stealing brief glimpses at the master's books) and a sense of purpose from the Bible: Baker includes text from the Turner/Gray *Confessions* ("Wrapped myself in mystery, devoting my time to fasting and prayer" [91]) that chronicles Turner's increasing dedication to a higher mission that will right slavery's wrongs. "Freedom" is chapter 3, a blow-by-blow chronicle of Turner's rebellion from its beginning (Turner and four men kill his master's family, in "the work of a moment" [117]) to its escalation and finally to its eventual defeat when Turner is captured by the white landowners. (This section of *Turner* begins with a white boy waving hello to Will, the bald, massive slave, and this is the boy beheaded by the same slave later in the chapter.)

In chapter 4, "Triumph," Turner is lynched in front of an audience of white revelers, and his dead body is dissected. But the book ends with hope. A maid sneaks off with a copy of the *Confessions*, an image that refers back to several moments concerning storytelling in *Turner*: Turner's mother speaks her experiences to the assembled slaves, a different maid earlier in the narrative is whipped for reading her master's animal book, and Nat acquires reading with "the most perfect ease": "so much so, that I have no recollection whatever of learning the alphabet" (86). At the beginning of chapter 2, an elderly slave transmits messages by playing a hidden drum, until he is caught by overseers who whip him, shove salt in his wounds, and cut off his hands. The drumbeat stops, but the books and stories continue to circulate.

The Critique

Nat Turner's reception has been mixed. One criticism of the book comes from Marc Singer, who in a March 2010 post on his blog criticized what he saw as *Turner's* uneasy mix of history, violence, and unrealistic action-adventure tropes. Singer accuses Baker of jazzing up slavery "with chases and fight scenes and huge Frank Miller heroes who battle dozens of guys in silhouette" and calls the book "not a history but a romantic fiction, a Frank Miller comic in slave-narrative drag." For Singer, this is especially true of the opening of *Turner*, where Baker invents a backstory that takes place before the time covered by

Gray's *Confessions*, particularly a dramatization of how Turner's parents were kidnapped from their African village by white slavers. A scene in the first chapter where Turner's mother hurls herself off a cliff—preferring death to capture and servitude—only to be lassoed in midair by a kidnapper is "absolutely ridiculous": "It's just an attempt to build Nat Turner's mom up into an action hero, to make Turner some sort of genetically pedigreed badass." Singer does not consider the irony here, in that Baker creates his own fantasy of a "genetic pedigree" to challenge the eugenics that justified American slavery.

For Singer, the last third of the book is more artfully complex, communicating the visceral impact of the violence of Turner's raid through such antiquated representational strategies as insets, faux photographs, and close-ups straight out of D. W. Griffith. Yet for Singer, this powerful formalism does not hide Baker's "troubling ethical positions," such as Baker's claim that he objectively portrayed the events of Turner's life—even while drawing those slaves who "acted to save white slave owners from Turner's followers" as minstrel stereotypes. And then Singer confesses that he, like me, is haunted by the image of the slave chopping off the child's head, and he asks, is this image "an admirable refusal to sugar-coat Turner's rebellion, an insistence on showing the true cost of a futile revolt whose victims were mostly children? Is it a fair and balanced depiction of what really happened in Southampton in 1831? Or does the sheer graphic overkill leaven the image with a perverse undercurrent of *joy*?"

The Response to the Critique

In "Drawing the Unspeakable: Kyle Baker's Slave Narrative," Conseula Francis contends that the indeterminacy of *Turner* that bothers Singer is actually one of the book's signature innovations. Francis places *Turner* in the context of such nineteenth-century prose slave narratives as Frederick Douglass's *Narrative of the Life of Frederick Douglass* (1845) and Harriet Jacobs's *Incidents in the Life of a Slave Girl* (1861), arguing that these older narratives are crafted to dramatize, in the words of the scholar Penny Tucker, the author's "achievement of respectability through literacy, literary eloquence, and reason" (Tucker 140, qtd. in Francis 116). They are stories of uplift against all odds, designed to lobby for the intellectual parity of the "Negro" and for abolition on moral grounds. Thus, they avoid the ambiguities of the true experience of slavery. As Francis writes, "If the goal of the slave narratives was to gain the sympathy of white readers, then the authors of slave narratives needed to be strategic about which details they offered and which they held back" (116). Which makes the "emotionless, detached, unapologetic description of unspeakable violence" (116) in the Turner/Gray *Confessions* remarkable: Turner does not try to curry favor with his white readers. He simply tells us, clinically, what he and his insurrectionists did—"There was a little infant sleeping in a cradle, that was forgotten, until we had left the house and gone some distance, when Henry and Will returned and killed it" (13)—and there is a similar bluntness in Baker's visuals, a bluntness that, unlike the well-crafted slave narrative, exposes the moral ambiguities of the horrors Turner committed in the name of revenge.

This is not to say, however, that Baker condemns Turner's actions. As Francis points out, Turner's revenge comes only after we have seen Turner's mother wrenched from Africa, branded, and put up for sale and Turner himself forcibly separated from his wife and children, who are auctioned off to another slaver. Following the destruction of his family, Turner experiences a wrenching vision of "white spirits and black spirits engaged in battle" (10), staged dramatically across two pages. We see Turner in a lightning storm, soaked by rain and lifting his fists to the sky. Francis comments on this scene thusly:

> Taken together, the words and the images on these two pages show a man caught up in the awesomeness of God, and surely this is true. Turner's own words suggest he is in constant awe at being chosen as one of God's prophets. Yet these words and images do not stand alone. They come immediately after the harrowing sequence of Turner's wife and children being sold away from him. The reader, then, can not help but read the storm as also a reflection of Turner's anger and despair. Again, while Baker does nothing in this story to discount Turner's claims to prophetic powers, he nonetheless takes great pains to place those powers into the body and mind of a man who feels deeply all the atrocities of slavery. (130–131)

Another interpretation is possible: perhaps Turner has been driven mad by the loss of his family, and his revelations are a symptom of his madness. Sane or mad, Turner is a victim of slavery, and Francis's point is that Baker's word-picture combinations lead us to understand his motivations, even while we wince as Turner strikes his slaver repeatedly with an axe.

The Polyphony

In response to Singer's criticism that *Turner* lacks a consistent authorial point of view, Francis praises how Baker leads us to feel sympathy for Turner *and* revulsion for the specifics of his revenge. Francis's position is a reminder of how *Turner* and all texts operate simultaneously on multiple levels of meaning, contingent on the form of the text and the subjectivities that individual readers bring to the text. This notion of multiple meanings has recently been supplemented by instances of criticism designed to explore the messy ways a comic might generate meaning through its formal construction and its intersections with history, ideology, and audience. Charles Hatfield's *English Language Notes* essay on the Jaime Hernandez stories "How to Kill a" (1982) and "Flies on the Ceiling" (1989–1990) addresses topics as diverse as Thierry Groensteen's ideas of "braiding" through a comics text and the effects that serialization of the Maggie and Hopey saga has had on both Hernandez's art and the reception of his work by readers. More recently, Ken Parille, in *The Dan Clowes Reader*, suggests "six interpretive frameworks" for dissecting Clowes's heavily symbolic short story "Black Nylon" (1996), including "the Freudian psychosexual origins of the heterosexual male superhero" (268) and the status of the story as an "impossible fiction" that has "no definable relationship to our world or to genre fiction" (269). This increased critical attention on multiple perspectives and interpretive strategies jibes with the complexities of my own reading processes and with the cognitive dissonance I sometimes experience when my own reading strategies diverge as I read a comic.

In that spirit, I want to return to the page from *Turner* that haunts me—Will's beheading of the child—and briefly suggest three "interpretive frameworks" for understanding the meanings of that image beyond Singer's self-confessed confusion and Francis's justification of moral ambiguity. That beheading can reveal how *Turner* functions as a horror comic, an example of the Milleresque violence in contemporary comics, and the first instance of a new style, the "incoherent comic," in Baker's oeuvre.

The Horror (The Horror!)

The axe as a weapon holds a special place in horror comics history, ever since the EC editor Bill Gaines tried to defend the cover of *Crime SuspenStories* #22 (April 1954) during the Senate Subcommittee on Juvenile Delinquency in April 1954.

Turner's connections to the horror genre go further than Will's choice of weapon. In *The Philosophy of Horror* (1990), Noël Carroll argues that horror texts subvert our understanding of the world by presenting us with hybrid "monsters." For Carroll, perception is inescapably connected to our ability to place the objects and people we perceive into familiar cognitive categories: our sense of smell helps us to quickly determine whether something is "edible" or "inedible," and when we look at someone, our first instinct is to identify the person as either "male" or "female." The monsters in horror media, however, are figures that refuse to fit into our traditional ways of defining and categorizing stimuli, and that is why they make us uneasy (31–32). Humans and animals are easy to tell apart in our everyday perceptions, but the werewolf splices together the incompatible characteristics of man and beast; likewise, the commonly obvious difference between life and death is undermined by monsters such as zombies and vampires. The habitual male/female gender dichotomy is challenged by Norman Bates, who is both mother and son, female and male, and Buffalo Bill in *Silence of the Lambs* (1991), a transsexual who sews women's flesh into a suit he can wear, to bring his physical body in harmony with his interior female identity. Buffalo Bill is in fact an example of the conservatism possible in the horror genre, how the genre cultivates in readers and audiences a mistrust of any hybridity beyond perceptual habit.

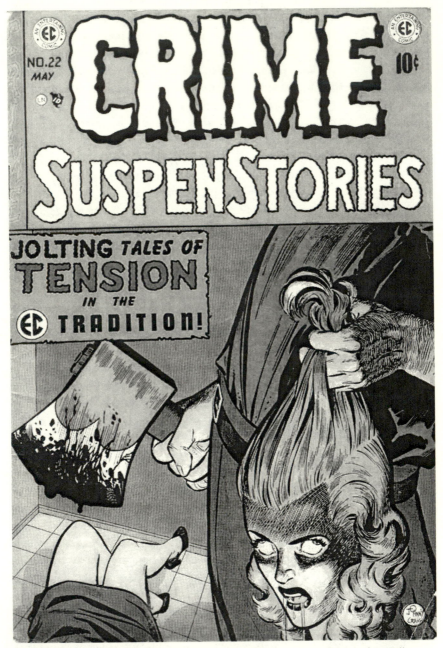

12.2 The axe holds a special place in horror comics history, ever since the EC editor Bill Gaines tried to defend this cover of *Crime SuspenStories* during the Senate Subcommittee on Juvenile Delinquency in April 1954.

If we accept Francis's argument that Baker shows us both the justification for Turner's raid (through the subjectivities of men *who can stand slavery no more*) and the savagery of the raid itself, then we understand Will's ideological double bind as he beheads the child. The "Freedom" chapter begins as Will forces a smile at the little boy whom he later kills, and this smile might hide several emotions: a fear of the master's punishments if he behaves rudely, a fear of acting on Turner's radical words, and/or a desire to masquerade as a good slave until the time is right for revenge. Once Will swings his axe, however, he becomes a monster in the Carrollian sense, a locus for the clash of incompatible ideologies. He is a hero, yet he murders a defenseless child; at the same moment that he becomes a freedom fighter, he also becomes a hulking golem, a visual crystallization of the Big, Black Buck figure used to justify slavery. (In chapter 4, Turner himself takes on similar symbolic weight, as his lynching becomes a public humiliation that restores the racist social order.) Perhaps on the most primal level, there is Singer's speculation that this image could provide readers "with a perverse undercurrent of *joy*," independent of narrative and ideological context, the interpretive paradigm (or absence of an interpretive paradigm) that Fredric Wertham despised most of all.

The director Paul Thomas Anderson defines the "gearshift movie" as one that changes tones abruptly, taking its audiences by surprise (Hyden et al.). Fans have since adopted Anderson's "gearshift" label and written their own lists of favorite movies that begin with one plot and/or character, only to lurch surprisingly in another direction later in the narrative. One such list is the A.V. Club's "Turning on a Dime: 15 Great Gearshift Movies" (Hyden et al.), which includes such horror and suspense films as *Psycho* (Alfred Hitchcock, 1960), *Audition* (Takashi Miike, 1999), *Something Wild* (Jonathan Demme, 1986), and *Lost Highway* (David Lynch, 1997). The gearshift aesthetic is a close cousin to monstrous hybridity: in horror films, the unease we feel when confronted with a category-defying zombie or werewolf is amplified when the text refuses to stick to dramatic unities and traditional storytelling rules, when it is instead sewn together like Frankenstein's monster.

Nat Turner is one such stitched-together narrative. As Singer points out, the action-movie idiom of the first two chapters—particularly the superheroic stunts of Turner's mother in chapter 1—abruptly shifts to the more sinister domestic status quo of slavery, and Turner's abrupt disruption of that norm, in chapter 3. If the action in chapter 1 is an idealization of resistance against slavery, chapter 3 is, in Singer's words, "a story of grotesque and largely pointless bloodshed." The title for chapter 3, "Freedom," teases us with an exalted goal, but the only freedom that Will, Turner's men, and ultimately Turner himself find is death.

The Mess

As we have seen, Marc Singer calls *Nat Turner* a "Frank Miller comic in slave-narrative drag," and several Baker works treat Miller's aesthetic as a source of homage, parody, and/or inspiration. The first page of Baker's "Hawkman" serial in DC's *Wednesday Comics* (2009) opens with captions representing the thoughts of eagles and other birds as Hawkman commands them to fly into the atmosphere and attack a hijacked plane. As the online critic Chris Sims notes, the staccato tone of these thoughts—"He fills us with faith, trust and confidence. / We flap."—is a parody of the terse narration of Miller's *300* (1998) (Hudson et al.).

There is, however, one way in which *Turner* follows, rather than satirizes, a Miller trope: both Miller and Baker portray violence in ink-soaked, indistinct ways. Ironically, the single passage that epitomizes and explicates this approach best is not from a Miller comic. In a long chapter in Alan Moore and Eddie Campbell's *From Hell* (1999), William Gull, the man responsible for the Jack the Ripper murders, carves apart a woman's body, and although much of the process is shown in disquietingly literal terms, there is a brief sequence where a knife plunging into flesh triggers an indistinct glimpse inside the woman's body (see fig. 12.3). When explicating this passage in the footnotes to *From Hell*, Moore notes that the inspiration for this scene came from the reaction that the comic artist Steve Bissette had to Stan Brakhage's *The Act of Seeing with One's Own Eyes* (1971), an experimental film that shows, in unflinching detail, pathologists performing autopsies in a Pittsburgh morgue. Moore writes, "As Steve experienced the film, initial understandable revulsion as the body's inner cavities were opened up soon gave way to a kind of fascinated awe at the magnificence and intricacy of our inner workings" (*From Hell* 35). To capture this "intricacy," Campbell photocopied images of the human heart and gave them to his assistant Pete Mullins to ink, and the result was, surprisingly, a page that, in Campbell's words, "looks almost abstract" (Moore and Campbell, *Companion* 218). The comics critic Matt Seneca echoes Campbell when he describes this page as "an incredibly beautiful bit of near-abstract art" that stands independent of narrative context as "seven beautiful pictures, each image both arresting and dynamic." Moore and Campbell (and Mullins), in their desire to create awe by opening for display the meat of the human heart, ended up with ink-soaked figuration rather than easily accessible art.

Contemporaneous with the serialization of *From Hell* was Miller's first *Sin City* arc, "The Hard Goodbye" (1991–1992 [2005]), which takes a similar pseudoabstract approach to violence. "The Hard Goodbye" tells the story of Marv, a noir superman who tears apart an urban landscape looking for the person responsible for the death of Goldie, the woman he loved. (The first part of Robert Rodriguez's *Sin City* film version [2005] adapts this tale, with Mickey Rourke in the role of Marv.) In chapter 5 of "The Hard Goodbye," during a

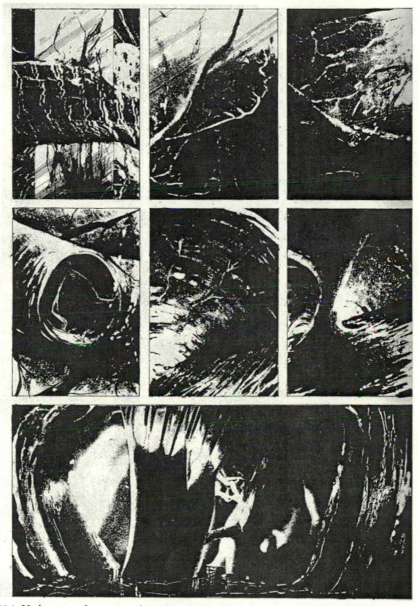

12.3 Violence may be portrayed in ink-soaked, indistinct ways, as seen in Alan Moore and Eddie Campbell's *From Hell*. Here is a brief sequence where a knife plunging into flesh triggers an indistinct glimpse inside the woman's body.

sequence where Marv rampages around the city beating up low-level thugs for information about Goldie, Miller inserts a panel that is built around a shape, an X composed of both Marv's and the victim's hands in the upper and lower quadrants of the panel (see fig. 12.4). Miller places the victim's bloody face square at the intersection of the lines of the X, and from this center blood flows,

12.4 In chapter five of "The Hard Goodbye," Miller relies on hyperstylization as in this X design of Marv beating up a low-level thug for information about Goldie.

although this blood is more of a design element than a scrupulous rendition of realistic gore; the hands in the panel are little more than white expanses of negative space, canvases against which the blood can splash. Miller's hyperstylization extends beyond the numerous moments of violence in *Sin City*—there are several pages in chapter 8 of "The Hard Goodbye" where Miller's interest in drawing rain as alternating lines of white and black dry brush overwhelm and almost render illegible other visual content—and it is this abstraction that influences Baker's art as Turner's raid escalates in the "Freedom" chapter of *Turner*.

Surrounded by a crowd of vengeful, armed slave owners, Will attacks the crowd head-on, and in two splash pages, we see him reduce bodies to a whirling mass of shadows, fabric wrinkles, and grime (see figs. 12.5 and 12.6). Though we can see specific violence in each splash page—a decapitated head in the first, a severed arm in the second—Baker's emphasis is on distressing the picture plane with so many marks, lines, and shadows that the mess itself, independent of referential content, comes to signify blood and gore. The beheading of the child is heavily crosshatched, but Baker used holding lines and tones to distinguish the child's arm from Will's leg, and Will's feet from the shadow he casts. Will's attack on the slave owners, however, is harder to read, much closer to the abstract representations of the heart in the *From Hell* passage and to the visual representations of Marv's rampages in Sin City than to the dark but legible storytelling in the rest of *Turner*.

12.5 In two splash pages of *Nat Turner*, as Will attacks a crowd, the bodies are reduced to a whirling mass of shadows, wrinkles, and grime.

The Incoherence

Robin Wood has written that all art has as its goal "the ordering of experience, the striving for coherence" (41). This can lead to a text (and a vision of the world) that is whole, complete, and understandable, where style, story, and theme meld together to transmit a coherent message or mood. Yet the story of modernism is partially about texts whose coherence is in the disruption of standards of the well-wrought work of art: think of Bertolt Brecht short-circuiting

12.6 Splash pages of *Nat Turner* (*continued*)

the identificatory illusion of the stage, or Kathy Acker scuttling over the history of literature like a packrat, picking out passages to steal and drop into her own rough-hewn prose collages. Compared to creators like Brecht and Acker, Baker's own subversions of coherence in *Turner*—his tonal shift between the first and second halves of the book, his willingness to define Will in complicated and ambiguous terms—do not seem that radical, except, perhaps, within a comic book culture whose readership prefers concrete expression and easily identifiable heroes.

Immediately after *Turner*, Baker created another, even more "incoherent" text, *Special Forces* (four issues published by Image Comics from 2007 to 2009, collected edition 2009), about an army platoon of misfits charged with destroying "the insurgent hideout in Baquba" and capturing "Khaled Ayub Mohamed, a.k.a. 'the Desert Wolf'" (first issue). The first image in *Forces* is that of the exploding head of an African American platoon member, Baker's rueful take on action films' tendency to kill off their Black characters as early as possible. Other soldiers—the overweight Doughboy, the cowardly Sarge, the flamboyantly gay Hummer—also die in combat, and soon the only survivors are Felony, our central protagonist, a "bad girl" whose thoughts guide us through the narrative, and Zone, an autistic platoon member whose obsession with routine (even if that routine is to kill "the Desert Wolf") makes him a strong warrior. Throughout the rest of the story, Felony and Zone, together and separately, have adventures in their thinly veiled analogue for the Iraq War's theater of operations.

There are similarities between *Turner* and *Forces*. In issue 3 of *Forces*, Felony escapes from the "Axis of Evil Mutants"—children deformed by unexploded cluster bombs and uranium munitions—by shooting at them (though Felony wounds the kids instead of killing them), and the Desert Wolf is, like Will, a huge, rock-hard, threatening Black man. The tone of *Forces*, however, is different from *Turner*; in *Forces*, Baker combines what appears to be straight-faced reverence for U.S. soldiers with as many politically incorrect jokes as he can come up with about the members of the platoon. Felony is our heroine, but Baker relentlessly draws her wearing almost no clothes, a ragged halter top stretched across her enormous breasts, leaping into action poses that often make her ass and crotch the most prominent objects inside a panel.

This strange combination of saluting and satirizing soldiers reaches a fever pitch on the very last page of the fourth issue of *Forces* (March 2009), where Baker presents an image of two American soldiers, a man and a woman, kissing in the pose of the famous V-E Day photograph, with other contemporary soldiers standing in the foreground. A caption praises the "mentally handicapped and/or felons" who have given their lives in the Iraq War, and the image as a whole reads as more of an indictment of army recruiting policies (elsewhere satirized in *Special Forces*) than genuine gratitude. On the next page, the inside back cover of *Forces* #4, a letter from Douglas Evans of Victoria criticizes Baker for "anti-American propaganda," while in another letter, the cartoonist and historian Trina Robbins is even more unfavorable: "So I gave [*Special Forces*] a chance and read it, and I have to say that I don't get it and I don't like it. This is not the Kyle Baker I know. It's not a statement against the war in Iraq; it's a violent action comic starring a sexy babe. What the hell?" Baker's response: "I thought you said you didn't get it. You TOTALLY get it!" Apparently Robbins understands (but does not appreciate) the fact that *Forces* is a Mixmaster of oddly incompatible elements, designed to antagonize and provoke the reader. Even the most stable rule of comic book creation—that characters should remain on model and that the drawing style should remain consistent (except for clearly defined narrative reasons) across a miniseries or single work—is abandoned in *Forces*, as the long interval between issues 3 and 4 (eight months) prompts Baker to abandon his earlier Kubert-scratchy art for a final chapter dense with sound effects, granularity on the picture plane, and candy-colored sleekness. Is nothing sacred?

The End

Pictures are mysterious and dense; the image of Will decapitating the child is a symptom of Baker's artistic confusion, a heinous but inevitable backlash against the dehumanization of slavery, an expression of the "monstrous" traditions of comic book horror, a cheap thrill, a parody of Frank Miller's work, an example of the visually abstracted violence of today's comics, an ambiguous part of a likewise "incoherent" and complex text, and more. Singer in his blog post briefly discusses teaching *Turner* to his students at Howard University and acknowledges that the book "furnished plenty of material for some rich class discussion." Singer wishes that *Turner* "has the courage to judge or condemn its hero as easily as it praises him," but the interpretive field goes beyond the praise/judge valence, and the result is a text that provokes dissent and response, an eminently teachable book. And I find myself succumbing to one more interpretive paradigm as I wonder, could *Turner* only be done by an artist deeply embedded in both mainstream and alternative comics traditions?

Works Cited

Baker, Kyle. *The Cowboy Wally Show*. New York: Doubleday, 1988.
———. "Hawkman." *Wednesday Comics* 1. Ed. Mark Chiarello. New York: DC Comics, 2009. N. pag.
———. *Nat Turner*. New York: Abrams, 2008.
———. *Special Forces*. Berkeley, CA: Image Comics, 2009.
———. *Special Forces* 4. Berkeley, CA: Image Comics, 2009.
———. *Why I Hate Saturn*. 1989. New York: Vertigo, 2004.
Brakhage, Stan. *The Act of Seeing with One's Own Eyes*. 1971. Film.
Carroll, Noël. *The Philosophy of Horror; or, Paradoxes of the Heart*. New York: Routledge, 1990.
Farago, Andrew. "Special: An Interview with Kyle Baker." *Comics Reporter* 1 May 2005. Web. http://www.comicsreporter.com/index.php/resources/interviews/2251/. Accessed 25 October 2013.
Francis, Conseula. "Drawing the Unspeakable: Kyle Baker's Slave Narrative." *Comics and the U.S. South*. Ed. Brannon Costello and Qiana J. Whitted. Jackson: University Press of Mississippi, 2012. 113–137.
Hatfield, Charles. "How to Read a . . ." *English Language Notes* 46.2 (2008): 129–150.
Hudson, Laura, Chris Sims, David Brothers, and David Uzumeri. "Roundtable Review: *Wednesday Comics* Hardcover, Part 2." Comics Alliance. 25 May 2010. Web.

comicsalliance.com/roundtable-review-wednesdaycomics-hardcover-part-2/. Accessed 25 October 2013.

Hyden, Steve, Chris Mincher, Keith Phipps, Leonard Pierce, Tasha Robinson, and Scott Tobias. "Turning on a Dime: 15 Great Gearshift Movies." A.V. Club 25 January 2009. Web. http://www.avclub.com/article/turning-on-a-dime-15-great-gearshift-movies-23015. Accessed 25 October 2013.

Kimball, Kurt. "Dial B for Blog #300: The Forbidden Comic Book." *Dial B for Blog* n.d. Web. http://www.dialbforblog.com/archives/300/. Accessed 25 October 2013.

Kunka, Andrew J. "Intertextuality and the Historical Graphic Narrative: Kyle Baker's *Nat Turner* and the Styron Controversy." *College Literature* 38.3 (2011): 168–193.

Mautner, Chris. "Collect This Now! *The Shadow.*" *Robot* 6 (blog), Comic Book Resources, 15 October 2010. Web. http://robot6.comicbookresources.com/2010/10/collect-this-now-the-shadow/. Accessed 25 October 2013.

McGruder, Aaron, and Reginald Hudlin. *Birth of a Nation: A Comic Novel*. New York: Three Rivers, 2005.

Miller, Frank. *The Frank Miller Library, Volume 1: The Hard Goodbye*. 1991–1992. Milwaukie, OR: Dark Horse Books, 2005.

Moore, Alan, and Eddie Campbell. *From Hell: Being a Melodrama in Sixteen Parts*. Marietta, GA: Top Shelf, 2006.

———. *The From Hell Companion*. Marietta, GA: Top Shelf, 2013.

Nolen-Weathington, Eric, ed. *Modern Masters, Volume 20: Kyle Baker*. Raleigh, NC: TwoMorrows, 2009.

Parille, Ken. "Decoding 'Black Nylon.'" *The Daniel Clowes Reader*. Ed. Parille. Seattle: Fantagraphics, 2013. 267–270.

Seneca, Matt. "Your Wednesday Sequence 40: Eddie Campbell." *Robot* 6 (blog), Comic Book Resources, 31 January 2012. Web. http://robot6.comicbookresources.com/2012/02/your-wednesday-sequence-40-eddie-campbell/. Accessed 25 October 2013.

Sinclair, Tom. "Black in Action." *Entertainment Weekly* 22 November 2002. Web. http://www.ew.com/ew/article/0,,390672,00.html. Accessed 25 October 2013.

Singer, Marc. "Week 8: *Nat Turner.*" *I Am Not the Beastmaster* (blog) 18 March 2010. Web. http://notthebeastmaster.typepad.com/weblog/. Accessed 25 October 2013.

Styron, William. *The Confessions of Nat Turner*. New York: Random House, 1967.

Tucker, Penny. "Traumatic Traces: Slave Narratives, Post-traumatic Stress, and the Limits of Resistance." *Representing Minorities: Studies in Literature and Criticism*. Ed. Larbi Touaf and Soumia Boutkhil. Cambridge: Cambridge Scholars, 2006. 139–149.

Turner, Nat, and Thomas Gray. *The Confessions of Nat Turner*. Baltimore: Thomas R. Gray, 1831.

———. *The Confession, Trial, and Execution of Nat Turner, the Negro Insurrectionist; Also a List of Persons Murdered in the Insurrection in Southampton County, Virginia, on the 21st and 22nd of August, 1831, with Introductory Remarks by T.R. Gray*. Petersburg, VA: John B. Ege, 1881.

Wertham, Fredric. *The Seduction of the Innocent: The Influence of Comic Books on Today's Youth*. New York: Rinehart, 1954.

Wood, Robin. *Hollywood from Vietnam to Reagan . . . and Beyond*. New York: Columbia University Press, 2003.

Worcester, Kent. "Kyle Baker." *Comics Journal* 219 (January 2000): 38–80.

Chapter 13

Performance Geography

• •

Making Space in Jeremy Love's
Bayou, Volume 1

HERSHINI BHANA YOUNG

Located in the vicinity of the fictional town of Charon, Mississippi, Jeremy Love's *Bayou*, volume 1 (2009), is site specific even as evokes other, more general landscapes haunted by plantation slavery. As a graphic novel, *Bayou* can enact a spectacular visuality with sweeping skies, rising suns over swamps, dense forests, and makeshift little towns. Page after page gives itself over to the landscape, whose water, rocks, and trees constitute both the text and the narrative in such fulfilling ways that one barely notices how sparse the words become in certain sections of the novel. It would be easy to give oneself over to the horrible beauty of a global South saturated by plantation economics and the relationships it engendered. It might even be easier to consider the terrain as a backdrop to the story of Lee Wagstaff, whose father, Calvin, has been arrested for the alleged murder of Lee's friend, the white Lily Westmoreland. As the events unfold that lead to Lee struggling to save her father from the lynching that is only hours away, one can dismiss the novel's geography as merely the stage on which the players act their part. However, Love shows the landscape to be essential to the story itself. Space is not simply occupied, nor is it mere backdrop that visually frames the story. Rather, the land palpably, sensually participates in the performances of blacks and whites haunted by violent geographies of domination that help create racial and gender hierarchies. *Bayou* carefully shows not only the geographic rituals that enact black subjugation but also alternate mappings of space that overlay and underlie black and native strategies of resistance. In its insistence on the terror and promise of the African diaspora, *Bayou* is an example of "performance geography."

Sonjah Stanley Niaah defines "performance geography" as the site where "physical, mental, emotional, and spiritual activity . . . enacts a human existence, specifically in the 'black Atlantic' space between violation, ruptured roots and self-reconstruction" (194). Black global space thus is not so much occupied by black people as forged through ritualistic enactments of black experiences. The focus on investing spaces of domination with black Atlantic meanings via the performative work of their inhabitants and their resistance to racial and gender hierarchies speaks to alternate geographies. Love's larger-than-life characters insist on mappings of space that produce liberatory meaning. The form of *Bayou* lends itself to this if we think of graphic novels (and one of its precursors, the panorama that I discuss later) as hybrid visual/textual performances that move through narratives in a way that unmoors the narrative from the textual. Perhaps the performance exists in the space between the visual and the text, in the sounding of the visual/aural panels that undercut linearity and posit a spatial way of being, a diasporic performance that reimagines the space of blackness itself?

This black performance of the graphic novel is not without precedent. Black graphic novelists such as Love, despite their relative scarcity, come from a long line of diasporic cartographers who link performance, narration, and the visual to repeat and remake black worlds.

The "Mirror of Slavery," or Tales from the Swamp

Henry Box Brown's escape from a plantation in Richmond, Virginia, via U.S. postal mail in 1849 was remarkable. But it is what he did with his freedom that specifically connects him to Jeremy Love's *Bayou*. The consummate performer, Brown quickly established himself on the abolitionist circuit, initially in the United States and later, after a run-in with slave catchers enforcing the Fugitive Slave Act, in England. His spectacular performances included textual narratives, singing, talks, and dramatic reenactments of his escapes in which he triumphantly sprung from a simulacrum of his original box. In 1850, Brown decided to add to his performance a moving panorama called the "Mirror of Slavery," produced in collaboration with the painter Josiah Walcott. The fifty-thousand-square-foot panorama provides a useful, mythic origin story for *Bayou*, swamp stories, and other performance geographies.

Moving panoramas consisted of a series of related scenes painted onto a roll of cloth, which was secured at either end of the stage by cylinders that assistants rolled and unrolled to give the impression of scenes moving across the stage.

The "Mirror of Slavery" was an appropriation of popular landscape, river, and other panoramas that painted scene after scene of national expansion based on putative American foresight, industry, and efficiency. But such a portrayal of the United States, as the "Mirror of Slavery" carefully showed, could only be achieved by overlooking the brutal and horrific system of slavery and coerced labor that enabled national expansion in the first place, something Brown's panorama hoped to address.

The moving panorama has several qualities that made it ideal for Brown's alternate histories of the nation and that link the genre of the panorama to the comics medium. Indeed one could argue for Brown's panorama as being one of the first black comics in its narrative and stylistic qualities. For one, the "Mirror of Slavery" was open-ended and circular, neither beginning nor ending at fixed points. Though its paintings were presented sequentially, they could be read in a variety of ways. The order of the paintings constructed narrative arcs, but those arcs could be multiplied by the viewer's juxtaposing of nonsequential images to see other stories. Similarly, the comics medium allows the reader to construct multiple narratives. The flow of images on a page can be read in numerous ways, especially in the instance of *Bayou*, whose story often progresses without words as one reads the various haunting images that fill the page. The hybrid form of the panorama, which combined the visual, the performative, textual narrative, and myth making, enabled Brown to move away from sanitized, glorified scenes of American life toward a spatialization of slavery and a deep awareness of how geographies construct and are constructed by race. A cursory overview of the scenes in the "Mirror of Slavery," parts 1 and 2, shows an overwhelming emphasis on racialized geographies. Only twenty-nine scenes are painted of events or activities that have no specific location in the scene title. The panorama thus consisted of serial portraits that were at once frozen and moving, insisting on "the need to tell stories not only from the inside of the 'modern' world but from its borders, . . . forgotten stories that bring forward at the same time a new epistemological dimension, an epistemology from the borders of the modern colonial world system" (Walter Mignolo 52, qtd. in Spencer 128). Love also wishes to tell forgotten stories via an alternate historical geography that personifies space, revealing its chasms, expanses, marsh gases, and bodies hanging from trees. However, both Brown and Love are not content with merely depicting black suffering and abjection. Brown portrayed resistance to slavery's violations by manipulating tropes of death and rebirth with scenes of his own escape alongside the escapes of William and Ellen Craft and Henry Bibb. He repeatedly used his own burial and then resurrection from the box as a trope for transnational political uprising; the revolutions of the panorama suggested a large-scale revolution that went beyond the abolitionist agenda. In many ways, Love's protagonist, Lee, functions similarly as fugitive/revolutionary body whose resistance to racial subjection remakes the space of the bayou through a confrontation of the specters of slavery that erupt from the landscape. From the vantage point of a present in which the Thirteenth Amendment has been passed, Love shows that the logic of slavery, in which human beings are converted into fungible objects, is not gone but is continually resurrected. Thus, it is not just the fugitive slave who steals away from containment, but it is also racist violence that erupts from its hiding places, escaping into the present with a new vengeance. Love's *Bayou* thus is a postabolitionist panorama that insists on the survival and reinvention of racist geographies.

It is no coincidence that both Brown and Love turn to the swamp. According to Daphne Brooks, the scene of the Dismal Swamp in the "Mirror of Slavery" functioned as a "liminal space between entrapment and freedom, between the excruciating labor and relentless sunlit fields of the 'Cotton Plantation' and the stealthy nocturnal routes of 'Nubians, escaping by Night'" (104). The terrain of the swamp bridged the spaces between black suffering and active black resistance, showing their inextricability. Brooks locates the Dismal Swamp in Brown's panorama on the borders of Virginia and North Carolina, linking it to Nat Turner's narrative, in which the unmapped swamp provided refuge from slave catchers. However, in response to an audience member's question as to the location of the Dismal Swamp, Brown did not mention Virginia or North Carolina but instead replied that he did not exactly know. A racist reviewer, convinced of Brown's ignorance, caricatured his response: "daint asotly know; taint somewhere in the middle of the state" (Spencer 134). While it is certain that Brown was protecting fugitive slaves and the secrecy of their escape routes by limiting how much information he passed on, his answer suggests something more. Brown's "not exactly knowing" where the Dismal Swamp lies insists that space does not merely exist neutrally or transparently and that it is not fixed in time. Rather, slavery and fugitive slave bodies produce space. "If *who* we see is tied up with *where* we see through truthful, commonsensical narratives, then the placement of subaltern bodies deceptively hardens spatial binaries, in turn suggesting that some bodies belong, some bodies do not belong, and some bodies are out of place" (McKittrick xv). Brown's refusal to materially map the Dismal Swamp even as his panorama dwells on it demonstrates that all space is produced via embodied performances of terror and resistance. Brown's panorama and *Bayou* disrupt the transparency of space (space that is just there to be occupied), showing how the very notion of transparency is predicated on a unitary vantage point (Wynter 355) that naturalizes dominant geographies and obscures resistant ones. "Geography's discursive attachment to stasis and physicality, the idea that space 'just is,' and that space and place are merely containers for human complexities and social relations, is terribly seductive: that which 'just is' not only anchors our selfhood and feet to the ground, it seemingly calibrates and normalizes where, and therefore who, we are" (McKittrick xi). Rather, place is an equal participant in the drama of geography, a key player in the unfolding of terror and resistance.

Bayou and the "Mirror of Slavery" are not randomly chosen examples of performance geography. Rather, they are part of the same genealogy that uses sequential art to remap black spaces and also to show that abolition could not and did not mark the end of racial subjugation. Brown's moving beyond an abolitionist agenda toward exposing how global systems of coerced labor enable national capital dovetails into Love's insistence that despite the official end of slavery, racial and gender violence cross-hatches the nation. Both show the living legacy of slavery to extend its reaches far beyond the nation-state and far beyond the official emancipation of slaves. Rather, the endurance in the way that space is hierarchically mapped and haunted by brutalized and suffering Africans and their ancestors maintains that geography can "serve as conduits of memory for social performances, providing a zone of play within which improvisatory variations may be staged" (Roach 90). Thus, while the sharecropper is not the same as the slave, both repeat with differences the scripts of black (female) subjugation. Linking various social performances that create space in this way necessitates alternate temporalities and other ways of knowing. We cannot construct a teleological narrative of forward progression from slavery to emancipation, but we have to turn, like Brown and Love do, to revolving scenes, backward and forward motion, simultaneous temporalities that cross-hatch the living and breathing landscape. Love's graphic novel set in 1933 uses contemporary aesthetic sensibilities to link sites of memory, or what Roach calls "vortices of behavior" (64) to various other time periods that all burst forth like strange fruit at the same time. "It is a moment of repetition, a moment in which the past returns to the present in expanded form, a moment in which present time finds stored and accumulated within itself a nonsynchronous array of past times" (Baucom 29). This retemporalization is key to performance geography.

Dominant Geographies, or Tragedy on the Bayou

Gillian Rose writes how the feminist subject "depends on a paradoxical geography in order to acknowledge both the power of hegemonic discourses and to insist on the possibility of resistance" (155). Applying this notion of contradictory and multiple space to Love, ones clearly sees the interplay between dominant geographies and resistant black spatial practices throughout *Bayou*'s pages. I wish to begin with one of the more striking examples: Jack Barbour's special commentary on the history of Charon and its surrounding areas that underpins the racist analysis of the arrest of Lee's father, Calvin Wagstaff. This commentary appears twice in the novel in different formats. The first time it appears is after a section in which Lee's Uncle Bedford bequeaths her his great-grandfather Enoch's axe. Enoch lived in an old Spanish fort in Florida, where "injuns, Choctaw, Seminole and negroes who run off from slavery . . . made a good life for themselves *in that swamp*" (Love; my italics). The blessed axe, used by a Choctaw warrior to rescue a few women and children from the fort when the "U.S. gub'ment" attacked, was passed down to Enoch, whose parents were killed by Jackson's attack. Enoch used that axe to storm Fort Wagner. The paradox of the same axe being used to fight against the U.S. government and then used in its defense should not be lost on us. Uncle Bedford movingly states, "This axe was baptized in the blood of the negro and the mighty Choctaw. The blood of my family . . . Reckon I was supposed to give it to Junior when he was of age, but it looks like you'll need it more than him." This moving section tells another history of slavery from the perspective of black and native peoples. It constructs a parallel legacy to that of slavery, one of resistance, of unbelonging and belonging to the nation, of being marginal and central as an "imminent threat to national security." Bedford passing on of the axe and the task of the warrior to a girl constitutes a profoundly feminist moment that works against the traditional sexism of the genre of the graphic novel as well as traditional patriarchal scripts of men rescuing women (often with a kiss). Wearing her cousin Junior's cap and coat and carrying her cousin Hattie's little doll Etta Mae, Lee (whose name could be either a girl's or a boy's) carries the axe through the night and into the dawn in a series of images that evoke the legacy of ancestral spirits who watch over us, who walk with us, who intervene in our lives.

The story of the axe is followed by a three-page spread. Each page contains Jack Barbour's written commentary on the left-hand side of the page and gorgeous images of Lee walking and running along the Yazoo River at dawn and finally reaching Charon. The rising sun, reflected in the water, tints the image a gorgeous lavender color. The second image (which evokes memories of runaway slaves) brings us closer to Lee, who is now running beside a train, with the same sky radiating through the gap between the cars. In the third image, in which Lee stands on a grassy bank near a tall tree overlooking the town of Charon, the sun has risen. All three images focus on sky, river, grass, and rising sun, and they are rendered all the more beautiful given that they are surrounded by Barbour's pseudohistories and racist analysis of the arrest of Calvin Wagstaff.

"The spatial form is an important element in the constitution of power itself" (Massey 22). Barbour reinstates the power of white privilege through his spatial practices. He begins by describing the South and the town of Charon from the perspective of the southern slaveholder defending his stronghold from "Sherman's Northern marauders" (Love). His commentary begins with, "From majestic plantations and mansions to the north, the sprawling cotton fields, and the haunting bayous in the south, there is one of the last bastions of Southern grandeur." He goes on to celebrate the Confederate general after whom the town is named: General Matthew Bogg, nicknamed Charon to honor his "sacrifice" during the war in which the North attempted to destroy the majestic South. Consider the juxtaposing of two stories. The first, located in a Floridian swamp and the mouth of Charlotte harbor, is told from the perspective of Choctaw and runaway slaves and their descendants, one of whom fought at Fort Wagner both against the Confederacy and also against northern racism. The second, located in the northwest corner of Mississippi on the alluvial plain, where cotton is king, is told from the perspective of slaveholders and their descendants, who see the decline of their southern way of life (i.e., plantation economies) as leading to "big and burly wretch[es], with long sinewy apelike arms and massive hands," free to wander around and murder innocent little white girls. Barbour concluded his commentary with a threat: "We can only pray that the surge of white anger does not boil over and seek to reclaim the glory of our slain ancestors." These words actually link Barbour's commentary with the images of Lee. Both Lee and Barbour are calling up a violent history of oppression, subjugation, coercion, and resistance in the name of their slain ancestors. However, while Barbour is unable to acknowledge the existence of multiple modes of belonging to the same land, Lee inhabits a paradoxical geography where her family and ancestors are denied and erased even as their labor and their performative geographies remap southern space and the nation.

It is no coincidence that to enter the town, Lee must walk by the statue of General Douglass M. "Hellhound" Bogg, "hero of the war of northern aggression" (Love). Just as the black codes after Emancipation or Jim Crow laws or even black ghettoes and housing projects attempt to fix the meaning of space into rigid hierarchies of white superiority (Tyner 218), so too do monuments structure the landscape. The statue of Bogg dominates the entrance to the town as he towers above everything, taking up the entire length of the page. His panoramic gaze from above, forcing Lee and the reader to look up, shows how the "dominant gaze constructs access to knowledge of geography as a white bourgeois heterosexual masculine privilege. And this gaze is not only the gaze at the land. . . . It is also a gaze at what are constituted as objects of knowledge, whether environmental, social, political or cultural" (Rose 109). A close-up of the *Yazoo Herald* featuring a section of Jack Barbour's commentary further emphasizes the reduction of blacks to objects of knowledge. The white patriarchal authority enacted via the layout and content of the town's official newspaper is made obvious by the headline—which reads, "Negro Held in Kidnapping"—and a police sketch of Calvin Wagstaff, flanked by stories of volunteers from surrounding counties helping to find Lily and another story on "Pretty Boy" Floyd killing four law enforcement officers. Not only are black men objects of knowledge, but they are also criminalized objects of surveillance and punishment. This notion of criminalized black men has obvious resonance in the present, when the number of black men tangled up in the criminal justice system is astronomical. Love counters the construction of black objects with an audacious Lee, who steps on the newspaper lying on the street before she reads it. She demonstrates this same audacity as she walks a gauntlet of angry white men, waiting around the jailhouse to lynch her father. Lee's steps, past the monument to Bogg, on the newspaper, up the jailhouse stairs to stand in front of her battered father behind bars, create what Michel de Certeau calls a "migrational, or metaphorical [town that] slips into the clear text of the planned and readable" town suggested in Barbour's history (93). Her walk toward her father (armed with a doll and an axe) constitutes a profound spatial practice that questions the designated sites of official memory like Bogg's monument and embeds new sites of memory that speak of gender/racial domination and the attempts to overcome it. Lee appropriates the logic of the plantation space, based on inequity and violence, and uses its vocabulary to speak new meaning. Lee's search for meaning, for the means to rescue her father, lead her straight to the swamp, where she dives down into the bayou toward the dark hole where she found her friend Billy Glass's body years ago.

"The Thing I Came For": Haunting the Bayou

Love's performative geographies push against many of the foundational binaries of Western geographical thought. He shows that distinctions between real and metaphorical space, between land and experience, emotion, and spirit cannot and do not hold true. Thus, uneven geographic development—as can be seen, for example, in the very different houses of the Westmorelands and the Wagstaffs—demonstrates the devastatingly real consequences of geography that keep one family in leisure smoking on the porch and Lee and her father pushing and pulling a mule. Yet these material realities of overdevelopment and underdevelopment, the black family's impoverishment (seen when Calvin Wagstaff offers to work off the price of the missing necklace and in the white family's excess wealth, such that a child can have such an expensive trinket) is linked to creative, metaphoric theories of space and race. Performative geographies actively link imaginative, embodied practices to material geography that "carries with it (and on it) all sorts of historically painful social encounters and all sorts of contemporary social negotiations" (McKittrick 18). In other words, material physical and metaphoric spaces flow into one another. To separate one from the other is like trying to separate history from the present.

Lee dives into the bayou to prevent her father from being mutilated and drowned like Billy Glass and in order to find Lily's necklace. She submerges herself into a literal/metaphoric bayou: the swampy water itself and the bayou as an embodiment of a violent, traumatic history of landscape. "Vortices of behavior tend to occupy liminal ground" (Roach 64), and thus it is under the water that performances of violence repeat as if for the first time. In a parody of Alice's entrance into Wonderland, Lee dives down into the hole and then attempts to rise to the surface, only to have her ankle grabbed by a golliwog. This grotesque caricature of Sambo, one of the aesthetic legacies of blackface minstrelsy, almost succeeds in drowning Lee (see fig. 13.1). She is nearly destroyed by the stranglehold of racism, by the red-lipped, bug-eyed golliwog in ragged clothes who supposedly represents her. The hand that reaches into the water to save her is the hand of (the) Bayou. An enormous man whom Lee initially mistakes for a monster, Bayou turns out to be a gentle, magical, mild-mannered man terrorized by someone he refers to as the Bossman. Bayou clearly does not belong to this time or place even as he haunts the landscape with his little dog. When Lee flees into the woods, he talks to himself, saying that he is not allowed to leave the bayou. The reason for his reluctance to leave the swamp and enter into the woods becomes clearer when a gnat buzzing in his ear reminds him what happened the last time he helped the wicked old rabbit. He insists that Bayou remain in his place and not actively remap space by walking beyond his boundaries.

Bayou's struggle as he decides what to do reminds us of the economy of slavery, in which simple acts can become unbearably complicated due to the violence elicited by any form of slave agency and by the use of kinship to control black bodies. "Bossman hurt Bayou real b-bad last time Buh-Bayou got in some mess. Bossman say, Bayou if n you git yo' self in another mess, you ain't never gonna see . . . gonna see . . . If n she is trouble, and Buh-Bayou don't help, it be just like Bayou KILLT her himself" (Love). Slaveholders often used "kinship ties in slavery as a guarantee of their continued compliance. . . . Slaveholders used the humanity and individuality denied under slave law to 'tether, bind, and

13.1 The grotesque figure of Sambo, one of the most notorious of racist images, almost succeeds in drowning Lee.

oppress.' They used those same affective social attachments that helped slaves to buffer themselves from brutalization in order to fetter them to slavery" (Wong 9). Thus, recognition of a slave's humanity aggravated instead of ameliorated his or her pain. Bayou cannot name who or what he might never see again. The ellipses in the narrative speak to the intensity of his fear and loss. The refusal to name the thing he fears the most is a strategy of protection, except that what he fears most has already happened—the loss of Nandi, his daughter. When Nandi appears in the story, she is a lovely vision in a flowing white dress with gold earrings and necklaces and her braided hair wrapped with gold ribbon. Her garb, the shining elegance of the little girl, evokes a Nandi before she was enslaved, a Nandi as she might have appeared before the seasoning of the trek to the coast, before the nightmare of the Middle Passage, before the ineffable, quotidian violence of southern slavery, in which she is a weapon used to control Bayou.

While Bayou tries to decide what to do, Lee falls into a trap and is impaled. Her body lies in a pool of blood, with the spike piercing her through the chest and coming out her back. This is where most stories would end. For Love, this is merely another beginning, a revolving panorama of entries and exits and reentries. Bayou slings Lee's body over his shoulder and takes her to his house on stilts deep in the bayou. There he fixes her with a little of this and a little of that, some of which includes his own blood. While Lee is laying on Bayou's table being sewn up, she meets her friend Billy Glass (with butterfly wings), who loses no time in telling her that she is dead and that Bayou's "n***** riggin'" isn't going to last long (Love). All Lee is concerned with is whether she will be alive long enough to help her father and Lily. For Lee, death is not a separate landscape. Rather, the dead and the living walk the same paths, mapping the terrain in historically specific ways. Love shows Lee as being able to see the past in the present, to tangibly see and experience the living histories that erupt all around her. Near the beginning of the graphic novel, we see her running with her friend Lily's shoe in her hand, only to stop when she comes to a clump of trees where bare feet dangle. The visual irony of shoe / bare feet should not be lost on us. The images move back to show us several lynched bodies in various states of mutilation (see fig. 13.2). Initially we are unsure if these bodies are "real," but we soon learn that the dichotomy between real and not real is misleading. Just like a giant panorama, historical events cycle through, performing multitemporal space. The lynched bodies are both here and there, absent and present—always tangible, always real. Strange fruit, butterfly spirits, a blues-singing monster who swallows Lily whole—by the time we get to Lee's impalement, we have accepted not only that the dead walk among us but that various sensual and historical experiences of the land are alive, allowing us to run our hands over them. Avery Gordon, in describing some of the most prominent features of African American intellectual and creative work, writes, "The capacity not only to live with specters, in order to determine what sort of people they were and could be, but also to engage the ghost, heterogeneously but cooperatively, as metaphor,

13.2 The strange fruit, peculiar to the South, haunts Lee.

as weapon, as salve, as a fundamental epistemology for living in the vortex of North America" (151). This behavioral vortex, where a house, a swamp, a tree becomes animated or haunted, reflects the complex social relations that make space itself. Thus, these ghosts, like us, do not inhabit the space as much as create the space. Bayou is not just the ghost of a slave haunting the bayou, but he is also the bayou itself: deep, gentle, strong, magical, and brutal. He is both the runaway slave hiding in the swamp remembering Nandi and the swamp itself, remembering. And the swamp, like Bayou, remembers Nandi through Lee. As the story progresses, Bayou begins to see Lee as Nandi at various moments. The two girls are juxtaposed; they haunt each other, and they haunt (the) Bayou. Ghosts do not represent a simple return to the past. If this was the case, Bayou could abandon the present to dwell on his loss of Nandi. Rather, ghosts incite and coax us to deal with the past's tangibility in the present. This past has less to do with individual trauma and more to do with the complex social forces that constitute the African diasporic landscape. Nandi's episodic appearances in the novel insist that Bayou help Lee, as inaction actively perpetuates the status quo.

The dead/alive Lee walks from Bayou's home on stilts to the home of Cotton-Eyed Joe, the Bossman's son, who swallowed Lily whole. The walk between the two houses across fields of grass shows the connections of slave and master, landowner and sharecropper, the liminal and the central. As Roach states, walkers "activate the spatial logic of a [terrain] built to make certain powers and privileges . . . perpetually reproducible. The [pedestrian] spaces become a performance machine for celebrating the occult origin of [racial] exclusions" (14). The resilience of plantation relations is embedded in geographies that Lee and other specters expose and undercut. "Inserting black geographies into our worldview and our understanding of spatial liberation and other emancipatory strategies can perhaps move us away from territoriality, the normative practice of staking a claim to place" (McKittrick and Woods 5). This is precisely what Lee does as she walks through the grass, almost as tall as she is, from the swamp to the big house, armed with a gun and surrounded by butterflies that represent the spirits of the dead. In many ways, this is the slaveholder's ultimate nightmare: the armed approach of an army of black folk, intent on protecting their own. Only this army consists of a powerful little girl and the dead that she gathers around her after the official end of slavery, in order to create a space of geographic reform where structures of kinship are not reduced to violent tools for controlling blacks.

Cotton-Eyed Joe's gothic house has long corridors and large rooms with orange medallion wallpaper. It is bigger than any of the other houses we have seen, evoking the decaying white, southern plantation grandeur that Jack Barbour, among others, mourns. This notion of decay is reinforced when Lee crosses the threshold and encounters an awful smell. This is not just the stench of the female skeleton that sits at the head of the table, surrounded by animal skulls and a plastic doll. This is the less literal, though still overwhelming, stench of the authoritarian consumption of (black) life that leads to decay and death. The Bossman's house, with family portraits on the wall, can be seen to represent the ultimate goal of racial hierarchy—rigid, unchanging boundaries that confine, delimit, and fix the players in their designated places. Thus, though the house is teeming with the dead, this is not the death that we encounter previously. These dead are not vibrantly alive like Billy Glass, attempting to create new black geographies alongside their living descendants. Instead, the deteriorating house attempts to produce an unwavering mirage of domination through fixed, racialized, and gendered rituals—most obviously the macabre tea party with female skeleton as host presiding over the table.

As Thavolia Glymph details, the plantation house was never a private space separated from the public political realm by the type of labor performed or by the sex of the plantation mistresses who regulated this labor force. While the authority of planter mistresses was ultimately subject to patriarchy, these women's violent exercise of power over black men and women cannot be underestimated. Black women constituted the majority of household labor and bore the brunt of white women's aggression. So severe was the psychological and physical brutality enacted on them that domestic workers were often the first to flee slavery as they actively rejected "the white household's symbolic and political meanings and its work. . . . No longer legally bound to the white household after the Civil War, former slaves set out to demolish the residue of that attachment, which legislation was powerless to efface, as one of their first political acts" (Glymph 7, 9). We have already encountered the vicious Mrs. Westmoreland, who resides over her home with no husband in sight, as well as Lily, whose treatment of Lee (despite calling her a friend) reveals her to be a mistress-in-training of a postwar plantation household. Lee's mother's refusal of domesticity in volume 2 illustrates not only the roles that black women played in distancing themselves from certain types of labor but also their key role in its destruction. Similarly, Lee refuses to perform any kind of role in the ritualistic enactment of white domesticity as she answers Cotton-Eyed Joe's invitation to tea by blowing his head off with her shotgun and shattering the dishes in the process. She follows this by burying her family axe in his skull and later in Joe's family portrait of a Confederate soldier on the wall, indirectly pointing toward how one's legacy of disenfranchisement and resistance relates to another's legacy of entitlement and privilege. Lee's destruction is thus not merely an individual form of redress or revenge but rather a geographic performance that undoes the social rituals that have long defined the southern plantation domestic space of labor.

Cotton-Eyed Joe—despite Lee's bullet through his head and her axe buried in his skull—remains alive until he leaves the closed, dead space of the house. Much to Lee's and Bayou's shock, he is immediately picked apart by Jim Crows, who Bayou tells us are a manifestation of the Bossman. The Jim Crows are also a manifestation of plantation geographies where both white and black face consequences for forgetting their place and traversing the performative boundaries of their roles. Joe is punished for his careless eating of a little *white* girl by being ripped open—the Jim Crows pluck Lily from his insides and carry her away to the Bossman's plantation. The rest of volume 1 describes the escalation of violence supposedly elicited by the various characters' transgressions of the segregated spaces of a plantation South.

The haunting appearance of a shackled Nandi and multiple butterfly and insect spirits leads to the next stage of the quest: the search for Bossman's plantation. The confrontation with Bossman's son, and not Bossman himself, could be seen as a step toward the reworking of racist terrains. But to paraphrase Bob Marley, one needs to shoot the sheriff and not the deputy, the master and not the son/overseer. This logic was especially relevant for slaves, who were fully cognizant that slavery was a many-headed hydra whose power lay embedded not within individual masters but within the institution of slavery itself, which created and enabled the role of the master. Thus, Bayou's ripping off of the arm of the Ku Klux Klan member appointed to whip him does little to change his situation overall. To do this, one needs to remap and rework the geography of the master's house. Volume 2, which has yet to be published in print, details Lee's attempt to find the master's plantation in order to save her father.

Mercy Mercy Me: The Geographic
Knowledge Produced by the Blues

"The blues poet has been where we are all afraid to go, as if there was a physical place, a forbidden place that corresponds to a place in ourselves where we experience the tragic sense of life and its amazing wonders. In that dive, in that all-night blues and soul club, we feel the full weight of our fate" (Simic 47).

In examining the interstices between the visual and narrative, one could overlook the role that sound plays in Love's performative geography. The idea of a culturally legible landscape has been located in "the ideology of the visual and has neglected the extent to which sound generally, and music in particular, structures space and characterises place. . . . [Even] writers using the idea of the landscape as a means of challenging the orthodoxy of scientific method in geography have reproduced the visual bias associated with positivism and empiricism in an otherwise welcome attempt" to expand the discipline beyond its traditional boundaries (Smith 232). We thus seldom think to listen to a photograph or listen to the images in a graphic novel. Love, however, insists that history in all its representations bears what Fred Moten describes as the "phonic substance" of the image. Looking at photographs of Emmett Till, Moten elaborates: the "arrangements of the photograph . . . anticipate a looking that cannot be sustained as unalloyed looking but must be accompanied by listening, . . . even though what is listened to—echo of a whistle or a phrase, moaning, mourning, desperate testimony and flight—is also unbearable" (197, 200). *Bayou* begins with Lee diving into the bayou and recovering Billy Glass's body. Upon her return to the surface, Lee is frightened so badly that she vows never to return to the bayou. Hiding her fear from her father, she tells the reader quietly, "I was hearing these voices. Sounded like people singin" (Love). It is not just the weight of the corpse in her arms or the sight of it that threatens to overwhelm her—it is also the sonic substance of death, violence, and loss that permeates the soundscape of the novel.

Soundscapes emerge from the interplay between the material environment that produces sound and the cultural environment in which sound accumulates meaning (Smith 232). The idea that what we hear is unmediated, that we all simply hear it as it is, grants sound a false universality. Emotionally or theoretically recognizing and understanding sound does not come naturally to all human beings, irrespective of cultural/racial positions. Rather, what we hear and who hears positions us in complex multisensory soundscapes in which performances of time, sound, and space intersect. Sound and place generate each other, providing us with a richer notion of geography and expanding what we consider as meaningful sound. The genre of the graphic novel is particularly well suited to drawing attention to sound—we read the "bzzzz" of the mosquito in Bayou's ear, "SNAP" as Lily's locket is yanked off her neck, music notes for a whistle, the "KRACK" as Lee wrings the chicken's neck. Text and image perform sound, which performs space, and vice versa.

Sound obviously includes but is not limited to music. Instead, the grunt of pain expelled from Bayou's mouth or the barking of a dog operates alongside the various performances of the blues that permeate the text. Love's southern soundscape thus vibrates as traditional blues music; splashes, shrieks, and snaps come together to form something more than symphonic noise. "To consider the place of music is not to reduce music to its location, to ground it down into some geographical baseline, but to allow a purchase on the rich aesthetic, cultural, economic and political geographies of musical language [and image]" (Leyshon, Matless, and Revill 425). Thus, the way that the blues is performed in the novel cannot be separated from the spatial traces of mythic origin and performance venues that cling to its contours, hence the different types of blues being named after specific locales, such as Delta blues, Kansas City blues, Memphis blues, and even swamp blues. Michelle Scott in her book *Blues Empress in Black Chattanooga* defines blues culture as "the various forms of communication and the creation of community that occur in such recreational environments as saloons, vaudeville houses, tent shows, juke joints, and street corners" (4, qtd. in Niaah 198). A brief historical digression regarding Mecca Flat Blues provides a useful illustration, not only of how the blues informs place but also of how the music and noise come together to create a genre. By linking blues to place, I do not mean to suggest that the blues originates in a particular locale. To assume that Chicago blues, for example, arose only in Chicago is to reduce the complexity of soundscapes. Swamp blues, though deeply imbued with the sensibility of small-town Louisiana, was a reinvention of Chicago sound, which was a reinvention of Delta blues.

Chicago musicians labeled their mix of St. Louis, Louisiana, and other types of blues Mecca Flat blues, not only to pun on the word *flat* but also to assert the importance of a specific site in Chicago to their music. To understand why an entire idiom of the blues was named after an apartment house, one needs to understand exactly what made the Mecca's design features unique and what facilitated the development of a black Chicago soundscape. The Mecca apartments faced outward toward a beautiful landscaped exterior courtyard and, most unusually, inward toward interior atria. Each of the two primary wings of the Mecca were focused around an enormous interior skylit atrium, each one measuring 33 by 170 feet (Bluestone 384). While the Mecca had multiple entrances that diffused the building's flow of residents, the promenade balconies and bay windows made the atria a public space where people could see and be seen. "Thus the Mecca design contained two rich but contrary tendencies. One tendency, captured in the exterior courtyard and separate entrances, responded to entrenched fear over the compromise of single-family living and familial privacy; the other tendency, represented in the skylit atria, cultivated the possibilities of a gregarious and cosmopolitan gathering of five hundred people under a single roof" (Bluestone 384–385). Put another way, the bourgeois ideology of private domesticity coexisted with the noisy performative space of the atria. Numerous factors facilitated a change in the occupants of the Mecca. Increased African American migration from the South, the extension of the railroads, the opening in 1865 of the Union Stockyards, and the development of the University of Chicago campus east of the Mecca meant pressure for the conversion of white residential spaces in order to accommodate black people who could no longer be contained in the Black Belt neighborhood.

Daniel Bluestone details how by the 1910s, the Mecca was actually only a block north from Chicago's predominant African American business and retail district, including the leading jazz clubs where musicians such as Louis Armstrong and Jelly Roll Morton played. Links between the now largely black-occupied Mecca and jazz were made overt by local bands playing and recording what they called "Mecca Flat blues," such as James Blythe's "Mecca Flat Blues," recorded in 1924 with Priscilla Stewart, or Albert Ammons's "Mecca Flat Blues" in 1939. Mecca Flat blues described characters such as the "Mecca Flat Woman" and the "Mecca Flat Man" whose sexual lives were the topic of great interest. The comings and goings, triumphs and tragedies, of the Mecca's residents were captured in the blues. This is where we see how place informs the blues and the blues shapes space itself. The urban spectacle of black men and women in the atria, living lives that could not be relegated to private, atomized, moral domestic spaces, was the perfect subject for Mecca Flat blues, in which the music of private memory and tribulation was translated into larger, socially remembered issues of disenfranchisement facing various black communities. Whereas for city planners, the chaotic performances of apartment-house living were indicative of urban blight, for the blues musicians, this was the stuff of legends. They told a story of black northern migration, community, and identity forged around the atria that functioned as a social stage for urban black cultural survival.

In 1950, an article written by John Bartlow Martin and illustrated by Ben Shahn appeared in *Harper's Magazine* titled "The Strangest Place in Chicago." Martin, in his attempt to have the Mecca demolished, wrote of residents spitting and toddlers urinating from the balconies to the atria below. He also wrote of stories in which a pimp threw a prostitute from the balcony and a man murdered the building's janitor in a jealous rage over a woman. Martin's essay describes the Mecca in much the same way as depicted in Mecca Flat blues, though for him this was a sign of the failure of high-density living and the need for more modern planning. For blues musicians, the sounds that filled the atria—of raised voices, the trickle of urine, residents calling down to each other—were a sign of African American cultural vitality. This example of the Mecca Flat blues insists that the relationship between space and the blues is not one of a singular origin but rather a complex interplay of the architecture of specific spaces and how music is made. Heightening our awareness of "the possible textures of music's geography" (Leyshon, Matless, and Revill 425), music and noise come together and repeat through the spaces of performance—the jazz club, the neighborhood, and the atria.

To return to *Bayou*, Love insists on the inextricability of spaces of performance and the blues. Lee's glamorous mother sings in the local juke joint onstage surrounded by (male) admirers. "My momma was beautiful and my daddy say she had a voice like a MOCKINGBIRD. Aunt Lucy said she was a loose woman but I don't care" (Love). In an obvious reference to Harper Lee's *To Kill a Mockingbird*, the famous story of another falsely accused black man in danger of being lynched, the music that Lee's mother sings is shaped by the sexual economy of the juke joint. But her song is also saturated by the big storm that floods the bayou and washes the juke joint into the river. In a nod to Hurricane Katrina and its victims, Lee's mother's blues are shaped by environmental catastrophe and the relegation of informal black business to real estate more likely to be flooded. Her blues are sensual, a claiming of her own sexuality within the narrow constraints of racism. Her blues conjure up floods, black people with white flags on roofs desperately calling out that their lives are just as worthy as their white counterparts'.

Bayou sings, "come to my house / find no' / body 'round! Me and my baby, we gon' / SHAKE EM ON DOOOWN / must I holler / YEEAAH / must I / SHAKE EM OOOOON DOWN," on the porch of his home. Bayou, though bound to the bayou, sings of the act of stealing away, the literal theft of oneself as property via the crossing of borders and boundaries. His song, like most of the blues, "emerges from, among other things, massive loss and massive resistance, only in order to reproduce agony as pleasure differently with every listening" (Moten 107). At the sound/sight of Lee's impalement early in the novel, Bayou reaches forward through time to softly chant "mercy mercy me." "Mercy Mercy Me (the Ecology)" was the second single off Marvin Gaye's 1971 album *What's Going On*. Contemporary readers would immediately be haunted by Gaye's sorrowful rendition, even though Bayou himself could not have known the song. Here is another moment when one sees how performative geographies evoke ritual enactments that traverse time. "Gaye produces that new space whose essence is the ongoing call for the production of New Space, of a new world, by holding—which is to say suspending, embracing—time" (Moten 225). Bayou's anachronistic words construct localized communities via recognizing and addressing sorrow and loss in the black diaspora. His words, like the voices that Lee hears at the beginning of the novel, are a sensual invocation of a New World characterized not by a false but by a "dynamic universality (which critically moves in, among other things, grief, anger, hatred, the desire to expose and eradicate savagery) whose organization would suspend the condition of possibility of deaths like Emmett Till's" or Billy Glass's (Moten 209). The voices of people singing are the haunting sonic traces of space as we live and die, creating and re-creating it.

Works Cited

Baucom, Ian. *Specters of the Atlantic: Finance Capital, Slavery, and the Philosophy of History.* Durham, NC: Duke University Press, 2005.

Bluestone, Daniel. "Chicago's Mecca Flat Blues." *JSAH* 57.4 (December 1998): 382–403.

Brooks, Daphne A. *Bodies in Dissent: Spectacular Performances of Race and Freedom, 1859–1910.* Durham, NC: Duke University Press, 2006.

Certeau, Michel de. *The Practice of Everyday Life.* Berkeley: University of California Press, 2002.

Glymph, Thavolia. *Out of the House of Bondage: The Transformation of the Plantation Household.* New York: Cambridge University Press, 2008.

Gordon, Avery. *Ghostly Matters: Haunting and the Sociological Imagination.* Minneapolis: University of Minnesota Press, 1997.

Leyshon, Andrew, David Matless, and George Revill. "The Place of Music: Introduction." *Transactions of the Institute of British Geographers* 20.4 (1995): 423–443.

Love, Jeremy. *Bayou.* Vol. 1. Zuda Comics, 2009. N. pag.

Massey, Doreen. *Space, Place, and Gender.* Minneapolis: University of Minnesota Press, 1994.

McKittrick, Katherine. *Demonic Grounds: Black Women and the Cartographies of Struggle.* Minneapolis: University of Minnesota Press, 2006.

McKittrick, Katherine, and Clyde Woods. "No One Knows the Mysteries at the Bottom of the Ocean." *Black Geographies and the Politics of Place.* Ed. Katherine McKittrick and Clyde Woods. Cambridge, MA: South End, 2007. 1–13.

Mignolo, Walter. *Local Histories/Global Designs: Coloniality, Subaltern Knowledges, and Border Thinking.* Princeton, NJ: Princeton University Press, 2000.

Moten, Fred. *In the Break: The Aesthetics of the Black Radical Tradition.* Minneapolis: University of Minnesota Press, 2003.

Niaah, Sonjah Stanley. "Mapping Black Atlantic Performance Geographies: From Slave Ship to Ghetto." *Black Geographies and the Politics of Place.* Ed. Katherine McKittrick and Clyde Woods. Cambridge, MA: South End, 2007. 193–217.

Roach, Joseph. *Cities of the Dead: Circum-Atlantic Performance.* New York: Columbia University Press, 1996.

Rose, Gillian. *Feminism and Geography: The Limits of Geographical Knowledge.* Minneapolis: University of Minnesota Press, 1993.

Scott, Michelle R. *Blues Empress in Black Chattanooga: Bessie Smith and the Emerging Urban South.* Urbana: University of Illinois Press, 2008.

Simic, Charles. "No Cure for the Blues." *The Unemployed Fortune-Teller: Essays and Memoirs.* Ann Arbor: University of Michigan Press, 1994. 46–52.

Smith S. J. "Soundscape." *Area* 26 (1994): 232–240.

Spencer, Suzette A. "Henry Box Brown, an International Fugitive: Slavery, Resistance, and Imperialism." *Black Geographies and the Politics of Place.* Ed. Katherine McKittrick and Clyde Woods. Cambridge, MA: South End, 2007. 115–136.

Tyner, James A. "Urban Revolutions and the Spaces of Black Radicalism." *Black Geographies and the Politics of Place.* Ed. Katherine McKittrick and Clyde Woods. Cambridge, MA: South End, 2007. 218–232.

Wong, Edlie. *Neither Fugitive nor Free: Atlantic Slavery, Freedom Suits, and the Legal Culture of Travel.* New York: NYU Press, 2009.

Wynter, Sylvia. "After/Word: Beyond Miranda's Meanings: Un/Silencing the 'Demonic Ground' of Caliban's 'Woman.'" *Out of the Kumbla: Caribbean Women and Literature.* Ed. Carole Boyce Davies and Elaine Savory Fido. Trenton, NJ: Africa World, 1994., 355–372.

Chapter 14

A Secret History of Miscegenation

••••••••••••••••••••

Jimmy Corrigan and the
Columbian Exposition of 1893

JAMES J. ZIEGLER

> History is what hurts.
> —Fredric Jameson

In a catalogue essay for the exhibition *Masters of American Comics*, Dave Eggers marvels at Chris Ware's meticulous artistry.[1] Even preliminary sketches for Ware's comic strips and graphic novels are, Eggers explains, "architectural in their precision and daunting in the complexity of their planning" (309). Of the appearance of the Columbian Exposition of 1893 in Ware's acclaimed graphic novel *Jimmy Corrigan, the Smartest Kid on Earth*, he writes, "The World's Fair images, some of Ware's best work, probably wouldn't have been included in the novel were they not so beautiful. They serve the plot only insomuch as they serve Ware's, and our, desire to see his protagonists—almost always brutally lonely men who never have hair—exist along with the most delicate and impermanent kind of architecture" (316).[2] Eggers contends that Ware's exact drawings of the buildings and grounds of the Exposition function cosmetically in the novel without substantially influencing the narrative or advancing the plot. In a full-page frame, Ware replicates the view of the "Court of Honor," reflecting pool, and surrounding buildings on display in this photograph (see fig. 14.1). The precision with which he copies the details of the Fair's most esteemed site may seem to suggest, with Eggers, that he borrows the imagery to incorporate beauty into his dispiriting narratives of the bald and lonely, but over the course of his novel, he relates tales of family dysfunction and national scandal that remark on the visual meaning of the monumental buildings of the World's Fair that gave it the name White City. Framed by the narrative of *Jimmy Corrigan*, the imagery of the White City becomes a cautionary tale in the hazard of aestheticizing history.[5] In other words, and contrary to Eggers, Ware's novel has a problem with the beauty of the Fair.

My concern in this chapter is the historiographical significance of Ware's metafictional graphic novel. More specifically, my intention is to show how *Jimmy Corrigan* critiques heroic public histories that narrate U.S. national identity as if it were free from the vexations of race. Ware's counternarrative cites the Columbian Exposition of 1893 as a paradigmatic instance of how the disavowal of interracial identity has been a defining feature of U.S. national culture. According to Homi Bhabha's formulation, "Counter-narratives of the nation that continually evoke and erase its totalizing boundaries—both actual and conceptual—disturb those ideological manoeuvres through which 'imagined

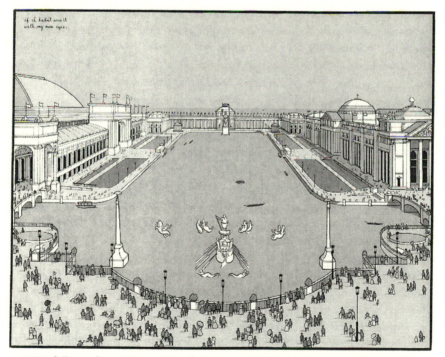

14.1 In a full-page frame, Ware replicates the view of the "Court of Honor," reflecting pool, and surrounding buildings at the Columbian Exposition of 1893.

communities' are given essentialist identities" (213). The essentialism disturbed by *Jimmy Corrigan* is the affiliation of American national identity with whiteness, which, following Richard Dyer, we understand to be historically a privileged marker of universality against which other, particular racial identities are measured (1–4).

After an initial phase in the reception of Ware's work that dealt mainly with the difficult brilliance of his approach to the form of comics art, recent work has begun to acknowledge the acumen with which his graphic narratives address cultural politics of gender and race.[4] *Jimmy Corrigan*, for instance, is a miscegenation narrative. It is an example of what Werner Sollors calls "interracial literature," in which texts of any genre "represent love and family relations involving black-white couples, biracial individuals, their descendants, and their larger kin" (3). The novel concentrates on the story of the hapless, thirty-six-year-old protagonist's journey to meet his father, Jim, for the first time. Interwoven with that tale set in the late 1980s is the story of Jimmy's grandfather, James Corrigan, who as a young boy was neglected, abused, and eventually abandoned by his ill-tempered father, William, in the middle of the Chicago World's Fair of 1893. William, James, Jim, and Jimmy represent a genealogy of failed paternity and increasing unease with the expectations of masculinity. The bright side of the family history is that the abusive, misogynist, and racist sensibilities of William turn aggressively inward four generations later as Jimmy's self-pitying attitude harms himself more than anyone else.

Having never communicated with his father, Jimmy receives a letter from Jim suggesting "its [sic] about time we fellas got to know each other, what do you say?" (Ware 13). Jimmy hides his plans from his overbearing mother and over the Thanksgiving holiday visits his father for two calamitous days in which the men talk awkwardly, thieves steal his father's car, a truck knocks Jimmy to the ground, and in a separate car accident, his father sustains injuries that result in his death. And Jimmy learns that during the years of his abandonment, his father has been married and raising an adopted daughter, Amy. Amy is African American. The Corrigan men are white, an identity underscored throughout the novel by the racist outbursts of William in the 1890s and his son James's puzzlement decades later over why his son, Jim, would elect to raise a black daughter after neglecting a white son. As irony would have it, the abandoned son and the adopted daughter meet for the first time in the hospital after their father's car accident. When their father dies, Jimmy flees from the hospital for his home in Chicago, never to see Amy again. At that point, two pages of genealogy interrupt the narrative and disclose that these two children of the recently deceased share a biological ancestor. William Corrigan, Jimmy's great-grandfather, is also the great-great-grandfather of Amy. During the time William was employed installing windows in the buildings for the World's Fair, he had sexual relations with the African American woman who worked as a maid in the Corrigan home. Amy, according to the old formula, is at least one-sixteenth white, though no character in the text has the recollection necessary to know that prior to her adoption she was already born into the Corrigan family. The mixed-race relations from which she, like so many Americans, has been engendered are not on the record.

The Columbian Exposition of 1893 is a telling backdrop for a history in which blood ties remain unknown even to the tenderly familiar Amy and her father. Intending to display before the world the greatness of the United States on the four hundredth anniversary of Columbus's "discovery" of the New World, the event's organizers rejected requests that a space be devoted to the accomplishments and progress of African Americans since the start of Reconstruction. Moreover, as the eldest James Corrigan matter-of-factly informs a young Amy when she interviews him for a school report, she would have only been permitted entry to the Fair on the single day set aside for "coloreds." The Exposition's scandalous disavowal of the significance and even the presence of African Americans incited leading black activists, most notably Ida B. Wells and Frederick Douglass, to coauthor a treatise against the organizers' willful ignorance toward the centrality of African Americans in the attainments of the United States. Ware's novel, I argue, extends their historic complaints by depicting how the imposition of secrecy on miscegenation enables both the denial of affiliations across racial lines and the insistence that such lines signify innate differences. In other words, Amy on her mother's side belongs to a lineage that the genealogy of Corrigan men has employed, at times unwittingly, to define their whiteness.

Corrigan Family History

Immediately before Jimmy and Amy finally meet, we see them reflecting separately on their racial differences. Jimmy's physical position accentuates his mental distress. Already waiting at the hospital when Amy receives notification of her father's accident, Jimmy is seated on a toilet when he hears his sister arrive in the waiting room (see fig. 14.2). As he listens to Amy pace on the other side of the bathroom door, he recalls the one photograph he has seen of her. Representing Jimmy's thoughts, the bottom left panel is a direct citation of a frame that conveys Jimmy's point of view when he first spies the photograph framed on a shelf at his father's apartment. The balloons and a modest string of flags in the background suggest that the young Amy and her parents are at a local fair. Coming soon after learning of Amy's existence, Jimmy's first encounter with this record of family intimacy compels him to try to arrange an earlier flight back to Chicago. With all seats booked, he instead retreats into sleep until awakened by the emergency services call regarding his father's accident. This second consideration of the picture of Amy with her parents prompts in Jimmy no reflex to flee, understated indignation about his abandonment, or questions for Amy about what she knew of his neglect. On the contrary, Jimmy worries about the impression he will make on her. He is especially intent on how race might play

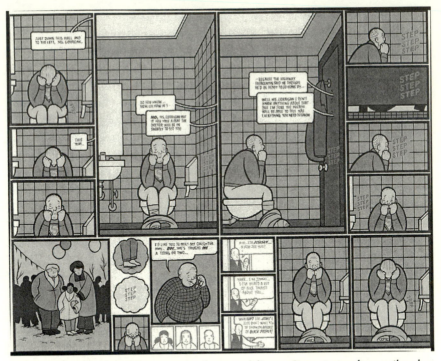

14.2 Jimmy's physical position accentuates his mental distress: Jimmy is seated on a toilet when he hears his sister arrive in the waiting room of the hospital.

when they introduce themselves. Monochromatic blue panels at center bottom display his speculations about how she might look and what he should say. The horizontal sequence imagines her with three different hairstyles. The distinctively African American braids in the second image come with a serious facial expression, and the even more pronouncedly African American–style cornrows in the third image come with an expression of hostility. In this private reverie, the anxious Jimmy associates blackness with anger. The vertical sequence sees him rehearsing greetings to complement each look. He practices meeting Amy of the cornrows with a vernacular "Whassup?" though in this third instance his rehearsal turns into self-parody. Cognizant of his fear that African Americans will think he is afraid of them, he imagines following "Whassup?" with the impolitic admission "I just don't want you to think I'm afraid of black people" (Ware 292). He reveals his tacit, circuitous racism: he is afraid of how black people might perceive him. He also suffers a more base anxiety. He is embarrassed to imagine that Amy can hear him; the final panel of the page shows him burying his face in his hands out of shame when "zrsp" sounds from his body poised above the commode.

Meanwhile, on the other side of the door, Amy worries about whether the hospital's failure to provide further information about her father might be the result of mistaken identification. What if, she wonders, there just happens to be an African American patient named Corrigan? Hospital personnel will assume she is related to a stranger rather than her father. Her anxieties about not being identified as Jim's legitimate daughter soon prove to be unfounded, but the awkwardness of her first conversation with Jimmy is exacerbated by this emergency situation in which the abandoned biological son presumably has more information about their father than does his doting, familiar adopted daughter. As a consequence, when she plies him for information about the accident, her questions eventually insinuate that Jimmy has somehow failed to take adequate care of their father. She asks what Jimmy knows about their father's condition, the nature of the crash, why their dad was driving by himself in the snow, whether Grandpa has been notified, and "what did you two talk about for the last day, anyway?" (298). Nothing in the exchange articulates the inappropriateness of Jimmy's being held accountable for how he has disposed of just over a day spent with a father he has never known, and when he later leaves, there is no one to acknowledge the tragic lack of resolution that he must suffer as a result of his father's dying hours after they first meet.

Jimmy's appearance punctuates the pathos of his situation with absurdity. Leaning on a crutch with one foot heavily bandaged, he wears a borrowed Superman sweatshirt. Amy recognizes it as her father's favorite of the iconic shirts she gives him for his birthday each year. The most recent reads, "#1 Dad." The novel is rife with tropes of Superman, though throughout Ware's work, in *Jimmy Corrigan* and elsewhere, DC's famed superhero is refigured as "The Super-Man"—a paunchy, masked superhero personality from comic books and television. While this facsimile of Superman is an especially meaningful satire for readers who follow Ware's various projects, Jimmy is not in on the joke. "The Super-Man" has been a sincere lifelong investment that occupies his time and shapes his imagination. A comic strip on the book jacket shows the adult Jimmy organizing a large collection of comics he keeps sleeved, boxed, and catalogued in his kitchen pantry. Throughout the novel, Ware supplements Jimmy's stammering, inexpressive efforts at dialogue with elaborate fantasy sequences that typically involve whatever woman has just treated him with kindness or even just perfunctory courtesy. In the fantasy narratives, Jimmy transforms from being initially unavailable to becoming a heroic, devoted partner; for example, Amy's curiosity about his interests prompts him to envision a postapocalyptic scenario in which as the only survivors of a nuclear war, they live happily with their new baby. The paternalism with which Superman takes responsibility for the well-being of others is absent from Jimmy's life, but it is the structuring conceit of his fantasies. However, his relationship with Superman is doubly ambivalent. Although Superman represents a quality of caring that Jimmy desires finally to receive and exercise but never has, he also embodies masculine qualities that Jimmy can hardly hope to emulate. In a social order dominated by expectations for masculinity that receive an ideal expression in Superman's strengths, Jimmy must feel alienated.

Jimmy is most ineffectual in his rapport with Amy when he seeks to comfort her after a doctor informs them of their father's death. He pats her arm only to have her push him away and shout, "get away from me" (348). In keeping with the coordination of Jimmy's body, her gesture topples him to the floor. A nurse helps him up and escorts him out of the small conference room into the hall. In the time it takes him to step into a taxi that someone else has called for a ride to the train station, Amy has recovered her composure and opens the door with an apology, only to find the hallway empty. The panel of Amy standing in the open door discovering that Jimmy is nowhere to be seen becomes on the following page the top-left-corner frame of the two-page genealogy that traces her ancestry back to William Corrigan and May, the African American woman who worked in the Corrigan home (356–358; see fig. 14.3). On the right page, the strip of three rectangular panels inset at the bottom of the unframed picture of the Corrigan home shows William seated at a table with James. Sperm and egg icons indicate that William and May conceived the baby girl who becomes the woman tending a baby son in the centermost panel of the page. William's white grandson, Jim, appears with Amy and her adoptive mother in the wedding photo at the top center of the left page. The sequence at the bottom left shows

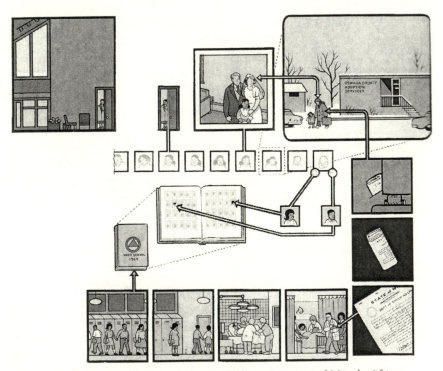

14.3 A genealogy traces Amy's ancestry back to William Corrigan and May, the African American woman who worked in the Corrigan home, with complex illustrations of various events and time frames.

that high school students conceived Amy; the father holds hands with another girl at the time that pregnancy begins to show on Amy's biological mother. The exclusively visual narrative hints that the young couple's breakup leads Amy's mother to give her up for adoption (see fig. 14.4).

The chart of Amy's Corrigan family relations functions as an elaborate and dark punch line at the end of the few hours that Jimmy and Amy ever spend together. With their short relationship already at an end, we learn of both their blood tie and how her mixed-race ancestry has become a secret. And while we know a fact of Amy's ancestry that will never be recovered in the storyworld of *Jimmy Corrigan*, we must also contend with a discomfiting lack of knowledge about the character of William's relationship with May, the maid. Their sexual relations are ambiguous. The sperm and egg icons that indicate their sexual congress diagram successive panels in which May merely serves dinner to William and his son. Whether or not William's relationship with the woman at the head of Amy's family history was consensual, the history of white slave owners raping black women, his standing as her employer, his propensity for violence, and his racist remarks toward other African Americans all make legible the possibility of sexual coercion.

The tracing of Amy's family lineage across generations replicates the style of an illustrated map that appears on the inside of the book jacket of the hardcover

14.4 The exclusively visual narrative hints that the young couple's breakup leads Amy's mother to give her up for adoption.

edition of *Jimmy Corrigan*. (The paperback edition reproduces the poster in smaller scale across two pages added just before the prologue.) In the middle of the poster is a globe with the Atlantic Ocean at its center. A line describes the path of a slave ship with its captives from the coast of West Africa to the southern United States; another line shows the course of a ship of immigrants traveling to New York City from Ireland. Brief comic strips surround the globe on all sides and in four different orientations. To study the map completely requires turning one's attention to all four sides in succession. The reiteration of the world-historical map's style in the genealogical chart of Amy's ancestry underscores that Corrigan family history is a narrative of how American national identity has been conferred and denied through the invention of racial differences and the concomitant disavowal of commonalities that belie those differences.

Dating from the last days of the Atlantic slave trade in the early nineteenth century and coming forward through the U.S. Civil War, the Chicago Fire of 1871, the World's Fair, and up to Jimmy's isolated adulthood in Chicago, the poster follows Corrigan family genealogy while mapping the coerced and compelled migrations of Africans and Irish, respectively. With the exception of a few conjunctions and prepositions that emphasize causality in two of the frame sequences, the poster employs wordless narrativity to communicate sweeping histories of the enslavement of Africans and the emigration of the famine-stricken Irish. A single frame brings these histories into direct, personal contact: a black woman who descends from a man sold at auction stands at a dresser in the bedroom of a small boy. The narrative within the book later identifies them as May and James. Like the chart that details Amy's genealogy, the poster labels with sperm and egg icons those men and women who have conceived children together, but no point on the poster reveals interracial sexual congress. When that disclosure comes in the genealogy that follows the terminus of Amy and Jimmy's brief rapport, it rectifies the impression from the poster that African American and Irish American histories can be related as discrete narratives of hard-won Americanization up from, respectively, bondage in the Americas and the famine in Ireland. Instead, William Corrigan's involvement with May suggests that the secret under erasure in American national history is that mixed-race progeny have been common and that generations later Amy's adoption need not have been understood to translate her across a racial divide. Reading the world-historical map from the later vantage of Amy's secret genealogy reminds us that the *necessity* of racial identity has never been natural history but instead derives from the social need to exercise power collectively. In the case of the histories to which the Corrigan story alludes most pointedly, to claim the advantages of whiteness in the latter half of the nineteenth century, the Irish needed to seem distant from and superior to African Americans.

American National Genealogy

Miscegenation is a peculiarly American term. It was coined and disseminated in an elaborate publishing hoax designed to deny President Abraham Lincoln reelection (Kaplan 225–226). The antiabolitionist journalists David Goodman Croly and George Wakeman of the *New York World* penned an anonymous treatise, *Miscegenation: The Theory of the Blending of the Races, Applied to the American White Man and Negro.* The 1864 pamphlet extols the virtue of interracial marriage and professes that the ultimate aspiration of Lincoln's Emancipation Proclamation is to promote miscegenation, a word Croly and Wakeman construct from the Latin *miscere* and *genus*: "to mix" and "kind," respectively (Kaplan 221). Distributed for free to select abolitionists and anti-abolitionist publications alike, the seventy-two-page statement was designed to dupe the former into endorsing its views and to induce the latter to rally vocifer-ously against the tract's vision of a thoroughly mixed-race America. Although the pamphlet failed to deny Lincoln the presidency, its semantic innovation made more coherent a discourse of racial difference that has endured ever since as a rhetorical resource for supremacist, segregationist, and reactionary politi-cal arguments that inveigh against integration and social equity as threats to the integrity of the nation. *Miscegenation* facilitated the further racialization of national belonging. Playing neatly into Anglophilic cultural narratives of national identity, it incited defiant expressions of how whiteness is the proper cast of American character.

The pamphlet was especially well crafted to ignite the antipathies of Irish Americans. With a veneer of scientific veracity, it reports that progress toward a thoroughly miscegenated America is well under way as a result of the proclivity of the Irish and African "races" to mate. Living together in the impoverished sections of northeastern cities, "black men" and "Irish women" naturally form "connubial relations." These relations, Croly and Wakeman claim, are of "infinite service to the Irish" because "they are a more brutal race and lower in civiliza-tion than the negro" (qtd. in Kaplan 224). With the pamphlet being circulated within a few months of the draft riots in New York City, passages denigrating the Irish by characterizing their race as lower than that of "the negro" were a provocation to renewed violence. As the historians Noel Ignatiev and David Roediger have documented, Irish immigrants to the United States in the middle of the nineteenth century were not regarded as white. They attained whiteness over the second half of the century. Active involvement on behalf of the Demo-cratic Party's antiabolitionist and, later, pro–Jim Crow policies was essential by the end of the nineteenth century to the eventual assimilation of Irish Ameri-cans into the potent social fiction of the white race (Ignatiev 137). Marrying the Irish to the Africans, the authors of *Miscegenation* had to know they would recall the animus of the draft riots, in which Irish immigrants expressed outrage at their conscription into the Union army by marauding in gangs through the streets beating and killing African Americans, the alleged cause of the Civil War.

Without including the events of the Civil War or the draft riots in the narratives that take place between the covers of *Jimmy Corrigan*, Ware nonetheless indicates their relevance to the disposition of race relations at the time of the World's Fair. William Corrigan is a veteran of the U.S. Civil War. During dinners, he assails his son with questions about the death count at the Battle of Shiloh, where he lost a finger. The book jacket's map of the transportation of Africans and Irish to the United States includes panels that show William enlisting in response to advertisements encouraging new Irish arrivals to avoid conscription by volunteering for the war. At the time, the susceptibility of Irish immigrants for the draft marked their difference from more established, Protestant whites, who could avoid military service by paying a $300 substitution fee, a price that recent Irish immigrants such as William and his parents could rarely afford. By the 1890s, when William lords over his son the sacrifice of his finger for the sake of the Union, the Irish have begun to enjoy the privileges of whiteness.

Inside the back cover of the novel, Ware includes two pages of corrigenda: "a list of errors with corrections, in a book. Arranged alphabetically." The juxtaposition of consecutive entries on "Draft Riots" and "Exposition" suggests that violence against African Americans has helped to incorporate Irish Americans into the Exposition's whitewashed version of American history. The first entry explains that in the "Civil War Draft Riots . . . angry mobs, (reportedly composed of primarily Irish citizens) murdered nearly one thousand Afro-Americans and caused over two million dollars worth of property damage over a period of four days." Immediately below that entry, an aerial view of the White City depicts the famed "Exposition," but the panel's additional wording refers not to the Fair but to "the main body of a work, esp. that which explicates a main theme, or introduced a fundamental motif." Locating the image of the Fair under a heading of the "main theme" of a work and just below the entry for "Draft Riots," Ware invites us to consider again what the Columbian Exposition was all about and to regard it as a reference in his book for which the Corrigan family genealogy provides clarification. Recall that Eggers regards the Fair to be merely a beautiful foil for the unappealing Corrigans. This supplemental page of corrections that appears at the end of the narrative proper impresses on us retrospectively that the tensions underlying the draft riots have been a subtext of *Jimmy Corrigan*. The design of the White City denied how U.S. national history has proceeded by way of lethal and costly explosions of racial violence.

Posturing for an ideological commitment that inverts the authors' actual convictions, *Miscegenation* reanimated a nativist fiction in which white Americans somehow enjoy original title to the identity, authority, and resources of the United States. Without the defensiveness or overt hostility of the pamphlet, the Columbian Exposition of 1893 was organized to relate a similar foundational fiction. Like the fabled "city on a hill" projected in John Winthrop's 1630 sermon before the Puritan founders of the Massachusetts Bay Colony, the White City was intended to represent the culmination of a providential narrative. The United States and its representative city Chicago were the most suitable hosts for all the world to observe modernity's greatest achievements in science, art, and commerce. An expression of American Exceptionalism by way of a massive construction project, the Exposition itself was perhaps the most impressive exhibit. In the scale and appearance of the buildings and grounds, they suggested that among the leading nation-states of the world, the United States was the ultimate realization of modernity's technological and cultural promise. This narrative of American accomplishment communicated by the Fair's design did not, however, acknowledge either the contributions to the United States by African American citizens in the decades since the Emancipation Proclamation or the unremunerated labor of enslaved Africans from the early seventeenth century until the end of the Civil War.

Whether or not providential narratives of national development are rooted in theology, they are possessed of a mystifying temporality. Bhabha explains in his work on the narrative dimensions of national identity that the inherently ambivalent character of national identity compels that its narratives be written in a "double time." National identity is a social fiction that professes continuity with a nation's founding. The problem that such an attachment to origins entails is that the persistence of a nation over time requires resiliency and change in response to shifting conditions. In the present, the nation must constantly invent its relationship to its past. Bhabha writes, "For the political unity of the nation consists in a continual displacement of its irredeemably plural modern space, bounded by different, even hostile nations, into a signifying space that is archaic and mythical, paradoxically representing the nation's modern territoriality in the patriotic, atavistic temporality of Traditionalism. Quite simply, the difference of space returns as the Sameness of time, turning Territory into Tradition, turning the People into One" (213). The design for the buildings and grounds of the Exposition was an exemplary strategy for narrating a romantic American national identity undisturbed and unsullied by counterfactual stories of atrocity perpetrated in the national interest. In line with Bhabha's statement, the narrative of the United States told by the Fair's appearance infused space with a sense of time. Key to the success of the Exposition as a monument to American Exceptionalism was a doubling of the temporal character of the area of the Fair designated the White City.

The White City appeared to be a utopian domain removed from the passage of time and, simultaneously, the endpoint in a developmental chronology of human history. The neoclassical architecture of the massive buildings gave the White City an unworldly feel, as if it were removed from the ordinary passage of time to a continuous present. In the illustrations that look down at the Fair when it is dense with patrons, Ware captures the scale of the centerpiece of the White City: the buildings around the reflecting pool with an allegorical statue, *Republic*, at the top of the water. As in the photograph above, people appear as minuscule shadows. But the area described by the photograph and Ware's drawing constitutes less than one-third of the White City, which itself covered only half the Fair's acreage. For people on the ground in the middle of the White City, Chicago disappeared. From observation decks atop the White City, Chicago appeared a shrunken, distant exterior to the monumental white buildings. The layout of the entire Fair in two primary sections, the White City and the Midway Plaisance, suggested that the White City's magisterial appearance should also be understood as the culmination of a developmental narrative in which humanity has progressed from primitivism to civilization. Patrons of the Fair visited the exhibition halls of the White City to educate themselves. The Midway, in contrast, was a site for amusement. A 280-foot Ferris wheel was the central attraction. While major European states sponsored exhibition halls in the White City, installations devoted to African culture were located in the Midway. The Fair, in other words, divided the world into a colonial hierarchy of core and periphery in which exotic, colonial locales served both as commercial entertainment and as ethnographic evidence of the superior development of nations with predominantly white populations.

The novel's longest continuous section of pages set in the time of the World's Fair culminates with an episode that indicates that William guided his young son, James, through the fairgrounds according to this path of development from the Midway to the White City (Ware 200–281). Cursive script provides a first-person voice-over narration that the text later suggests has been the voice of the elderly James responding to an interview with his adoptive granddaughter, Amy, who has been assigned a family genealogy project for fourth grade. In the sequence that recounts the young James's single trip to the Fair, the narrative follows his progress through the crowded Midway. His father leads them past a sign pointing toward "Dwelling of the Cannibals," which is how many of the Fair's attendees would have thought of the "Dahomey Village" exhibition. That "White City" to this day remains a metonym for the entire Columbian Exposition of 1893 recalls how the Midway's symbolic purpose was to serve as a foil for American civilization even as its commercial purpose was to excite attendance, which over the months of the fair totaled 27,529,400 adults and children (Rydell, *All* 40). The prominent, dignified representation of African Americans within the White City would have disrupted the efficiency with which the relegation of African culture to the Midway alongside the Ferris wheel and other commercial amusements invested in the appearance of racial difference a visual narrative of human progress from primitive to civilized, from the Midway to the White City, from appetite to education, and from black to white. This final attribution censures the full enfranchisement of nonwhites in the ultimate achievement of modernity, American national identity. Public appearances by African American performers on the Midway were, however, encouraged. The

most popular was Nancy Green's debut portrayal of "Aunt Jemima," the plantation mammy that R. T. David Milling Company created to promote its pancake
mix (Rydell, "Editor's" xix). In the manner of minstrel shows, the one-woman
performance used homespun agrarian wisdom to assure the Fair's patrons that
she had slaved over their pancake batter and knew that her proper place was on
the Midway.

The Exposition supplemented its strategic arrangement of space with ceremonial events that reinforced the narrative of America's exemplarity, which is to
say how the nation sets itself apart from all others and also serves as a model for
others to emulate. Removed from ordinary time and at the end of history, the
United States appears in the White City to be the realization of ideals that must
be conserved and defended. Schoolchildren were enlisted to that end for the
public dedication of the Fair on October 12, 1892. In Ware's novel, James Corrigan is one of four children selected from his class to represent his school in the
"Living Flag." Dressed in a red cap and vest, James becomes a part of the American flag. "The Pledge of Allegiance to the Flag" was written for the Exposition's
dedication. Ware does not include this detail or have the children recite the
pledge, but his account of James's participation in the Living Flag shows how
the dedication of the World's Fair involved a theatrical nationalist pedagogy.
And we see the exclusion of African Americans when James, waiting for the cue
to don his red costume, worries over an isolated boy in a red cap until he realizes that "it's only a negro" boy selling newspapers. African American children
had no part in the Living Flag. We see in the novel how their visible exclusion
from the grandstand instructs in the child James a racist sensibility that decades
later will see him genuinely perplexed about how his son could be a conscientious parent to an adopted black girl but a stranger to his biological white son.
Circulated to schools throughout the United States by the Federal Bureau of
Education, the Pledge of Allegiance allowed millions of children to participate
virtually in ceremonies that more than one hundred thousand people attended
in Chicago (Rydell, *All* 46). That the Pledge of Allegiance is still recited each
morning by children in many public schools throughout the United States
without any reference to its original occasion or exclusions is evidence of how
novel performances that reinvent national belonging become pedagogical routines, presumed in their traditionalism to have always been part of a citizen's
responsibility.[5]

To protest the injury of omitting African American history and the insult
of according black Americans a single day to patronize the Fair and perform in
the White City, Ida B. Wells, Frederick Douglass, and other prominent African
American activists authored *The Reason Why the Colored American Is Not in the
World's Columbian Exposition*.[6] Published on August 30, 1893, five days after
"Colored People's Day," the pamphlet does more than protest the exclusion
of African Americans. It presents a counterargument to the visual narrative of
national identity described by the White City. Douglass's introduction counters

the conceit that American history has been a story of unfolding progress. He catalogues the falsehoods of the Exposition:

> There are many good things concerning our country and countrymen of which we would be glad to tell in this pamphlet, if we could do so, and at the same time tell the truth. We would like for instance to tell our visitors that the moral progress of the American people has kept even pace with their enterprise and their material civilization; that practice by the ruling class has gone hand in hand with American professions; that two hundred and sixty years of progress and enlightenment have banished barbarism and race hate from the United States; that the old things of slavery have entirely passed away, and that all things pertaining to the colored people have become new. (Wells et al. 8)

Douglass reinforces the substance of his complaints with the form of his second sentence: a bravura succession of independent clauses. I have quoted four, but the sentence extends to a total of twenty-two. Each asserts an aspiration for social justice that remains unrealized; each conveys that forces in the United States act violently to deny those aspirations. In the reiteration of vivid examples of justice denied, the sentence is a contrapuntal refutation of the unabashed providential history of the White City, which in the final clause Douglass wishes was not a "whited sepulcher" (9).

For anyone who read one of the twenty thousand copies of *The Reason Why* circulated in August 1893, Ida B. Wells's chapter on lynching confronted the imagery of the White City with lurid, visual evidence that the lynching of African American men by white mobs was a resurgent cultural practice in the United States. She lists the offenses through which African Americans might instigate a lynch mob, and she identifies how many African Americans have been lynched annually for each offense in the years preceding the Exposition. The number of "negroes murdered by mobs" reported in the United States rose each year, from 52 in 1882 to 169 in 1891. A third of the murdered were black men charged with raping white women. Other crimes that routinely put African Americans at risk included murder, robbery, burglary, race prejudice, quarreling with white men, making threats, rioting, miscegenation, or no reason at all (Wells et al. 30–31). Reprinting postmortem photographs of lynch mobs and their victims as souvenir postcards was also a common cultural practice. Wells includes a copy of such a card that commemorates an 1891 lynching in Clanton, Alabama. The image shows a black male victim hanging dead or soon to be so above the heads of a group that addresses its civil decorum directly to the camera as if finished with any feelings about the man hanging above them. A girl and three boys stand prominently before the assembly of mostly men; a few women are barely visible in the background; all the crowd is white. With their expressions fixed on the camera rather than the body of the dead man, the image projects a sense of uniform purpose. Lynchings served to place all African

Americans under a tacit threat of sudden execution, and they functioned as rituals of communal identification for white Americans. They were scenes in which a principle of white commonality was enacted through the violent purgation of black life from the social order. Insofar as the White City purged African Americans from U.S. history and fixed national identity to whiteness, in grand style the World's Fair shared in the cultural logic by which lynching produced white solidarity through the theatrical enactment of convictions of white supremacy.

With the young, abused James Corrigan cast as the subject of his father's racist example and the Exposition's instruction in white national identity, Ware's embedded narrative of 1893 draws on the conventions of bildungsroman to show how racism became institutionalized in a romantic national narrative that holds up superior technological development and incomparable cultural achievement as the unique providence of the United States. The White City narrative of an exceptional America does not admit explanations for the global standing of the United States that do not refer principally to the quality of American national character: never minding historical factors such as the advantages of colonial authority or the cost-beneficial legacy of slavery. The novel's counternarrative to the triumphalism of the Exposition climaxes when William abandons James at the highest point in the White City: the observation deck on the roof of the Manufacturing and Liberal Arts Building, which was promoted as the largest building in the world. The awesome view of the fairgrounds, the city beyond, and the expanse of Lake Michigan would be daunting and then frightening for a nine-year-old boy who finds himself alone on this purchase. His abrupt isolation at a dizzying height and the opportunities the Fair presents for William to escape his son's or anyone else's notice turns the story of the Columbian Exposition into a massive emblem of responsibility disavowed, a "whited sepulcher" in which William might as well have left James for dead.

Conclusion: Uncommon Chicago

The timing of the World's Fair was fortuitous for its investors. On either side of its dates, events provided immediate counterpoints to the affluence of the Exposition and its representation of the transcendence of the United States from social distress and state violence. In *The Incorporation of America*, Alan Trachtenberg identifies the Exposition as the culmination of a transformation in the political culture and governance of the United States that positioned the corporation as the most powerful institution in public life. He points out that the long summer of the Fair fell between the financial panic of 1893 and the Pullman strike of 1894. The largest of many labor actions incited in the 1890s by the Gilded Age immiseration of the working classes, the Pullman strike was a response to severe wage cuts and the approximately two thousand fatal industrial accidents among railway workers between 1888 and 1893 (Goldfield 158). Federal military intervention against the strike and an attack on the

American Railway Union prompted a citywide general strike. Had it occurred a few months earlier, the general strike would have revised the narrative of the White City. Rather than a temporality that attributed subsistence living to primitive, remote locales fixed in the past, an Exposition absent its striking workers would have exposed how much wage labor was required for the White City to operate and, by extension, to return to the investors their share of the more than $1 million profit from the Fair's ticket sales and vendor fees.

Aside from following William Corrigan's deterioration as he loses his family's home and must move with James into a single room at a boarding house, *Jimmy Corrigan* does not depict directly the economic crises of the 1890s that surrounded the World's Fair. But by juxtaposing images of the White City with the commercial landscape inhabited by Jimmy decades later, the novel extends its critique of racist historiographies to examine the consequences of entrusting the public good and national narratives to corporations that are beholden to shareholders rather than citizens. In the final representation of the Columbian Exposition that appears in the narrative, the Manufacturing and Liberal Arts Building fills the entire left page (see fig. 14.5). Nearly indiscernible, the abandoned James remains on the roof, peering over the railing at the people on the ground. This monumental depiction of the Fair contrasts with the modest, nearly contemporary public street composed in multiple panels on the right page (see fig. 14.6). If we were to view these two pages in isolation from Ware's narrative, the opposition of the Fair's grandeur and the snowy, unassuming street would suggest a historical devolution. In contrast to the contemporary street scene, the White City looks majestic. But our realization that William has abandoned James at the height of the Fair—a fact related in the cursive script, "Of course he never did [return]"—and our familiarity with the temporary construction of the Exposition buildings from cheap material allow us to recognize a continuity between the seemingly magnificent Exposition and the ubiquitous icon of corporate privilege, McDonald's golden arches. Equally missing from the left and right pages is an image of noncommercial public space, and in the absence of a commons, history cannot be shared free of charge. This impression that the White City is an early landmark in a long American century during which commercial interests have persistently incorporated the times and places of ordinary social relations—as well as the histories we may imagine ourselves to share—punctuates the work that Ware's graphic novel undertakes to illustrate how "miscegenation" has typically been elided in conventional histories of the United States. What hope does *Jimmy Corrigan* offer us when it affirms the extent to which white privilege has been invested in the denial of the truly interracial character of U.S. history? Rather than encourage us to believe that demystifying the whitewash of American history pronounced by the Columbian Exposition and reiterated since will lead to the redress of racial discrimination, Ware's novel amplifies the dispiriting facts of the secret history of miscegenation with the suggestion that, at present, recognition of

14.5 In the final representation of the Columbian Exposition that appears in the narrative, the Manufacturing and Liberal Arts Building fills the entire left page.

how American citizenship has been yoked unconscionably to whiteness is hopelessly belated. It arrives at a time in which the diminishing value of white racial identity, embodied by Jimmy, corresponds to the pervasive spread of social insecurities and the reduction of information, including historical knowledge, to its value as a commodity.

I have argued that *Jimmy Corrigan* shows how whiteness flourishes through the artifice of inventing racial differences and that such invention is especially pernicious when integrated into narratives of American national identity. Critiques of the privilege of whiteness and the racialization of national belonging are by now all too familiar, and still they bear repeating. Moreover, Ware's depiction of a critical genealogy of the racial formation of the United States across the long twentieth century enjoys special pertinence because he joins it visually to a landscape in which we also witness the emergence of a service economy and the disappearance of the kind of industrial manufacturing and building initiatives that were announced as the future at the 1893 Exposition. The novel

14.6 The monumental depiction of the Fair contrasts with the modest, nearly contemporary public street composed in multiple panels on the right page.

implies that the bleak consequence of that change in venue is that, even as indigence remains racialized statistically, the dividing lines of the twenty-first century will be rooted in a socioeconomic insecurity that will deny even the traditional assurances of racial identity. "The possessive investment in whiteness," as George Lipsitz terms it, may become unsustainable. Sourced to the extension of unsustainable degrees of risk to virtually everyone, the seemingly laudable and certainly overdue devaluation of whiteness would signal not the expansion of equality across racial divisions but instead a redistribution of insecurity that would see virtually no one immune from the kind of precarious social standing that Jimmy seems to channel in practically his every word, gesture, and misadventure. Read in this way as a figure of unwitting prescience, Jimmy's story is a personal record of public history that smarts.

Notes

1 *Masters of American Comics* was sponsored between 2005 and 2007 by the Hammer Museum and the Museum of Contemporary Art, Los Angeles. Born in 1967, Ware was the youngest comics artist selected for the exhibit, which also included Winsor McKay, Lyonel Feininger, George Herriman, E. C. Segar, Frank King, Chester Gould, Milton Caniff, Charles M. Schulz, Will Eisner, Jack Kirby, R. Crumb, Art Spiegelman, and Gary Panter.

2   *Jimmy Corrigan* won an American Book Award and the Guardian First Book Award in 2001. For the latter, it was the first graphic novel to be chosen for a major literary prize over conventional, pictureless texts. In 2002, Ware was the first comics artist to exhibit at the Whitney Museum of American Art biennial exhibition.

3   The *Masters of American Comics* exhibit and catalogue might be taken as an example of how aestheticizing history can function as an alibi for willful exclusion or accidental neglect of the already marginalized. George Herriman is the sole person of color among the fifteen masters. Stanley Crouch's essay describes Herriman's ambivalent personal relationship to ethnicity and offers discerning remarks about the resonance of race matters in *Krazy Kat*. The exhibition catalogue provides no account of how the list of masters includes no women.

4   For a review of scholarship on Ware, see David Ball and Martha Kuhlman's "Introduction: Chris Ware and the 'Cult of Difficulty.'" Gene Kannenberg's "The Comics of Chris Ware" and Daniel Raeburn's monograph *Chris Ware* are examples of formalist treatments of Ware's work. Juda Bennett and Cassandra Jackson's "Graphic Whiteness and the Lessons of Chris Ware's *Jimmy Corrigan*" addresses the novel's representation of race. Following Dyer, they identify the novel as a critique of how whiteness passes invisibly as if it were a neutral, universal standard. My argument is sympathetic to Bennett and Jackson's article, and I share their interest in the novel's references to Superman and the 1893 World's Fair. My characterization of the novel as historiographical metafiction that remarks on the racialization of national identity ultimately differs from their account of how Ware's text represents personal identity as composed recursively through error and amendment. *The Comics of Chris Ware: Drawing Is a Way of Thinking*, an anthology of recent scholarship edited by Ball and Kuhlman, includes articles that associate Ware's work with critical race studies. Of particular relevance to my argument is Joanna Davis-McElligatt's "Confronting the Intersections of Race, Immigration, and Representation in Chris Ware's Comics." She considers how Ware addresses comics' problematic formal reliance on caricature as it corresponds to the history of racist stereotypes, especially those of Irish and African Americans. Concluding that *Jimmy Corrigan* is critical of how American national identity has involved the disavowal of interracial "family relationships that have been, and forever will be, lost to view" (144), she remarks on how normative formulations of racial difference that would neglect, for example, Amy's blood tie to the Corrigan men elide those histories of immigration that would expose the punishing obligations that have confronted minority populations endeavoring to assimilate. My argument also notices how *Jimmy Corrigan* recalls that antiblack racism was essential for Irish immigrants to attain the status of whiteness in the United States by the end of the nineteenth century, and I offer the further suggestion that Ware's novel is suggestive about how a public culture dominated by corporations will diminish the significance of white privilege.

5   My references to "pedagogical" and "performative" borrow from Bhabha's elaboration of his theory of national narratives and counternarratives (212). The ambivalence between national pedagogies that reinforce traditional identification and performances that renew national attachment is a resource for the critical practice of counternarratives. Such critiques may seize on how the disjunction between the pedagogical and performative dimensions of national identification allow for the observation that national identity is irreducibly contingent and therefore subject to revision.

6   Wells and Douglass actually disagreed with each other about the proper response to the invitation to attend Jubilee Day at the World's Fair. Wells published her objection

to attendance, urging other African Americans to reject the Exposition altogether. Douglass determined that the chance to present leading African American intellectuals and artists could make the single day valuable for the public image of African Americans (Rydell, "Editor's" xxx).

Works Cited

Ball, David M., and Martha B. Kuhlman, eds. *The Comics of Chris Ware: Drawing Is a Way of Thinking*. Jackson: University Press of Mississippi, 2010.

———. "Introduction: Chris Ware and the 'Cult of Difficulty.'" *The Comics of Chris Ware: Drawing Is a Way of Thinking*. Ed. David M. Ball and Martha B. Kuhlman. Jackson: University Press of Mississippi, 2010. ix–xxiii.

Bennett, Juda, and Cassandra Jackson. "Graphic Whiteness and the Lessons of Chris Ware's *Jimmy Corrigan*." *ImageTexT: Interdisciplinary Comics Studies* 5.1 (2010). Web. http://www.english.ufl.edu/imagetext/archives/v5_1/bennett-jackson/. Accessed 2 Jan. 2013.

Bhabha, Homi. *The Location of Culture*. London and New York: Routledge, 1994.

Croly, David Goodman, and George Wakeman. *Miscegenation: The Theory of the Blending of the Races, Applied to the American White Man and Negro*. New York: H. Dexter Hamilton, 1864.

Crouch, Stanley. "Blues for Krazy Kat." *Masters of American Comics*. Ed. John Carlin, Paul Karasik, and Brian Walker. Los Angeles and New Haven, CT: Hammer Museum and the Museum of Contemporary Art / Yale University Press, 2005. 194–201.

Davis-McElligatt, Joanna. "Confronting the Intersections of Race, Immigration, and Representation in Chris Ware's Comics." *The Comics of Chris Ware: Drawing Is a Way of Thinking*. Ed. David M. Ball and Martha B. Kuhlman. Jackson: University Press of Mississippi, 2010. 135–145.

Dyer, Richard. *White*. London and New York: Routledge, 1997.

Eggers, Dave. "Chris Ware." *Masters of American Comics*. Ed. John Carlin, Paul Karasik, and Brian Walker. Los Angeles and New Haven, CT: Hammer Museum and the Museum of Contemporary Art / Yale University Press, 2005. 308–317.

Goldfield, Michael. *The Color of Politics: Race and the Mainsprings of American Politics*. New York: New Press, 1997.

Ignatiev, Noel. *How the Irish Became White*. New York and London: Routledge, 1995.

Jameson, Fredric. *The Political Unconscious: Narrative as a Socially Symbolic Act*. Ithaca, NY: Cornell University Press, 1981.

Kannenberg, Gene, Jr. "The Comics of Chris Ware." *A Comics Studies Reader*. Ed. Jeet Herr and Kent Worcester. Jackson: University Press of Mississippi, 2009. 306–324.

Kaplan, Sidney. "The Miscegenation Issue in the Election of 1864." *Interracialism: Black-White Intermarriage in American History, Literature, and Law*. Ed. Werner Sollors. Oxford: Oxford University Press, 2000. 219–265.

Lipsitz, George. "The Possessive Investment in Whiteness." *White Privilege: Essential Readings on the Other Side of Racism*. Ed. Paula S. Rothenberg. New York: Worth, 2005. 67–90.

Raeburn, Daniel. *Chris Ware*. New Haven, CT: Yale University Press, 2004.

Roediger, David. *The Wages of Whiteness: Race and the Making of the American Working Class*. London: Verso, 2007.

Rydell, Robert. *All the World's a Fair: Visions of Empire at American International Expositions, 1976–1916*. Chicago: University of Chicago Press, 1984.

———. "Editor's Introduction: 'Contend, Contend!'" *The Reason Why the Colored American Is Not in the World's Exposition: The Afro-American's Contribution to Columbian Literature*. Ed. Rydell. Urbana: University of Illinois Press, 1999. xi–xlviii.

Sollors, Werner. *Neither Black nor White yet Both: Thematic Explorations of Interracial Litera-ture*. Oxford: Oxford University Press, 1997.

Trachtenberg, Alan. *The Incorporation of America: Culture and Society in the Gilded Age*. New York: Hill and Wang, 1982.

Ware, Chris. *Jimmy Corrigan, the Smartest Kid on Earth*. New York: Pantheon, 2000.

Wells, Ida B., Frederick Douglass, Irvine Garland Penn, and Ferdinand L. Barnett. *The Reason Why the Colored American Is Not in the World's Exposition: The Afro-American's Contribu-tion to Columbian Literature*. 1893. Ed. Robert Rydell. Urbana: University of Illinois Press, 1999.

Chapter 15

It's a Hero?

• •

Black Comics and
Satirizing Subjection

REBECCA WANZO

Protagonists in comics often represent ideal citizens, but these archetypes signify varied kinds of fantasies about the nation's power or innocence. In the comic book, the traditional superhero is the embodiment of U.S. power; in the comic strip, the precocious youngster is a symbol of childhood and nuclear families. In superheroes' origins, their bodies are ones of excess, always of excessive musculature and sometimes of atypical goodness.[1] Idealized white children, as pictured in comic strips such as *Peanuts*, *Family Circle*, or *Archie*, are ideal in their average travails; domestic concerns do not connect to national political issues. I am not implying that there have not been more complicated representations in either kind of comic. Instead, I am establishing a baseline for traditional representations in the genre.[2] These representations of U.S. ideal citizenship are shaped by the relationship between word and image, but once the images of the characters have been imprinted on the imagination, it is the repetitive image that becomes the immediate referent for Americana. In comics, bodies "occupy a position of primacy over text" (Eisner 103). Thus, Superman's red cape and Charlie Brown's simple silhouette are what comics readers expect: the gaze knows the body because it is the expected image; the words work in concert with what the image tells the comics reader.

Comic has a double generic meaning; sequential art is obviously not always humorous. However, its root is the interpretation of body into a simplified line, a practice that can easily lead to the production of stereotypes. Stereotypes have long been a tool of producing laughter. But it is often not the stereotypical expected body that can serve as an object of humor, particularly when the superhero is the referent. Instead, as is often the case with humor, the contrast between the superhero's body and one configured as less than ideal can be the source of comedy. Will Eisner's groundbreaking comic strip *The Spirit* (1940) blended mystery, romance, adventure, and comedy, and a source of comedy was often the actions of the heroic title character's sidekick, Ebony White. Eisner drew White as a blend of ape and man, immediately evoking the traditional stereotypes of African Americans as subhuman (even as Eisner understood himself as lovingly bestowing a humanity on White that was rare in the period [Cooke; Benson]). Ebony White's dialect and buffoonery were a foil to the Spirit's bodily and elegant perfection. While Eisner was conscious of the stereotyping and later attempted to change the character and added another black character that moved beyond stereotype, White was similar to centuries of derogatory images of blacks.

Decades later, the disconnect between traditional ideal citizens and the idea of black heroism has been a source of humor for comics with African American main characters. Comics creators have sometimes played on the distance between black bodies and models of ideal Americans, satirizing the impossibility of black bodies as representatives of heroism or patriotism. However, the implied disconnect can also be a source of melancholia; the humor in African American comics that builds on the difference between the expected ideal citizen and the African American counterideal is informed by the racist histories that can overdetermine representational possibilities for black bodies.

In this chapter, I explore how two comics creators explored the tensions between varied citizenship ideals, unpacking citizenship models in comics through the black counterideal in the 1990s. In the comic book *Icon* (1993–1997), the late African American comic book and television writer Dwayne McDuffie and varied artists tell the story of Raquel Ervin, a black teenager who is an unwed single mother but crafts herself and an alien with supernatural powers into a black superhero and role model. While *Icon* is, in many ways, a traditional superhero comic, McDuffie and the artists often call attention to the impossibility of Raquel's body in relationship to dominant narratives of U.S. heroism. In another comics genre, the comic strip, the dissonance between the ideal child-citizen body and the contrasting black child body was perhaps most provocatively realized in Aaron McGruder's *The Boondocks* (1999–2006). McGruder's protagonist, Huey, is a precocious ten-year-old black radical who blends the traditional comic strip domestic scenes with cultural criticism and, quite often, nationalist discourse. In different ways, *Icon* and *The Boondocks* both satirize what it means that their bodies and speech cannot or should not be imagined in discourses of citizenship, that they should not exist in the genre they inhabit, and critique what black heroic models have previously circulated. Using what I call *critical race humor*, the creators of both texts address the erasure of their black bodies in citizenship discourse.

My discussion of critical race humor draws on critical race theory, a body of scholarship that blends critical theory with studies of race, privileging race in interrogations of institutional inequities.[3] Critical race theorists have at the forefront of their analyses both the material raced body and allegedly ephemeral psychological harms that other kinds of scholars, particularly those utilizing an objective and allegedly color-blind legal hermeneutic, often address tangentially or reductively. However, there are other modes of production that call attention to the harms affecting raced bodies, and visual artists have often taken on the project of addressing the damaging histories of these representations.[4] The tyranny of racist representation has made stereotypical images of people of color an important tool of cultural and political imperialism. Stereotypical images of black bodies can be found around the world—from U.S. film to Japanese manga. Humor, as a genre that often depends on representations of the body as incongruent or somehow out of place in order to achieve laughter, is an appropriate site to attack visual imperialism. By calling attention to the history of representation and, importantly, crafting new representations, those who work in visual media can challenge these visual histories. Those who have been wounded by the legacies of racist humor can turn the traditional visual objects of humor into a source of critical engagement with nationalist representations that have traditionally erased or misrepresented bodies that are counter to traditional images of ideal citizens. Many scholars, as others in this volume explain, have called attention to the ways in which humor can function as a site of political resistance, and graphic storytelling has also been a place of cultural production that offers some critiques similar to those offered in more scholarly spaces.

In *Icon* and *The Boondocks*, critical race humor is a primary mode of intellectual intervention into traditional nationalist narratives, and their texts also draw attention to how critical humor can be informed by affects other than amusement. In the midst of one-liners and punch lines, these are creations of hope and desire, willing into being and proliferation that which was previously unimaginable. Tied to such a weighty cause, critical race humor is often tied to melancholia. The melancholic is, as Anne Anlin Cheng describes it in her discussion of racial melancholia, "psychically stuck" (8). Both consumers and objects of racial stereotypes are often "stuck" with the history of these representations, constantly negotiating images that are culturally imprinted. Those who attempt to produce new models of black bodies are often burdened by a history of stereotype, particularly in genres that have never imagined them as anything other than that. To move beyond that, and to constantly struggle against the conventions of the medium, is an effort to transform the expectations of audiences and to make the hypervisible visible in a wholly other way. A starting point for critical race humor is thus racist representational histories, and creators are often psychically stuck in the attempts to defeat this erasure, crafting visual humor in a world where the burden of degrading historical representations is the precursor to laughter.

Up and Up and Unwed Mother? Reframing the Superhero Body

The superhero body, in its origins of hyperembodied musculature, fetishizes force and treats myth-making as the path to ideal citizenship. Superman is the archetypal superhero; created by two Jewish men in the 1930s, his is the story of an immigrant outsider who becomes an ideal icon of the nation. Of course, Superman's iconicity spread beyond the comic book frame, and he became an iconographic image in the United States (Wright 1). The costumed superhero is a thoroughly American genre—in the nationalist sense of America that displaces the continents that construct the region. As a sign of America, Superman's chiseled silhouette, white skin, and idealization of the nation became the standard superhero archetype. But as domestic political unrest became a major national concern, mainstream comic book creators began to create antiestablishment comic book heroes who might question the nation state (Wright 226–247). Comic books became more critical of the nation and nationalism as a project in the 1960s and 1970s, taking a definitive turn toward the antihero when Frank Miller depicted Batman as a vigilante in *The Dark Knight Returns* in 1985 and Alan Moore interrogated the romance of power, secrecy, and state surveillance embodied by superheroes in *Watchmen* (1985–1987).

Superhero comics have not become a bastion of progressivism, but there has been evidence of a struggle, a struggle that is the result of the comic book superhero representing, at its foundations, power that more often than not makes violent and nationalist interventions. But interrogating the intersectional role of race, gender, and masculinity in state power has not been central to the fairly mainstream strand of critique of U.S. nationalism offered in superhero comics. As signs of both manhood and nation, the U.S. superhero body has paradigmatically been white and male, leaving women and people of color to possess liminal status. There have been women superheroes, but with the exception of Wonder Woman, they are marginal figures (and even Wonder Woman has lacked the high-profile cinematic life of her male counterparts). There have been black superheroes, but since comics characters are hyperphysical, the excesses of their body are always present. Since black bodies are always already hyperembodied, how transgressive is it to stage protest in a genre that typically depicts characters as caricature and/or physically violent?

As scholars of black comics have noted, black superheroes have often struggled to escape stereotype (see Brown; Singer). While headlining characters such as Black Panther and Luke Cage received their own comics in the 1970s and were aimed at representing the rhetoric of the Black Power movement and offering critiques of institutional racism, their heroism was still shaped by a hypermasculine stereotype. Such representations did not end in the 1970s. For example, the 1990s relaunch of *Black Panther* depicts the perfect leader as an unbeatable, incorruptible king of the nation Wakanda, which is scientifically advanced nationally far beyond everything else in the world. Its perfect model, however, often fails to challenge the nexus of male force and nation as ideal. While it challenges narratives about Africa, what is missing is the necessary ambivalence around the nature of citizenship, a kind of subjectivity that means not only being the subject *who* has powers but being subject *to* larger powers. The *Black Panther* comic book often plays with the notion that black superheroes are unimaginable, that they could not possibly exist or do what they do, but such narratives still often depend on glossing over the nature of power dynamics in the state by privileging muscular power as the ideal fantasy of agency. Black comic books thus raise the question that black comedians in film and hip hop performers often evoke: how do cultural producers transcend the history of black representation, as these representations inform productions and readings of bodies? Can a comic book character not be read as a stereotype?

Thus, while African American superheroes have often satirized the subjection of black characters in recent years, critiquing the impossibility of imagining black heroism or African American iconic status, the already overdetermined meanings of black masculinity, combined with the overdetermined meaning of superhero musculature, all too often produce more stereotypes of hypermasculine black subjectivity. The comic book *Icon* offered one of the greatest interventions into this tradition of cut and sinewy agency by presenting an atypical female superhero body. Raquel Ervin / Rocket, the fifteen-year-old protagonist of the 1990s Milestone comic book *Icon*, is the sidekick but actual brains behind the construction of the black superhero Icon. As Raquel Ervin, she meets the superpowered Augustus Freeman III when she accompanies her boyfriend and his friends in an attempt to rob Freeman's house. Freeman, like Superman, crashed in a field and was adopted by the family that found him. Unlike Superman, the alien had lived many years as an adult on his home planet before his crash and adapted by taking on the infant form of the people who found him. He was found by southern slaves in the nineteenth century and, immortal on Earth, lived for many years, periodically leaving where he lived and returning as his own son. After his years of living through slavery and Jim Crow segregation, he believed that African Americans were not taking advantage of the gains of the civil rights movement and became a black conservative. After witnessing Freeman's superpowers during the thwarted robbery, Raquel returns to convince Freeman that he has an obligation, as an African American with such gifts, to be a role model for others. Throughout the series, she constantly reminds him through her words and material circumstances of the realities of structural racism in a post-civil-rights culture. Raquel is the heart of the series, the character who invites the reader's identification.

Making Raquel a point of identification is a radical departure from most comics given what the creators do to her character and body. While her body is chiseled when in uniform, outside of the costume, Raquel is a very normal figure. In fact, writer Dwayne McDuffie and the artists quickly transform her body into one of the most abject in U.S. culture—the teenage, black, unwed, single mother. In a genre of hyperembodiment, her pregnant body would appear the ultimate counterideal to the U.S. citizen. Raquel personifies all that cannot possibly be read as heroic in U.S. culture. While unwed mothers are sometimes read as admirable after they have overcome their status, Raquel, perhaps because of the limited run of the series, continued to personify someone of limited opportunity. Bright but living in housing projects, struggling to balance school, motherhood, and work, Raquel's melancholy at not only her subjection but that of the other inhabitants of Paris Island, a low-income section of the fictional city of Dakota, informs much of the comic. But it is a melancholia about class and race relations that is cut by optimism and a satirical gaze on what the impossibility of being able to imagine Raquel means in the context of the heroic citizen-making imaginary of the United States. By constantly calling attention to the tension between Icon and traditional superheroes and, in particular, between her body and the traditional superhero or sidekick, Raquel's character is the voice of critical race humor.

"Brother from Another Planet"

In a critique of black superhero comics, Anna Beatrice Scott claims that there is "absolutely nothing new" about *Icon*: "an alien who falls to earth and takes on the form of an African slave, . . . a black Republican brought out of the closet, so to speak, by a soon-to-be unwed teenage mother, who is also his sidekick" (311). While I have not run into many black single-mother superheroes, let alone those who create the heroes they assist and read Toni Morrison, I do take her point that "black bodies are already stories, mythological beasts with epic powers and tragic presaged endings in the faulty perspectivism of the white supremacist world" and, moreover, that "an artist's perception of a necessity of representing the 'real' when rendering a black body as fiction character almost always reveals the creator's intention of getting it right or righting a wrong, but rarely writing a story" (312). And indeed, *Icon* and some other black comics can be sites of didacticism, or as a Milestone reader in Jeffrey Brown's study claimed, be "preachy" (40). However, the fact that the comics occasionally told traditional comic book stories and could be preachy did not mean that the creators were not also capable of self-referential complexity and humor.

The wry and peppy cover of issue 31 is an explicit double of an early Batman comic book cover depicting Batman and Robin, the most iconographic superhero and sidekick in the history of comics. The famous Bob Kane cover in 1940 features a jaunty yellow background with Batman and Robin soaring through the air over the rooftops (issue 1, Spring 1940). They look at each other, with Robin clearly smiling, and the cover informs us that we will be treated to the "THE ALL BRAND NEW ADVENTURES OF THE BATMAN AND ROBIN, THE BOY WONDER." Issue 31 of *Icon* duplicates the original cover, down to the shape of the title on the page, but the visual humor is made explicit by the combination of duplication and the subtle difference in images and text. On the cover of *Icon*, we see black bodies and are told that we will be rewarded with the "ALL BRAND NEW ADVENTURES OF ICON AND ROCKET, THE UNWED MOTHER!" (see fig. 15.1). The dissonance between "the boy wonder" and "the unwed mother" draws attention to the incongruity of the old-fashioned frame with the new-fashioned heroine. This refashioning of conventions is common in *Icon*, which produces dramatic or situational irony in relationship to both comic book conventions and common narratives about African American subjects.

At the end of the inaugural issue of *Icon*, Icon and Rocket rush in to save a group of hostages, and this scene plays on historical representations of super-heroes, the role of black characters in comics, and the relationship between African Americans and the police. As they begin their adventure in issue 1, Rocket says to Icon, "Let's go set a positive example for the downtrodden"— the situational irony lying in Rocket's consciousness of the problematic, hyperbolic role of the hero and the fact that this is, in fact, what Raquel asked Augustus Freeman to do (25). Raquel's critical race humor is based on her knowledge of the incongruity of her body, and she calls attention to the tyranny of visual representation and how that history will challenge their attempts to make political interventions. She evokes the status of older black sidekicks to white heroes when she questions Icon's belief that he can "land in the middle of eighty bazillion cops and ask if they need a hand." She exclaims, "Hey I'M the sidekick. I'M supposed to be the naïve one!" As the sidekick who created the ideological purpose of Icon, she draws attention to the ways in which the sidekick often stands for the consciousness and hopes of the everyday citizen, a consciousness that black sidekicks such as Ebony White to the Spirit were often denied. Raquel has knowledge of the limitations of black citizens having iconic or heroic status. She asks, "you think the cops are sitting around waiting for a flying nigger to drop out of the sky and do their job for them?" (26). Icon is distant from the real challenges facing black citizenship and resists the idea that there will be a racial reading of Icon's body. But of course, when they enter the fray, they find themselves confronted by the gun barrels of countless police officers. Wryly commenting on how illegible they are as saviors and how easily they are read as enemies of the state, Rocket declares, "I bet this never happens to Superman!" (see fig. 15.2). She is satirizing their status as objects of abjection; they are radical Others who challenge white citizens' visions of themselves as the only possible source of true heroism. Her humor reflexively gestures toward the history of black bodies as the antithesis of national heroes.

15.1 The cover of *Icon* #31 clearly imitates the cover of *Batman* #1 (Spring 1940), except for the dissonance between "the boy wonder" and "the unwed mother."

15.2 "I bet this never happens to Superman!" Rocket wryly notes, a comment on how they are easily mistaken for the bad guys due to their race.

Readers have fewer affective connections to Icon in his perfection; in this very Superman-like perfection, embodying self-determination and selfless virtue, he illustrates how the iconographic ideal might not be the ideal representative of real citizens. Rocket must teach him about the material reality of black existence at the end of the twentieth century. Living in the projects, her story and body are thoroughly of the present, resisting conservative narratives that suggest that African Americans do not experience structural racism in contemporary culture. As the sidekick, she is the voice that checks the conservatism that Icon embodies. The incongruity between the conservatism embedded in the superhero iconography and real citizenship is illustrated in issue 8, when Icon gives her the full story of his origins. Rocket exclaims, "I think I just figured out how a black man could be a conservative Republican—You're from OUTER SPACE!"[5] While the creators have rejected the idea that Icon is a black double of Superman, the narrative of immigration, adoption, and iconographic and straight-laced status holds many parallels to the Superman story. And in the invocation of Rocket as the true heart and ideological conscience of the construction of the superhero narrative, her character challenges not only Icon but the traditional comic book narrative that frames the Superman model as the ideal and fantastic representative of the United States. Raquel's body stands as the real body in the frame that must deal with the material constraints of her heroic labor. As she struggles to get her costume on before going on maternity leave, the realness of her body does not prevent her from using the energy-absorbing utility belt that protects her from harm and allows her to direct the force used against her. However, it *does* make it more difficult (see fig. 15.3). Rocket thus is never an idealized fantasy.

This visual humor in the scene of the pregnant Raquel putting on her utility belt is a radical variation on traditional frames depicting superhero activity— the mysterious or heroic silhouette, the costume change, and physical labor. Because the chiseled musculature of the superhero is so iconic, the image of Raquel's slight form and protruding belly is a radical visual challenge to the source of heroic power. The source of her *physical* power is not inherent—it is the belt—and thus reminds the reader of the fact that what produced a space for Raquel Ervin's heroism was outside the traditional stories about inherent power or skill sets produced by accidents. Her work as a superhero is very much shaped by her own specialized labor—her ability with words to convince Freeman of his responsibilities and her compassion, energy, and dedication. As she huffs and puffs in an effort to fasten her belt, showing the everyday labor of her work, her face mimics the expression that she would actually have giving birth. When women's labor (giving birth) entails the same signifier as heroic labor, it challenges the naturalization of chiseled masculinity as the only kind of heroic body. Most importantly, the comic does not confine women's heroism to the romance of childbirth, suggesting that the domestic is the most important place of women's heroism. Instead, the creators displace a signifier of women's labor

15.3 The reality of Raquel's/Rocket's pregnancy: she has difficulty putting on the utility belt that gives her super powers.

(the pregnant face that huffs and puffs) and places it in the public, heroic sphere. In placing the everyday in the heroic sphere, the creators invite identification as well as humor. Rocket's pregnant body makes her a more representative citizen, not less.

Rocket's encumbered body stands in contrast to the fantasies of organic, authentic black strength represented by characters such as Luke Cage and the Black Panther. In *Icon*, the character Buck Wild stands for an earlier, Blaxploitation version of this kind of authentic black masculine subject (see fig. 15.4). Clearly evoking early Luke Cage comics, Buck Wild is a mercenary for hire, whose dialect cannot escape tortuous linguistic caricature. His first phrase on the splash page in issue 13 is "Alright, you mother-lovin', finger licking, chicken pluckers. You done messed up now! Cause I'm Buck Wild, Mercenary Man!" He is introduced via Rocket's narration; he is an "old, played out record" that she cannot escape. We get frames of his "belief defying strength" and his struggles with Lysistrata Jones in hip huggers, mastering him with the P-Whip (2–4). As we see Buck Wild's adventure unfold, Rocket's narration goes on to say that "the record's played out, alright, but nothing ever came along to take its place ... It ain't much. It ain't even good. But it might be all there is. And that's better'n' nothin' ain't it?" (3). Buck Wild stands for the compromised possibilities offered by black images in comics, a stagnation of production that has been facilitated by mainstream comics publishers. He stands for "psychically stuck" representations. McDuffie suggests that rather than try to revamp the old stereotype, it is time to develop new paradigms. At the end, Buck Wild says, "Seein you two taught me a lot. Lookin at you makes me think, mebbe if I hadn't been frozen, I wouldn't have to be like this. Mebbe I can Still be more than What I is now." But

15.4 Buck Wild, a mercenary, clearly recalls the imagery of Blaxploitation as well as the early imagery of Luke Cage.

Rocket humorously rejects the idea that he can be productively reimagined: "I wouldn't count on it, Buck. You are what you is. And 1972 was a long time ago. Maybe it's just time to move on" (30).

McDuffie is nonetheless respectful of the role that such stereotypical heroes played. Buck Wild dies in issue 30 and has a funeral, and the creators evoke many prominent black characters in superhero comics—from Black Goliath to Brother Voodoo. In delivering Buck Wild's eulogy, Icon delivers a melancholic meditation on black representation in the midst of the satirical evocation of this history:

> He spent his life fighting for what is right, all the while struggling with questions of identity and public perception that we STILL do not have answers for. He reinvented himself time and again, searching for a comfortable way to present himself to the world. And while we winced on occasion at his embarrassing speech and demeaning behavior, more often we cheered him on. Because whatever else he was, he was always a hero. A hero for those of us who had no heroes. Were it not for him we would not be here today.

Melancholia is about a subject's attempt to deal with invisibility and his or her status as an object, as well as the loss of a desired object, and Icon's words gesture toward that feeling. He is attempting to reconcile the absence of some representations and the loss of a representation that black subjects need to discard if they are to move out of melancholia, even as they mourn the loss of the only representation they had (Cheng 14). In the midst of a fairly humorous issue, filled with excessive representations of black stereotypes, McDuffie inserts a fairly serious speech, blending humor with melancholia, illustrating the affective makeup of critical race humor.

Icon's words apply to the content of the comic in other ways as well, because *Icon*, and the Milestone project in general—of comics producers coming together briefly to form their own imprint—struggled with "questions of identity and public perception that we STILL do not have answers for." And one of the most compelling questions is why Rocket could not have been the Icon herself. Rocket was the new paradigm that Icon evoked in his speech. And yet the only way Raquel Ervin could be the protagonist was for her to be sidelined. Nevertheless, *Icon*, through Raquel, began to imagine some answers for some of the questions that can plague cultural producers, particularly if they represent black people in visual humor. How can representations of black bodies or black humor move beyond stereotype to progressive political commentary, when the history of black representation is one that is always already comical, hyperphysical, and outside of narratives about "universal" concerns in the United States? How does a text escape, or negotiate with, its historical antecedents? How can bodies that are perpetually cast as antithetical to citizenship claim representative status in a country that alleges the valuing of diverse citizenship? Is the heroic narrative that takes pleasure in iconographic citizenship so aligned with muscular nationalism that there is no room for the kind of thoughtful, progressive, black heroic lead that is outside of the traditional paradigm? Rocket, calling attention to the visual incongruity between her body and the U.S. heroic ideal, was a truly alternative superhero. But the irony of her new kind of ideality, representing a more diverse citizen, is that she was still not the subject at the center.

Refusing the Black Smile

Aaron McGruder's comic strip *The Boondocks* also negotiated these questions and issues, and while this model also places male citizen-subjects at the center (rarely valuing the perspectives of women in the strip), it is resistant to the nationalist recuperative models of the comic strip genre. As opposed to producing something like *Curtis* or *Jump Start*, which are traditional family-centered strips featuring African American characters, McGruder resisted the frame of the genre in a way that *Icon* did not. McGruder was often accused of perpetuating stereotypes, but such accusations are often informed by bad reading practices produced by the demand for uplift ideology in all black cultural productions (see Cornwell and Orbe). Early criticisms of the comic often elided the difference between satire and perpetuation of stereotypes. A few black comic strip artists have broken through the glass gutter of the funny pages, but none of them have been as controversial as Aaron McGruder's strip.[6] Nothing quite like *The Boondocks* had ever achieved national circulation.[7] It featured the radical ten-year-old Huey, who moves to the suburbs with his grandfather and "thug" little brother, Riley. Huey is constructed as the rational subject who gazes on unreason. Like *Icon*, *The Boondocks* sometimes made conservatism the object of its critique. When the strip began, it focused on local and domestic racial politics. But as it progressed, McGruder more often had a national focus. Huey is a progressive black nationalist, critiquing the sins of Black Entertainment Television, the black celebrities worthy of his "Most Embarrassing Black Person" award, and the foibles of the two-party political system. While many readers expressed offense at what they viewed as stereotypes of African Americans, the strip's creator became a national star after 9/11. McGruder did not shy away from criticizing President Bush or his administration after the event, and a number of newspapers pulled his strip when they deemed it too offensive (Hoad 32).

Like Raquel, Huey is positioned as a fairly powerless citizen-subject, but as he does not live in a world with brothers from another planet who can perform acts of supernatural heroism, he utilizes the traditional methods of visibility. Letters of protest, phone calls, speaking out against ideological indoctrination (while at school), and educating family and friends are his means of protest. Mirroring a pose we often seen in Gary Trudeau's *Doonesbury*, the most common image is of Huey lounging in an armchair, taking in the absurdities of U.S. politics and popular culture. But because he is a child and not an adult, he is an atypical national critic in a space that typically presents children as precocious or awkward youngsters challenging adults in the domestic sphere. Huey embraces a role in the public sphere, but a recurring source of the comic strip's humor is the depiction of Huey fruitlessly sending protests into the void—venting to family and friends or making protests through the phone, Internet, or letters. As he is ten years old, his invisibility and voicelessness is heightened, and yet the child's voice also illustrates the toothless power of many citizens. However, the strip makes Huey visible—he is a markedly black body and loud radical voice in a space that has traditionally lacked such a presence. McGruder constructs Huey as a heroic figure fighting against national absurdity and totalitarianism. Huey is both funny in his exhausted radicalisms that cannot change the world and definitively not a traditional black humorous subject.

McGruder, in his first strip after 9/11, again challenges the notion of black bodies as objects of humor, as well as the question of comedy after such a national trauma, a common question in the entertainment industry in the weeks after the attacks. These frames represent a common sequence in *The Boondocks*, depicting Huey in contemplation, moving to a moment of silence in shadow before the punch line of the strip. The moment of silence mimics the moments of silence that the nation took in mourning after the terrorist attacks. But with the assertion that Huey "never" laughed or smiled before the attacks, it actually calls attention to narratives that suggest that laughter and smiling was easy for the nation before 9/11. There was terror and struggle before the events, and Huey's innocence was not disrupted by the attacks—he was never allowed innocence.

The kind of strips that resulted in *The Boondocks'* removal from some papers was scathing attacks on the logic of patriotism after the events. McGruder suggested that the administration encouraged fear and also called attention to long histories of U.S. support of groups that then would engage in terrorist activities. Huey was depicted screaming to those who would not listen, but of course the strip itself had an audience in a space where such critiques were rarely found. Some papers reacted by placing the strips on the editorial page, while others removed them entirely.

In response to the strips being pulled, McGruder created the characters Flagee and Ribbon. Flagee and Ribbon are an interesting double for Huey and the desired recipients of his politics. Huey plays the role of elder statesmen, wise in the ways of the nation-state (albeit often to the cluelessness or derision of those whom he addresses). Ribbon is the kind of protégé that Huey might enjoy, one who soaks in the knowledge that he produces. The movement of Flagee also connotes jauntiness, moving in ways foreign to the serious protagonist of *The Boondocks*. Flagee and Ribbon exhibit a kind of inherent joy that Huey never possesses. At the same time, the strokes that convey jauntiness also connote Flagee's and Ribbon's rage and fear, respectively. When Ribbon tells Flagee, "I heard someone say on radio that if we kill innocent people, we're not better than the terrorists," Flagee leans threateningly down on Ribbon, stating that he would drag Ribbon out to the street and shoot him if he said anything like that again. The line between patriot and fascist, joy and fear, is thin here. Huey identifies the continuum of these ideas, in a space where child characters traditionally only exhibit joy or disappointment at everyday childhood challenges.

Flagee's and Ribbon's "joy" can only be conveyed by a reified patriot; the flag is the signifier of a particular kind of ideal subject. McGruder constructs the ideal citizen-subject in the post-9/11 imaginary as disembodied. Not only is there no room for Huey's body in the ideal construction of U.S. citizens; all citizens get displaced under the weight of ideology. This ideal U.S. citizen mindlessly parrots jingoistic phrases, incapable of recognizing that the construction of citizenship that they perpetuate depends on disregarding real bodies, exhibited by the actual erasure of Huey and the characters who usually fill McGruder's strip. Thus, replacing bodies with the trappings of patriotism suggests that the path of post-9/11 national discourse romanticizes neither real bodies nor real minds but instead ideas that ignore real bodies. The world does not make room for Huey. It silences him, desires his erasure. In erasing him, McGruder shows what is left: Flagee and Ribbon; jingoism and his sidekick, parrot.

The metacritique produced by "The Adventures of Flagee and Ribbon" also poses the question of what the possibilities for humor are in such a climate. The idea of Flagee and Ribbon is funny, but only through the delivery of lines that are decidedly not humorous. While McGruder has been accused of stereotyping, this devolution of bodies into the tools of U.S. nationalist discourse illustrates another kind of erosion of complex differences: the desire for homogeneity through the panopticon of the Patriot Act. In that world, there is little room for humor or any other kinds of intellectual production that fails to match the script disseminated by Fox News broadcasters.

Huey, like Raquel, is an example of what Lani Guinier and Gerald Torres call the miner's canary in U.S. culture. They are the most vulnerable kinds of citizens, and attendance to their struggles places the risks facing all citizens into stark relief. Huey's silence, invisibility, and incongruity in relationship to U.S. narratives of citizenship are examples of widespread erasures of diverse citizenship models and problems in U.S. culture. Moving their bodies from margin to center, the creators also place silence and invisibility at the center of a genre that traditionally ignores these kinds of citizens. As opposed to allowing someone with a body like Superman's to speak for "truth, justice, and the American way," bodies that are traditionally marginalized speak the truth, decry injustice, and challenge the American way.

Humor becomes essential to this project because of the ways in which these types of bodies are often sites of humor and not taken seriously. Huey is not the pickaninny, eating watermelon or smiling with wide eyes. The fact that Huey never smiles in the strip is one of the sites of visual resistance. As he is never the smiling pickaninny, who is never to be taken seriously, presenting a serious image in the comedic frame, he challenges traditional representations of black children—from the nameless black babies eaten by alligators in early twentieth-century material culture to late twentieth-century black sitcoms that treat lazy and back-talking black children as a source of laughter. While other representations of black children treat them as a source of threat, Huey also challenges the ways in which black children can be a threat. He is an intellectual threat and not a physical one. His diminutive presence is a challenge because of his persistent radicalism, not because of weaponry or gang life. His body resists the ways in which black bodies are traditionally framed, just as Raquel as Rocket exploded outside the frame with her pregnant body.

There are certainly examples of graphic storytelling that exhibit more aesthetically transgressive characteristics than these comics. From Art Spiegelman's *Maus* to the artistry in more mainstream comics, writers and artists have played with narrative and form in more adventurous and avant-garde ways. However, *Icon* and *The Boondocks* are useful for attempting to imagine alternative representations in more traditional spaces—the traditional superhero comic and the comic strip in the daily newspaper. Utilizing genres so tied to nationalist, masculinist, and escapist histories, their struggle to present something within the conventional frame may offer the most challenges to it. As opposed to announcing, from the inception, through form or context, that their representations are revisions, other to the narratives that are supposed to be mainstream and representative of the nation's desires, these text revise within the conventional frame. By staying within the traditional framework, instead of suggesting that they are counter to the representative, these texts suggest that their characters are the most representative, replacing one set of ideal bodies with other kinds of bodies.

The joke is in the incongruity of such a replacement. And the laughter that the creators of these comics evoke when gesturing to the incongruity is grounded in topics of deadly seriousness. Raquel Ervin and Huey are characters desperately screaming out for help, demanding action, and resenting their voicelessness in the state. In many ways, the issues they address are no laughing matter, but humor is often their response to their disenfranchisement. These texts suggest that critical race humor might often be a productive approach, until the state can imagine the political productivity of disenfranchised citizens. When that day comes, comic book creators will be able to work in a world where the impossibility of their heroism is not the foundation of so much laughter.

Notes

1 Jeffrey Brown argues that "classical comic book depictions of masculinity are perhaps the quintessential expression of our cultural beliefs about what it means to be a man" (26). Aaron Taylor acknowledges that both male and female superheroes are sites of excess and even fetishes, but he suggests that these bodies actually challenge traditional gender identities because they are so capable of supernatural transformation.

While his provocative argument works well in considering many of the revisions of the comic book genre, I respectfully disagree with the idea that the immediate association and invited identifications in comics have encouraged the cultivation of nonideal bodies.

2   In "Chronicling the Culture: The American Comic Strip and the Constitution," Garyn G. Roberts discusses the history of comics that think critically about nationalism, with texts such as *Bloom County* and *Doonesbury* standing as some of the most powerful examples of nationalist critique. However, he does not systematically prove that most comic strips are satirical and politically engaged. Perhaps most interestingly, Roberts argues that *Bloom County* was successful because the satire was easier to take because the creator used children and animals who seemed distant from the readers' experiences. If this interpretation of reader response is true, it contributes to a discussion about what displacing and/or less important bodies do to citizenship discourse in comic strips.

3   For an introduction to critical race theory, see Delgado and Stefancic; Crenshaw et al.

4   In *Colored Pictures: Race and Visual Representation*, Michael D. Harris explores how African American artists have addressed stereotypes through their work.

5   Incidentally, Clarence Thomas was a big *Icon* fan, much to the consternation of Dwayne McDuffie, and the writer has a very funny essay about his disconcerted response to Thomas's admiration of *Icon* on his website, called "Here Comes the Judge."

6   The *gutter* is a term that refers to the space between comic book frames.

7   In fact, black characters were often not present or stereotypical. For a quantitative and qualitative analysis of representations of black characters in comics, see White and Fuentez.

Works Cited

Benson, John. "Will Eisner: Having Something to Say." *Comics Journal* 267 (April–May 2005). http://www.tcj.com/will-eisner-having-something-to-say/.

Brown, Jeffrey A. "Comic Book Masculinity and the New Black Superhero." *African American Review* 33.1 (1999): 25–42.

Cheng, Anne Anlin. *The Melancholy of Race: Psychoanalysis, Assimilation and Hidden Grief*. New York: Oxford University Press, 2001.

Cooke, Jon B. "A Spirited Relationship: Will Eisner Discusses His Experiences with Warren." *Comic Book Artist* 4 (Spring 1999). http://www.twomorrows.com/comicbookartist/articles/04eisner.html.

Cornwell, Nancy C., and Mark P. Orbe. "'Keepin' It Real' and/or 'Sellin' Out to the Man': African-American Responses to Aaron McGruder's *The Boondocks*." *Say It Loud! African American Audiences, Media and Identity*. Ed. Robin R. Means Coleman. New York: Routledge, 2002. 27–44.

Crenshaw, Kimberlé W., Neil Gotanda, Gary Peller, and Kendall Thomas, eds. *Critical Race Theory: The Key Writings That Formed the Movement*. New York: New Press, 1995.

Delgado, Richard, and Jean Stefancic, eds. *Critical Race Theory: The Cutting Edge*. 2nd ed. Philadelphia: Temple University Press, 2000.

Eisner, Will. *Comics and Sequential Art*. Tamarac, FL: Poorhouse, 1985.

Guinier, Lani, and Gerald Torres. *The Miner's Canary: Enlisting Race, Resisting Power, Transforming Democracy*. Cambridge, MA: Harvard University Press, 2002.

Harris, Michael D. *Colored Pictures: Race and Visual Representation*. Chapel Hill: University of North Carolina Press, 2003.

Hoad, Phil. "Talk of the Toon." *Observer* October 31, 2004: 32.

McDuffie, Dwayne. "Here Comes the Judge." McDuffie's website n.d. http://dwaynemcduffie .com/opinions/archives/BTYB10.php (accessed November 8, 2008).

McDuffie, Dwayne (writer), M. D. Bright (penciler), Mike Gustovich (illustrator), Noelle Giddings (colorist). "She's Got Your Hero Right Here." *Icon* #1 (May 1993). Milestone (DC Comics).

McDuffie, Dwayne (writer), Mark Bright (penciler), Mike Gustovich (illustrator), James Brown (colorist). "Brother from Another Planet." *Icon* #8 (December 1993). Milestone (DC Comics).

McDuffie, Dwayne (writer), Mark Bright (penciler), Mike Gustovich (illustrator), James Brown and David Montoya (colorist). "Buck Wild: Mercenary Man." *Icon* #13 (May 1994). Milestone (DC Comics).

McDuffie, Dwayne (writer), Mark Bright (penciler), John Paul Leon (illustrator, colorist), James Scott Jones (colorist). "The Big Bang Theory." *Icon* #20 (December 1994). Milestone (DC Comics).

McDuffie, Dwayne (writer), Mark Bright (penciler), Mike Gustovich, P. Rollins, Caesar Ravil, and Mark Bright (illustrator), J.S.J., Julia Lacquement, Burrell, Micheline Hess, David Montoya, and Craig Rippon (colorist). "Cancel Christmas." *Icon* #30 (October 1995). Milestone (DC Comics).

McDuffie, Dwayne (writer), Mark Bright (penciler), Romeo Tanghal (illustrator), and Jason Scott Jones (colorist). "Space Is the Place." *Icon* #31 (November 1995). Milestone (DC Comics).

McGruder, Aaron. *The Right to Be Hostile: The Boondocks Treasury*. New York: Three Rivers, 2003.

Roberts, Garyn G. "Chronicling a Culture: The American Comic Strip and the Constitution." *Journal of American Culture* 13.2 (1990): 57–61.

Scott, Anna Beatrice. "Superpower vs. Supernatural: Black Superheroes and the Quest for Mutant Reality." *Journal of Visual Culture* 5.3 (2006): 295–314.

Singer, Marc. "'Black Skins' and White Masks: Comic Books and the Secret of Race." *African American Review* 36.1 (2002): 107–120.

Taylor, Aaron. "He's Gotta Be Strong and He's Gotta Be Fast and He's Gotta Be Larger than Life: Investigating the Engendered Superhero Body." *Journal of Popular Culture* 40.2 (2007): 344–360.

White, Sylvia, and Tania Fuentez. "Analysis of Black Characters in Comic Strips, 1915–1995." *Newspaper Research Journal* 18.1–2 (1997): 72–85.

Wright, Bradford W. *Comic Book Nation: The Transformation of Youth Culture in America*. Baltimore: Johns Hopkins University Press, 2003.

Contributors

REYNALDO ANDERSON is an assistant professor of humanities and teacher education at Harris-Stowe State University. He also serves as a member of the Executive Board of the Missouri Arts Council and, in 2010, received a community leadership award in the humanities from Governor Jay Nixon of Missouri. Anderson has published extensively in the fields of communication studies, Africana studies, social media, rhetoric, and more recently Afrofuturism.

ANDRE CARRINGTON is a minority dissertation fellow in American studies at Skidmore College in Saratoga Springs, New York. He is a PhD candidate in American studies at New York University, where he is writing a dissertation titled "Speculative Fiction and Media Fandom through a Lens, Darkly." He is a lifelong reader of comics and a science fiction fan, and he has taught history and literature at the Fashion Institute of Technology and the City University of New York. His work has appeared in the online journal *Politics and Culture*, and he is the archivist for the fan-fiction website Remember Us: Dreaming in Color.

ROBIN R. MEANS COLEMAN is an associate professor of communication studies and AfroAmerican and African studies at the University of Michigan. She is the author of *African-American Viewers and the Black Situation Comedy: Situating Racial Humor* and *Horror Noir: Blacks in American Horror Films from the 1890s to the Present*. She is the editor of *Say It Loud! African American Audiences, Media, and Identity* and coeditor of *Fight the Power! The Spike Lee Reader*. Coleman's additional publications include articles in *Television and New Media*, *Popular Communication*, *Journal of Black Studies*, *Journal of Popular Film and Television*, *African American Research Reports*, and *Qualitative Research Reports in Communication*.

BLAIR DAVIS has a PhD from the Department of Communication Studies at McGill University in Montreal and has taught courses in film and cultural studies at Simon Fraser University since 2003. He has essays featured in the anthologies *Caligari's Grandchildren: German Horror Film since* 1945, *Horror Film: Creating and Marketing Fear*, and *Reel Food: Essays on Film and Food* and in the *Canadian Journal of Film Studies* and the *Historical Journal of Film, Radio and Television*.

CRAIG FISCHER is an associate professor of English at Appalachian State University. He has served on the Executive Committee of the Society for Cinema and Media Studies, the editorial board of *Cinema Journal*, and the Executive Committee of the International Comic Arts Forum at the Library of Congress. His work has appeared in the *Iowa Journal of Cultural Studies* and *Stay Tooned*. Fischer is a frequent contributor to the *Comics Journal* and the *International Journal of Comic Art*.

CONSEULA FRANCIS used to be oblivious to the world of superheroes until she married a Marvel zombie ten years ago. She now spends way too much of her time reading *Wizard* magazine and waiting for the latest issue of *Ultimates*. When she is not reading comics, Conseula is an assistant professor of English and director of African American Studies at the College of Charleston in South Carolina. She writes about twentieth-century Black intellectual thought, African American literary movements, and contemporary African American literature. She is the author of *Conversations with Octavia Butler*. Her random musings on all things Black and geeky can be found at http://afrogeekmom.blogspot.com.

FRANCES GATEWARD teaches courses on film and popular culture in the Department of Cinema and Television Arts at California State University–Northridge. Her research interests include African American cinema and other forms of Black expressive culture, feminist media theory, youth cultures, and Korean cinema. She has published on African Americans and speculative film, anime, kung fu and hip hop, and issues of gender and race identity and the cinema. Her work includes the anthologies *Sugar, Spice, and Everything Nice: Cinemas of Girlhood*, *Where the Boys Are: Cinemas of Masculinity and Youth*, and *Seoul Searching: Cultural Identity and Contemporary Korean Cinema*. Her current project is *A Powerful Thang! Agency and Identity in African American Women's Films*.

NANCY GOLDSTEIN is the author of *Jackie Ormes: The First African American Woman Cartoonist*. In 2008, the American Library Association's *Booklist* included Goldstein's book in its "Top 10 Biographies of the Year" and also its "Top 10 Books on the Arts"; and the *Village Voice* listed it in its "Best Books of 2008."

JOHN JENNINGS is an associate professor of visual studies at the University at Buffalo, the State University of New York. His research and teaching focus on the analysis, explication, and disruption of African American stereotypes in popular visual media. He is an accomplished designer, curator, illustrator, cartoonist, and award-winning graphic novelist. Jennings is coauthor of the graphic novel *The Hole: Consumer Culture* and of *Black Comix: African American Independent Comics* and cocurator of "Out of Sequence: Underrepresented Voices in American Comics." He is also coauthor (with longtime collaborator Damian Duffy) of the upcoming graphic novel adaptation of Octavia Butler's classic dark fantasy novel *Kindred*. Along with collaborator Stacey Robinson, Jennings has also created an arts collective called Black Kirby, which is dedicated to studying black visual culture and celebrating the legacy of Jack Kirby's monumental career in American comic book culture.

SALLY MCWILLIAMS is an associate professor of English and director of the Women's and Gender Studies Program at Montclair State University. Her teaching and research interests include Chinese women's literature, literature of the African diaspora, and transnational feminism. She has published articles on feminist pedagogy, narrative strategies, and international women's literature.

KINOHI NISHIKAWA is an assistant professor of English at the University of Notre Dame, where he specializes in African American literary and popular culture. Kinohi's recently completed book manuscript traces the rise of black-authored pulp fiction (by the likes of Iceberg Slim and Donald Goines) from its material roots in postwar men's literature to its cultural influence on contemporary hip hop. A new research project will examine black-owned bookshops' historic but overlooked contributions to African American social and political life. Kinohi's work has appeared in the journals *PMLA*, *American Literature*, and *Book History*.

PATRICK F. WALTER is an instructor of English at the University at Buffalo, the State University of New York. His areas of study are popular culture, popular literature, race, regionalism, gothic fiction, and horror film. He is currently working on projects that involve the production of the rural body in American gothic fiction and the contemporary horror film.

REBECCA WANZO is an associate professor in the Women, Gender and Sexuality Studies Program at Washington University, St. Louis. Her research interests include African American literature, history, and culture; theories of affect; popular culture (particularly the history of popular genre fiction and graphic storytelling in the United States); critical race theory; and feminist theory. She is the author of *The Suffering Will Not Be Televised: African American Women and Sentimental Political Storytelling*.

QIANA WHITTED is an associate professor of English with a joint appointment in African-American Studies at the University of South Carolina. Her research and teaching interests focus on African American literature, black cultural studies, and American comics and graphic novels. Whitted is coeditor of *Comics and the U.S. South*, a collection that includes her essay on postmodern slave-narrative conventions in horror comics. Other academic publications include the book *"A God of Justice?" The Problem of Evil in Twentieth-Century Black Literature* as well as articles in the *Journal of Graphic Novels and Comics*, *African American Review*, and *Southern Literary Journal*.

DANIEL F. YEZBICK is an assistant professor at St. Louis Community College–Forest Park, where he teaches English and media studies. He has lectured and published on diverse topics in literature, performance, and media studies, including Victorian stereoscopic views, radio drama, Blaxploitation cinema, and New Deal theater. Yezbick recently edited R. C. Harvey's critical biography of the legendary American cartoonist Milton Caniff and is currently expanding his own research of the classic American children's author, illustrator, and cartoonist George Carlson.

WILLIAM LAFI YOUMANS is an assistant professor in the School of Media and Public Affairs at George Washington University. His research interests are global news media, media law, and social movements. His writings have appeared in *Journal of Communication*, *Middle East Journal of Culture and Communication*, and *Journal of Intercultural Communication Research*.

HERSHINI BHANA YOUNG is an associate professor at the University at Buffalo, the State University of New York, where she teaches classes in literature and art of the African diaspora. Her first book, *Haunting Capital: Memory, Text and the Black Diasporic Body*, looks at the black female body as living text that remembers the injury of dislocations and enslavements necessitated by capital. She is completing her second book, titled *Coercive Performances: Illegible Will in Southern African Spectacular Performances of Labor*.

JAMES J. ZIEGLER teaches in the Department of English at the University of Oklahoma, where he specializes in American literature after 1900, literary theory, and rhetoric. His research concentrates on the culture of the early years of the Cold War, with particular attention to the effect of anticommunism on both liberal political philosophy and the civil rights movement.

Index